Political Competition

Political Competition

Theory and Applications

JOHN E. ROEMER

Harvard University Press

Cambridge, Massachusetts

London, England

2001

Library of Congress Cataloging-in-Publication Data

Roemer, John E.
    Political competition: theory and applications / John E. Roemer.
        p. cm.
    Includes bibliographical references and index.
    ISBN 0-674-00488-4 (alk. paper)
    1. Political parties—Mathematical models.   2. Democracy—Mathematical models.   I.
    Title.

    JF2051 .R64 2001
    324.2'01'51—dc21   00-047246

To Joaquim Silvestre
patient teacher, dear friend

Contents

Preface   *xi*

Introduction   *1*

2/26/02 1. Political Competition over a Single Issue:
         The Case of Certainty   *13*

    1.1 Citizens, Voters, and Parties   *13*
    1.2 The Downs Model   *16*
    1.3 The Wittman Model   *28*
    1.4 Conclusion   *36*

3/27 2. Modeling Party Uncertainty   *38*

    2.1 Introduction   *38*
    2.2 The State-Space Approach to Uncertainty   *39*
    2.3 An Error-Distribution Model of Uncertainty   *45*
    2.4 A Finite-Type Model   *47*
    2.5 Conclusion   *51*

3/27 3. Unidimensional Policy Spaces with Uncertainty   *52*

    3.1 Introduction   *52*
    3.2 The Downs Model   *52*
    3.3 The Wittman Model: An Example   *55*
    3.4 Existence of Wittman Equilibrium   *61*
    3.5 Properties of Wittman Equilibrium   *69*
    3.6 Summary   *71*

4. Applications of the Wittman Model   73

    4.1 Simple Models of Redistribution: The Politics of Extremism   73
    4.2 Politico-Economic Equilibrium with Labor-Supply Elasticity   76
    4.3 Partisan Dogmatism and Political Extremism   81
    4.4 A Dynamic Model of Political Cycles   82
    4.5 Conclusion   89

5. Endogenous Parties: The Unidimensional Case   90

    5.1 Introduction   90
    5.2 Average-Member Nash Equilibrium   91
    5.3 Condorcet-Nash Equilibrium   94
    5.4 Conclusion   101

6. Political Competition over Several Issues:
The Case of Certainty   103

    6.1 Introduction   103
    6.2 The Downs Model   103
    6.3 The Wittman Model   116
    6.4 Conclusion   122

7. Multidimensional Issue Spaces and Uncertainty:
The Downs Model   124

    7.1 Introduction   124
    7.2 The State-Space and Error-Distribution Models of Uncertainty   124
    7.3 The Coughlin Model   127
    7.4 The Lindbeck-Weibull Model   130
    7.5 Adapting the Coughlin Model to the Case
       of Aggregate Uncertainty   134
    7.6 Conclusion   144

8. Party Factions and Nash Equilibrium   145

    8.1 Introduction   145
    8.2 Party Factions   148
    8.3 PUNE as a Bargaining Equilibrium   155
    8.4 A Differential Characterization of PUNE   159
    8.5 Regular Wittman Equilibrium   163
    8.6 PUNEs in the Unidimensional Model   166
    8.7 PUNEs in a Multidimensional Euclidean Model   167
    8.8 Conclusion   170

9. The Democratic Political Economy of Progressive Taxation   *172*

    9.1 Introduction   *P U N E*   *172*
    9.2 The Model   *173*
    9.3 The Equilibrium Concepts   *178*
    9.4 Analysis of Party Competition   *179*
    9.5 Calibration   *186*
    9.6 Conclusion   *187*

10. Why the Poor Do Not Expropriate the Rich in Democracies   *189*

    10.1 The Historical Issue and a Model Preview   *189*
    10.2 The Politico-Economic Environment   *192*
    10.3 Analysis of PUNEs   *195*
    10.4 Empirical Tests   *198*
    10.5 Proofs of Theorems   *202*
    10.6 Concluding Remark   *207*

11. Distributive Class Politics and the Political
    Geography of Interwar Europe   *209*

    11.1 Introduction   *209*
    11.2 The Luebbert Model   *212*
    11.3 Testing Luebbert's Theory   *218*
    11.4 Introducing the Communists: A Three-Party Model   *230*
    11.5 Conclusion   *241*
    11.6 Methodological Coda   *242*
        Appendix 11A   *244*

12. A Three-Class Model of American Politics   *251*

    12.1 Introduction   *251*
    12.2 The Model   *253*
    12.3 Characterization of PUNEs   *254*
    12.4 Results   *256*
    12.5 Conclusion   *257*

13. Endogenous Parties with Multidimensional Competition   259

    13.1 Introduction   259
    13.2 Endogenous Parties   260
    13.3 Taxation and Race   261
    13.4 Fitting the Model to U.S. Data   263
    13.5 Quadratic Taxation   269
    13.6 Private Financing of Parties   276
    13.7 A Technical Remark on the Existence of PUNEs   277
    13.8 Conclusion   279
    13.9 Why the Poor Do Not Expropriate the Rich: Reprise   279

14. Toward a Model of Coalition Government   281

    14.1 Introduction   281
    14.2 The Payoff Function of a Wittman Party   282
    14.3 An Example of Coalition Government:
          Unidimensional Wittman Equilibrium   290
    14.4 Multidimensional Three-Party Politics   296
    14.5 Coalition Government with a Multidimensional Issue Space:
          An Example   299
    14.6 Conclusion   304

    Mathematical Appendix   309

    A.1 Basics of Probability Theory   309
    A.2 Some Concepts from Analysis   318

    References   323

    Index   327

Preface

I began thinking about political competition while reading Adam Przeworski and John Sprague's *Paper Stones*, in the early 1990s. Their book was a model of careful analysis of the strategic behavior of socialist parties in Europe during the first half of the twentieth century. It at once made painfully clear the inadequacy for historical analysis of the prevalent Downsian model of political competition, in which parties are assumed to have no policy preferences, and the need for a fully strategic model of party competition. For the Przeworski-Sprague analysis was incomplete: the Socialists were presumed to react strategically to bourgeois and Communist parties whose behavior was exogenously given. One might say the drama they described was marred by incomplete character development of several of the main actors.

I have gained from discussions of these topics with many people since that time. In particular, I wish to thank David Austen-Smith, Jon Elster, John Ferejohn, Stephen Holmes, Roger Howe, Eric Maskin, Klaus Nehring, Ignacio Ortuño-Ortín, Adam Przeworski, Herbert Scarf, Joaquim Silvestre, and Michael Wallerstein. Many seminar participants have made comments which have doubtless influenced the final product, although I cannot make appropriate attributions. I especially thank Ignacio Ortuño-Ortín who has provided a valuable critique of many, if not most, of the ideas in this book. And I am deeply indebted to Woojin Lee and Humberto G. Llavador, who, as research assistants, wrote much of the Mathematica code for the computations, and read a number of chapters. In addition, Lee wrote the appendix to Chapter 11. My thanks, finally, go to Elizabeth Gilbert at Harvard University Press, whose judicious editing has improved the present text as well as several others I have previously authored.

I have made substantial revisions in drawing on several of my previously published articles: "The Democratic Political Economy of Progressive Income Taxation," *Econometrica* 67, no. 1 (©1999 by the Econometric Society): 1–19; "Why the Poor Do Not Expropriate the Rich in Democracies," *Journal of Public Economics* 70 (©1998; reprinted with permission from Elsevier Science): 399–442; "Political Cycles," *Economics and Politics* 7 (©1995 by Blackwell Publishers): 1–20; and, both in *Social Choice and Welfare,* "A Theory of Policy Differentiation in Single-Issue Electoral Politics," 11 (1994): 355–380, and "Political-Economic Equilibrium When Parties Represent Constituents," 14 (1997): 479–502. I thank the journals for permission to use these materials here.

This book, however, was written while I was a fellow at the Russell Sage Foundation in New York, and was revised while I taught a course based on it at the Politics Department at New York University. I am most grateful to Eric Wanner, Russell Sage's president, and to that foundation's support and kitchen staff, for providing an ideal environment in which to cogitate and write. And I thank George Downs, chair of the NYU Politics Department, for allowing me to experiment with the text upon his graduate students.

I take great pleasure in dedicating this book to my wise colleague, frequent collaborator, subtle critic, and friend, Joaquim Silvestre.

August 2000

Political Competition

Introduction

The formal model of political competition almost ubiquitously employed, to date, by students of political economy is one in which political parties play no role. That model, introduced by Anthony Downs (1957) over forty years ago, portrays a competition between two candidates whose sole motivation for engaging in politics is to enjoy the power and perquisites of officeholding. Although voters care about policies, the candidates do not; for them, a policy is simply an instrument to be used, opportunistically, as an entry ticket to a prosperous career. Political parties, however, perhaps because they are formed by citizens' interest groups, have, throughout the history of democracy, cared about policies. Therefore the Downsian model cannot be viewed as a historically accurate model of party competition.

Democratic history is one of competition between parties that represent, perhaps imperfectly, contesting interest groups among the polity. Contesting interest groups can be represented, abstractly, as possessing different preferences regarding policies that are to be implemented by the government. A historically accurate model should therefore represent political competition as occurring between parties, each of which has preferences over policies and each of which seeks, in the "game" of political competition, to propose the policy that maximizes its preference order, or utility.

Such a model was indeed introduced by Donald Wittman (1973), but it was not carefully developed until recently, and has only been used in applications by a small number of researchers. The Wittman model is less user-friendly than the Downs model, in two ways: first, more data are required to specify the political environment with Wittman politics than with Downs politics (for instance, one must specify the preferences of the active political parties) and, second, the computation of equilibrium, at least in the interesting case of the presence of uncertainty, is more complex in the Wittman model. But as Albert Einstein said, good science consists in constructing models that are as simple as possible, but no simpler. In this case, I contend that the Downs model is too simple—the price of its simplicity is the elimination of politics from political competition.

In this book I attempt to develop, in a systematic and rigorous fashion, a theory of competition between political parties in a democracy. Although the Downs model is not the one of choice, I develop the Downs theory as well, for it has played an important role in formal political theory. It is, moreover, important to understand when the theory of competition between *parties* produces political equilibria that differ from the Downs equilibrium in the competition between *opportunistic politicians*, for it does not always do so. Thus it is the case, in certain situations, that although competition occurs between partisan parties, the result is no different than it would have been had the competition been between policy-disinterested candidates. I shall argue, however, that the two models only predict the same equilibrium policies in cases that are historically unrealistic, ones in which there is no uncertainty surrounding elections.

We begin with a model of a polity composed of citizens who possess preferences over a policy space. I assume a continuum of citizens; this is the model of choice when we seek to understand political competition with large polities. There are two political parties, whose preferences (or payoff functions) are first specified sufficiently abstractly that both Downs politics and Wittman politics are special cases. We model political equilibrium as the Nash equilibrium of the game in which each party maximizes its payoff function over a strategy space which is the policy space. A party's payoff, under both the Wittman and the Downs specifications, depends, inter alia, upon its probability of victory, given the policies played by it and its competitor.

The book is a further articulation of this general model. In Chapters 1–8, we study the properties of the Nash equilibria of the political game, under eight different specifications of the model. These specifications are the eight possibilities in the cross-product of models:

$$\{\text{Downs, Wittman}\} \times \{\text{certainty, uncertainty}\}$$

$$\times \{\text{unidimensional, multidimensional}\}.$$

"Downs/Wittman" refers to the motivation of the political actors—whether they seek to maximize the probability of victory (Downs) or the expected utility associated with a preference order over the policy space (Wittman).

"Certainty/uncertainty" refers to whether parties know for certain the distribution of voter types or have only a probability distribution over the possible distributions of voter types. Parties are certain about how the vote will be distributed between the parties, once policies have been announced, if and only if they are certain about the distribution of voter types. "Unidimensional/multidimensional" refers to the dimension of the policy space.

The classical "median voter theorem" is a description of the Nash equilibrium in political competition in the case {Downs, certainty, unidimensional}, and probably 95% of the formal literature in political economy since Downs has employed this particular specification. In my view, this model is ahistorical in all three ways: democratic politics are never Downsian, parties are never certain about the mapping from policy pairs (proposed by the two parties) to the vote distribution, and, I contend, (national) politics are never unidimensional.

The structure of the book is given in Figure I.1. Chapter 1 characterizes political equilibrium in the cases {Downs, certainty, unidimensional} and {Wittman, certainty, unidimensional}. In both cases, there is a "median voter theorem," but it is a different theorem in each—in particular, additional premises are needed to prove the theorem in the Wittman context. The conclusion of both theorems is that both parties announce the same policy at equilibrium, which is the ideal policy of the voter whose ideal point is median in the distribution of voter ideal points. If we believe that parties never propose the same policies in actual democracies, then these models must be inaccurate.

It may, however, be a good approximation to say that in some elections, both parties proposed the same policy. Chapter 1 tells us, importantly, that such an observation is not indirect evidence for the validity of the Downs characterization of politics, for Wittman politics will produce the same result. In a world of certainty, Downs and Wittman politics are observationally equivalent (unless we can somehow observe party motivations).

Chapter 2 introduces party uncertainty about voter behavior. There are, indeed, a variety of methods for modeling this kind of uncertainty, and three are described in this chapter. All three approaches to uncertainty deliver *aggregate uncertainty,* despite the fact that there is a continuum of voters. Thus it will not do to assume that each voter behaves stochastically and that the random variables that describe the behavior of individual voters are independently distributed, for in that case, uncertainty at the aggregate level would disappear. Even though we have a continuum of voters, parties do not know for sure the mapping from pairs of policies to the vote distribution.

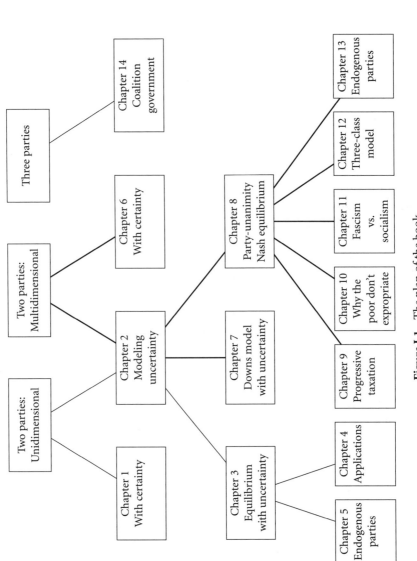

Figure I.1 The plan of the book

Let $\pi(t^1, t^2)$ be the probability that party 1 defeats party 2 at the policy pair (t^1, t^2). The three approaches to uncertainty offered here each provide microfoundations (to varying extents) which allow us to *compute* the function π. That function is not a datum of our problem, but is deduced from more primitive assumptions. This philosophically desirable approach renders our analysis somewhat difficult at times, because it is often the case that the computed function π is rather badly behaved, even when the underlying primitives are unexotic. For instance, π is typically not everywhere continuous, nor everywhere differentiable where it is continuous; nor does π standardly possess the kind of convexity properties that are useful in equilibrium theory.

Armed with these several approaches to uncertainty, Chapter 3 studies the cases {Downs, uncertainty, unidimensional} and {Wittman, uncertainty, unidimensional}. Now the Downs and Wittman formulations *do* generate equilibria which are different: while the Downs model continues to predict that both parties propose the same policy in equilibrium, the Wittman model predicts that equilibrium policies will be differentiated.

Thus of the four model types we have studied in the unidimensional case—{Downs, certainty}, {Wittman, certainty}, {Downs, uncertainty}, {Wittman, uncertainty}—only the last one generates the realistic outcome that parties offer different policies in equilibrium. We can conclude that both the Downs assumption and the certainty assumption are poor ones, if we believe that in reality policies are differentiated in elections.

Although a theorem proving the existence of political equilibrium in the {Wittman, uncertainty, unidimensional} case is presented in Chapter 3, it is not fully satisfactory or general, for its premises are complex in the sense of not being stated in terms of the primitive data of the model. Here the unpleasant behavior of the function π comes home to roost. It is nevertheless the case that in many applications of the model, these equilibria exist and can be calculated, even if we do not have a fully general theorem asserting the existence of equilibrium. Chapter 4 offers four applications of the {Wittman, uncertainty, unidimensional} model and computes equilibria. These applications are offered for two reasons: first, to show that the model is indeed tractable, and can be used as a tool in political economy and, second, for the particular substantive results deduced.

Until now we have taken the preferences of parties as given, much as the Arrow-Debreu model takes the technologies of firms as given. In Chapter 5 we relax this assumption and propose two models in which the parties'

preferences, in the Wittman model, are endogenously derived from the preferences of the citizens. Our conception is one of "perfectly representative democracy," an ideal type that is not realistic when parties are financed by private
contributions, as they are in the United States; nevertheless, there is value in
comparing what these models predict with what we observe.

Thus we propose notions of "equilibrium in the process of party formation";
one of these we dub "Condorcet-Nash equilibrium." With these models we
have a relatively *complete* theory of political economy, one which derives political equilibrium beginning only with knowledge of the distribution of voter
preferences. (Of course, the classical Downs model does that as well, but we
are dissatisfied with it as a model of politics.) The section on Condorcet-Nash
equilibrium can therefore be viewed as the first oasis in our trek across this
landscape. As an application, we show how at least one important claim about
the relationship between taxation and income distribution, which is true when
politics are Downsian, is not true in this setting of endogenous Wittmanesque
parties. This provides another reason to reject the Downs model of politics.
We also calculate the Condorcet-Nash equilibrium for a Euclidean model, and
demonstrate an interesting relationship between the preferences of parties and
the voters who support them.

Chapter 5 concludes the unidimensional analysis. In Chapter 6 we study
the models {Downs, certainty, multidimensional} and {Wittman, certainty,
multidimensional}. The story in these cases is that, except under singular specifications of the data, political equilibria do not exist. In the Downs case, this fact
is well known, and is essentially equivalent to the nonexistence of Condorcet
winners (when the policy space is multidimensional). Altering the specification of party payoff functions from Downs to Wittman does not enable us to
escape the failure of the model in offering a prediction of political equilibrium
in the multidimensional context.

Chapter 7 studies the {Downs, uncertainty, multidimensional} model. Several authors (Coughlin 1992; Lindbeck and Weibull 1987) have shown that
political equilibria exist in models of this type. We present their results. Their
models assume, however, a finite polity, and the uncertainty that exists in the
environments they postulate disappears when the polity approaches the continuum. Nevertheless we are able to use the finite-type model (introduced in
Chapter 2) to show that equilibria continue to exist in a model with a continuum of voters. As before, in Downs equilibrium, both parties offer the same
policy.

Although we have shown that equilibrium can exist in the {Downs, uncertainty, multidimensional} case, it is a fragile existence: equilibrium does not exist in this case if we model uncertainty in the other two ways described in Chapter 2.

The fact that equilibrium does not exist in the models of Chapter 6, and exists only fragilely in the environment of Chapter 7, has induced many researchers to depart from equilibrium analysis and study "cycling." Cycling behavior is what presumably occurs in a real-world game with no Nash equilibrium: party 1 plays t, party 2 plays a best response to t, party 1 plays a best response to what party 2 played, and so on. If a Nash equilibrium does not exist, this process will never converge; it continues ad infinitum.

We take, however, a different point of view—that when a model has no equilibrium, it is probably a misspecification of the real-world phenomenon it is meant to portray. In Chapter 8, which is, in a dramatic sense, the center of our story, we offer a way of thinking of multidimensional political competition under uncertainty in which Nash equilibria do exist.

That conception marries the Downs and Wittman approaches. It conceives of a party as consisting of three factions—militants, opportunists, and reformists. The opportunists are the dramatis personae of the Downs model—they desire only to maximize the probability of the party's victory. The reformists are the actors in the Wittman model—they desire to maximize the expected utility associated with the party's preference order over policies. The militants are new characters: they desire to propose a policy as close as possible to the party's ideal point, and have little or no interest in winning the election at hand. I argue that political histories are replete with descriptions of these three kinds of party activist—for instance, Schorske ([1955] 1993) calls them, when describing the German Social Democratic Party, the party bureaucrats, the trade union leadership, and the radicals. To paraphrase, in a word, the opportunists, reformists, and militants are interested, respectively, in *winning, policy,* and *publicity.*

Each party is now postulated to be a coalition of these three factions. We propose that the *party's* preference order over policy pairs is the intersection of the preference orders of its three factions. Political equilibrium—christened "party-unanimity Nash equilibrium" (PUNE)—is now defined as a Nash equilibrium where each equipped with the preferences just described. In words, this means that, at a policy pair (t^1, t^2), party 1 will deviate from t^1 to a policy t^* only if all three of its factions (weakly) prefer (t^*, t^2) to (t^1, t^2). We show that we should expect a (two-dimensional) continuum of such equilibria to exist in multidimensional party competition.

Once armed with the PUNE concept, we are also able to resolve the question of existence of equilibrium in the {Wittman, uncertainty, multidimensional} model—an issue that, until now, has remained open.

The existence of a continuum of equilibria in the {multifaction, uncertainty, multidimensional} model means that the model is underdetermined—if we believe that real political equilibria are locally unique. I argue, in Chapter 8, that the multiplicity of equilibria is the price we pay for not specifying a particular bargaining game among the factions of a party. There are, however, reasons not to specify such a game. Perhaps the main one is that bargaining among factions requires compromises, and compromises are easiest to motivate in a multiperiod game—for example, the militants will compromise today in return for a promise that the reformists will compromise in the next election. Bargaining among factions, in any case, is only coherent in a more complex model, one played over many periods, or one complexified in some other way.[1]

It turns out, nevertheless, that in many applications, the cost we pay for not refining the equilibrium set is small, either because the PUNEs turn out to be quite locally concentrated in the policy space, and so the model gives us quite good predictions of the characteristics of equilibrium, or because we are able to establish characterizations of the entire equilibrium set. Chapters 9–12 present a sequence of applications of the {multifaction, uncertainty, multidimensional} model.

Chapter 9 considers the problem of multidimensional taxation. The question why income taxation is progressive in almost all democracies has never received a fully satisfactory answer in the political economy literature, because a specification of a multidimensional political contest in which equilibria exist has been lacking. We assume that the set of admissible income tax policies consists of quadratic functions of income, with certain properties (for example, monotonicity of after-tax income in pretax income). The policy space is two-dimensional, after taking account of a budget-balancing constraint. There are two political parties, one representing relatively rich citizens, the other relatively poor citizens. The polity is one in which median income is less than mean income (as in all actual democracies). We show that in all PUNEs of the game

---

1. Another way of modeling compromise among factions without an intertemporal story would be to allow transfers of some good among factions: we'll assent to your proposal if you pay us.

where parties compete by announcing tax policies, a *progressive* tax policy wins with probability one. This application demonstrates that even though we have a continuum of equilibria, we can say something interesting about all of them.

Chapter 10 attacks a venerable question in political economy, one of concern since the foundation of democracy. In a democracy, why do the poor not expropriate the rich through the tax system? Various answers have been offered; this chapter proposes a new formulation of an old answer that depends upon the multidimensionality of the policy space. That old answer is that the voters— in particular, the poor—care about other things as well as income, for example, religion. If the conservative party is religious and the labor or socialist party is not, a section of the poor will vote for the conservatives, despite its conservative policy on income redistribution.[2] This chapter proposes a polity in which each citizen type has a preference order over income and the religious position of the government; the polity is characterized as a distribution of these types. We ask: Is there a condition on the distribution of types under which it will be the case that, if religion is sufficiently salient, *all* PUNEs will involve *both left and right* political parties' proposing low tax rates? We indeed discover such a condition. Here is, again, an application in which the infinite multiplicity of PUNEs turns out not to sabotage the possibility of analysis. We go on to show, empirically, that if the "religious" issue is read as the race issue in the United States, then the condition in question holds for the U.S. polity. Thus to the extent that race is a salient issue for U.S. voters, we should expect *neither* political party to propose highly redistributive policies.

This result shows that multidimensional politics can be, at first glance, coun- terintuitive or, as some would say, paradoxical. We show, in Chapter 10, that if religion is sufficiently salient for voters, both parties will propose a *zero* tax rate, in all PUNEs, even though a majority of the population has an ideal tax rate of unity! The source of the paradox is that policies are voted on not inde- pendently, but as a package, under party competition. (This is in contrast to the referendum process, where, presumably, each dimension of policy can be voted on independently.)

In Chapter 11 we apply the PUNE concept to another historical question: why did socialists win in some countries, and fascists in others, in interwar Europe?

---

2. This is not quite the same thing as Marx's view that "religion is the opium of the people." For Marx, religion kept the masses from rebelling; here religion may deter many workers from voting for the party that champions their economic interests.

The chapter is inspired by the rich analysis of this question by Luebbert (1991). Although Luebbert's analysis is complex, a rather simple story is its dominating feature. That story is one of multiclass, competitive politics. Luebbert models countries as consisting of four classes: the urban workers (W), the urban middle class (M), the rural landed peasantry (P), and the agricultural laborers (A). (Of course urban and rural upper classes existed too, but were too few in number to matter in terms of voting.) The key to political victory (whether by election or through some other form of popular support) was to forge an alliance either between the workers and landed peasants or between the middle class and the landed peasants. Presumably the Left would win if the former alliance were cemented, and the Right would win if the latter alliance were cemented. Luebbert goes on to argue that the Left succeeded in forging the worker-peasant alliance only in countries in which peasant–agricultural worker class struggle was quiescent. The three European countries where that struggle was active were Germany, Italy, and Spain, which all became fascist.

We design a model to test Luebbert's conjecture, which becomes a formulation about the probability of victory by the Left in an electoral competition between Left and Right, where rural class struggle is either quiescent or active. The "Luebbert conjecture" is that this probability should be significantly larger when rural class struggle is quiescent. The policy space in this model is four-dimensional. We deduce strong but not ironclad support of the Luebbert conjecture.

Chapter 12 presents a rather schematic, three-class model of U.S. politics, whose purpose is to study the question: why are the interests of large capital represented in both the Democratic and the Republican parties? (We presume this to be the case, without argument.) The economy consists of three types of individuals: capitalists, who own a large firm 'and hire labor; workers, who sell their labor power to the large firm; and the petite bourgeoisie, who work in their own shops and hire no labor. It is supposed that the large firm uses government-provided infrastructure an an input, besides capital and labor, while the petit bourgeois shops use only the labor of their owners. The political problem is to determine a uniform tax rate on the income of all three classes, and to divide tax revenues between a lump-sum transfer to all citizens and spending on infrastructure. This is a two-dimensional policy space, after taking account of the government's budget constraint.

We presume that the petite bourgeoisie and large capital are both represented in the Republican Party. (This party turns out to have five factions.) We study two alternative membership scenarios for the Democratic Party: either it represents only workers (Scenario One), or it is a coalition of workers and large capital (Scenario Two). These alternatives are easily captured with the machinery of factions. We show that capitalists do better in the political equilibria (PUNE) of Scenario Two than in those of Scenario One, which provides an explanation of the presence of both large capital and labor in the Democratic Party. Why does large capital not join the British Labour Party and the Scandinavian social democratic parties? Perhaps it has. If not, this analysis would suggest that entry of the capitalist class into those parties is forbidden.

Chapter 13 revisits the problem of (endogenous) party formation , but now in the multidimensional context. We begin with a distribution of types and assume that two parties will form. We compute what the preferences of those parties will be under the assumption of a perfectly representative democracy that was introduced in Chapter 5. We develop two applications. First, we estimate the distribution of U.S. voter preferences on the two issues of taxation and race, using data from the National Election Survey, and then compute the endogenous parties that would form in a perfectly representative democracy. Second, we take the model of Chapter 9, in which the set of policies is quadratic income taxes, and compute what parties should arise, given the distribution of income in the United States and assuming that all voters are interested in maximizing their after-tax income. We show, in both of these examples, that the parties are quite polarized in their preferences and that policies in political equilibrium are quite far apart. We end the main body of this chapter with a short section that contemplates the nature of party formation in an imperfectly representative democracy, where the preferences of parties are determined by their financial contributors. A reprise takes up, once again, the issue of why the poor don't expropriate the rich in democracies, and summarizes what we have learned.

Chapter 13 presents our most complete theory of political economy, for parties emerge endogenously from political competition, given only the distribution of preferences and endowments of the citizenry. As such, the chapter competes with the median-voter model, which also claims to explain political outcomes given only those same primitives.

Chapter 14 begins an exploration of the theory of three-party competition. It is assumed that, if no party wins a majority of the vote, then a majority coalition, consisting of two parties, must form. We now introduce two kinds of voter—sincere and strategic—and model political equilibrium as a Nash equilibrium of a game that takes place at three dates: first, when parties announce policies; second, when citizens vote (perhaps after a series of opinion polls); and third, when a coalition government forms and announces a policy. The main purpose of the chapter is to show that, under the supposition of uncertainty about voter behavior, the main concepts introduced in the two-party model generalize to the three-party case—that is, with a unidimensional policy space, a generalized Wittman equilibrium exists, and with a multidimensional policy space, a generalized PUNE exists. As in the two-party case, the policies of parties are differentiated at these equilibria.

Throughout this book there is an emphasis on the computation of political equilibrium. We wish to show the reader that the models we study can be fit to data, and can be useful tools of analysis in empirical work—in particular, the PUNE concept liberates formal political economy from the handicap of having to conceive of politics as unidimensional. Although the computation of multidimensional political equilibria is more complex than finding the ideal policy of the median voter, it can be mastered by studying the examples we present. We have used Mathematica to compute equilibria, but of course other programs can be used as well. We strongly recommend that the student learn to compute. Our tools can be used to unearth concrete answers to problems involving political competition, but mastering computation is essential to that end.

The mathematics employed in this book is almost all covered in a course in linear algebra and an advanced calculus course. Concepts or theorems invoked that do not fit that characterization, such as Farkas' lemma and other terminology of elementary convex analysis, and the basic elements of probability theory, are briefly presented in the Mathematical Appendix. As is often said, a certain level of mathematical sophistication is desirable, for which an advanced calculus course is a proxy. Any student who has completed the first-year Ph.D. course in microeconomic theory will be adequately prepared, but that preparation is probably not necessary. Some significant exposure to economic modeling is, however, surely necessary. A number of examples assume a familiarity with the concept of general economic equilibrium, but those examples are fairly simple. The game theory used in the book is elementary: the only equilibrium concept used is Nash equilibrium. Nevertheless, the reader will develop a good understanding of the equilibrium approach if she or he masters the text.

1

Political Competition over a Single Issue: The Case of Certainty

1.1 Citizens, Voters, and Parties

We begin with a classical example in political economy, to illustrate the basic components from the theory of rational individual decision making that our theory must include. There is a population of voters, in an economy with two goods: a private good, to be thought of as an amalgam of consumption commodities and measured in dollars, and a public good, provided by the state and financed through taxation. All voters have the same preferences over these two goods, represented by a *direct utility function*

$$u(x, G) = x + 2\alpha G^{1/2},$$

where x is the individual's consumption level of the private good and G is the level of the public good provided to all. Voters are differentiated by their wage-earning capacity; a voter with a wage of h earns enough to purchase h units of the private good in, say, a year. Suppose that h is distributed among voters according to a probability measure $\mathbf{F}$, whose mean is μ. The public good is measured in units of the private good that are needed to produce it per capita: thus if T dollars per capita are raised in tax revenue, then T units of the public good can be produced.

The *policy* that voters must choose is a proportional income tax rate to fund the public good. We stipulate that the *policy space* is the interval [0, 1], which is to say the tax rate must be at least zero and no larger than one. If the tax rate is t, then taxes raised will be in the amount $t\mu$ per capita, since

$$\int th \, d\mathbf{F}(h) = t\mu.$$

(This formula embeds an assumption that voter-workers do not alter their labor supply depending upon what the tax rate is.) At tax rate t, the voter of "type h" will consume $(1 - t)h$ units of the private good (her after-tax income) and $t\mu$ units of the public good. We now define the voter h's *indirect utility function* over policies, which is

(1.1) $v(t, h) = (1 - t)h + 2\alpha(t\mu)^{1/2};$

v measures the utility of type h as a function of the tax rate.

Notice that voters of different types (where type is h) have different preferences over policies. The *ideal policy* of voter h is the value of t which maximizes his utility. Since v is concave in t, we may find this point by setting $\partial v / \partial t$ equal to zero, which gives

(1.2) $\hat{t}^h = \min[\dfrac{\alpha^2 \mu}{h^2}, 1],$

where we denote by $\hat{t}^h$ the ideal policy of h. (We must use the "min" operator, since when $\alpha^2 \mu / h^2$ is greater than one [for small h], the best feasible policy for h is to set the tax rate at unity.) It follows from the above expression that high-wage voters want low tax rates, and low-wage voters want high tax rates.

The political problem that will occupy us henceforth is how tax policy (more generally, any policy that is determined politically) is determined through political competition and, in particular, through competitive elections.

We may generalize from the example. We postulate a set of *types H*, where the generic *citizen* is denoted by $h \in H$. A citizen's type may be thought of as a vector of traits, which characterizes her preferences and endowments. All citizens are eligible to vote. We will always assume that H is a subset of some real space—for example, $\mathbf{R}$, $\mathbf{R}^2$, and so on. If, for instance, $H \subset \mathbf{R}^2$, then each citizen is relevantly characterized by two traits, perhaps her income and her religion. The population of citizens is characterized by a probability measure $\mathbf{F}$ on H. Thus if S is a (measurable) subset of H, then $\mathbf{F}(S)$ is the fraction of the population who have traits $h \in S$. $\mathbf{F}$ could be a probability distribution with finite or infinite support. In the former case, we speak of a *finite-type* polity. In most of this book we will work with distributions where the support is a continuum, for this will allow us to use the calculus. The infinite-type model is the appropriate one to capture the idea that each citizen has negligible effect on the political outcome, and that there are a very large number of vectors of types in the population.

The set of *voters* will be some subset of the set of citizens; in this chapter we assume that every citizen votes. There is a space of *policies, T. T* is a subset of some real space. In this chapter, we study the case where T is a real interval; this is the case of a *unidimensional policy* (or issue) *space*. When $T \subset \mathbf{R}^n, n > 1$, we say the policy space is *multidimensional*.

Every citizen has a preference order over policies, represented by a utility function $v : T \to \mathbf{R}$. We denote the utility function of a citizen of type h as $v(\cdot, h)$. When faced with two policies to choose from, a voter votes for the one he prefers. If he is indifferent, he votes for each policy with probability one-half.

There are two political *parties*, here denoted 1 and 2. Party i has a *payoff function* Π^i, which gives a payoff or utility for the party as a function of the pair of policies announced by both parties, (t^1, t^2). Thus

(1.3) $\Pi^i : T \times T \to \mathbf{R}, \qquad i = 1, 2.$

The payoff functions are, at this point, taken to be primitives, but we will, in this chapter, study two special cases where the payoff functions are derived from prior assumptions.

Definition 1.1 A *political equilibrium* is a Nash equilibrium in the game played by the two parties, where the payoff functions are $\Pi^i, i = 1, 2$, and T is their common strategy space.

That is, a political equilibrium is a policy pair (t^{1^*}, t^{2^*}) such that

$$\forall t \in T \quad \Pi^1(t^{1^*}, t^{2^*}) \geq \Pi^1(t, t^{2^*})$$

$$\forall t \in T \quad \Pi^2(t^{1^*}, t^{2^*}) \geq \Pi^2(t^{1^*}, t).$$

All political equilibria in this book are special cases of this general definition. Thus we use the most basic concept in game theory as our concept of political equilibrium.

In this chapter we assume not only that all citizens vote in elections, but that both parties know the distribution $\mathbf{F}$ of types and the utility function v. There is nevertheless some uncertainty as to the electoral outcome, due to the possibility of a tie. We assume that in this case a fair coin is flipped, so that each party wins with probability one-half.

Let $\underline{\Omega}(t^1, t^2) \subset H$ be the set of types who prefer t^1 to t^2, and let $I(t^1, t^2)$ be the set of types who are indifferent between t^1 and t^2. (The set of types who prefer t^2 to t^1 is the complement of $\Omega(t^1, t^2) \cup (I(t^1, t^2))$ in H.) Then the fraction of voters who vote for t^1, when facing the choice between t^1 and t^2, is

(1.4) $\rho(t^1, t^2) = \mathbf{F}(\Omega(t^1, t^2)) + \frac{1}{2} \cdot \mathbf{F}(I(t^1, t^2)).^1$

This fraction is either more than, equal to, or less than one-half. In the first case, party 1 wins the election, in the third case it loses, and in the case where $\rho = \frac{1}{2}$, each party wins with probability one-half. Summarizing, we denote by $\pi(t^1, t^2)$ the probability that party 1 wins the election. We have:

(1.5) $\pi(t^1, t^2) = \begin{cases} 1 & \text{if } \rho(t^1, t^2) > \frac{1}{2} \\ \frac{1}{2} & \text{if } \rho(t^1, t^2) = \frac{1}{2} \\ 0 & \text{if } \rho(t^1, t^2) < \frac{1}{2} \end{cases}.$

certainty We call this case—where voters are perfectly rational and parties know everything about them—the *case of certainty.* Empirically this case never occurs, but it is the obvious benchmark at which to begin our analysis.

1.2 The Downs Model

Anthony Downs (1957) applied the model of spatial equilibrium of Hotelling (1929) to the case of political competition. His model, succinctly stated, is the special case of political equilibrium (section 1.1) in which

(1.6)
$$\Pi^1(t^1, t^2) = \pi(t^1, t^2).$$
$$\Pi^2(t^1, t^2) = 1 - \pi(t^1, t^2).$$

Thus each party desires to maximize its probability of victory. A political equilibrium of this model will be called a *Downs political equilibrium.*

---

1. Formula (1.4) assumes that there is a continuum of traits, and that **F** is absolutely continuous with respect to Lebesgue measure. Thus if $\mathbf{F}(I) > 0$, there is a continuum of agents who are indifferent between t^1 and t^2, and if each flips a coin to decide how to vote, exactly one-half of them will vote for each policy. This justifies the formula.

In this model, the parties' payoff functions are *not* derived from preferences over policies. Parties are neither left nor right, secular nor confessional. A party's goal is solely to win office.

There are two interpretations of this model. The first is that of a competition between candidates, not parties, who desire to win the election solely because of the perks of office. If those candidates are chosen by parties, which do have policy preferences, the parties are unable to influence the candidates to act as their agents in respecting those preferences. Under this interpretation, the candidate is a completely unaccountable agent of his or her party. The second interpretation is that the parties themselves desire only to win office. They may do so either for venal reasons (the perks of office) or because, once holding office, a party can implement the policies of its choice. But if the latter were the case, then voters would be choosing between parties which would implement policies different from the ones announced—and this is not the Downsian assumption. In Downs's model, voters vote for the policy they prefer between the two announced: the assumption of voter rationality implies voters expect the announced policy to be implemented.

Because actual political parties are always partisan—in the sense of possessing preferences over policies—the Downs model does not appear to capture actual political history. Nevertheless the model has been extremely influential, in spite of its lack of realism, because it provides a clean, simple prediction about the nature of political equilibrium, to which we now turn.

Definition 1.2 A *Condorcet winner* is a policy $t^* \in T$ which defeats or ties all other policies in pairwise elections. In the case of this chapter, we may write:

$$\forall t \in T \qquad \pi(t^*, t) \geq \tfrac{1}{2}.$$

A *strict Condorcet winner* is a policy t^* which defeats all other policies in pairwise elections. In this chapter, we may write:

$$\forall t \neq t^* \qquad \pi(t^*, t) = 1.$$

Now observe:

Lemma 1.1 *Let t^* be a strict Condorcet winner. Then (t^*, t^*) is the unique Downs political equilibrium.*

Proof:

1. Existence. (t^*, t^*) is clearly a political equilibrium, for $\Pi^1(t^*, t^*) = \pi(t^*, t^*)$ $= \frac{1}{2}$, and $\Pi^2(t^*, t^*) = \frac{1}{2}$ as well, and if either party deviates, its probability of victory falls to zero.

2. Uniqueness. Suppose (t^{1^*}, t^{2^*}) were a Downs equilibrium where $t^{1^*} \neq t^* \neq t^{2^*}$. Both parties cannot win for sure at (t^{1^*}, t^{2^*}). Suppose $\pi(t^{1^*}, t^{2^*}) < 1$. Then party 1 should deviate to t^*, for $\pi(t^*, t^{2^*}) = 1$.

Now suppose $t^{1^*} = t^*$ and $t^{2^*} \neq t^*$. Then $\Pi^2(t^{1^*}, t^{2^*}) = 0$ but $\Pi^2(t^{1^*}, t^*) = \frac{1}{2}$. So party 2 should deviate. ∎

We leave as an exercise for the reader what political equilibria look like when there are several Condorcet winners.

Definition 1.3   A function $v : T \rightarrow \mathbf{R}$ is *single-peaked* iff it possesses a unique local maximum on T.

Remark   An alternative, and indeed preferable, definition is:

Definition 1.3*   A function $v : T \rightarrow \mathbf{R}$ is *single-peaked* iff it is strictly quasi-concave[2] on T.

Suppose T is not compact—say $T = \mathbf{R}$. The function graphed in Figure 1.1 has a unique local maximum on T, but it is not quasi-concave. We want to eliminate functions like this one from the family of "single-peaked" functions— hence the superiority of Definition 1.3*. If T is compact and v is continuous, then the two definitions are equivalent. Since the term "single peaked" clearly suggests the formulation of Definition 1.3, it is actually a misnomer.

If T is compact, and if $v(\cdot, h)$ is continuous, then it has a maximum on T. If $v(\cdot, h)$ is also single-peaked, this is its unique local maximum.

We now formally assume:

A1 $v(t, h)$ is continuous in its arguments.
A2 $v(\cdot, h)$ is single-peaked (in t) for all $h \in H$.

---

2. Concepts like quasi-concavity, with which the reader may not be familiar, will generally be defined in the Mathematical Appendix.

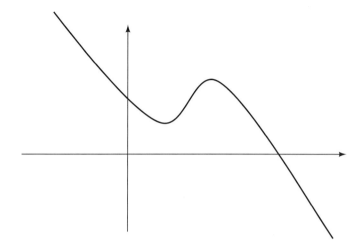

Figure 1.1   A non-quasi-concave function with a unique local maximum

A3 If $t^1 \neq t^2$, the set of types indifferent between t^1 and t^2 has **F**-measure zero.
A4 **F** is equivalent to Lebesgue measure,[3] λ.

The key property of single-peaked functions which we employ is stated in:

Lemma 1.2   *If $v : T \to \mathbf{R}$ is continuous and single-peaked on T and if v achieves its maximum at $\hat{t}$, then v is monotone decreasing for all $t > \hat{t}$ and v is monotone increasing for all $t < \hat{t}$.*

Proof:
We prove the first statement. Suppose, to the contrary, there are points t' and t'' such that $\hat{t} \leq t' < t''$, and $v(t'') > v(t')$. Let $k = v(t') + \frac{1}{2}(v(t'') - v(t'))$. Then $v(t'') > k$ and $v(\hat{t}) \geq v(t'') > k$, so $\hat{t}$ and t'' both lie in v's upper contour set at value k. However, $v(t') < k$, and t' lies between $\hat{t}$ and t''—this contradicts that fact that v is quasi-concave.

The second claim is proved in like manner.   ∎

---

3. See the Mathematical Appendix for the definition of the equivalence of two measures. If H is unidimensional, and F is the (cumulative) distribution function of **F**, then A4 is equivalent to F's being continuous and strictly increasing.

Definition 1.4 An *ideal policy* of citizen h is a policy $\hat{t}^h$ such that $\forall t \in T$, $v(\hat{t}^h, h) \geq v(t, h)$. An ideal policy $\hat{t}^h$ is a best policy for h.

We next define a function $\Psi : T \to [0, 1]$. Let H^t be the set of citizens in H whose ideal policy is less than t. Define

(1.7) $\Psi(t) = \mathbf{F}(H^t)$.

$\Psi(t)$ is the fraction of the population whose ideal policies are less than t.

Note that Ψ is an increasing function, since $t' > t \Rightarrow H^{t'} \supset H^t$.

Lemma 1.3 *Suppose A1, A2, and A3. If Ψ is continuous and strictly increasing then there is a policy t^* that is a strict Condorcet winner. In fact, $\Psi(t^*) = \frac{1}{2}$.*

Proof:

1. Since Ψ is continuous and strictly increasing, there is a unique t^* such that $\Psi(t^*) = \frac{1}{2}$. We shall show that t^* is a strict Condorcet winner.

2. Let $t < t^*$. Since $\Psi(t^*) = \frac{1}{2}$, exactly one-half the citizenry have ideal points greater than or equal to t^*. All these prefer t^* to t, by Lemma 1.2. It remains to show that *more* than one-half prefer t^* to t. Suppose to the contrary that this were false: then one-half the population either prefer t to t^* or are indifferent between t and t^*. By A3, those who are indifferent make up a null set, so exactly one-half the citizenry must prefer t to t^*. That is, $\mathbf{F}(\Omega(t, t^*)) = \frac{1}{2}$.

3. Let h^* be any type whose ideal point is t^*: by single-peakedness, $v(t^*, h^*) - v(t, h^*) > 0$. By continuity of v in h, there is an open ball, B, about h^* in H, such that

$$h \in B \Rightarrow v(t^*, h) - v(t, h) > 0.$$

4. Since $\mathbf{F}(\Omega(t, t^*)) = \frac{1}{2}$, $\Omega(t, t^*)$ contains types whose ideal points are arbitrarily close to t^*. So we may choose a sequence $\{h^i\}$ of types in $\Omega(t, t^*)$ whose ideal points converge to t^*; by continuity, the limit of this sequence, call it h^*, has ideal point t^*.

5. But this contradicts step 3, which shows that an open ball B about h^* can be constructed which excludes all points in $\Omega(t, t^*)$. It follows that the supposition in step 2 is false, and so a majority of types prefer t^* to t.

6. A similar argument shows that if $t > t^*$, a majority of types prefer t^* to t. Thus it is established that t^* is a strict Condorcet winner. ■

Theorem 1.1 *Suppose A1, A2, and A3 hold. Let $T \subset R$. Then there exists a political equilibrium in the Downs game. Moreover, if Ψ is continuous and strictly increasing on T, then the equilibrium is unique, and consists in both parties playing the same policy, the median ideal policy.*

Proof:

1. T is an interval, which we denote $T = [\underline{t}, \bar{t}]$.

2. We prove the first claim first. There are two cases.

Case (i)   There is a policy t^* such that $\Psi(t^*) = \frac{1}{2}$. In this case (t^*, t^*) is a political equilibrium. To see this, we must check whether either party can profitably deviate. Each party wins with probability one-half at (t^*, t^*). Suppose party 1 deviates to $t > t^*$. We know that one-half the population have ideal policies less than t^*: by Lemma 1.2, all those people prefer t^* to t. To fix this important observation in the mind, see Figure 1.2. Consequently party 1 now wins with probability at most one-half, so the deviation is not profitable. Now suppose $t < t^*$. The set of citizens with ideal policy greater or equal to t^* makes up at least one-half the population, and these citizens all prefer t^* to t, by Lemma 1.2: consequently party 1 now wins with probability at most one-half. Hence this deviation is not profitable.

The same argument applies to possible deviations by party 2. Hence (t^*, t^*) is a political equilibrium.

Case (ii)   There is no policy t such that $\Psi(t) = \frac{1}{2}$. Suppose the set $\{t \mid \Psi(t) \geq \frac{1}{2}\}$ is nonempty. Then, let $t^* = \inf\{t \mid \Psi(t) \geq \frac{1}{2}\}$. Then (t^*, t^*) is a political equilibrium. We must check the possible deviations. Suppose party 1 deviates to $t > t^*$. We know that at least half the population prefer t^* to t, because for any small $\epsilon > 0$, $\Psi(t^* + \epsilon) > \frac{1}{2}$, and so this deviation is unprofitable. Now suppose $t < t^*$. All the citizens who prefer t to t^* have ideal point less than t^*. But since $t' < t^*$ implies $\Psi(t') < \frac{1}{2}$, less than half the citizenry prefer t to t^*. By A3, more than half the citizenry prefer t^* to t, so t is an unprofitable deviation.

3. On the other hand, suppose $\{t \mid \Psi(t) \geq \frac{1}{2}\} = \emptyset$. Then $(\bar{t}, \bar{t})$ is a Downs equilibrium. Since $H(\bar{t}) < \frac{1}{2}$ by hypothesis, more than half the polity prefer $\bar{t}$ to any other policy. This concludes the proof of the first statement.

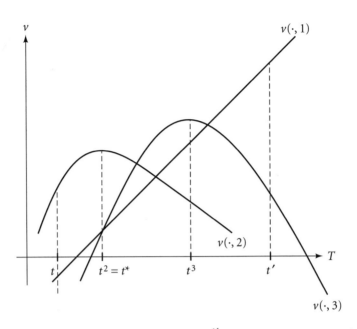

Figure 1.2   All citizens with ideal policies $\hat{t}^h \geq t^*$ prefer t^* to any $t < t^*$

4. Now suppose that Ψ is continuous and strictly increasing on T. It follows by Lemma 1.3 that the median ideal policy, t^*, is a strict Condorcet winner. It follows by Lemma 1.1 that t^* is the unique Downs equilibrium. ∎

In the case where Ψ is continuous and increasing, the policy t^* (where $\Psi(t^*) = \frac{1}{2}$) is the *median ideal policy* in the sense that one-half the voters have ideal policies less than or equal to t^* and one-half have ideal policies greater than or equal to t^*. There is no sense, however, in which the *voters* who have t^* as their ideal policies are median in the type space H. For note that Theorem 1.1 does not assume $H \subset \mathbf{R}$. If H lies in a higher dimensional space, then its median is not well defined. Hence the so-called median voter theorem, in which t^* is the ideal policy of a voter with the median trait, is a special case of Theorem 1.1. Let us illustrate this point with some examples.

Example 1.1   We continue the analysis of the introductory example. Citizens are endowed with (scalar) incomes $h \in H$. The distribution of income is given by $\mathbf{F}$ on H. We assume A4. All citizens have identical preferences over income, x, and a public good, G. Their preferences are represented by the utility function

(1.8) $u(x, G) = x + 2\alpha\sqrt{G},$

where $\alpha > 0$, and α is the same for all individuals. If $h^2 \geq \alpha^2\mu$ for all types, then, from (1.2) we have, for all h:

(1.9) $\hat{t}^h = \mu \left(\dfrac{\alpha}{h}\right)^2.$

Note that $\hat{t}^h$ is a strictly decreasing, continuous function of h. Hence Ψ is continuous and strictly increasing. Check that there is a unique type who is indifferent between any pair of distinct policies. Theorem 1.1 tells us that the unique Downs political equilibrium is (t^*, t^*) where $\Psi(t^*) = \frac{1}{2}$. But the set of citizens whose ideal tax rate is t^* or less, because it consists of one-half the population, is exactly the set of citizens whose endowment is greater than or equal to m, where m is the median income of the population.

Let F be the cumulative distribution function (CDF) of the probability measure $\mathbf{F}$. Then m is defined by the equation

$$F(m) = \tfrac{1}{2}.$$

Having solved for m, we immediately get t^* via (1.9).

In this example, we see that the Condorcet winner t^* is associated with the "median voter."

Example 1.2   Just as in the first example, we assume utility is given by (1.8), except we now suppose that α varies in the population. h remains a citizen's income. Now a citizen is characterized by the *pair* of traits (h, α). Let B be the domain of types (h, α) and let $\mathbf{G}$ be the probability measure on B characterizing the distribution of types. We assume that $\mathbf{G}$ is absolutely continuous with respect to Lebesgue measure on B.

Just as before, we have

$$v(t, \alpha, h) = (1 - t)h + 2\alpha(t\mu)^{1/2}$$

and so $\hat{t}^{h,\alpha} = \mu\left(\frac{\alpha}{h}\right)^2$. Assume that α takes on values in an interval $[\underline{\alpha}, \bar{\alpha}]$ and h takes on values in an interval $[\underline{h}, \bar{h}]$. Then Ψ is a continuous, strictly increasing function (by the absolute continuity of $\mathbf{G}$ with respect to Lebesgue measure), and so Theorem 1.1 tells us there is a unique Downs political equilibrium,

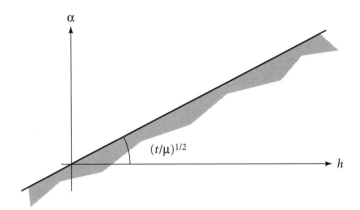

Figure 1.3   The set of types in Example 1.2 with ideal tax rate less than t

(t^*, t^*). Let B^t be all citizens whose ideal tax rate is less than or equal to t. There is a unique t^* defined by

$$\mathbf{G}(B^{t^*}) = \tfrac{1}{2}.$$

Let us solve for t^*. The set of all citizens whose ideal tax rate is less than t is, by (1.9),

$$\left\{ (h, \alpha) \mid \frac{\alpha}{h} < \left(\frac{t}{\mu} \right)^{1/2} \right\}.$$

This is the set of all citizens whose trait pair (h, α) lies below a line through the origin in the (h, α) plane with slope $(t/\mu)^{1/2}$: see Figure 1.3. The Condorcet winner t^* is that tax rate at which this half-plane has $\mathbf{G}$-measure one-half. If we specified $\mathbf{G}$, we could compute t^*.

In this example, the set of voters with ideal tax rate t^* is the line $\alpha = h(t^*/\mu)^{1/2}$. Granted, this line separates the type space into two equal masses, but there is no well-defined median voter.

Example 1.3   We now have a one-dimensional type space again, where $h \in H$ is income. In this example, taxes do not fund a public good: rather tax revenues (from proportional taxation) are redistributed equally on a per capita basis. Let F have mean μ and median $m < \mu$. (Thus, as is always true in actual societies, median income is less than mean income.) An individual's utility is given by her after-tax income. We have

(1.10) $v(t, h) = (1 - t)h + t\mu.$

The per capita tax revenue is $t\mu$ at tax rate t. This time, we must be more careful in computing ideal tax rates. We have $\partial v/\partial t = -h + \mu$. Thus, if $h > \mu$, then $\partial v/\partial t$ is negative for all t, so $\hat{t}^h = 0$. If $h < \mu$, then $\partial v/\partial t$ is positive for all t, so $\hat{t}^h = 1$. The individuals with $h = \mu$ are indifferent among all tax rates. If $\mathbf{F}$ is absolutely continuous with respect to Lebesgue measure, then $\{h = \mu\}$ is a set of measure zero in the population, which we can ignore.

Thus there are only two ideal tax rates for the polity: zero and one. The function Ψ is given by

$$\Psi(0) = 0$$

$$\Psi(t) = 1 - F(\mu) \qquad \text{for all } t, 0 < t \leq 1.$$

This says the fraction of society whose ideal tax is less than t, for any $t \leq 1$, is precisely the fraction whose income is greater than μ.

Now $F(\mu) > F(m) = \frac{1}{2}$, so $\Psi(t) < \frac{1}{2}$ for all t. This is a case where $\{t \mid \Psi(t) \geq \frac{1}{2}\}$ is empty, and so the proof of Theorem 1.1 tells us that $(1, 1)$ is a Downs political equilibrium. The reader may verify that the equilibrium is unique. In words, this example says that, if the majority of citizens have income (or wealth) less than the mean income (wealth) and if income redistribution is the only issue, then the unique Downs political equilibrium entails a complete redistribution of income to the mean.

Examples 1.1 and 1.2 make the point that what is key for Theorem 1.1 is the unidimensionality of the policy space. The dimension of the type space can be large. The term "median voter" conjures up a voter whose *trait* is median in the space of types: but this only makes sense for unidimensional type spaces. Theorem 1.1 is thus more general than the "median voter theorem." Nevertheless, its logic is almost the same as the classical median voter theorem (with unidimensional type spaces).

Part of the confusion in the literature between the type space and the policy space is due to the following example, which is perhaps the most popular illustration of the Downsian logic.

Example 1.4   The preferences of voters are given by

$$v(t, a) = -1/2(t - a)^2,$$

where $a \in A$, A is a real interval, and the population is distributed according to **F** on A.

These preferences are called *Euclidean*, because a citizen's utility is just minus one-half the square of the Euclidean distance to his ideal point, a. Thus *his ideal policy is his type*. (Note that $\partial v / \partial t = a - t$, so a's ideal point is a.) If **F** is absolutely continuous with respect to Lebesgue measure then Ψ is continuous, and Theorem 1.1 says that the unique Downs political equilibrium is (t^*, t^*) where $t^* = a^*$ and $F(a^*) = \frac{1}{2}$.

It is pedagogically unfortunate that political scientists use Euclidean preferences so frequently, for their use obscures the important distinction between the type space and the policy space.

Some authors work with a variant of the Downs model, in which each party's goal is to maximize the fraction of the vote it receives. We have defined $\rho(t^1, t^2)$ as the fraction of the vote received by party 1, and so under this formulation

(1.11) $\Pi^1(t^1, t^2) = \rho(t^1, t^2)$ and $\Pi^2(t^1, t^2) = 1 - \rho(t^1, t^2)$.

Call this the *vote-maximizing model*.

It is easy to see that Theorem 1.1 also characterizes the equilibria of the vote-maximizing model. For consider the pair (t^*, t^*), which is a Downs equilibrium. At this policy pair, each party receives $\rho = \frac{1}{2}$ the vote. If either party deviates, it receives at most one-half the vote. So (t^*, t^*) is a vote-maximizing political equilibrium as well. Conversely, the reader can convince herself that if (t^{1^*}, t^{2^*}) is a vote-maximizing equilibrium it is also a Downs equilibrium.

The identity between the vote-maximizing equilibria and Downs equilibria fails to hold, however, when uncertainty is introduced (see Chapter 2). At that point, one must decide which model is preferable.

In my view, any model that predicts that parties propose the same policy in equilibrium is inconsistent with other background postulates of a realistic theory: that voters are rational and that party building requires commitment, financial or otherwise, from groups of citizens. For if both parties propose the same policy and voters know this will occur, why should anyone spend resources building a *particular* party? So the Downs model is only coherent within a broader framework if running elections and building parties are cost-less enterprises.

Nevertheless the Downs model has had tremendous influence in the development of formal theories of politics, because for years it was the only game in town. This chapter in the history of political science shows the impact that a single, formal model can have on the work *and perceptions* of social scientists.

The Downs model is one of *opportunist* politics, because it assumes that parties or candidates are motivated only by the desire to win office, not the desire to implement particular policies. As Downs wrote,

> [Party members] act solely in order to obtain the income, prestige, and power which come from being in office. Thus politicians in our model never seek office as a means of carrying out particular policies; their only goal is to reap the rewards of holding office per se.
>
> . . . Upon this reasoning rests the fundamental hypothesis of our model: parties formulate policies in order to win elections, rather than win elections to formulate policies. (Downs 1957, 28)

Thus for Downs, policies were merely instrumental devices for putting candidates into office. Yet from political history, it appears that parties are formed by interest groups (and coalitions thereof) to advance their interests. If this is so, then, as I wrote earlier, one could interpret the Downs model as one of competing *candidates,* where—for some reason—parties completely lack control of their candidates.

There is a notable contrast here with the development of formal economic theory. The general equilibrium model, which developed roughly over the century 1880–1960, assumed that firms maximize profits. Only in the early 1970s, with the first formal models of the "principal–agent problem," did the distinction between the manager and the owner of the firm enter *formal* economic theory. (Of course Berle and Means (1932) had introduced the distinction informally decades earlier.) Thus until 1970, formal economic theory assumed the manager of a firm to be a perfect agent of the firm's owners. In formal political theory, however, exactly the opposite occurred. The first formal political model (Downs) assumed that candidates were completely imperfect agents of their parties.

In my view, the trajectory of the history of political thought, on this issue, is unfortunate. For history tells us, I believe, that the main feature of party competition is the competition between interest groups in the polity, not the competition between opportunist politicians. The latter competition may be important, but it is not the *first* aspect of political competition one should attempt to model.

1.3 The Wittman Model

Almost contemporaneously with Downs, Seymour Martin Lipset ([1960] 1994) argued, in another influential book, that political parties are the instruments of various economic classes or, more generally, interest groups. Lipset studied the political history of the first half of the twentieth century, where parties were socialist, fascist, communist, or liberal—names deriving from their preferences over policies. Lipset's book, however, made no imprint on formal political theory, a misfortune due—in large part, I believe—to his not having formulated a simple mathematical model of electoral equilibrium. As I noted earlier, Downs was able to do that by applying the elegant spatial model of Hotelling. Lipset does not refer to Downs's book, surely evidence of the lack of cross-fertilization between different methodological schools. Their views on the nature of party competition were diametrically opposed.

It was not until 1973 that Donald Wittman proposed the first formal model of political competition in which parties are partisan or ideological in the sense of possessing preference orders over the policy space T. Let $v^i : T \rightarrow \mathbf{R}$, $i = 1, 2$, be the von Neumann–Morgenstern (vNM) utility functions representing the preferences of parties 1 and 2. (Thus the parties will be ranking lotteries on policy space.) Wittman postulated that each party's goal is to maximize its expected utility; that is,

$$(1.12a) \quad \Pi^1(t^1, t^2) = \pi(t^1, t^2)v^1(t^1) + (1 - \pi(t^1, t^2))v^1(t^2),$$

$$(1.12b) \quad \Pi^2(t^1, t^2) = \pi(t^1, t^2)v^2(t^1) + (1 - \pi(t^1, t^2))v^2(t^2).$$

A political equilibrium of this model will be called a *Wittman* (later, a *reformist*) *political equilibrium*. In this section we analyze only the model with certainty, where the function π is given by (1.3), and T is unidimensional.

One may interpret the Wittman model as one of parties that represent different interest groups: here, v^1 and v^2 represent the policy preferences of two groups of citizens—or some aggregation of the preferences of groups of citizens.

Although the Wittman model seems more faithful to political history, it does not enable us to escape the unfortunate conclusion that political equilibria consist in both parties playing the same policy.

Our environment is the same as in section 1.2. T is the policy space, a real interval, H is the sample space of citizen types, in some real space, and $\mathbf{F}$ is the probability distribution on H characterizing the citizenry. We next state an assumption.

A5 (Monotonicity)   For any pair of policies $t^1, t^2 \in T$, where $t^1 < t^2$, there exists a policy t' such that $\Omega(t^1, t^2) = H^{t'}$.

That is, the set of citizens who prefer t^1 to t^2 is precisely the set whose ideal policy is less than some number t'. Call this the *monotonicity* axiom, which says, informally, that the set of types who prefer a small policy to a large policy are all those whose ideal policies are not too large. This assumption holds in most applications.

Let τ^1 be the ideal policy of party 1 and τ^2 the ideal policy of party 2. Let t^* be such that $\Psi(t^*) = \frac{1}{2}$. We now state:

Theorem 1.2   *Let A1, A2, A3, and A5 hold. Furthermore, suppose that*

(a) the function Ψ is continuous and strictly increasing on T, and
(b) $\tau^1 < t^* < \tau^2$.

Then (t^*, t^*) is the unique Wittman political equilibrium.

The form of Theorem 1.2 is similar to that of Theorem 1.1. t^* is the "median policy" in the sense that exactly one-half the population have ideal policies less than t^*. Here, however, we postulate a new property, monotonicity, and also that the parties are "polarized" in the sense that their ideal policies lie on opposite sides of the median policy.

We first prove a lemma.

Lemma 1.4   *Let the premises of Theorem 1.2 hold. Let $t^1 < t' < \hat{t} < t^2$ be four policies such that $\Omega(t^1, t^2) = H^{\hat{t}}$. Then $\mathbf{F}(\Omega(t', t^2)) > \mathbf{F}(\Omega(t^1, t^2))$.*

Proof:

1. Define the function $t(\epsilon)$ by

$$\Omega(t^1 + \epsilon, t^2) = H^{t(\epsilon)},$$

for ϵ in the domain $[0, t^2 - t^1)$. $t(\epsilon)$ is well defined by A5.

2. We show $t(\epsilon)$ is strictly monotone increasing. It cannot be monotone decreasing because as $\epsilon \to t^2 - t^1$, it is clear that $t(\epsilon) \to t^2$. But $t^2 > \hat{t} = t(0)$.

3. Therefore, unless $t(\epsilon)$ is strictly monotone increasing, there must be values ϵ_1, ϵ_2 in $[0, t^2 - t^1)$ such that $t(\epsilon_1) = t(\epsilon_2)$: that is,

$$\Omega(t^1 + \epsilon_1, t^2) = \Omega(t^1 + \epsilon_2, t^2) \equiv \Omega,$$

where $\Omega \neq H$. It follows that the closure of the set Ω contains a type who is indifferent among three points: $t^1 + \epsilon_1, t^1 + \epsilon_2$, and t^2. This contradicts single-peakedness. Consequently $t(\epsilon)$ must be strictly monotone increasing.

4. By A5, there exists a policy $\tilde{t}$ such that

$$\Omega(t', t^2) = H^{\tilde{t}}.$$

By paragraph 3, it follows that $\tilde{t} > \hat{t}$, and since Ψ is strictly increasing, it follows that $\Psi(\tilde{t}) > \Psi(\hat{t})$. But this means that $F(\Omega(t', t^2)) > F(\Omega(t^1, t^2))$. ∎

We are now ready to prove the theorem.

Proof of Theorem 1.2:

1. We first show that (t^*, t^*) is a Wittman equilibrium. Assumption (a) implies (Lemma 1.3) that t^* is a strict Condorcet winner. We have

$$\Pi^1(t^*, t^*) = v^1(t^*)$$
$$\Pi^2(t^*, t^*) = v^2(t^*).$$

Suppose party 1 deviates to $t \neq t^*$. Then $\pi(t, t^*) = 0$ and so $\Pi^1(t, t^*) = v^1(t^*)$. Hence there is no profitable deviation for party 1; likewise for party 2. Hence (t^*, t^*) is a Wittman political equilibrium.

2. The remainder of the proof shows uniqueness. We first observe that if (t^1, t^2) were another equilibrium, then $t^1 < t^* < t^2$. Suppose to the contrary that t^1 and t^2 were located on the same side of t^*—say $t^2 > t^1 > t^*$. Consider the coalition of citizens $H^{t^*+\epsilon}$, for small $\epsilon > 0$. These form a majority coalition, by assumption (a), and by single-peakedness (A2) they all prefer t^1 to t^2. Hence t^1 defeats t^2 for sure. Thus

$$\Pi^i(t^1, t^2) = v^i(t^1) \qquad i = 1, 2.$$

But party 1 can profitably deviate to t^*; it will still be the case that $\pi(t^*, t^2) = 1$, and so

$$\Pi^1(t^*, t^2) = v^1(t^*) > v^1(t^1),$$

by single-peakedness.

Next consider the case $t^2 > t^1 = t^*$. A strict majority prefers t^1 to t^2. By continuity a strict majority prefers $t^* - \epsilon$ to t^2 for small $\epsilon > 0$. Therefore $\pi(t^* - \epsilon, t^2) = 1$. By continuity of v^1,

$$v^1(t^* - \epsilon) > v^1(t^1),$$

and so we have

$$\Pi^1(t^* - \epsilon, t^2) = v^1(t^* - \epsilon) > v^1(t^*) = \Pi^1(t^*, t^2).$$

So party 1 can profitably deviate to $t^* - \epsilon$. The other possible cases can be similarly disposed of (a good exercise for the reader), showing that any other Wittman equilibrium (t^1, t^2) must be of the form $t^1 < t^* < t^2$.

3. Suppose, then, we have a Wittman equilibrium (t^1, t^2) where $t^1 < t^* < t^2$. It must be the case that $\pi(t^1, t^2) = \frac{1}{2}$. For if $\pi = 0$, then party 1 can deviate to t^* and increase its payoff from $v^1(t^2)$ to $v^1(t^*)$. And if $\pi = 1$ then party 2 can, in like manner, increase its payoff by deviating from t^2 to t^*. Hence $\Pi^i(t^1, t^2) = \frac{1}{2}(v^i(t^1) + v^i(t^2))$.

4. Note that party 1 cannot prefer t^2 to t^1, or it would deviate to t^2. Similarly, party 2 cannot prefer t^1 to t^2.

5. Since $\pi(t^1, t^2) = \frac{1}{2}$, it follows that $\mathbf{F}(\Omega(t^1, t^2)) = \frac{1}{2} = \mathbf{F}(\Omega(t^2, t^1))$. All we need to note here is that, by A3, the set of citizens who are indifferent between t^1 and t^2 has measure zero.

6. By A5, it follows that there is a policy t' such that $\Omega(t^1, t^2) = H^{t'}$. It therefore follows, by step 5, that $\Psi(t') = \frac{1}{2}$, which, by (a), uniquely determines t': in fact, $t' = t^*$.

7. We next remark that party 1 strictly prefers t^1 to t^2. We know by step 4 it cannot strictly prefer t^2 to t^1, but it could conceivably be indifferent between t^1 and t^2. Suppose $v^1(t^1) = v^1(t^2)$. Then, by single-peakedness of v^1, $t^1 < \tau^1 < t^2$. By (b), $t^1 < \tau^1 < t^* < t^2$. Lemma 1.4 now applies, and tells us that $\mathbf{F}(\Omega(\tau^1, t^2)) > \mathbf{F}(\Omega(t^1, t^2)) = \frac{1}{2}$. Thus $\pi(\tau^1, t^2) = 1$, and hence if party 1

deviates to τ^1 (from t^1) its payoff increases from $\frac{1}{2}(v^1(t^1) + v^1(t^2))$ to $v^1(\tau^1)$, its ideal! Hence (t^1, t^2) would not be an equilibrium. Thus $v^1(t^1) > v^1(t^2)$.

8. Now apply Lemma 1.4 to the four policies $t^1 < t^1 + \epsilon < t^* < t^2$, where ϵ is small and positive. We conclude $\mathbf{F}(\Omega(t^1 + \epsilon, t^2)) > \mathbf{F}(\Omega(t^1, t^2)) = \frac{1}{2}$, and so $\pi(t^1 + \epsilon, t^2) = 1$. Therefore a deviation by party 1 from t^1 to $t^1 + \epsilon$ increases its payoff from $\frac{1}{2}(v^1(t^1) + v^1(t^2))$ to $v^1(t^1 + \epsilon)$. Since $v^1(t^2) < v^1(t^1)$, this is an unambiguous increase in payoff for ϵ sufficiently small.

Hence (t^1, t^2) is not a Wittman equilibrium, which concludes the proof. ∎

Note that we never assumed that H is unidimensional (but see below). Thus again—as in Theorem 1.1—we see that the "median policy" result is a feature of the unidimensionality of the policy space, not the unidimensionality of the space of types.[4]

Note that assumption (b) is essential to the conclusion of Theorem 1.2. Suppose, to the contrary, that $t^* < \tau^1 < \tau^2$. Then it is easy to see that (τ^1, τ^1) is a Wittman equilibrium. There are other Wittman equilibria (the reader should check), but they all deliver τ^1 as the elected policy.

Although H need not lie in $\mathbf{R}$, monotonicity does imply that H is "essentially unidimensional." To be precise, if monotonicity holds, then types may be "reparameterized" in terms of their ideal points—that is, points in the unidimensional set T. For suppose h^1 and h^2 are two types that have the same ideal point, t. Let t^1 and t^2 be any two policies, such that $t^1 < t^2$; by monotonicity, there is a policy t' such that $\Omega(t^1, t^2) = H^{t'}$. If $t < t'$, then both h^1 and h^2 must prefer t^1 to t^2; if $t > t'$ then both h^1 and h^2 must weakly prefer t^2 to t^1. But in this case it follows that either both are indifferent between t^1 and t^2, or both prefer t^2 to t^1; for suppose, to the contrary, that $v(t^1, h^1) = v(t^2, h^1)$ and $v(t^1, h^2) < v(t^2, h^2)$. Then we can find a policy t^3 near t^1 such that h^1 prefers t^3 to t^2 and h^2 prefers t^2 to t^3, which contradicts monotonicity. It therefore follows that h^1 and h^2 have identical (ordinal) preferences on the policy space. We can therefore reparameterize types, naming a type by its ideal point. This, of course, would change the probability measure on the set of types.

Despite this remark, it is convenient to have Theorem 1.2, because often the set of types presents itself as a multidimensional set. Although the list of

---

4. An easier theorem is available if we assume that $H \subset \mathbf{R}$: see Roemer (1994a, Theorem 2.1).

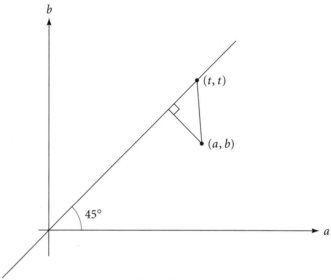

b

(t, t)

(a, b)

$45°$

a

Figure 1.4

premises of Theorem 1.2 is fairly long, they are all satisfied in many models. Following are some examples.

Example 1.5 Let H be a convex, compact set in $\mathbf{R}^2$, let T be an interval in $\mathbf{R}$, and, for $(a, b) \in H$, let

$$v(t, a, b) = -\tfrac{1}{2}(t - a)^2 - \tfrac{1}{2}(t - b)^2.$$

Let $\mathbf{F}$ be a probability measure on H which is equivalent to Lebesgue measure. The ideal point of type (a, b) is the policy $\hat{t}^{(a,b)} = (a + b)/2$. (Compute this by solving $\partial v / \partial t = 0$.) To avoid problems, assume that T is sufficiently large that every type's ideal policy lies in the interior of T. Geometrically, (a, b)'s utility at t is minus one-half the distance squared from (a, b) to the point (t, t): see Figure 1.4. Thus, (a, b)'s ideal policy is the coordinate of the point on the 45° line closest to (a, b).

Let t^* be defined by

$$(1.13) \qquad \mathbf{F}\left(\left\{(a, b) \mid \frac{a + b}{2} \leq t^*\right\}\right) = \frac{1}{2}.$$

Here t^* is well defined, because $\mathbf{F}$ is equivalent to Lebesgue measure. Thus exactly half the population have ideal policies less than t^*. Therefore $\Psi(t^*) = \frac{1}{2}$. More generally, we have

$$\Psi(t) = \mathbf{F}\left(\left\{(a, b) \mid \frac{a+b}{2} \leq t\right\}\right).$$

Next choose (a_1, b_1) and (a_2, b_2) such that

$$\frac{a_1 + b_1}{2} < t^* < \frac{a_2 + b_2}{2},$$

and define

$$v^i(t) = v(t, a_i, b_i), \qquad \text{for } i = 1, 2.$$

This defines the parties' preferences.

We check the axioms of Theorem 1.2. A1 is obvious. A2 is true because $v(\cdot, a, b)$ is strictly concave. Premise (a) is true because $\mathbf{F}$ is equivalent to Lebesgue measure: that is,

$$t^1 > t^2 \quad \Rightarrow \quad \lambda\left(\left\{(a, b) \mid \frac{a+b}{2} \leq t^1\right\}\right) > \lambda\left(\left\{(a, b) \mid \frac{a+b}{2} \leq t^2\right\}\right),$$

and so the same inequality holds when we substitute $\mathbf{F}$ for λ, which means Ψ is strictly increasing. Continuity of Ψ is obvious. Premise (b) is true by choice of (a_1, b_1) and (a_2, b_2).

We are left with A3 and A5; we check A3 first. A type (a, b) is indifferent between policies t^1 and t^2 exactly when

$$(t^1 - a)^2 + (t^1 - b)^2 = (t^2 - a)^2 + (t^2 - b)^2,$$

which reduces to

$$t^1 + t^2 = a + b.$$

For given (t^1, t^2), the set $\{(a, b) \mid a + b = t^1 + t^2\}$ is a line in $\mathbf{R}^2$, which has Lebesgue measure zero, and hence $\mathbf{F}$-measure zero. Finally, we check A5. Let t^1

and t^2 be a pair of distinct policies, $t^1 < t^2$. Then we may compute that

$$\Omega(t^1, t^2) = \{(a, b) \mid a + b \le t^1 + t^2\}.$$

But this is identical to the set

$$\left(\left\{(a, b) \mid \frac{a + b}{2} \le t'\right\}\right) = H^{t'},$$

where $t' = \frac{1}{2}(t^1 + t^2)$. Hence $\Omega(t^1, t^2) = H^{t'}$, as required.

All the premises are satisfied. It follows that the unique Wittman equilibrium is (t^*, t^*).

Although our theorem permits H to be multidimensional, as in the previous example, the most common applications are to problems where H is an interval in $\mathbf{R}$.

Example 1.6 The environment is as in Example 1.1, except that we have two parties whose preferences are given by

$$v^1(t) = (1 - t)h^1 + 2\alpha(t\mu)^{1/2}$$
$$v^2(t) = (1 - t)h^2 + 2\alpha(t\mu)^{1/2},$$

where $h^1 < m < h^2$. (Recall that m is median income in this example.) Thus, party 1 "represents" a poor citizen, and party 2 a rich citizen.

We let the reader check all the premises of Theorem 1.2 except for A5, which we proceed to check together. The set of types who prefer t^1 to t^2, where $t^1 < t^2$, is the set of h for whom

$$(1 - t^1)h + 2\alpha(t^1\mu)^{1/2} > (1 - t^2)h + 2\alpha(t^2\mu)^{1/2},$$

which reduces to

$$h > \frac{2\alpha\mu^{1/2}}{\sqrt{t^1} + \sqrt{t^2}}.$$

Thus

$$\Omega(t^1, t^2) = \left\{ h \mid h > \frac{2\alpha\mu^{1/2}}{\sqrt{t^1} + \sqrt{t^2}} \right\}.$$

Equivalently, we can write this as

$$\Omega(t^1, t^2) = \left\{ h \mid \left(\frac{\sqrt{t^1} + \sqrt{t^2}}{2} \right)^2 > \mu \left(\frac{\alpha}{h} \right)^2 \right\}.$$

Now let

$$t' = \left(\frac{\sqrt{t^1} + \sqrt{t^2}}{2} \right)^2.$$

Then, referring to equation (1.9), we see that $\Omega(t^1, t^2)$ is exactly $H^{t'}$, and A5 is demonstrated.

Consequently, the unique Wittman political equilibrium is (t^*, t^*).

Example 1.7   This is the same environment as in Example 1.3, where $H \subset \mathbf{R}$, and $v(t, h) = (1 - t)h + t\mu$. We take

$$v^i(t) = (1 - t)h^i + t\mu \qquad i = 1, 2,$$

where $h^1 < m < h^2$, and m is the median income. $\mathbf{F}$ is equivalent to Lebesgue measure on H. Recall that this example fails to satisfy premise (a) of Theorem 1.2, so the theorem does not apply. Let us compute the Wittman equilibria. Here there is a continuum of equilibria. Recall that $t = 1$ is the ideal policy of all types $h < \mu$, and this set constitutes a strict majority since $m < \mu$. Any pair of the form $(1, t)$ where $t \in [0, 1]$ is a Wittman equilibrium: the policy $t = 1$ wins for sure. These are the only Wittman equilibria.

1.4 Conclusion

We have examined the two principal formal models of political competition in an environment where parties are certain about voter behavior, and the policy space is unidimensional. The Downs model is ahistorical in not recognizing that political competition is almost always between parties that have policy preferences. That the model yields a unique equilibrium in which policies are undifferentiated is therefore not too upsetting. We then introduced parties that are partisan, à la Lipset and Wittman, but did not succeed in escaping the Downsian conclusion. At this point, the "median policy" result seems quite robust. As we shall see in Chapter 3, the introduction of uncertainty into these two models does produce a clear differentiation between the predictions they make.

2

Modeling Party Uncertainty

2.1 Introduction

It hardly need be said that uncertainty is paramount in political competition. If parties were certain of voter behavior, then they would know, after announcing their policies, that either one party would win for sure or there would be a tie. In the former case, it would be difficult for the losing party to carry out electioneering activities. And in the latter case, the parties might as well flip a coin to see which one would take office, rather than carrying out an expensive campaign. So party uncertainty about voter behavior is necessary to understand why the expensive process of running elections is undertaken.

Perhaps the degree of uncertainty about voter behavior has decreased during the last generation, when polling techniques have become more sophisticated. Indeed, there may be very little uncertainty on election day concerning which party will win. But election-day uncertainty is not the relevant uncertainty: rather, we are concerned with the uncertainty about which party will win at the point that the parties announce their policies. Of course if parties could costlessly change their announced policies up to the day of the election, then election-day uncertainty would be relevant. But they cannot: constantly changing its policy in reaction to polls would harm the party's credibility with the voters. After all, what kind of principles could *that* kind of party have?

Indeed, in the European case at least, party manifestos are written at conventions some months prior to the election, and some researchers claim that the policies parties run on are very close to what their manifestos announce (see Klingermann, Hofferbert, and Budge 1994). Because voters' views will change during the process of debate between parties, there is often a significant degree of uncertainty as to the probability of victory at the time that manifestos are published.

In this chapter we shall present three models of electoral uncertainty that will be used in the rest of the book. All three models derive the probability-of-victory function, π, from prior assumptions. Indeed, that is the only reason for this chapter. If we were willing simply to postulate a function $\pi : T \times T \to [0, 1]$, we could avoid the work we shall undertake here. It is, however, clearly desirable to derive the function π from more basic assumptions about voter behavior and party beliefs. Nevertheless, our models of uncertainty will not go "all the way down" in trying to understand the uncertainty at the level of the individual voter. They will, if you wish, be "macro" models of uncertainty regarding the response of the electorate to pairs of policies.

Why have three models? Because sometimes one model is easier to handle in theoretical analysis than another and sometimes one model is more tractable than another in a particular application. We cannot expect any single model to do all jobs well, and so it is wise to have a toolkit with more than one tool.[1] The next three sections develop what I call the state-space model of uncertainty, the error-distribution model, and the finite-type model.

2.2 The State-Space Approach to Uncertainty

We assume, as usual, a policy space $T \subset \mathbf{R}^n$, a sample space of types H, and a function $v : T \times H \to \mathbf{R}$ with the usual properties. We assume in addition that there is a set of states S, equipped with a probability distribution σ. For each state $s \in S$ there is given a probability measure $\mathbf{F}_s$ on H. The interpretation is that in state of the world s, the distribution of voter types is given by $\mathbf{F}_s$ on H.

What are the possible interpretations of this model? The simplest is that the set of voters is different in different states. What is relevant for electoral victory is the set of voters, not the set of citizens. If some voters abstain on election day, and the set of abstainers is subject to a stochastic element, then the distribution of *voter* types is uncertain. For instance, s might be a proxy for the weather, which is stochastic: on rainy days, wealthy citizens might be disproportionately represented among the voters. The parties may know the exact relation between turnout and the weather ($\mathbf{F}_s$), but they do not know what the weather (s) will be.

Another interpretation is that all citizens vote, but their preferences over policies are not known with certainty by the parties. Voter preferences over policies may indeed alter during the course of political debate. This does not

---

1. See Aumann (1987), who makes this point with respect to game theory.

mean that voters are irrational in the sense of not having stable preferences. We may suppose that each voter has stable preferences over fundamentals—such as private consumption and consumption of public goods—but that she may very well be uncertain about which *policies* to prefer because she is uncertain about the mapping from policies to fundamentals. This may be so because she is uncertain about some parameters of the economy, such as the efficiency with which the government converts tax revenues into public goods or the elasticity of labor supply with respect to tax rates. This parameter uncertainty induces uncertain policy preferences in voters, even if they have stable preferences over fundamentals. I believe it is for this reason that much political debate between parties takes place over the values of economic parameters—that is, how the economy will respond to particular policies. (See Roemer 1994b; Schultz 1995.)

We may proceed, given these data, to write down the probability-of-victory function π. As before, let $\Omega(t^1, t^2)$ be the set of types who prefer t^1 to t^2. We shall from now on suppose that if $t^1 \neq t^2$, then $\lambda(I(t^1, t^2)) = 0$. We shall further suppose that all measures $\mathbf{F}_s$ are absolutely continuous with respect to λ, and so $t^1 \neq t^2$ implies $\mathbf{F}_s(I(t^1, t^2)) = 0$ for all s. The fraction of voters who prefer t^1 to t^2 in state s is $\mathbf{F}_s(\Omega(t^1, t^2))$. Policy t^1 wins the election when $\mathbf{F}_s(\Omega(t^1, t^2)) > \frac{1}{2}$. Let

$$S(t^1, t^2) = \left\{ s \in S \mid \mathbf{F}_s(\Omega(t^1, t^2)) > \tfrac{1}{2} \right\}.$$

$S(t^1, t^2)$ is the set of states in which t^1 defeats t^2. What is the probability that the event $S(t^1, t^2)$ will occur? Precisely $\sigma(S(t^1, t^2))$, and so

(2.1) $\pi(t^1, t^2) = \sigma(S(t^1, t^2)).$

(Note that t^1 would also win one-half the time in those states s for which $\mathbf{F}_s(\Omega(t^1, t^2)) = \frac{1}{2}$. In all interesting cases, this set has σ-measure zero, and so we may disregard it. We do so in order not to clutter up formula (2.1).)

Example 2.1 H is a real interval, $T = [0, 1]$, the mean population income is known to be μ, but the set of voters depends on the weather, indexed by $s \in S = [0, 1]$. Let σ be the uniform measure on S. Preferences and policies are as in Example 1.7: the issue is to choose a proportional tax rate to redistribute income. Thus $v(t, h) = (1 - t)h + t\mu$.

We can specify the uncertainty as follows. In state s the median *voter's* income is m_s; this is all we must know about $\mathbf{F}_s$. We assume m_s is a strictly decreasing continuous function of s. (Perhaps $s = 0$ means inclement weather and $s = 1$ means fine weather.)

As we computed in Example 1.6,

$$t^1 > t^2 \Rightarrow \Omega(t^1, t^2) = \{h \mid h < \mu\}.$$

Now $\mathbf{F}_s(\{h < \mu\}) > \frac{1}{2}$ if and only if $m_s < \mu$. Thus

(2.2) $\pi(t^1, t^2) = \sigma(\{s \mid m_s < \mu\}).$

Now suppose $m_0 > \mu > m_1$. Since m_s is strictly decreasing and continuous in s, there exists a (unique) number s^* such that $m_{s^*} = \mu$. It follows that

$$\{s \mid m_s < \mu\} = \{s \in [0, 1] \mid s > s^*\}.$$

But since σ is the uniform measure, the probability of this event is

(2.3) $\pi(t^1, t^2) = 1 - s^*.$

The reader should check, as an exercise, that

$$m_0 > m_1 \geq \mu \Rightarrow \pi(t^1, t^2) = 0$$

$$\mu \geq m_0 > m_1 \Rightarrow \pi(t^1, t^2) = 1.$$

Thus the interesting case is $m_0 > \mu > m_1$.

Note that, in this simple example, the probability of victory is constant as long as $t^1 > t^2$, for s^* is a datum of our problem. We can state formally:

$$\pi(t^1, t^2) = \begin{cases} 1 - s^* & \text{if } t^1 > t^2 \\ \frac{1}{2} & \text{if } t^1 = t^2 \\ s^* & \text{if } t^1 < t^2. \end{cases}$$

Thus although all the data of our problem are continuous functions and well behaved, the function π is *discontinuous* (unless, singularly, $s^* = \frac{1}{2}$).

This shows the danger of taking π as a primitive and endowing it with nice properties, like continuity. Even in this extremely nonpathological model, π is discontinuous.

Example 2.2   Here we return to Example 1.1, where $T = [0, 1]$, H is a positive real interval, and

$$v(t, h) = (1 - t)h + 2\alpha(t\mu)^{1/2}.$$

We will again assume that $S = [0, 1]$, σ is the uniform measure, and m_s is strictly decreasing and continuous in s. Recall that

$$(2.4) \qquad t^1 < t^2 \Rightarrow \Omega(t^1, t^2) = \left\{ h \mid h > \frac{2\alpha\mu^{1/2}}{\sqrt{t^1} + \sqrt{t^2}} \right\}.$$

It follows that $F_s(\Omega(t^1, t^2)) > \frac{1}{2}$ exactly when

$$(2.5) \qquad m_s > \frac{2\alpha\mu^{1/2}}{\sqrt{t^1} + \sqrt{t^2}}.$$

For in states where (2.5) holds, the set $\Omega(t^1, t^2)$ includes more than one-half the voters. Consequently

$$S(t^1, t^2) = \left\{ s \mid m_s > \frac{2\alpha\mu^{1/2}}{\sqrt{t^1} + \sqrt{t^2}} \right\}.$$

Let us assume that there exists an s^* such that

$$(2.6) \qquad m_{s^*} = \frac{2\alpha\mu^{1/2}}{\sqrt{t^1} + \sqrt{t^2}}.$$

Then $S(t^1, t^2) = \{s < s^*\}$ and so $\pi(t^1, t^2) = s^*$.

But note, unlike Example 2.1, s^* is now a function of (t^1, t^2), from (2.6).

Since we have the function m_s, we can solve for s^* of (2.6): call the solution $s^*(t^1, t^2)$. Because m_s is continuous, so is the function $s^*(\cdot, \cdot)$. We have

$$\pi(t^1, t^2) = \begin{cases} s^*(t^1, t^2) & \text{if } t^1 < t^2 \\ \frac{1}{2} & \text{if } t^1 = t^2 \\ 1 - s^*(t^1, t^2) & \text{if } t^1 > t^2. \end{cases}$$

Is the function π continuous? The only question is about π's behavior on the line $t^1 = t^2$. Clearly π is discontinuous on this line, because π is constantly $\frac{1}{2}$

on it, but the s^* that solves (2.6) when $t^1 = t^2 = t$ depends upon the particular value of t. Elsewhere, π is continuous.

This example shows that the simple step-function nature of π in Example 2.1 was an artifact of the linearity of v.

Example 2.3 A two-dimensional trait space
We return to Example 1.2, where

$$v(t, \alpha, h) = (1 - t)h + 2\alpha(t\mu)^{1/2}.$$

$H = [0, \bar{h}]$ is a positive (income) interval, and α also varies over an interval $A = [0, \bar{\alpha}]$. The set of types $\{(\alpha, h)\}$ is a set $B \subset \mathbf{R}^2$. Let $\mathbf{G}_s$ be the probability distribution of traits in state s; again take $S = [0, 1]$, and σ the uniform distribution. We suppose as well that $\mathbf{G}_s$ has a density function $g_s(\alpha, h)$. We know that

(2.7) $t^1 < t^2 \Rightarrow \Omega(t^1, t^2) = \left\{ (\alpha, h) \mid h > \dfrac{2\alpha\mu^{1/2}}{\sqrt{t^1} + \sqrt{t^2}} \right\}.$

Define $\phi(t^1, t^2) = \dfrac{2\mu^{1/2}}{\sqrt{t^1} + \sqrt{t^2}}$. In state s, the fraction of voters in $\Omega(t^1, t^2)$ is $\mathbf{G}_s(\Omega(t^1, t^2))$, which we may write, using (2.7), as:

(2.8) $\displaystyle \int_A \int_{\alpha\phi(t^1,t^2)}^{\bar{h}} g_s(\alpha, h) dh\, d\alpha.$

As we have previously noted, this is the fraction of types above the line

$$h = \alpha\phi(t^1, t^2)$$

in the (α, h) plane. We now impose an assumption (to simplify life) that the fraction of types above any line of positive slope through the origin in the (α, h) plane is decreasing in s. Then there will be a number $s^*(t^1, t^2)$ such that

(2.9) $\displaystyle \int_A \int_{\alpha\phi(t^1,t^2)}^{\bar{h}} g_s(\alpha, h) dh\, d\alpha = \tfrac{1}{2},$

and t^1 will defeat t^2 whenever $s < s^*(t^1, t^2)$. Therefore, as before

$$\pi(t^1, t^2) = \begin{cases} s^*(t^1, t^2) & \text{if } t^1 < t^2 \\ \frac{1}{2} & \text{if } t^1 = t^2 \\ 1 - s^*(t^1, t^2) & \text{if } t^1 > t^2. \end{cases}$$

where $s^*(t^1, t^2)$ is the function implicitly defined by equation (2.9).

Example 2.4 A two-dimensional issue space and trait space.
Suppose voters care about two things, their income (x) and the position of the government on race (z). A voter of type (h, a) has a pretax income of h and a racial view of a. Her utility function is

$$u(x, z) = x - \tfrac{1}{2}\alpha(z - a)^2.$$

A policy is a pair (t, z), where t is a uniform income tax rate, and z is the racial position of the government. Thus, the citizen (h, a)'s indirect utility function over tax rates and racial positions is

$$(2.10) \quad v(t, z; h, a) = (1 - t)h + t\mu - \tfrac{1}{2}\alpha(z - a)^2.$$

Type (h, a) lies in a set $B \subset \mathbf{R}^2$, where $h \in H$ and $a \in A = [\mathbf{R}, \bar{a}]$, and in state s, the set of voters is distributed according to the probability distribution $\mathbf{G}_s$ with density g_s.

We may compute that voter (h, a) prefers policy (t_1, z_1) to (t, z_2), iff:

$$(2.11a) \quad \bar{z} + \frac{\Delta t(h - \mu)}{\alpha \Delta z} > a \quad \text{if } \Delta z > 0,$$

$$(2.11b) \quad \bar{z} + \frac{\Delta t(h - \mu)}{\alpha \Delta z} < a \quad \text{if } \Delta z < 0,$$

$$(2.11c) \quad h < \mu \qquad\qquad\qquad \text{if } \Delta z = 0 \quad \text{and} \quad \Delta t < 0,$$

$$(2.11d) \quad h > \mu \qquad\qquad\qquad \text{if } \Delta z = 0 \quad \text{and} \quad \Delta t > 0,$$

where $\Delta z \equiv z_2 - z_1$, $\Delta t \equiv t - t_1$ and $\bar{z} \equiv (z_1 + z_2)/2$.

Because there are four cases, there are four different expressions for the function π, depending upon the region of (t, z) space in which the policy is located. For instance, in the case of (2.11a), the fraction of voters in state s who prefer (t_1, z_1) to (t, z_2) is given by

$$(2.12) \quad \int_H^{\bar{z} + \frac{\Delta t(h - \mu)}{\alpha \Delta z}} \int_{-\infty} g_s(h, a) \, da \, dh.$$

With a suitable monotonicity assumption on the behavior of $\{G_s\}$, we can derive a formula for π as a function of the policies (t_1, z_1) and (t, z_2), as in the earlier examples.

I have gone into some detail to indicate that, if we can estimate the distribution of traits (in an application), and also propose a probability measure on the state space, then we can compute the function π. The state-space approach is, moreover, tractable for theoretical investigations, as will be seen in later chapters.

There are, however, somewhat less abstract approaches to uncertainty, which may therefore be more appealing, to which we now turn.

2.3 An Error-Distribution Model of Uncertainty

This model is the simplest of the three discussed in this chapter. We postulate, now, only one probability distribution $\mathbf{F}$ on H. Thus given two policies t^1 and t^2, there is an unambiguous number $\mathbf{F}(\Omega(t^1, t^2))$, the fraction of citizens who prefer t^1 to t^2. But we now say that parties are only confident about this number up to a margin of error: they believe that the true fraction of citizens who prefer t^1 to t^2 lies in an interval $E(t^1, t) = (\mathbf{F}(\Omega(t^1, t^2)) - \beta, \mathbf{F}(\Omega(t^1, t^2)) + \beta)$, for some $\beta > 0$ and is distributed—let us say—uniformly on this interval. Thus $\pi(t^1, t^2)$ is the probability that a random variable uniformly distributed on $E(t^1, t^2)$ is greater than one-half.

Hence

$$(2.13) \quad \pi(t^1, t^2) = \begin{cases} 0 & \text{if } \mathbf{F}(\Omega(t^1, t^2)) + \beta \leq \frac{1}{2} \\ \frac{\mathbf{F}(\Omega(t^1, t^2)) + \beta - \frac{1}{2}}{2\beta} & \text{if } \frac{1}{2} \in E(t^1, t^2) \\ 1 & \text{if } \mathbf{F}(\Omega(t^1, t^2)) - \beta \geq \frac{1}{2} \end{cases}.$$

The formula above applies in the standard case that $t^1 \neq t^2$ and $\mathbf{F}(I(t^1, t^2)) = 0$. In the case when $t^1 = t^2$, the formula does not apply, and we define $\pi = \frac{1}{2}$. As in the state-space model, the function π is not generally continuous on the line $t^1 = t^2$. Consider, for instance, Example 2.1 with the present model. If $m < \mu$ for $\mathbf{F}$, we have

$$t^1 > t^2 \Rightarrow \mathbf{F}(\Omega(t^1, t^2)) = \mathbf{F}(\mu) > \tfrac{1}{2}.$$

If $F(\mu) > 1/2 + \beta$, then $\pi(t^1, t^2) = 1$. Now let t_j^1 approach t^2 from above. On this sequence of pairs (t_j^1, t^2), π is constantly 1, but in the limit its value is one-half.

One attractive feature of the error-distribution model is that it clarifies the distinction between the *probability* of victory and the *expected fraction of the vote* for a party. Suppose that $\mathbf{F}(\Omega(t^1, t^2)) = .519$ and $\beta = .02$. Then the probability of a victory by party 1 is approximately .97, while its expected vote share is only .519. Thus it is perfectly consistent to say that we expect a party to win by only a 1% margin, but we are almost sure it will win.

This shows that the two characterizations of the Downs model, as one where parties (i) maximize the probability of victory, and (ii) maximize the expected vote fraction, are very different. Consider the following example. A party has a choice of two actions (strategies), A and B. Under A, there are two possible outcomes: with probability $\tfrac{1}{2}$, the party receives 49% of the vote, and with probability $\tfrac{1}{2}$, it receives 60% of the vote. Under B it receives 51% of the vote for sure. The expected vote fraction under A is 54.5%, but it only wins with probability $\tfrac{1}{2}$, while under B, it wins for sure. The rational action for a Downsian party, I claim, is B.

The view that a Downsian party should maximize its expected vote is only coherent if in addition we stipulate that the election is not of the "winner takes all" type. For instance, under proportional representation, a Downsian party might well want to maximize its expected vote fraction.

We state a more general form of the error-distribution model of uncertainty. The share of the vote received by party 1 will be $\mathbf{F}(\Omega(t^1, t^2)) + \epsilon$, where ϵ is a random variable distributed according to a probability measure $\mathbf{X}$ on support $[-\beta, \beta]$, with distribution function X. Then[2]

$$\pi(t^1, t^2) = 1 - X(\tfrac{1}{2} - \mathbf{F}(\Omega(t^1, t^2))),$$

where it is understood that $X(y)$ is zero (one) for $y < -\beta (y > \beta)$.

---

2. The derivation is $\mathbf{F}(\Omega) + \epsilon > \tfrac{1}{2} \Leftrightarrow \epsilon > \tfrac{1}{2} - \mathbf{F}(\Omega)$; thus $\pi(t^1, t^2) = \text{Prob}\left[\epsilon > \tfrac{1}{2} - \mathbf{F}(\Omega)\right] = 1 - X\left(\tfrac{1}{2} - \mathbf{F}(\Omega)\right)$.

2.4 A Finite-Type Model

In the examples given thus far, there has always been a continuum of types. But there are times when it is appropriate to model a polity as consisting of a finite number of types. A finite-type polity might be either one with a finite population or one with a continuum of individuals for each of a finite number of types. For instance, in Chapter 11, we shall model a polity as consisting of four classes, while all members of each class are identical (same preferences, same endowments), up to the degree of resolution in the model.

In this case the error-distribution model of uncertainty often does not work well, because it may almost always deliver probabilities of either zero or one. (Consider the case of three types, no one of which constitutes a majority. For any arbitrary pair of policies (t^1, t^2), it will usually be the case that the members of two types will prefer t^1 to t^2 (or vice versa). Then, with the error-distribution model, $\pi(t^1, t^2) = 1$ (respectively, zero).)

An alternative is as follows. Let $H = \{h^1, h^2, \ldots, h^M\}$. Suppose that the fraction of population that is of type h^m is ω_m. Let us restrict $v(t, h)$ to be non-negative. Facing a policy pair (t^1, t^2), we say that the smaller the ratio $v(t^2, h^m)/v(t^1, h^m)$, the larger the fraction of citizens of type h^m who will vote for t^1. In particular, we might suppose that if $v(t^2, h^m) = v(t^1, h^m)$, then exactly one-half of type m citizens will vote for each policy.[3]

Consider the function $f : [0, \infty] \to [-1, 1]$ defined by

(2.14) $$f(x) = \frac{1 - x}{1 + x}.$$

The function f has the following properties:

(a) $f(0) = 1, f(1) = 0$, and $f(\infty) = -1$;
(b) f is monotone decreasing from 1 to -1 as x increases from 0 to infinity;
(c) f is continuous and differentiable;
(d) $f(1/x) = -f(x)$.

I suggest that f is the simplest function with these four characteristics.
Denote

$$\frac{v(t^2, h)}{v(t^1, h)} = x(t^1, t^2, h).$$

---

3. For this model to be coherent, it is necessary that the utility function v be "ratio-scale measurable." For an explanation, see Roemer (1996, chap. 1).

We now assume that the fraction of the population that will vote for t^1 over t^2 is a random variable of the form

(2.15) $\phi(t^1, t^2; \epsilon^1, \ldots, \epsilon^M) = \sum_{i=1}^{M} \frac{1}{2}\omega_i(1 + \epsilon^i f(x(t^1, t^2, h^i)))$,

where ϵ^i are i.i.d. real random variables on the support $[0, 1]$.

To understand formula (2.15) first notice that for any policy t, $\phi(t, t; \epsilon) = \frac{1}{2}$. (This follows from the fact that $f(1) = 0$.) Thus if both parties propose the same policy, they split the vote equally.

The ith term, $\frac{1}{2}\omega_i(1 + \epsilon^i f(x(t^1, t^2, h^i)))$, is the mass of type h^i voters who will vote for t^1. This mass can vary from zero to ω^i. If type i is indifferent between t^1 and t^2 then $x(t^1, t, h^i) = 1$, and so exactly mass $\frac{1}{2}\omega_i$ votes for t^1. The more favorable t^1 is to type h^i relative to t, the higher the fraction of its members that will, on average, vote for t^1. Suppose that the mean of ϵ^i is $\frac{1}{2}$. Then the mass of type i who are *expected* to vote for t^1 is $\frac{1}{2}\omega_i(1 + \frac{1}{2}f(x(t^1, t, h^i)))$, which is, of course, decreasing in x, as it should be.

There is a consistency check we must make. For the model to make sense, the fraction who vote for t^2 over t^1 should be

$$\phi(t^2, t^1; \epsilon) = \sum_{i=1}^{M} \frac{1}{2}\omega_i \left(1 + \epsilon^i f\left(\frac{1}{x(t^1, t^2, h^i)}\right)\right),$$

By property (d) above, we have

$$\phi(t^2, t^1; \epsilon) = \sum_{i=1}^{M} \frac{1}{2}\omega_i(1 - \epsilon^i f(x(t^1, t^2, h^i))),$$

from which it immediately follows that

(2.16) $\phi(t^2, t^1; \epsilon) + \phi(t^1, t^2; \epsilon) = 1$.

The model is consistent.

Now the probability that t^1 defeats t^2 is $\text{Prob}[\phi(t^1, t^2; \epsilon) > \frac{1}{2}]$. By (2.15) this is

(2.17) $\pi(t^1, t^2) = \text{Prob}[\sum \epsilon^i \omega^i f(x(t^1, t^2, h^i)) > 0]$.

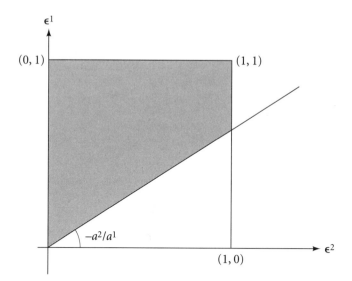

Figure 2.1

To gain further intuition, let us take an example in which $M = 2$. Let $a^i = \omega^i f(x(t^1, t^2, h^i))$. Then

$$\pi(t^1, t^2) = \text{Prob}[a^1 \epsilon^1 + a^2 \epsilon^2 > 0].$$

Suppose further that ϵ^i are uniformly distributed on $[0, 1]$. If $a^1 > 0$ and $a^2 < 0$ then $\pi(t^1, t^2) = \text{Prob}[\epsilon^1 \geq -a^2/a^1\epsilon^2]$, which is just the area in the square above the line of slope $-a^2/a^1$ in Figure 2.1. Clearly, this is simple to compute, given the data.

Like the two previous models, this one also produces a discontinuous function π. Consider a sequence $t_j^1 \to t^2$. Although $x(t_j^1, t^2; h) \to 1$ for all h, it is possible that all types prefer t_j^1 to t^2 for all j, and so $f(x(t_j^1, t^2; h)) > 0$ for all j, h. In this case $\pi(t_j^1, t^2) = 1$ for all j, but in the limit $\pi = \frac{1}{2}$.

An alternative to assuming that ϵ^i are i.i.d. random variables is to assume that (ϵ^1, ϵ^2) is a vector-valued random variable uniformly distributed on the positive orthant of the unit circle. Still assuming that $a_1 > 0$ and $a_2 < 0, \pi(t^1, t^2)$ is now the area shaded in Figure 2.2. Since $\theta = \arctan(-a^2/a^1)$, we have[4]

$$(2.18) \quad \pi(t^1, t^2) = \frac{\pi/2 - \theta}{\pi/2} = 1 - \frac{2}{\pi} \arctan\left(-\frac{a^2}{a^1}\right).$$

---

4. Note that the symbol "π" on the r.h.s. of (2.18) denotes the number "pi," not the function π.

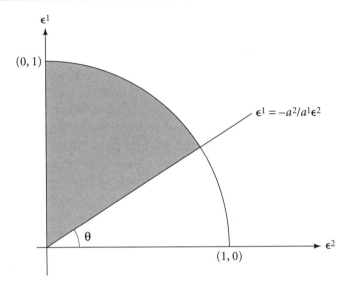

Figure 2.2

The relative virtue of this approach, over the formulation giving rise to Figure 2.1, is that, in that earlier formulation, the formula for the shaded area (hence, π) takes two different forms, depending on whether the line $\epsilon^1 = -(a^2/a^1)\epsilon^2$ lies above or below $(1,1)$. In Figure 2.2, however, the circle has no corners, and so formula (2.18) always works.

Turning to motivation, why is it not the case that, whenever $x(t^1, t^2, h) < 1$, all type h citizens vote for t^1? We can say that this fails to occur because our model is incomplete. Parties have many characteristics that voters care about that are not captured in our policy space T. What we hope to do in a model is to capture the most important characteristics of policy in the specification of T. Voters of type h are not really identical: they share a common set of traits (h) that we believe is important for determining their preferences, but they in fact have other noncommon characteristics that influence preferences and behavior.

Finally, we may say that politicians or parties do not always communicate policies unambiguously, and so different voters may interpret a party's policies differently.

We could (as with the error-distribution model) probably represent the finite-type model as a special case of the state-space model, but the representation presented in this section is more felicitous for applications.

There are plenty of justifications for adopting the present model in a finite-type economy. They all seem to say that the economy really has an infinite number of types, but for analytical reasons, it may be the prudent research strategy to ignore much of the variation.

2.5 Conclusion

It is important to note that the approaches to modeling uncertainty proposed in this chapter deliver uncertainty at the aggregate level, even when there is a continuum of voters. It would not do to postulate that each citizen-type's behavior is stochastic, but that the random variables that describe individual behavior are independent, for then uncertainty in the aggregate would disappear. For example, if there is a continuum of citizens of a given type, and each votes for policy t with probability .4, and the individual random variables are i.i.d., then exactly 40% of the type votes for policy t—aggregate uncertainty has disappeared. Uncertainty in the aggregate appears, generally speaking, when the behaviors of members of a type are correlated, and are also correlated to some random event (the "state"). It is aggregate uncertainty that is important for politics.

There are many models in the literature that work with a finite set of citizens and postulate uncertainty at the individual level that is uncorrelated across citizens. Because the set of voters is finite, these models will deliver uncertainty in the aggregate. But these models do not generalize to models with uncertainty when the set of citizens is "large," and are therefore of limited interest.

3

❋

Unidimensional Policy Spaces with Uncertainty

3.1 Introduction

Let the policy space T be unidimensional: $T = [\underline{t}, \overline{t}]$. As Chapter 1 showed, if parties are certain about voter behavior, then political equilibria exist in both the Downs and the Wittman models, and in them both parties propose the same policy, the median ideal policy. In this chapter we introduce party uncertainty about voter behavior and show that we now (in one case) escape the tyranny of the median policy.

3.2 The Downs Model

We postulate a function $v(t, h)$ obeying A1 and A2. Let us first work with the error-distribution model of uncertainty. We therefore postulate a distribution of traits $\mathbf{F}$ on H, and A3.

To be precise, we assume that the fraction of the vote for party 1, given the policy pair (t^1, t^2), is $\mathbf{F}(\Omega(t^1, t^2)) + \epsilon$ where ϵ is a random variable with support $[-\beta, \beta]$. We further suppose that ϵ is distributed according to a continuous probability measure $\mathbf{X}$ on $[-\beta, \beta]$, with a distribution function X. We suppose that $\mathbf{X}$ is symmetric with mean zero. (This implies that $X(0) = \frac{1}{2}$.)

The probability that t^1 defeats t^2, for $t^1 \neq t^2$, is thus

$$\pi(t^1, t^2) = \text{Prob}[\mathbf{F}(\Omega(t^1, t^2)) + \epsilon > \tfrac{1}{2}]$$

$$= \text{Prob}[\epsilon > \tfrac{1}{2} - \mathbf{F}(\Omega(t^1, t^2))]$$

(3.1) $$= 1 - X(\tfrac{1}{2} - \mathbf{F}(\Omega(t^1, t^2)))$$

Of course, for any t we define $\pi(t, t) = \frac{1}{2}$.

Let t^* be the median ideal policy. We have:

Theorem 3.1 *With the error-distribution model of uncertainty, (t^*, t^*) is the unique Downs equilibrium.*

Proof:

1. We first verify that (t^*, t^*) is a Downs equilibrium. Suppose party 1 were to deviate to t. Now $\pi(t, t^*) = 1 - X(\frac{1}{2} - \mathbf{F}(\Omega(t, t^*)))$. But $\mathbf{F}(\Omega(t, t^*)) < \frac{1}{2}$ and so $\frac{1}{2} - \mathbf{F}(\Omega(t, t^*)) = \gamma > 0$. But $X(\gamma) > \frac{1}{2}$ since $X(\gamma) > X(0) = \frac{1}{2}$. Therefore $\pi(t, t^*) < \frac{1}{2}$.

Consequently there are no profitable deviations for either party.

2. The reader can check, as an exercise, that if (t, t) is a Downs equilibrium, then $t = t^*$.

3. Finally, suppose that (t^1, t^2) is a Downs equilibrium and $t^1 \neq t^2$. Since $\pi(t^1, t^2) = \frac{1}{2}$ it follows that $X(\frac{1}{2} - \mathbf{F}(\Omega(t^1, t^2))) = \frac{1}{2}$ and hence, since $X(0) = \frac{1}{2}$, $\mathbf{F}(\Omega(t^1, t^2)) = \frac{1}{2}$.

Therefore either $t^1 < t^* < t^2$ or $t^2 < t^* < t^1$. It immediately follows that either party can profitably deviate to t^*.

This concludes the proof. ∎

We now turn to the state-space model of uncertainty. Thus we have a continuum of probability measures $\{\mathbf{F}_s \mid s \in S\}$. We assume $S = [0, 1]$ and s is distributed according to a continuous probability measure σ on S, with CDF σ.

We further suppose A4 and A5 as restrictions on ν.

Let $\hat{t}^{m(s)}$ be the median ideal policy in state s. That is,

$$\mathbf{F}_s(H^{\hat{t}^{m(s)}}) = \tfrac{1}{2}.$$

We finally assume:

A6 $\hat{t}^{m(s)}$ is strictly monotonic in s.

We shall further suppose, without loss of generality, that $\hat{t}^{m(s)}$ is *increasing* in s.

We now derive the function π. In the state-space model, if $t^1 \neq t^2$ then:

$$\pi(t^1, t^2) = \sigma \left(\{s \mid \mathbf{F}_s(\Omega(t^1, t^2)) > \tfrac{1}{2}\} \right).$$

By A5, there exists a policy t' such that $H^{t'} = \Omega(t^1, t^2)$, and so

$$\pi(t^1, t^2) = \sigma\left(\left\{s \mid F_s(H^{t'}) > \tfrac{1}{2}\right\}\right).$$

But $F_s(H^{t'}) > \tfrac{1}{2}$ if and only if $t' > \hat{t}^{m(s)}$. Now invoke the fact that $\hat{t}^{m(s)}$ is increasing in s. There are three cases.

   Case (1) $\hat{t}^{m(0)} > t'$. Then $\pi(t^1, t^2) = 0$.
   Case (2) $t' > \hat{t}^{m(1)}$. Then $\pi(t^1, t^2) = 1$.
   Case (3) There exists a number $s^* \in [0, 1]$ such that $t' = \hat{t}^{m(s^*)}$. In this case we have

(3.2) $\pi(t^1, t^2) = \sigma\left(\left\{s \mid s \le s^*\right\}\right) = \sigma(s^*).$

Of course, s^* is a function of t' which is a function of (t^1, t^2), so we should write $s^* = s^*(t^1, t^2)$.
   Let $\tilde{s}$ be the median state (that is, $\sigma(\tilde{s}) = \tfrac{1}{2}$), and define $t^* = \hat{t}^{m(\tilde{s})}$.

Theorem 3.2 *With the state-space model of uncertainty, the unique Downs equilibrium is (t^*, t^*).*

   Proof:

   1. We first show that (t^*, t^*) is a Downs equilibrium. Let us examine whether party 1 can profitably deviate to $t < t^*$. For $s \ge \tilde{s}$, we have

$$t < \hat{t}^{m(\tilde{s})} \le \hat{t}^{m(s)},$$

and so in those states a majority vote for t^* against t, and so t loses. By continuity of m and v, it follows that t^* also defeats t for s in an interval $(\tilde{s} - \delta, \tilde{s})$, for small $\delta > 0$. Therefore $\pi(t, t^*) < \tfrac{1}{2}$, and the deviation is unprofitable. A similar argument establishes that $t > t^*$ is not a profitable deviation for party 1 either. Of course the same reasoning applies to party 2, and the claim is established.

   2. Let (t, t) be a Downs equilibrium. The reader can verify that, if $t \ne t^*$, either party can profitably deviate to t^*.

   3. Let (t^1, t^2) be a Downs equilibrium, $t^1 \ne t^2$. Of course, $\pi(t^1, t^2) = \tfrac{1}{2}$, and so it follows that $s^*(t^1, t^2) = \tilde{s}$. (See (3.2).) Let , $H^{t'} = \Omega(t^1, t^2)$, by A5.

Then t' must be the ideal policy of the median voter in state $s^*(t^1, t^2)$—that is, $t' = \hat{t}^{m(\bar{s})}$. It follows that either party can profitably deviate to $\hat{t}^{m(\bar{s})}$ and win with probability greater than one-half. ∎

One might call Theorem 3.2 the "double median" theorem. The unique political equilibrium consists in both parties' proposing the median ideal policy in the median state.[1]

Our conclusion is that introducing uncertainty into the unidimensional model does not enable us to escape the conclusion that, with Downsian politics, policy differentiation fails to occur.

3.3 The Wittman Model: An Example

We begin with two examples which illustrate the essential property of the Wittman model with uncertainty—that it engenders equilibria in which the parties propose different policies.

Example 3.1   All citizens have preferences over income (x) and a public good (G) given by

$$u(x, G) = x - \frac{\alpha}{2}(G - \mu)^2,$$

where μ is the mean of **F**, the population distribution of income. Provision of \$1 worth of the public good requires an expenditure of \$1 per capita. The single issue is the level of proportional income tax, t, which finances the public good. Thus the indirect utility function of type h is

$$v(t, h) = (1 - t)h - \frac{\alpha}{2}(t\mu - \mu)^2 = (1 - t)h - \frac{\alpha\mu^2}{2}(t - 1)^2.$$

We shall use the error-distribution model of uncertainty. We have

$$\pi(t^1, t^2) = \frac{\mathbf{F}(\Omega(t^1, t^2)) - \frac{1}{2} + \beta}{2\beta}.$$

---

1. Naturally this theorem depends upon the fact that the state space S is unidimensional.

We assume that party i represents a voter with income h^i, where $h^1 < \mu < h^2$. Thus party i maximizes the expected utility of a voter with vNM utility function $v(t, h^i)$. We compute that

$$t^1 > t^2 \Rightarrow \Omega(t^1, t^2) = \{h \mid h < \alpha \mu^2 (1 - \bar{t})\},$$

where $\bar{t} = (t^1 + t^2)/2$.

Now assume that $\alpha = 4$, $\mu = \frac{1}{2}$, and that **F** is the uniform distribution on $[0, 1]$. It follows that

$$\pi(t^1, t^2) = \frac{(1 - \bar{t}) + \beta - \frac{1}{2}}{2\beta}.$$

The first-order conditions for a Wittman equilibrium (t^{1*}, t^{2*}) are

$$\frac{\partial \Pi^1}{\partial t^1}(t^{1*}, t^{2*}) = 0, \qquad \frac{\partial \Pi^2}{\partial t^2}(t^{1*}, t^{2*}) = 0.$$

We may compute that the F.O.C.s reduce to

(3.3)
$$\Delta t(h^1 - (1 - \bar{t})) = 2(\beta + \tfrac{1}{2} - \bar{t})(h^1 + t^1 - 1)$$
$$\Delta t(h^2 - (1 - \bar{t})) = 2(\beta + \bar{t} - \tfrac{1}{2})(h^2 + t^2 - 1),$$

where $\Delta t = t^1 - t^2$.

Let us now specialize to the case where $h^1 = \frac{1}{2} - \epsilon$ and $h^2 = \frac{1}{2} + \epsilon$, for some number $\epsilon > 0$. Symmetry suggests we try for a solution of the form $t^1 = \frac{1}{2} + \frac{1}{2}\delta$, $t^2 = \frac{1}{2} - \frac{1}{2}\delta$. Substituting these values into (3.3) yields a solution

$$\delta = \frac{2\epsilon\beta}{\beta + \epsilon},$$

and so

(3.4) $$t^{1*} = \frac{1}{2} + \frac{\epsilon\beta}{\beta + \epsilon}, \qquad t^{2*} = \frac{1}{2} - \frac{\epsilon\beta}{\beta + \epsilon}.$$

Thus (t^{1^*}, t^{2^*}) satisfies the F.O.C.s for equilibrium, but it remains to show that t^{1^*} is indeed a maximum of the conditional payoff function $\Pi^1(t, t^{2^*})$, with a similar statement for t^{2^*}.

We now specify $\beta = 0.2$. Figure 3.1 plots the conditional payoff functions (there labeled V^1 and V^2) for several values of ϵ; by inspection, we see that t^{1^*} and t^{2^*} are indeed maxima for their respective conditional payoff functions.

As promised, the Wittman model with uncertainty delivers a political equilibrium with differentiated policies.

We also note that although the data of this model are as simple and smooth as one could ask for—including a function π that is linear in the policies—the conditional payoff functions (see Figure 3.1) are not quasi-concave. Thus the Wittman model is intrinsically "badly behaved." The standard approach to proving the existence of Nash equilibrium is to show that the conditional payoff functions in the game are quasi-concave, and then to apply Kakutani's fixed-point theorem. (Elaboration will follow below.) But that straightforward approach cannot work here, because even the simplest example does not display the desired property of quasi-concave payoff functions. Thus a general proof of existence of Wittman equilibrium will necessarily be "hard."[2]

Example 3.2 Let $H = [0, 1]$, $T = \mathbf{R}$, and $v(t, h) = -\mid t - h \mid$. Let h be distributed according to $\mathbf{F}$ on H with density f. We use the error-distribution model of uncertainty, where the random variable is uniformly distributed on $[-\beta, \beta]$, so

$$\pi(t^1, t^2) = \frac{F(\frac{t^1 + t^2}{2}) + \beta - \frac{1}{2}}{2\beta}, \quad \text{for } t^1 < t^2.$$

Let party i have utility function $v(t, h^i)$, where $h^1 < m < h^2$, and m is the median type.

---

2. The existence proofs in Wittman (1983) and Wittman (1990) are incorrect. For discussion, see Roemer (1997).

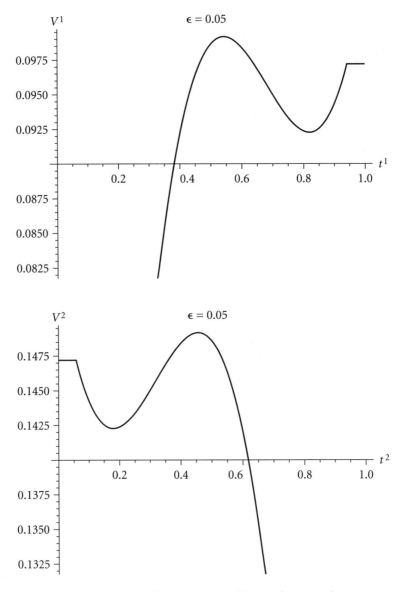

Figure 3.1a   Conditional payoff functions at equilibrium for Example 3.1,
$\epsilon = 0.05$ ($t^{1*} = 0.54$, $t^{2*} = 0.46$)

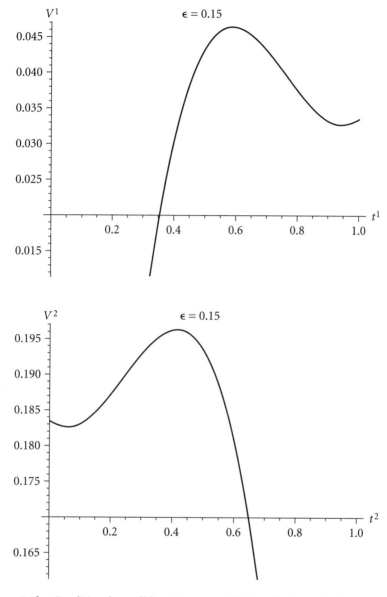

Figure 3.1b Conditional payoff functions at equilibrium for Example 3.1, $\epsilon = 0.15$ ($t^{1^*} = 0.59$, $t^{2^*} = 0.41$)

Let (t^{1*}, t^{2*}) be a Wittman equilibrium, and assume that $h^1 < t^{1*} < t^{2*} < h^2$. Then the parties' payoff functions, near (t^{1*}, t^{2*}) can be written

$$\Pi^1(t^1, t^2) = \left(\frac{1}{2} + \frac{F\left(\frac{t^1 + t^2}{2}\right) - \frac{1}{2}}{2\beta}\right)(h^1 - t^1) + \left(\frac{1}{2} - \frac{F\left(\frac{t^1 + t^2}{2}\right) - \frac{1}{2}}{2\beta}\right)(h^1 - t^2),$$

$$\Pi^2(t^1, t^2) = \left(\frac{1}{2} + \frac{F\left(\frac{t^1 + t^2}{2}\right) - \frac{1}{2}}{2\beta}\right)(t^1 - h^2) + \left(\frac{1}{2} - \frac{F\left(\frac{t^1 + t^2}{2}\right) - \frac{1}{2}}{2\beta}\right)(t^2 - h^2).$$

The reader can compute that the F.O.C.s for Nash equilibrium reduce to

$$(t^{2*} - t^{1*})f(\bar{t}) - 2\beta = 2(F(\bar{t}) - \tfrac{1}{2}),$$

$$(t^{1*} - t^{2*})f(\bar{t}) + 2\beta = 2(F(\bar{t}) - \tfrac{1}{2}),$$

where $\bar{t} = (t^{1*} + t^{2*})/2$. These two equations imply that

$$2(F(\bar{t}) - \frac{1}{2}) = 0,$$

and so $F(\bar{t}) = \tfrac{1}{2}$, which means that $\bar{t} = m$. It follows that

$$\frac{t^{1*} + t^{2*}}{2} = m \quad \text{and} \quad \frac{t^{2*} - t^{1*}}{2} = \frac{\beta}{f(m)},$$

from which we deduce

$$t^{1*} = m - \frac{\beta}{f(m)}, \qquad t^{2*} = m + \frac{\beta}{f(m)}.$$

The policy pair (t^{1*}, t^{2*}) satisfies the F.O.C.s for a Wittman equilibrium; indeed, the pair form a Wittman equilibrium when $h^1 < t^{1*}$ and $t^{2*} < h^2$. It is a peculiar (indeed, Downsian) feature of this example that the equilibrium is independent of (h^1, h^2).

The example illustrates the fact that, unlike Downs equilibrium, Wittman equilibrium depends in general on the nature of the distribution **F**, not simply on its median value, m. Thus if we alter $\mathbf{F}$ so that the median remains un-changed, but $f(m)$ changes, then the Wittman equilibrium changes, while the Downs equilibrium does not. This is why Wittman equilibrium is an inherently more complex idea than Downs equilibrium—and, incidentally, why there are few examples where one can calculate Wittman equilibrium (as we have done in this section) by hand.

Note that as β approaches zero, we approach "median-voter politics" in this example's equilibrium.

3.4 Existence of Wittman Equilibrium

We shall assume through this section that A1, A2, A3, and A4 hold, and that T and H are intervals in $\mathbf{R}$. Let $H = [\underline{h}, \bar{h}]$. Let the parties have single-peaked vNM utility functions v^1 and v^2 on T.

In addition, we shall assume:

A7   For any pair (t^1, t^2) with $t^1 > t^2$, the function $v(t^1, h) - v(t^2, h)$ is strictly decreasing[3] in h.

A8 v is differentiable.

Consider the condition:

Single-crossing property (SCP)   For any distinct pair $t^1, t^2 \in T$, the equation $v(t^1, h) = v(t^2, h)$ has at most one solution in h.

We denote the solution to the equation in SCP, if there is one, by $h(t^1, t^2)$.

The name "single-crossing property" derives from the fact that if $v(t^1, h) = v(t^2, h)$, then the pair $\{t^1, t^2\}$ is an "indifference curve" for h. Single-peakedness implies it is the complete indifference curve. If there were two values of h for which this equation held, then two types would have indifference curves intersecting in two points. Hence SCP says that any two indifference curves of two types intersect at most once. Note that:

Lemma 3.1 $A7 \Rightarrow$ SCP.

---

3. We could more generally assume strict monotonicity; "decreasing" is assumed for the sake of concreteness.

Proof:

For any $t^1 > t^2$, $v(t^1, h) - v(t^2, h)$ is strictly decreasing in h. There is therefore at most one h at which that function is zero. ∎

Lemma 3.2 *A2, A7, and A8 imply that $h(\cdot, \cdot)$ is differentiable,*

$$\frac{\partial h}{\partial t^1}(t^1, t^2) < 0 \quad \text{and} \quad \frac{\partial h}{\partial t^2}(t^1, t^2) < 0.$$

Proof:

1. First assume $t^1 > t^2$.

The function $h(t^1, t^2)$ is defined by

$$(3.5) \qquad v(t^1, h(t^1, t^2)) = v(t^2, h(t^1, t^2)).$$

Differentiating (3.5) implicitly w.r.t. t^1 yields

$$(3.6) \qquad \frac{\partial h}{\partial t^1}(t^1, t^2) = \frac{\frac{\partial v}{\partial t}(t^1, h)}{\frac{\partial v}{\partial h}(t^2, h) - \frac{\partial v}{\partial h}(t^1, h)},$$

where $h \equiv h(t^1, t^2)$. By the implicit function theorem, the function h is therefore differentiable as long as the denominator in (3.6) does not vanish. The denominator of (3.6) is *positive* by A7, and the numerator is negative. (To see the last claim, note that t^1 must be on the decreasing branch of $v(\cdot, h)$, since $v(t^1, h) = v(t^2, h)$ and $t^1 > t^2$.) Therefore $\frac{\partial h}{\partial t^1}(t^1, t^2) < 0$.

Similarly, we have

$$(3.7) \qquad \frac{\partial h}{\partial t^2}(t^1, t^2) = \frac{\frac{\partial v}{\partial t}(t^2, h)}{\frac{\partial v}{\partial h}(t^1, h) - \frac{\partial v}{\partial h}(t^2, h)}.$$

The denominator of (3.7) is negative and the numerator is positive.

2. Now let $t^1 < t^2$. Then the denominator of (3.6) is negative and the numerator is positive. Likewise the denominator of (3.7) is positive and the numerator is negative. ∎

We shall now specialize to the model in which π is defined by the error-distribution model of uncertainty. Let ϵ be a random variable distributed according to a continuous distribution X, and

$$\pi(t^1, t^2) = \text{Prob}[\mathbf{F}(\Omega(t^1, t^2)) + \epsilon > \tfrac{1}{2}]$$

(3.8)
$$= \text{Prob}[\epsilon > \tfrac{1}{2} - \mathbf{F}(\Omega(t^1, t^2))]$$

$$= 1 - X(\tfrac{1}{2} - \mathbf{F}(\Omega(t^1, t^2))).$$

A7 and A8 permit another useful lemma:

Lemma 3.3 *Assume A2, A7 and A8. Let $\bar{t}^1 > \bar{t}^2$. Then $\pi(t, \bar{t}^2)$ and $\pi(\bar{t}^1, t)$ are decreasing in t at $\bar{t}^1$ and $\bar{t}^2$, respectively. If $\bar{t}^1 < \bar{t}^2$, then $\pi(\bar{t}^1, t)$ and $\pi(t, \bar{t}^2)$ are increasing in t at $\bar{t}^2$ and $\bar{t}^1$ respectively.*

Proof:

1. $\bar{t}^1 > \bar{t}^2$ implies, by A7, that $\Omega(\bar{t}^1, \bar{t}^2) = [\underline{h}, h(\bar{t}^1, \bar{t}^2))$. Thus $\pi(\bar{t}^1, \bar{t}^2) = 1 - X(\tfrac{1}{2} - \mathbf{F}(h(\bar{t}^1, \bar{t}^2)))$. Since h is decreasing in t^1, π is decreasing in t^1.

Similarly, π is decreasing in t^2.

2. Let $\bar{t}^1 < \bar{t}^2$. Then A7 implies that $\Omega(\bar{t}^1, \bar{t}^2) = (\underline{h}(\bar{t}^1, \bar{t}^2), \overline{h}]$. Now we see that $\pi(t, \bar{t}^2)$ is increasing in t at $\bar{t}^1$, and so on. ∎

Define

$$\Psi^1(t^1, t^2) = v^1(t^1) - v^1(t^2)$$

$$\Psi^2(t^1, t^2) = v^2(t^2) - v^2(t^1),$$

and note that we can write the payoff functions of the parties as

$$\Pi^1(t^1, t^2) = \pi(t^1, t^2)\Psi^1(t^1, t^2) + k_1$$

$$\Pi^2(t^1, t^2) = (1 - \pi((t^1, t^2))\Psi^2(t^1, t^2) + k_2,$$

where k_i is not a function of t^i. Since party i wishes to choose t^i to maximize Π^i given a policy by the other party, we may without harm replace the payoff function by the functions $\pi\Psi^1$ and $(1 - \pi)\Psi^2$, respectively.

Definition 3.1 Given a policy t^2, the *set of decent responses by party 1* is

$$\Delta^1(t^2) = \{t \mid \pi(t, t^2)\Psi^1(t, t^2) > 0\}.$$

Similarly, given t^1, the set of decent responses of party 2 is

$$\Delta^2(t^1) = \{t \mid (1 - \pi(t^1, t))\Psi^2(t^1, t) > 0\}.$$

A decent response by party 1 to t^2 is a policy t that party 1 prefers to t^2 (that is, $\Psi(t, t^2) > 0$) and that has positive probability of defeating t^2 ($\pi(t, t^2) > 0$). Clearly, in considering a response to t^2, party 1 might as well limit its search to $\Delta^1(t^2)$. If $\Delta^1(t^2) = \varnothing$, party 1 can do no better than to respond with t^2.

We have

Lemma 3.4 *Assume A2 and A7, and assume the error-distribution model of uncertainty. Then, for any policy t^2, the set $R(t^2) = \{t \mid \pi(t, t^2) > 0\}$ is convex.*

Proof:

1. Let $t > t^2$. Let $h(t, t^2)$ be the unique type h that is indifferent between t and t^2 (if there is one). Then, by A7, $\Omega(t, t^2) = \{h < h(t, t^2)\}$.

2. Let $t', t'' \in R(t^2)$. We must show that any point in the interval (t', t'') is also in $R(t^2)$.

There are two cases to consider.

Case (i) $t' > t'' > t^2$.

Let $t \in (t'', t')$. It suffices to show that $\mathbf{F}(\Omega(t, t^2)) \geq \mathbf{F}(\Omega(t', t^2))$. By step 1, it suffices to show that $h(t, t^2) > h(t', t^2)$. Note that type $h(t', t^2)$ prefers t to t^2, by single-peakedness. This proves that $h(t, t^2) > h(t', t^2)$.

Case (ii) $t' > t^2 > t''$.

The argument given in Case (i) shows that if $t \in (t^2, t')$ then $t \in R(t^2)$. It remains only to show that $t \in (t'', t^2)$ also lies in $R(t^2)$. Now, $\Omega(t'', t^2) = \{h > h(t'', t^2)\}$, by A7. Thus it suffices to show that $h(t, t^2) < h(t'', t^2)$, since $\Omega(t, t^2) = \{h > h(t, t^2)\}$. But the required inequality is true by virtue of the fact that type $h(t'', t^2)$ prefers t to t^2 (again, invoke single-peakedness).

3. The other possible cases are identical to one of these two. ■

As a consequence of Lemma 3.4, we have

Corollary 3.1 *Let A1, A2, and A7 hold. Then for all $t^1, t^2 \in T$, the sets $\Delta^1(t^2)$ and $\Delta^2(t^1)$ are convex (intervals).*

Proof:

We prove the corollary for $\Delta^1(t^2)$. Let t, $t' \in \Delta^1(t^2)$. Then $\pi(t, t^2) > 0$, $\pi(t', t^2) > 0$, $\Psi^1(t, t^2) > 0$, and $\Psi^1(t', t^2) > 0$. Since v is single-peaked in t, so is Ψ^1, in its first argument, and hence, for any $\lambda \in [0, 1]$, $\Psi^1(\lambda t + (1 - \lambda)t', t^2) > 0$.

By Lemma 3.4, it follows that $\pi(\lambda t + (1 - \lambda)t', t^2) > 0$. Hence $\lambda t + (1 - \lambda)t' \in \Delta^1(t^2)$, proving that $\Delta^1(t^2)$ is convex and hence an interval. ∎

We can now state the existence theorem.

Theorem 3.3 *Let A1, A2, A3, A7, and A8 hold. Let* **X** *be a continuous distribution. Suppose that* Π^1 *is a quasi-concave function of* t^1, *for any* t^2, *on* $\Delta^1(t^2)$, *and* Π^2 *is a quasi-concave function of* t^2, *for any* t^1, *on* $\Delta^2(t^1)$. *Then a Wittman equilibrium exists.*

Let $\hat{r}^1(t^2)$ be the set of best responses by party 1 to t^2 and $\hat{r}^2(t^1)$ be the set of best responses by party 2 to t^1. We define the following refinements of $\hat{r}^1$ and $\hat{r}^2$:

$$r^1(t^2) = \begin{cases} \hat{r}^1(t^2) & \text{if } \Delta^1(t^2) \neq \varnothing \\ t^2 & \text{if } \Delta^1(t^2) = \varnothing \end{cases}$$

$$r^2(t^1) = \begin{cases} \hat{r}^2(t^1) & \text{if } \Delta^2(t^1) \neq \varnothing \\ t^1 & \text{if } \Delta^2(t^1) = \varnothing \end{cases}$$

To see that r^i is a refinement of $\hat{r}^i$, we need only note that when $\Delta^1(t^2) = \varnothing$, t^2 is a best response (by party 1) to t^2; a similar statement holds when $\Delta^2(t^1) = \varnothing$.

Now define

$$r(t^1, t^2) = r^1(t^2) \times r^2(t^1).$$

Then $r : T \times T \rightarrow\rightarrow T \times T$. If r is upper hemicontinuous, everywhere nonempty, and convex valued, then by Kakutani's fixed-point theorem, it has a fixed point. A fixed point of r is Wittman equilibrium. For $t^1 \in r(t^2)$ means that t^1 is a best response to t^2 and $t^2 \in r^2(t^1)$ means t^2 is a best response to t^1.

The point is: we shall be able to show that r is indeed convex valued, a fact that we know, from Example 3.1 and Figure 3.1, is not generally true of the correspondence $\hat{r}(t^1, t^2) = \hat{r}^1(t^1) \times \hat{r}^2(t^2)$. By definition the function r is nonempty. Hence Theorem 3.3 will be proved by proving:

Lemma 3.5   *Under the assumptions of Theorem 3.3, the correspondence r is upper hemicontinuous and convex valued.*

Proof:

1. If $\Delta^1(t^2) = \varnothing$, then $r^1(t^2)$ is a point, and hence a convex set. If $\Delta^1(t^2) \neq \varnothing$, then $\hat{r}^1(t^2)$ is the set of maximizers of $\Pi^1(\cdot, t^2)$ on the interval (see Corollary 3.1) $\Delta^1(t^2)$. Since $\Pi(\cdot, t^2)$ is quasi-concave on an interval, its maximizers form a convex set. Therefore $r^1(t^2)$ is convex in this case also. Similarly, $r^2(t^1)$ is convex valued; it follows that r is convex valued on $T \times T$.

2. It remains to show that r is upper hemicontinuous. This will follow if r^1 and r^2 are upper hemicontinuous. We demonstrate this for r^1.

Let $t_k^2 \to \bar{t}^2$ and $t_k^1 \in r^1(t_k^2)$, where $t_k^1 \to \bar{t}^1$. We must show $\bar{t}^1 \in r^1(\bar{t}^2)$.

3. We may view Π^1 as a function of t^1 with parameter t^2. According to the theorem of the maximum (see Mathematical Appendix), the mapping from t^2 to the maximizers of $\Pi^1(\cdot, t^2)$ is an upper hemicontinuous correspondence. (Observe that Π^1 is a continuous function.) Since $r^1(t^2)$ is exactly the set of maximizers of $\Pi^1(\cdot, t^2)$ when $\Delta^1(t^2) \neq \varnothing$, we need only worry about the cases where for infinitely many k, $\Delta^1(t_k^2) = \varnothing$, and/or $\Delta^1(t^2) = \varnothing$.

Thus we have two cases to consider.

Case (i)   For infinitely many k, $\Delta^1(t_k^2) = \varnothing$.

Case (ii)   For finitely many k, $\Delta^1(t_k^2) = \varnothing$, and $\Delta^1(\bar{t}^2) = \varnothing$.

4. *Case (i)* We may assume that $\Delta^1(t_k^2) = \varnothing$ for all k. Then $t_k^1 = t_k^2$ for all k. Since $t_k^2 \to \bar{t}^2$ and $t_k^1 \to \bar{t}^1$, it follows that $\bar{t}^1 = \bar{t}^2$. Suppose that $\bar{t}^2 \notin r^1(\bar{t}^2)$; then decent responses to $\bar{t}^2$ exist, and so there exists $\hat{t}^1$ such that $\pi(\hat{t}^1, \bar{t}^2)\Psi^1(\hat{t}^1, \bar{t}^2) > 0$, which implies that, for large k, there exists $\hat{t}_k^1$ such that $\pi(\hat{t}_k^1, t_k^2)\Psi^1(\hat{t}_k^1, t_k^2) > 0$. But this contradicts the supposition that $\Delta^1(t_k^2) = \varnothing$.

5. *Case (ii)* By continuity of Π^1, we have

$$\lim_{k \to \infty} \pi(t_k^1, t_k^2)\Psi^1(t_k^1, t_k^2) = \pi((\bar{t}^1, \bar{t}^2)\Psi^1(\bar{t}^1, \bar{t}^2) = 0.$$

This limit is non-negative, since for every k, the product $\pi(t_k^1, t_k^2)\Psi^1(t_k^1, t_k^2)$ is positive, because $\Delta^1(t_k^2) \neq \varnothing$. Therefore it must be zero, since $\Delta^1(\bar{t}^2) = \varnothing$. Since $\bar{t}^2 = r^1(\bar{t}^2)$ (because $\Delta^1(\bar{t}^2) = \varnothing$), we must show $\bar{t}^1 = \bar{t}^2$.

6. Moreover, the limit argument also shows that $\pi(\bar{t}^1, \bar{t}^2) \geq 0$ and $\Psi^1(\bar{t}^1, \bar{t}^2) \geq 0$, since $\pi(\bar{t}_k^1, \bar{t}_k^2)$ and $\Psi^1(\bar{t}_k^1, \bar{t}_k^2)$ are positive for all k.

7. Suppose, on the contrary, that $\bar{t}^1 \neq \bar{t}^2$. Without loss of generality, suppose $\bar{t}^1 > \bar{t}^2$. From step 5, either $\pi(\bar{t}^1, \bar{t}^2) = 0$ or $\Psi^1(\bar{t}^1, \bar{t}^2) = 0$.

Suppose first that $\pi(\bar{t}^1, \bar{t}^2) = 0$; since, for points (t_k^1, t_k^2) very close to $(\bar{t}^1, \bar{t}^2)$ we know that $\pi(t_k^1, t_k^2) > 0$, it follows that[4]

$$\mathbf{F}(\Omega(\bar{t}^1, \bar{t}^2)) = \tfrac{1}{2} - \beta.$$

We know as well that $\Omega(\bar{t}^1, \bar{t}^2) = \{h < h(\bar{t}^1, \bar{t}^2)\}$, and so $F(h(\bar{t}^1, \bar{t}^2)) = \tfrac{1}{2} - \beta$.

8. If we decrease $\bar{t}^1$ to $\bar{t}^1 - \delta$, then by Lemma 3.2, $h(\bar{t}^1 - \delta, \bar{t}^2) > h(\bar{t}^1, \bar{t}^2)$, and so, since $\mathbf{F}$ is continuous, $F(h(\bar{t}^1 - \delta, \bar{t}^2)) > \tfrac{1}{2} - \beta$; therefore $\pi(\bar{t}^1 - \delta, \bar{t}^2) > 0$. Hence it must be the case that $\Psi^1(\bar{t}^1 - \delta, \bar{t}^2) \leq 0$, or else $\bar{t}^1 - \delta$ would be a decent response to $\bar{t}^2$.

Because this holds for all small $\delta > 0$, it must be that $\Psi^1(\bar{t}^1, \bar{t}^2) \leq 0$; by step 6, $\Psi^1(\bar{t}^1, \bar{t}^2) = 0$. But by single-peakedness, this implies that $\Psi^1(t, \bar{t}^2) > 0$ for all points $t \in (\bar{t}^2, \bar{t}^1)$—contradicting the fact that $\Psi^1(\bar{t}^1 - \delta, \bar{t}^2) \leq 0$. This disposes of the possibility that $\pi(\bar{t}^1, \bar{t}^2) = 0$.

9. The final possibility is that $\Psi^1(\bar{t}^1, \bar{t}^2) = 0$. Again, we have $\Psi^1(t, \bar{t}^2) > 0$ for all $t \in (\bar{t}^2, \bar{t}^1)$. We know that $F(h(\bar{t}^1, \bar{t}^2)) \geq \tfrac{1}{2} - \beta$. We know that $h(\bar{t}^1 - \delta, \bar{t}^2) > h(\bar{t}^1, \bar{t}^2)$ by Lemma 3.2, and so $F(h(\bar{t}^1 - \delta, \bar{t}^2)) > \tfrac{1}{2} - \beta$, which implies that $\pi(\bar{t}^1 - \delta, \bar{t}^2) > 0$. Therefore, $\bar{t}^1 - \delta$ is a decent response to $\bar{t}^2$, an impossibility. This proves the lemma. ∎

The discussion prior to the statement of Lemma 3.3 shows that Theorem 3.4 is now proved.

Our next task is to provide conditions under which the conditional payoff functions $\Pi^1(\cdot, t^2)$ and $\Pi^2(t^1, \cdot)$ are quasi-concave on the sets $\Delta^1(t^2)$ and $\Delta^2(t^1)$, respectively.

As we have noted, party 1 chooses t to maximize $\pi(t, t^2)\Psi^1(t, t^2)$. In turn, this function is quasi-concave on $\Delta^1(t^2)$ if $\log[\pi(t, t^2)\Psi^1(t, t^2)]$ is concave on $\Delta^1(t^2)$, since applying a strictly monotonic transformation to a function will not disturb its maxima. Therefore it suffices that $\log \pi(t, t^2) + \log \Psi^1(t, t^2)$ be a concave function on t. $\log \Psi^1(t, t^2)$ is concave if v is concave in t; a sufficient condition is therefore that $\log \pi(t, t^2)$ and v^1 be concave in t since the sum of concave functions is concave.

---

4. Here we assume for simplicity of exposition that $\mathbf{X}$ is the uniform distribution on $[-\beta, \beta]$.

Similarly, a sufficient condition for $(1 - \pi(t^1, t))\Psi^2(t^1, t^2)$ to be quasi-concave on $\Delta^2(t^1)$ is that $\log(1 - \pi(t^1, t))$ and v^2 be concave in t. Thus we have

Corollary 3.2 *Let A1, A2, A3, A7, and A8 hold; let $\log \pi(t, t^2)$ and v^1 be concave on $\Delta^1(t^2)$, and $\log(1 - \pi(t^1, t))$ and v^2 be concave on $\Delta^2(t^1)$. Then a Wittman equilibrium exists.*

Let us return to Example 3.1. A1, A2, A3, A7, and A8 hold. We have

$$\log \pi(t, t^2) = \log \left[\frac{1 - \frac{t + t^2}{2} + \beta - \frac{1}{2}}{2\beta} \right], \quad \text{and}$$

$$\log(1 - \pi(t^1, t)) = \log \left[\frac{-1 + \frac{t^1 + t}{2} - \beta + \frac{1}{2}}{2\beta} \right].$$

These are both concave functions of t, as are v^1 and v^2. Thus Corollary 3.1 suffices to prove the existence of a Wittman equilibrium in that example.

It would surely be more satisfactory to supply sufficient conditions for the existence of Wittman equilibria that were stated directly in terms of the data of the model, $\{\mathbf{F}, \mathbf{X}, \beta, v^1, v^2\}$, instead of the derived function π. No simple condition stated in terms of these primitives is known.

A theorem similar to 3.3 may be proved for the state-space model of uncertainty (see Roemer 1997).

In sum, we find that in most interesting examples Wittman equilibria exist, but a truly satisfactory general existence theorem is not known.

As a final remark, we note that A5, the monotonicity axiom, and A7 are closely related.

Proposition 3.1 *Let $\hat{t}^h$ be decreasing in h, $\dim T = \dim H = 1$, and A1 and A2. Then A7$\Rightarrow$A5.*

Proof:
Let $t^1 < t^2$. A7 implies that $\Omega(t^1, t^2) = (h(t^1, t^2), \overline{h}]$. Since $\hat{t}^h$ is decreasing, $(h(t^1, t^2), \overline{h}]$ is the set of types whose ideal points are less than the ideal point of $h(t^1, t^2)$. But this implies A5.

If there is no h indifferent between t^1 and t^2, then $\Omega(t^1, t^2)$ is either $\oslash$ or H, which again implies the existence of t' such that $\Omega(t^1, t^2) = H^{t'}$. (Take $t' = \underline{t}$ or $\bar{t}$.) ∎

3.5 Properties of Wittman Equilibrium

We shall continue to employ the error-distribution model of uncertainty in this section.

Proposition 3.2 *Assume A3, A7, and A8. Assume the error-distribution model of uncertainty, and assume that X is a continuous distribution. If $h(t^1, t^2)$ is defined at (t^1, t^2) then π is differentiable at (t^1, t^2).*

Proof: We have either

$$\pi(t^1, t^2) = 1 - X(\tfrac{1}{2} - F(h(t^1, t^2))) \quad \text{or}$$

$$\pi(t^1, t^2) = 1 - X(\tfrac{1}{2} + F(h(t^1, t^2))),$$

depending on whether $t^1 > (<)t^2$. The distribution functions X and F, being continuous, possess densities (that is, derivatives) x and f, respectively. The derivative of $h(\cdot, \cdot)$ is given by (3.6) and (3.7) as long as the denominators in those expressions do not vanish. They do not vanish, by A7.

Consequently, the chain rule implies that π is differentiable at (t^1, t^2). ∎

Definition 3.2 A Wittman equilibrium (t^1, t^2) is *trivial* if either $t^1 = t^2$ or $\pi(t^1, t^2)$ is zero or one.

We now introduce the idea that the two parties are in some sense polarized in their interests. Let $\hat{t}^1$ and $\hat{t}^2$ represent the ideal policies of party 1 and party 2, and let $\hat{t}^m$ be the median ideal policy.

A9 $\hat{t}^1 > \hat{t}^m > \hat{t}^2$.

Theorem 3.4 *Assume A2, A3, A7, and A9, and the continuity of X. Then there exists no trivial Wittman equilibrium.*

Proof:

1. We need only consider equilibria (t^1, t^2) where $t^1, t^2 \in [\hat{t}^2, \hat{t}^1]$. It follows that $t^2 \leq t^1$, for if $t^1 < t^2$ then party 1 could increase its payoff by deviating to t^2.

2. Suppose there is a Wittman equilibrium where $t^1 = t^2 = t^* \neq \hat{t}^m$. Let $t^* > \hat{t}^m$. Then party 2 can increase both its probability of victory and its utility by decreasing its proposal to $t^* - \delta$.

A similar argument holds if $t^* < \hat{t}^m$.

3. Suppose $t^1 = t^2 = \hat{t}^m$. Because $\hat{t}^m$ is a best response of party 1 to $\hat{t}^m$, we have

$$\text{for all } t \quad \pi(t, \hat{t}^m)\Psi^1(t, \hat{t}^m) \leq 0,$$

because the product $\pi \Psi^1$ is zero at $t = \hat{t}^m$. But the continuity of $\mathbf{X}$ and $\mathbf{F}$ imply that π is positive at $t = \hat{t}^m \pm \delta$ for small $\delta > 0$. Therefore $\Psi^1(\hat{t}^m \pm \delta, \hat{t}^m) \leq 0$, which means that $\hat{t}^m$ is the maximum of v^1, contradicting A9.

4. Finally, let (t^1, t^2) be a Wittman equilibrium where $\pi(t^1, t^2) = 0$ and $t^2 < t^1$. Party 1's payoff is $v^1(t^2)$. It follows that $\hat{t}^m < t^2$: for if $t^2 \leq \hat{t}^m$ then party 1 could play $t^2 + \delta$, which would give it a positive probability of winning and, indeed, a higher payoff than $v^1(t^2)$.

We therefore must have $\hat{t}^m < t^2$. It must therefore be the case that $\mathbf{F}(\Omega(t^1, t^2)) = \frac{1}{2} - \beta$: for if $\mathbf{F}(\Omega(t^1, t^2)) < \frac{1}{2} - \beta$ then party 2 could deviate slightly toward $\hat{t}^m$ without lowering its probability of victory from one, and increase its payoff. But this means that if party 1 deviates to $t^1 - \delta$, it has a positive probability of winning—and its payoff at $(t^1 - \delta, t^2)$ is greater than $v^1(t^2)$, a contradiction.

A similar argument works if $\pi(t^1, t^2) = 1$. ∎

Theorem 3.4 tells us that when parties are polarized in the sense of A9, then *all Wittman equilibria involve differentiated policies:* the escape from the "tyranny of the median voter" is achieved.

We should expect that as uncertainty decreases, Wittman equilibrium converges to the Wittman equilibrium under certainty, in which both parties play $\hat{t}^m$ (Theorem 1.2). To study this question in the error-distribution uncertainty model, let $\mathbf{X}$ be the uniform measure on $[-\beta, +\beta]$; then "decreasing uncertainty" is easily modeled as "decreasing β."

Theorem 3.5 *Assume A2, A3, A7, and A9. Let π be defined according to error-distribution uncertainty where $X(\epsilon) = (1/2\beta)\epsilon + 1/2$. Let $(t^1(\beta), t^2(\beta))$ be a Wittman equilibrium, viewing β as a parameter. Then*

$$\lim_{\beta \to 0} t^i(\beta) = \hat{t}^m \quad \text{for} \quad i = 1, 2.$$

Proof:

1. From Theorem 3.4, we know that, for all β,

$$0 < \pi(t^1(\beta), t^2(\beta)) < 1.$$

It follows that

$$F(h(t^1(\beta), t^2(\beta))) - \beta < \tfrac{1}{2} < F(h(t^1(\beta), t^2(\beta))) + \beta.$$

Hence, $\lim_{\beta \to 0} h(t^1(\beta), t^2(\beta)) = m$.

2. There are two possibilities: either $t^i(\beta) \to m$ for $i = 1, 2$, or there is a subsequence $\beta^j \to 0$ such that $t^1(\beta^j) \to \bar{t}^1, t^2(\beta^j) \to \bar{t}^2, \bar{t}^1 > \bar{t}^2$, and $v(\bar{t}^1, m) = v(\bar{t}^2, m)$. We must show that the second case is impossible.

3. Suppose, then, that such a subsequence $\{\beta^j\}$ exists. The payoff of party 1 tends to $\tfrac{1}{2}(v^1(\bar{t}^1) + v^1(\bar{t}^2))$ as $j \to \infty$. Let δ be a small positive number; I claim that for large j, party 1 should deviate to $\bar{t}^1 - \delta$. We know that $F(h(\bar{t}^1 - \delta, \bar{t}^2)) > \tfrac{1}{2}$, so for small enough β^j, $\pi(\bar{t}^1 - \delta, t^2(\beta^j)) = 1$. Consequently, for large j, by this deviation, party 1 can assure itself of the payoff $v^1(\bar{t}^1 - \delta) > \tfrac{1}{2}(v^1(\bar{t}^1) + v^1(\bar{t}^2))$.

This contradicts the fact that $(t^1(\beta^j), t^2(\beta^j))$ is a Wittman equilibrium.

∎

3.6 Summary

We summarize the main results of Chapters 1 and 3 in Figure 3.2. Of the four models obtained by varying the choices of "party type" and "information," only one produces the realistic result that parties propose different policies in equilibrium. Since divergence is a fact of political life, this is a strong argument for the claim that parties are not Downsian, but are interested in policies.

That inference, however, is not watertight, because there is at least one other way of generating policy differentiation without discarding the Downsian

	Certainty	Uncertainty
Downs	Policy convergence	Policy convergence
Wittman	Policy convergence	Policy divergence

Figure 3.2

assumption. That way assumes the potential for a third party to enter the competition. If all parties are Downsian, the possibility of entry can produce equilibria with two parties in the race, and policy differentiation at equilibrium (Palfrey 1984; Osborne 1995).

Furthermore, there are ways of inducing equilibrium policy differentiation without uncertainty if parties have policy preferences. Ortuño-Ortín (1997) does so by postulating that parties care about the fraction of votes that they get, perhaps because representation is proportional or because a higher vote fraction will facilitate the party's ability to implement its policy once in office. Llavador (2000) also achieves policy differentiation with partisan parties, but without uncertainty, by introducing the possibility of voter abstention. Nevertheless, in his model, policy convergence is the norm.

4

Applications of the Wittman Model

4.1 Simple Models of Redistribution: The Politics of Extremism

Reconsider Example 2.1. Citizens vote on a purely redistributive proportional income tax t; we worked with the state-space model of uncertainty. We showed that, for $t^1 > t^2$, $\pi(t^1, t^2) = s^*$, a constant, where $s^* \in (0, 1)$.

Now assume that the parties have utility functions

$$v^i(t) = v(t, h^i) = (1 - t)h^i + t\mu, \qquad i = 1, 2$$

where $h^1 < \mu < h^2$. We have

Proposition 4.1 *There is a unique Wittman equilibrium, $(t^{1^*}, t^{2^*}) = (1, 0)$.*

Proof:
The payoff functions for the parties are equivalent to

$$\Pi^1(t^1, t^2) = s^* t^1(\mu - h^1) + (1 - s^*)t^2(\mu - h^1)$$

$$\Pi^2(t^1, t^2) = s^* t^1(\mu - h^2) + (1 - s^*)t^2(\mu - h^2).$$

Thus

$$\Pi^1(t^1, 0) = s^* t^1(\mu - h^1)$$

$$\Pi^2(1, t^2) = s^*(\mu - h^2) + (1 - s^*)t^2(\mu - h^2)$$

Since $\mu - h^1 > 0$, it follows that $\Pi^1(t^1, 0)$ is maximized at $t^1 = 1$; since $\mu - h^2 < 0$, it follows that $\Pi^2(1, t^2)$ is maximized at $t^2 = 0$, which shows that (t^{1^*}, t^{2^*}) is a Wittman equilibrium. It is left as an exercise to show that the equilibrium is unique. ∎

According to Theorem 3.2, the Downs equilibrium of this model is (t^*, t^*), where t^* is the ideal policy of the median voter in the median state. That could be either $(0, 0)$ or $(1, 1)$, depending on whether that "double median" voter has income greater or less than μ.

There is thus a sharp contrast between the prediction of the Downs and Wittman models in this example. The starkness of the polarity of equilibrium policies in the Wittman model is due to π's being constant. Note as well that the Wittman equilibrium does not depend on the relative position of the citizens with median and mean income, in contrast to the Downs model.

Here is a second example exhibiting political extremism. Suppose a polity must choose a quadratic income tax to finance public services in a given amount R per capita. Let $H = [0, \bar{h}]$. An individual with income h will pay a tax of $ah^2 + bh$ under the tax schedule (a, b). Denote the second moment of *population* income by $\mu_2 = \int h^2 d\mathbf{F}$, where $\mathbf{F}$ is the distribution of types in the population. Thus the budget-balancing constraint is

$$a\mu_2 + b\mu = R.$$

Writing $a = (R - b\mu)/\mu_2$, we now think of tax policies as unidimensional, represented by the marginal tax rate at zero income, b.

No one can pay more taxes than his income, so

$$a\bar{h}^2 + b\bar{h} \leq \bar{h},$$

where $\bar{h}$ is maximum income. This implies

$$b > \frac{R\bar{h} - \mu_2}{\mu\bar{h} - \mu_2}.$$

On the other hand, by looking at small h, we have

$$b \leq 1,$$

and so the bounds on b are

$$\frac{R\bar{h} - \mu_2}{\mu\bar{h} - \mu_2} \leq b \leq 1.$$

An individual prefers that policy which minimizes his tax liability; thus h prefers b_1 to b_2 exactly when

$$\frac{R - b_1\mu}{\mu_2}h^2 + b_1h < \frac{R - b_2\mu}{\mu_2}h^2 + b_2h,$$

or when

$$h < \frac{\mu_2}{\mu} \quad \text{if} \quad \Delta b > 0,$$

$$h > \frac{\mu_2}{\mu} \quad \text{if} \quad \Delta b < 0,$$

where $\Delta b \equiv b_2 - b_1$.

Let $b_2 > b_1$. Then b_1 defeats b_2 in state s iff

$$m_s < \frac{\mu_2}{\mu},$$

where m_s is the median of $\mathbf{F}_s$.

Now assume m_s is increasing in s, and let s be uniformly distributed on $[0, 1]$. Define s^* by

$$m_{s^*} = \frac{\mu_2}{\mu}.$$

Then the probability that b_1 defeats b_2 is s^*.

Since $\pi(b_1, b_2)$ is constant, it follows that the Wittman equilibrium consists in each party's proposing its ideal point, as in the previous example.

Let's check the ideal points. Type h wants to choose b to

$$\min \left(\frac{R - b\mu}{\mu_2}h + b\right)$$

or

$$\min b \left(1 - \frac{h\mu}{\mu_2}\right).$$

Hence

$$h > \frac{\mu_2}{\mu} \Rightarrow \hat{b}^h = 1$$

$$h < \frac{\mu_2}{\mu} \Rightarrow \hat{b}^h = \frac{R\bar{h} - \mu_2}{\mu\bar{h} - \mu_2}.$$

Thus the party representing the wealthy proposes the highest feasible marginal tax rate—and hence the least progressive income tax, since the associated value of a will be as small as possible—and the party representing the poor proposes the lowest marginal tax rate and the most progressive tax policy.

Some authors (for example, Calvert 1985) have claimed that the policies in Wittman equilibrium are close to the policies of Downs equilibrium. These examples show that this claim is in general false.

4.2 Politico-Economic Equilibrium with Labor-Supply Elasticity [1]

Let $H = [c, \infty)$, where h is interpreted as the skill level of type h, which means that output (y) can be produced from skill (h) according to the personal production function

$$y = hL,$$

where L is units of labor time expended by individual h.

We suppose that all citizens share the same vNM preferences over output and labor, represented by a utility function $u(y, L)$.

The policy shall be a redistributive income tax, t.

In this example, there is uncertainty about the distribution of types in the citizenry—that is, in the tax base. All citizens vote. We work with the state-space approach to uncertainty. The states, s, are uniformly distributed on $[0, S]$, where S is a positive number. In state s, the probability distribution of types is $\mathbf{F}_s$, the Pareto distribution on H whose density is

$$f_s(h) = \frac{s+3}{c} \left(\frac{c}{h} \right)^{s+4}.$$

---

1. This application is taken from Roemer (1994).

As usual, denote the distribution function of $\mathbf{F}_s$ by F_s. The mean and median of $\mathbf{F}_s$ are given by

$$(4.1) \qquad \mu_s = \frac{(s+3)c}{s+2}, \qquad m_s = 2^{\frac{1}{s+3}}c.$$

Thus larger s are associated with distributions of citizen types with lower means and medians.

The formula for the second moment of $\mathbf{F}_s$, which we denote $\tilde{\mu}_s$, is:

$$(4.2) \qquad \tilde{\mu}_s = \int_c^\infty h^2 f_s(h)\,dh = \frac{s+3}{s+1}c^2.$$

Let t be the tax rate and I be the level of tax revenue per capita; those revenues are redistributed in a lump-sum manner to all citizens. Then the utility of a citizen who earns y and works L is $u((1-t)y + I, L)$. We proceed to define an economic equilibrium.

Definition 4.1   An *economic equilibrium at tax rate t* is a function $L : H \to \mathbf{R}_+$ and a function $I : [0, S] \to \mathbf{R}_+$ such that:

(i) For all $h \in H$, $L(h)$ solves

$$\max_L \int_0^S u((1-t)hL + I(s), L)\frac{1}{S}\,ds.$$

(ii) For all $s \in [0, S]$,

$$I(s) = \int_H thL(h)\,d\mathbf{F}_s(h).$$

This is an equilibrium of the rational expectations type. Statement (i) says that, if every citizen of any type h expects the lump-sum payment to be $I(s)$ in state s, then she maximizes expected utility by supplying labor in amount $L(h)$. Statement (ii) says that if every type h supplies labor $L(h)$, then in state s, per capita tax revenues will be exactly $I(s)$. Thus labor-supply decisions of individuals are consistent with income expectations.

Suppose that $(L(\cdot), I(\cdot))$ is the unique economic equilibrium at tax rate t. Then a citizen of type h has an indirect utility function

(4.3) $$v(t, h) = \int_0^s u((1 - t)hL(h) + I(s), L(h))\frac{1}{S}ds.$$

If we now assume that party i represents a type h^i [that is, has vNM preferences $v(\cdot, h^i)$], then the political game is defined, as is its Wittman equilibrium.

We proceed to specify the model further in order to compute Wittman equilibria. We let $u(y, L) = y - (\alpha/2)L^2$, a quasi-linear utility function. We immediately compute that, for any t and I, the solution of

$$\max_L u((1 - t)hL + I, L)$$

is given by $\hat{L}(t, h) = \frac{(1-t)h}{\alpha}$. Thus quasi-linearity tells us that a citizen's labor supply is independent of the size of the lump-sum payment.

Define

$$1^t(s) = \int_c^\infty h\hat{L}(t, h)d\mathbf{F}_s(h) = \frac{1-t}{\alpha}\tilde{\mu}_s,$$

and note that

$$\int_0^1 I^t(s)ds = \frac{1-t}{\alpha}\int_0^s \tilde{\mu}_s\frac{1}{S}ds.$$

Then we have

Proposition 4.2 *For each $t \in [0, 1]$, there is a unique economic equilibrium* (L^t, I^t) *given by*

$$L^t(h) = \frac{(1 - t)h}{\alpha}, \quad I^t(s) = \left(\frac{1 - t}{\alpha}\right)\tilde{\mu}_s.$$

Proof:
This follows immediately from the discussion above. ∎

Using (4.2), we compute that

$$\int_0^S \tilde{\mu}_s \frac{1}{S} ds = c^2 \left(1 + 2\frac{\text{Log}(1+S)}{S}\right) \equiv M(S).$$

From (4.3) and Proposition 4.2, we compute that

(4.4) $$v(t, h) = \frac{(1-t)^2 h^2}{2\alpha} + \frac{t(1-t)}{\alpha} M(S).$$

We are now ready to compute the function π. The set of voter types $\Omega(t^1, t^2)$ who prefer t^1 to t^2, where $t^1 < t^2$, is given by

$$\Omega(t^1, t^2) = \{h \mid h^2 > 2M(S)\Psi(t^1, t^2)\},$$

where

$$\Psi(t^1, t^2) = \frac{t^2(1-t^2) - t^1(1-t^1)}{(1-t^1)^2 - (1-t^2)^2}.$$

It follows that the set $\Omega(t^1, t^2)$ is a majority coalition precisely in those states s for which $m_s \geq (2M(S)\Psi(t^1, t^2))^{1/2}$, where m_s is the skill level of the median voter in state s. But this is the set of states $\{s \mid 2^{2/(s+3)} c^2 \geq 2M(S)\Psi(t^1, t^2)\}$, by (4.1). It follows that $\pi(t^1, t^2) = (s^*(t^1, t^2))/S$ where

$$s^*(t^1, t^2) = \frac{\text{Log } 4}{\text{Log } \frac{2M(S)\Psi(t^1,t^2)}{c^2}} - 3.$$

We can now write down explicitly the payoff functions $\Pi^i(t^1, t^2)$, where party i represents a type with skill level h^i; hence we can write down the F.O.C.s $\partial \Pi^i / \partial t^i = 0$.

Parameterize the model as follows: $c = 20$, $\alpha = 5$, $h^1 = 1{,}000$, $h^2 = 20$. Thus party 2 represents the least-skilled type, and party 1 represents a type who is in the top 1% of the skill distribution for all Pareto measures $\{F_s \mid s \in [0, S]\}$, for values of S presented in Table 4.1. The table reports the Wittman equilibria for various values of S. The larger the value of S, the greater the uncertainty parties face. We note that (1) policy differentiation increases with the degree of uncertainty, and (2) both equilibrium policies appear to converge to the ideal policy of the median voter in the median state as uncertainty decreases.

Table 4.1 Wittman equilibria in model of section 4.2

S	t^1	t^2	π	$\hat{t}^{h^1}$	$\hat{t}^{h^2}$	$\hat{t}^{m(S)}$
0.1	0.31218	0.315944	0.493515	0	0.396102	0.314087
0.2	0.304612	0.312117	0.48723	0	0.392391	0.308462
0.3	0.297384	0.30859	0.481139	0	0.388844	0.303204
0.4	0.290464	0.305318	0.475234	0	0.385445	0.298273
0.5	0.283827	0.302265	0.469508	0	0.382179	0.293633
1	0.254131	0.289423	0.443306	0	0.367465	0.273931
2	0.207007	0.270678	0.400561	0	0.343614	0.24592
3	0.170226	0.256549	0.366947	0	0.324462	0.226486
4	0.140082	0.24493	0.339607	0	0.308388	0.211889
5	0.11459	0.234951	0.316793	0	0.294527	0.200322
6	0.092553	0.226163	0.297374	0	0.282351	0.190795
7	0.0731893	0.218294	0.280582	0	0.271507	0.18272
8	0.055958	0.211168	0.265874	0	0.261747	0.175725
9	0.0404683	0.204659	0.252864	0	0.252888	0.169561
10	0.0264282	0.198671	0.241225	0	0.244788	0.164056
11	0.0136131	0.193132	0.230757	0	0.23734	0.159086
12	0.00184697	0.187985	0.221273	0	0.230456	0.154557
13	0	0.183182	0.224022	0	0.224064	0.1504
14	0	0.178684	0.228196	0	0.218108	0.146561
15	0	0.17446	0.231605	0	0.212537	0.142996

Note: $m(S)$ is the median type in the median state when the set of states is $[0, S]$.

4.3 Partisan Dogmatism and Political Extremism

Imagine a polity concerned with two issues: the first is economic redistribution and the second is "religion." A citizen type has two traits, $h = (w, r)$, where w is its income and r is its religious position. Thus $\mathbf{F}$ is a probability distribution on $H \subset \mathbf{R}^2$. Let $v(t, z; w, r) = (1 - t)w + t\mu - (\alpha/2)(z - r)^2$, where (t, z) is a policy and μ is mean population income. Thus preferences are linear in income and Euclidean in the religious position (z) of the government.

Suppose there are two parties which are each dogmatic on the religious issue: this is an issue on which the parties will brook no compromise. Each party puts forth a dogmatic (constant) position on the religious issue, $\bar{z}^1$ and $\bar{z}^2$. Suppose $\bar{z}^1 < \bar{z}^2$. We use the error-distribution model of uncertainty.

We easily compute that

$$\Omega((t^1, \bar{z}^1), (t^2, \bar{z}^2)) = \left\{ (w, z) \mid z \leq \frac{\bar{z}^1 + \bar{z}^2}{2} - \frac{(w - \mu)(t^1 - t^2)}{\alpha(\bar{z}^2 - \bar{z}^1)} \right\}.$$

Of course, we have

$$\pi((t^1, \bar{z}^1), (t^2, \bar{z}^2)) = \frac{\mathbf{F}\left(\Omega((t^1, \bar{z}^1), (t^2, \bar{z}^2))\right) + \beta - \frac{1}{2}}{2\beta}.$$

Let w take values on a bounded interval; of course, $t^i \in [0, 1]$. Now suppose that $\bar{z}^2 - \bar{z}^1$ is large: then the term $((w - \mu)(t^1 - t^2))/\alpha(\bar{z}^2 - \bar{z}^1)$ will be small, which is to say the probability that $(t^1, \bar{z}^1)$ defeats $(t^2, \bar{z}^1)$ will be essentially independent of the tax policies t^1 and t^2. Indeed, as $(\bar{z}^2 - \bar{z}^1) \to \infty$, π becomes independent of the tax policies.

But we know what happens when π is independent of the policies: each party proposes its ideal policy in Wittman equilibrium (see §§ 4.1). Thus we conclude: the farther apart the two parties are on their dogmatic issue, the closer will their *economic* policies be to their ideal points, in Wittman equilibrium.

Although we have phrased this problem as one with two policy dimensions, it is, formally speaking, a unidimensional problem, because the positions $\bar{z}^1$ and $\bar{z}^2$ are fixed, and hence are simply parameters of the problem. If parties were not dogmatic but strategic with respect to both issues, we could not use the unidimensional model in analysis.

4.4 A Dynamic Model of Political Cycles [2]

In this section we model an idea of Albert Hirschman, that political moods shift regularly from a public orientation, a concern with large social issues, to a private orientation, a concern with the material well-being of the individual or family. Disappointment is the psychological key: "The world I am trying to understand in this essay is one in which men think they want one thing and then upon getting it, find out to their dismay that they don't want it nearly as much as they thought or don't want it at all and that something else, of which they were hardly aware, is what they really want" (Hirschman 1982, 21). Hirschman gives an interesting piece of linguistic evidence for man's asymmetrical penchant for disappointment: he can find no single word for its opposite (pleasurable surprise) in any language.

There is, as usual, a population distribution of types, **F**, characterized by their members' endowment of income, h. Denote mean income by μ and median income by m. All voters have the same preferences over private income (x) and a public good (G) given by the utility function

$$u(x, G) = x + a(s)G^{1/2},$$

where $a(s)$ is a parameter whose value will be specified presently. We suppose that all voters have the same preferences, that is, the same value of $a(s)$. We shall use, in this example, the state-space approach to uncertainty. We define $a(s) = a_0 + a_1 s$, where $a_1 > 0$. Parties are uncertain about the value of s, which is a random variable whose distribution is governed by a probability measure **S** on the sample space $[0, 1]$; with distribution function S.

There are two political parties; the Left represents a voter with income h^1 and the Right, a voter with income h^2, where $h^1 < \mu < h^2$. The single issue is the tax rate on income; thus

$$v(t, h; s) = (1 - t)h + t\mu + a(s)(t\mu)^{1/2},$$

and $v^i(t, s) = v(t, h^i; s)$, for $i = 1, 2$, are the parties' utility functions. Thus in this model, preferences depend on the state, s.

---

2. This application is taken from Roemer (1995).

We compute that

(4.5) $t^1 > t^2$ implies $\Omega(t^1, t^2) = \left\{ h \leq \dfrac{a(s)\sqrt{\mu}}{\sqrt{t^1} + \sqrt{t^2}} \right\}.$

Define the r.h.s. of the inequality in (4.5) to be $h(t^1, t^2; s)$. It follows that a majority vote for t^1 if and only if $h(t^1, t^2; s) > m$, which is equivalent to

(4.6) $a(s) > \dfrac{\left(\sqrt{t^1} + \sqrt{t^2}\right) m}{\sqrt{\mu}}.$

(The intuition is clear. The Left wins when preferences are sufficiently "publicly oriented.") Since $a(s)$ is strictly monotonic, the probability that (4.6) holds is just

$$\pi(t^1, t^2) = 1 - S\left(a^{-1}\left(\frac{\left(\sqrt{t^1} + \sqrt{t^2}\right) m}{\sqrt{\mu}} \right) \right),$$

where $a^{-1}(X) = (X - a_0)/a_1$ is the inverse function of $a(s)$. Define:

$$s(t^1, t^2) = a^{-1}\left(\frac{\left(\sqrt{t^1} + \sqrt{t^2}\right) m}{\sqrt{\mu}} \right).$$

We next describe the payoff functions of the parties. The party does not know the state s, so it does not know the preferences of its constituent in this model; thus the expected utility of the voter h^1, from the Left party's viewpoint, at the policy pair (t^1, t^2), is

(4.7a) $\Pi^1(t^1, t^2) = \displaystyle\int_{s(t^1, t^2)}^{1} v^1(t^1, s) dS(s) + \int_{0}^{s(t^1, t^2)} v^1(t^2, s) dS(s).$

The first integral averages the utility of voter h^1 over the various possible values of s in the region where t^1 is victorious, and the second integral averages the utility of voter h^1 over the various possible values of s in the region where t^2 is victorious. Similarly, the expected utility of voter h^2 from the Right party's viewpoint is

$$(4.7b) \qquad \Pi^2(t^1, t^2) = \int_{s(t^1,t^2)}^{1} v^2(t^1, s)dS(s) + \int_{0}^{s(t^1,t^2)} v^2(t^2, s)dS(s).$$

We next introduce a dynamic element in the determination of the probability distribution **S**. The idea here is that the likely value of the parameter a is determined by the past experiences of the population with regard to the level of public goods. Let time—more precisely, elections—be indexed by $r = 1, 2, 3 \dots$. I choose S_r, the distribution of states at election r, to be a beta distribution $\mathbf{B}(2, b_r)$—these are convenient unimodal distributions defined on the interval $[0, 1]$. The mean of this beta distribution is $2/(2 + b_r)$. Recalling that $a_1 > 0$, we can see that it follows that the larger s is, the greater is the population's relative preference for the public good, that is, the value $a(s)$. So if b_r is *small*, then the random variable s has a high mean, and so the public have a *high* relative preference for the public good.

Now think of a sequence of elections $r = 1, 2, 3, \dots$. Define r_r^R as the number of consecutive elections just before election r that the Right has won, and r_r^L as the number of consecutive elections just before r that the Left has won. (For example, if the Right wins election $t = 1, 2, 3$ then $r_4^R = 3$ and $r_4^L = 0$). For any r, either r_r^L or r_r^R is zero. I define

$$(4.8) \qquad b_r = 2 + m_r t_{r-1},$$

where t_{r-1} is the victorious policy at election $r - 1$, and where

$$(4.9) \qquad m_r = \begin{cases} m_{r-1} - r_r^R, & \text{if } r_r^R > 0 \\ m_{r-1} + r_r^L, & \text{if } r_r^L > 0. \end{cases}$$

(The sequence m_r begins with some fixed value m_0.) The effect of (4.8) and (4.9) is to *increase* the value of b_r if the Left has been in power, thus *decreasing* society's relative preference for the public good, and to *decrease* the value of b_r if the Right has been in power, thus *increasing* society's relative preference for the public good. Furthermore, according to (4.9), the longer a particular party has been in power, the more radically do public preferences shift "away" from the kind of good it advocates (the Left advocates the public good and the Right advocates the private good). This is the Hirschman effect.

We are now ready to simulate electoral histories. I chose the parameter values $m = 30$, $\mu = 50$, $h^1 = 20$, $h^2 = 70$, $a_0 = 3$, $a_1 = 2$, $m_0 = 1.28$, and $t_0 = 0.27$. Thus b_1 is determined (by equation (4.8)), and so is the probability distribution $\mathbf{S}_1 = \mathbf{B}(2, b_1)$. This allows us to solve for a Wittman equilibrium (t_1^1, t_1^2, π_1) in the first period, where $\pi_1 = \pi(t_1^1, t_1^2)$. Now we generate a random number η in the interval $[0, 1]$ according to the uniform distribution on $[0, 1]$: if $\eta \leq \pi_1$, we declare the Left party the winner of the election, and if $\eta > \pi_1$, then the Right party is the winner. (These events occur with probabilities π_1 and $1 - \pi_1$, respectively.) Now the values r_2^R and r_2^L, and hence m_2 and b_2, are determined, and so we have the new probability distribution $\mathbf{S}_2 = \mathbf{B}(2, b_2)$. Thus we can compute an electoral equilibrium in period 2. The recursion proceeds for as many periods as we wish to simulate.

Table 4.2 presents the first twenty and last twenty elections for a typical simulation which ran for 100 elections. "Probab" is π; the next two columns report the equilibrium policies of the Left and Right; "Govt" is the party that won the election, M is m_r, and "Avergs" is the mean of the beta distribution $\mathbf{B}(2, b_r)$.

Figure 4.1 graphs three-year moving averages of the Right and Left tax policies (that is, the value of the top figure at time r is $\frac{1}{3}(t_{r-1}^1 + t_r^1 + t_{r+1}^1)$) for the experiment of Table 4.2. What is remarkable is the occurrence of apparent electoral cycles, of various periods. There is, for example, a long upward trend in tax rates from period 40 to period 73, and then a long downward trend to period 85. In fact, these downward and upward trends are not characterized by a single party's being in power.

Figure 4.1 is a typical history of electoral politics over a "century." About one-tenth of the time, however, we simulate a history like the one in Figure 4.2, with apparently *regular* political cycles between relatively high and relatively low public provision. Were one a political scientist living in a century such as the one in Figure 4.2, one might conjecture that a certain regularity in political cycles was an immutable law of democracy. That, however, would not be the case. Cycling will always be a property of stochastic dynamic

Table 4.2 Wittman equilibria in Hirschman model

Year	Probab	TaxL	TaxR	Govt[a]	M	Avergs
1	.437165	.284606	.135974	0	1.28	.460236
2	.460498	.313151	.135596	0	0.28	.495286
3	.431142	.321102	.137704	1	−1.72	.530958
4	.36951	.294245	.14027	1	−0.72	.530672
5	.432323	.281133	.13609	1	1.28	.456972
6	.493665	.266285	.131892	0	4.28	.384375
7	.499694	.304251	.132775	0	3.28	.451202
8	.475151	.310349	.134564	1	1.28	.479622
9	.452462	.272325	.134529	1	2.28	.424845
10	.494376	.267928	.131916	1	4.28	.38718
11	.53811	.256469	.128895	1	7.28	.336105
12	.582101	.246531	.125935	0	11.28	.290151
13	.567471	.289182	.12775	0	10.28	.377743
14	.550545	.292739	.12902	1	8.28	.395431
15	.56157	.244344	.127134	0	9.28	.297769
16	.550534	.292963	.129026	0	8.28	.39583
17	.53186	.296999	.130414	0	6.28	.415776
18	.500026	.304671	.132764	0	3.28	.451696
19	.447904	.317548	.136533	1	−0.72	.512241
20	.401366	.285682	.138059	1	0.28	.489128
81	.49193	.262163	.131824	0	4.28	.377202
82	.499709	.304271	.132775	1	3.28	.451225
83	.491929	.262159	.131824	0	4.28	.377196
84	.499709	.304271	.132775	1	3.28	.451225

Table 4.2   *(continued)*

Year	Probab	TaxL	TaxR	Govt[a]	M	Avergs
85	.491929	.262159	.131824	1	4.28	.377196
86	.525074	.261453	.129846	1	6.28	.35421
87	.561765	.251186	.127303	0	9.28	.311222
88	.550537	.292902	.129024	1	8.28	.395721
89	.561568	.24431	.127134	0	9.28	.297702
90	.550534	.292964	.129026	1	8.28	.395831
91	.561568	.244298	.127133	0	9.28	.297676
92	.550534	.292964	.129026	0	8.28	.395831
93	.53186	.296999	.130414	0	6.28	.415776
94	.500026	.304671	.132764	1	3.28	.451696
95	.4919	.26209	.131822	0	4.28	.377075
96	.499709	.304271	.132775	1	3.28	.451225
97	.491929	.262159	.131824	0	4.28	.377196
98	.499709	.304271	.132775	1	3.28	.451225
99	.491929	.262159	.131824	1	4.28	.377195
100	.525074	.261453	.129846	0	6.28	.35421

a. 0 = Right victory; 1 = Left victory.

models such as this one, but the apparent regularity of Figure 4.2 is just a matter of luck. It is important to note that Figures 4.1 and 4.2 were generated by exactly the same "seed"; only the realization of the random element (who wins each particular election) differs. And of course the history of who holds power determines the distribution of the stochastic element in the next period.

Finally, it should be noted that there is a built-in stabilizer in the present model: the longer the polity experience low tax rates in the immediate past, the

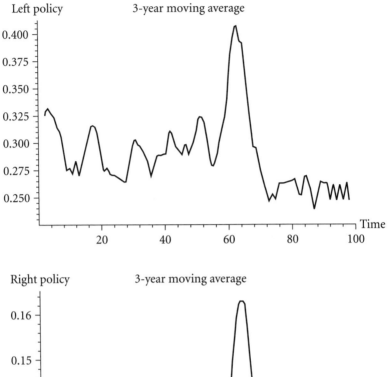

Figure 4.1 Long-term electoral cycles in the Hirschman model

more their preferences tilt *toward* the public good, and inversely. Despite this stabilizer, quite dramatic long-run political cycles are inherent in the process.

The reader is referred to Roemer (1995) for a further discussion of the genesis of cycles in this model. There it is shown that cycles are due precisely to the stochastic element inherent in the elections.

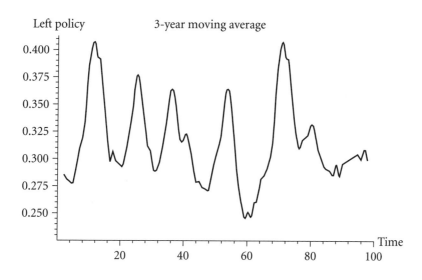

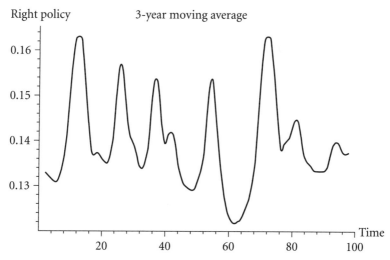

Figure 4.2   Regular long-term electoral cycles in the Hirschman model

4.5 Conclusion

We have shown that although the Wittman model is, in most cases, too complex to permit solving for the political equilibrium by hand, solutions are easily computable by machine. It is usually not easy to do analytical comparative statics with Wittman equilibrium, because of the complexity of the equations that determine it, but one can often do empirical comparative statics by simulation.

5

✳

Endogenous Parties: The Unidimensional Case

5.1 Introduction

In the applications of Chapter 4, the preferences of parties are exogenously given. We can think of those models as analogous to the Arrow-Debreu general equilibrium model, where firms are taken as given. A complete explanation of the politico-economy should, however, attempt to derive what parties come into being from more primitive assumptions about citizen preferences and endowments. In this chapter we begin the study of deriving parties endogenously.

We shall not, however, attempt to endogenize "all the way down"; in particular, we shall assume that only two parties will form. A more complete theory would endogenize the number of parties as well. We know that the number of parties is influenced by political institutions, laid out in the constitution (for example, Duverger's Law and single-member districts). We shall not proceed, however, to the deeper level of taking the constitution as an exogenous datum and deriving the number of parties from there. Clearly, if we wished to leave open the number of parties, we would have to have a theory of what political equilibrium looks like if there are n parties, for a new entrant into the party formation process would have to compute the political equilibrium that would result were it to enter. The natural approach would be to model the party formation process as Nash, in the sense that a stable set of parties is one in which no party wants to fold, given the existence of the others, and no new party has an incentive to form.

In this chapter we propose two theories of endogenous parties, both of which model a conception of *perfectly representative democracy*. Such a democracy is one in which:

(1) Every citizen belongs to one and only one party.
(2) Each party member receives "equal weight" in the determination of the party's preferences.

The phrase "equal weight" is vague, and the two theories referred to make that phrase concrete in different ways.

A perfectly representative democracy is clearly an ideal, and reality departs from that ideal most obviously because of the role of private contributions to parties. Presumably, large contributors have more influence on a party's preferences than do other citizens. We shall propose a general model of endogenous parties when there is party financing in section 13.6.

5.2 Average-Member Nash Equilibrium [1]

Our first model is based upon the idea that each party represents its "average member." We shall present the model using a specific example and then calculate equilibria for that example.

Suppose that h is a type's income, $\mathbf{F}$ is the distribution of income on $H = [\underline{h}, \overline{h}]$, and all citizens have preferences over income and public good, $u(x, G) = x + kG^{1/2}$. As usual, the policy is a proportional income tax, t, and so $v(t, h) = (1 - t)h + k\mu^{1/2}t^{1/2}$. As we have calculated, if $t^1 > t^2$ then

$$\Omega(t^1, t^2) = \{h < h(t^1, t^2)\},$$

where $h(t^1, t^2) = k\sqrt{\mu}/(\sqrt{t^1} + \sqrt{t^2})$.

We now suppose that every citizen belongs to one party. Suppose party 1's members are those citizens with $h \leq h^*$ and party 2's members are those citizens with $h > h^*$, for some "separating" type h^*. Further suppose that the party's preferences are those of the average type among its members. Thus define

(5.1) $$h^1 = \frac{\int_{\underline{h}}^{h^*} h d\mathbf{F}}{F(h^*)}, \qquad h^2 = \frac{\int_{h^*}^{\overline{h}} h d\mathbf{F}}{1 - F(h^*)}.$$

Then $v^i(t) = v(t, h^i)$, for $i = 1, 2$.[2] Now let $(\overline{t}^1, \overline{t}^2)$ be the Wittman equilibrium for the game so defined, and let $h(\overline{t}^1, \overline{t}^2)$ be the type who is indifferent between $\overline{t}^1$ and $\overline{t}^2$. Suppose it is the case that $h(\overline{t}^1, \overline{t}^2) > h^*$. Then some members of party 2 will vote for party 1 (that is, those h in the interval $(h^*, h(\overline{t}^1, \overline{t}^2))$). This

---

1. This application is based on joint work with Ignacio Ortuño-Ortin. See Ortuño-Ortin and Roemer (1998).

2. A variant of (5.1) is to define $v^i(t)$ as the average of the utility functions of party i's members: $v^1(t) = \int_{\underline{h}}^{h^*} v(t, h^1)d\mathbf{F}(h)$.

cannot be a stable situation. A stable situation—an equilibrium in the process of party formation—occurs precisely when $h^* = h(\bar{t}^1, \bar{t}^2)$. Only if this is so will every member of each party vote for her party in the election.

Formally, we define:

Definition 5.1 An *average-member Nash equilibrium (AMNE)* is a triple $(h^*, \bar{t}^1, \bar{t}^2)$ such that:

(1) $v^1(t)$ and $v^2(t)$ are defined by (5.1),
(2) $(\bar{t}^1, \bar{t}^2)$ is the Wittman equilibrium of the political game,
(3) $h^* = h(\bar{t}^1, \bar{t}^2)$.

The idea here—that malcontents "vote with their feet" by defecting to the other party—follows Caplin and Nalebuff (1997), and Baron (1993) first uses it in the context of political parties.

To simulate a version of this model, we choose **F** to be a Burr-Singh-Maddala distribution, a probability measure with three degrees of freedom, whose density function is

$$f(h; \alpha, \delta, \gamma) = \frac{\alpha \delta \gamma h^{\delta - 1}}{(1 + \alpha h^\delta)^{\gamma + 1}}.$$

(The reason for this choice will be explained later.) The formulae for the mean (μ), median (m), and Gini coefficient are

$$\mu = \frac{\Gamma\left(1 + \frac{1}{\delta}\right) \cdot \Gamma\left(\gamma - \frac{1}{\delta}\right)}{\Gamma(\gamma)\alpha^{1/\delta}},$$

$$m = \left(\frac{2^{1/\gamma} - 1}{\alpha}\right)^{1/\delta}, \quad \text{and}$$

$$\text{Gini} = 1 - \frac{\Gamma(\gamma)\Gamma\left(2\gamma - \frac{1}{\delta}\right)}{\Gamma(2\gamma)\Gamma\left(\gamma - \frac{1}{\delta}\right)},$$

where Γ is the Euler gamma function. We define π with the error-distribution model of uncertainty:

$$\pi(t^1, t^2) = \frac{F(h(\bar{t}^1, \bar{t}^2)) + \beta - \frac{1}{2}}{2\beta}.$$

Thus an AMNE is defined by the three equations

$$\frac{\partial \Pi^1}{\partial t^1}(\bar{t}^1, \bar{t}^2) = 0,$$

$$\frac{\partial \Pi^2}{\partial t^2}(\bar{t}^1, \bar{t}^2) = 0,$$

$$h^* = h(\bar{t}^1, \bar{t}^2),$$

where we understand that h^1 and h^2 are defined by (5.1).

Table 5.1 presents a series of AMNEs where $k = 4.5$ and $\beta = 0.20$. Each row of the table is an AMNE for a different choice of the parameters (α, δ, γ). Indeed, we have chosen a series of values of (α, δ, γ) to maintain $(\mu, m) = (40, 30)$, but to vary the Gini coefficient: this is possible because we are using a three-parameter family of density functions.[3] The columns of the table are self-explanatory; $t^{\exp}$ denotes the expected tax rate, $\pi \bar{t}^1 + (1 - \pi)\bar{t}^2$.

We now motivate this simulation. In the political-economy literature, there is a popular view that, as the skewness of the income distribution, measured as the ratio μ/m, increases, tax rates should increase. (For statements of this view, see Meltzer and Richard 1983 and Persson and Tabellini 1994.) This conclusion is based on the Downs model of political equilibrium, that the equilibrium tax rate will be the ideal tax rate of the median voter. With the voter preferences given by the utility function of the present section, Downs equilibrium consists in both parties proposing $t^* = (k^2/4)(\mu/m^2)$, so if μ is constant while m decreases (thus increasing skewness), the equilibrium tax rate will increase. But Table 5.1 shows that, in AMNE, this conclusion is in general false. For the table displays a sequence of economies with constant skewness in which expected tax rates decrease (read the table from the bottom to the top). Since the equilibrium is continuous in the parameters (α, δ, γ), we can now perturb those parameters slightly to produce a sequence of economies with constant mean and *increasing* median in which the expected tax rate (still) *decreases*.

Thus one of the most well known items of conventional wisdom in the political economy of growth ceases to hold when we move from Downs to Wittman politics. Exhibiting this phenomenon required a three-parameter

---

3. Recall that mean household income in the United States in 1990 was approximately $40,000, and median income was approximately $30,000.

Table 5.1 Wittman equilibria, endogenous parties

μ	m	Gini	h^*	t^1	t^2	π	$t^{\exp}$
40.0	30.0	0.434653	28.75	0.383653	0.139902	0.443255	0.247
40.0	30.0	0.444351	28.75	0.408851	0.138002	0.428176	0.253
40.0	30.0	0.449082	27.75	0.424958	0.137461	0.418763	0.257
40.0	30.0	0.451864	27.75	0.433305	0.13672	0.415342	0.259
40.0	30.0	0.453692	27.25	0.442597	0.136976	0.409473	0.262
40.0	30.0	0.454984	27.25	0.446924	0.136637	0.407854	0.263
40.0	30.0	0.455945	27.25	0.450236	0.136385	0.406638	0.264
40.0	30.0	0.456688	27.25	0.452854	0.136191	0.405691	0.264
40.0	30.0	0.457279	27.25	0.454974	0.136037	0.404932	0.265
40.0	30.0	0.45776	27.25	0.456725	0.135912	0.404311	0.265

Note:. The values of h^* are accurate to 0.25.

family of probability distributions—two to hold μ and m constant, and a third to force variation in the Wittman equilibrium.

More generally, we can say this is a consequence of the fact that Downs equilibrium depends only on the preferences of the "median voter," while Wittman equilibrum depends more intimately on the distribution of voter preferences, as we have already noted.

5.3 Condorcet-Nash Equilibrium

The concept of AMNE can be criticized because the stipulation of a party's preferences as the preferences of its average member is ad hoc. What intraparty political process determines this outcome? No justification has been provided. The equilibrium concept of the present section rectifies this inadequacy by specifying a process of internal party politics which determines the party's preferences.

If the present section improves on the preceding section, why have I presented the idea of average-member Nash equilibrium? Because the equilibrium concept of *this* section only works when the policy space is unidimensional, whereas the AMNE idea works even with multidimensional issue spaces, as we show in Chapter 13. Here again is an illustration of the principle that "no tool works well for all jobs," and so it is advisable to fashion several tools.

Indeed the reader may have wondered why we defined the party's preferences in section 5.2 by an averaging process rather than by a median process. The answer is that choosing the median player as the party's representative only works when policy space is unidimensional, but we can average utility functions over a party's members regardless of the dimensionality of the issue space.

We proceed to the definition of Condorcet-Nash equilibrium (CNE). Here we adapt the notion of the "citizen-candidate," introduced by Osborne and Slivinski (1996) and Besley and Coate (1997). (Some differences between our and their approach will be remarked upon below.) First, there will be a separating type, h^*, as in section 5.2, that partitions the set of types into two groups, which shall constitute, in equilibrium, two parties. Instead of determining the parties' preferences by the averaging process, however, we imagine that coalitions of party members propose specific party members as candidates. If a particular individual is chosen to be the candidate, then that individual uses his own preferences in the interparty competition. Thus after each party has chosen a citizen-candidate, those two individuals (types) arrive at a Wittman equilibrium, where each maximizes her own expected utility.

Suppose the candidates of parties 1 and 2 are of types h^1 and h^2, respectively. When will such a choice of candidates be "in equilibrium"? When no majority coalition in party 1 (that is, a coalition comprising a majority of party 1's members) would prefer to substitute an alternative member type for h^1, given that party 2's candidate is of type h^2, and when the analogous statement holds for party 2. Thus the *choice of candidates* is "Condorcet" within each party, while the equilibrium in the interparty competition is Nash.

We proceed to write down a set of equations which characterize such an equilibrium. Let $v(t, h)$ be the utility function of types H on the (unidimensional) policy space T. We shall assume, as well, that H is unidimensional, and that the ideal points of types h are monotonic in h.[4] Then we write the payoff function of Mr. h, should he be the party's candidate, as

$$\Pi(t^1, t^2; h) = \pi(t^1, t^2)v(t^1, h) + (1 - \pi(t^1, t^2))v(t^2, h).$$

---

4. The assumption that H is unidimensional is not necessary, but it simplifies the presentation. We can carry out the entire construction working with ideal points, and not with types, but the notation would add another layer of complexity to the presentation.

If m^1 and m^2 are the citizen-candidates of the two parties, then, at any Wittman equilibrium of the game so defined (that is, a Nash equilibrium where the players have payoff functions $\Pi(\cdot, m^1)$ and $\Pi(\cdot, m^2)$), there are differentiable functions $t^1(h^1, h^2)$ and $t^2(h^1, h^2)$ which describe what the equilibrium would be as we vary the pair (h^1, h^2) in a neighborhood of (m^1, m^2). This is a straightforward implication of the implicit function theorem. Thus the functions $t^1(\cdot)$ and $t^2(\cdot)$ are defined implicitly by the equations

$$(5.2) \qquad \frac{\partial \Pi(t^1, t^2; h^1)}{\partial t^1} = 0$$

$$(5.3) \qquad \frac{\partial \Pi(t^1, t^2; h^2)}{\partial t^2} = 0,$$

in some neighborhood of (h^1, h^2) in $H \times H$.

Now let h^1 and h^2 be citizen-candidates who emerge and let h^* be the type that separates the set of types into the two parties (recalling that H is an interval). Let t^1 and t^2 be the equilibrium policies. We must have

$$(5.4) \qquad v(t^1, h^*) = v(t^2, h^*),$$

which simply says that h^* is indifferent between the two policies.

We next define h^{1^*} and h^{2^*} as the median types of the two parties, that is, by the equations

$$(5.5) \qquad F(h^{1^*}) = \tfrac{1}{2} F(h^*),$$

and

$$(5.6) \qquad F(h^{2^*}) - F(h^*) = \tfrac{1}{2}(1 - F(h^*)).$$

These equations use the fact that party 1 consists of $\{h < h^*\}$ and party 2 of $\{h > h^*\}$.

We now come to the most delicate issue, of characterizing the fact that h^1 must be a Condorcet winner for the choice of party 1's citizen-candidate, given that party 2 has chosen that h^2, and that h^2 is a Condorcet winner for the choice of party 2's citizen-candidate, given that party 1 has chosen that h^1. We shall capture this by saying that it will be the case that exactly one-half of party 1's members would prefer to replace h^1 with a *larger* type, and exactly one-half of party 1's members would prefer to replace h^1 with a *smaller* type. This will happen only if the *median* type in party 1, namely h^{1*}, does not want to replace h^1 with either a larger or a smaller type: that is, Mr. h^1 is the *ideal* type to represent the party, as far as Ms. h^{1*} is concerned. This we write as the first-order condition:

(5.7)
$$\frac{d}{dh^1}[\pi(t^1(h^1, h^2), t^2(h^1, h^2))v(t^1(h^1, h^2), h^{1*})$$

$$+ (1 - \pi(t^1(h^1, h^2), t^2(h^1, h^2))v(t^2(h^1, h^2), h^{1*})] = 0.$$

Equation (5.7) says that the expected utility of h^{1*} at the Wittman equilibrium determined by the choice of party candidates (h^1, h^2) is at a local maximum, as we vary the choice of party 1's candidate (h^1). Note that we must write t^1 and t^2 as functions of the two candidate types in order to write the statement properly, for h^{1*} must think about the consequences, in terms of equilibrium policies, of varying the choice of his party's candidate.

Equation (5.7) is a necessary condition for the statement "types in party 1 who are smaller than h^{1*} desire to *decrease* the type that represents party 1, and types who are larger than h^{1*} in party 1 desire to *increase* the type that represents party 1"—and so h^1 will be a Condorcet winner, in the sense that no majority coalition in party 1 will be able to agree on a substitute for him. We should, of course, check that this statement is true once we have located a candidate solution to our problem.

In like manner, h^{2*}, the median citizen in party 2, must be happy with the choice of h^2 as his party's representative, in the precise sense that

(5.8)
$$\frac{d}{dh^2}[\pi(t^1(h^1, h^2), t^2(h^1, h^2))v(t^1(h^1, h^2), h^{2*})$$

$$+ (1 - \pi(t^1(h^1, h^2), t^2(h^1, h^2))v(t^2(h^1, h^2), h^{2*})] = 0.$$

Let us now count equations. Equations (5.2)–(5.8) constitute seven equations in seven unknowns $(t^1, t^2, h^1, h^2, h^{1*}, h^{2*}, h^*)$. This looks good. The only remaining problem is that we do not know the implicit functions $t^1(\cdot)$ and $t^2(\cdot)$ that appear in equations (5.7) and (5.8). We work our way around this problem as follows (this is a standard method for solving this kind of problem). First, write down equation (5.2) and (5.3) explicitly:

(5.2) $\dfrac{\partial \pi}{\partial t^1}(v(t^1, h^1) - v(t^2, h^1)) - \pi \dfrac{\partial v}{\partial t}(t^1, h^1) = 0,$

(5.3.) $-\dfrac{\partial \pi}{\partial t^2}(v(t^2, h^2) - v(t^1, h^2)) + (1 - \pi)\dfrac{\partial v}{\partial t}(t^2, h^2) = 0.$

Next, viewing t^1 and t^2 in the above equations as functions of (h^1, h^2)—these are the defining equations for those implicit functions—we differentiate (5.2) and (5.3) with respect to h^1. We record here only the first of these differentiations:

(5.9a)

$$\left(\frac{\partial^2 \pi}{\partial t^{12}}\frac{\partial t^1}{\partial h^1} + \frac{\partial^2 \pi}{\partial t^1 \partial t^2}\frac{\partial t^2}{\partial h^1}\right)(v(t^1, h^1) - v(t^2, h^1)) +$$

$$\frac{\partial \pi}{\partial t^1}\left(\frac{\partial v}{\partial t}(t^1, h^1)\frac{\partial t^1}{\partial h^1} + \frac{\partial v}{\partial h}(t^1, h^1) - \right.$$

$$\left.\frac{\partial v}{\partial t}(t^2, h^1)\frac{\partial t^2}{\partial h^1} - \frac{\partial v}{\partial h}(t^2, h^1)\right) +$$

$$\left(\frac{\partial \pi}{\partial t^1}\frac{\partial t^1}{\partial h^1} + \frac{\partial \pi}{\partial t^2}\frac{\partial t^2}{\partial h^1}\right)\frac{\partial v}{\partial t}(t^1, h^1) +$$

$$\left(\pi \frac{\partial^2 v}{\partial t^2}(t^1, h^1)\frac{\partial t^1}{\partial h^1} + \frac{\partial^2 v}{\partial t \partial h}(t^1, h^1)\right) = 0.$$

Note that the expression (5.9a) is linear in the terms $\partial t^1/\partial h^1$ and $\partial t^2/\partial h^1$. When we differentiate (5.3) w.r.t. h^1, we likewise get an expression—call it equation (5.9b)—which is linear in $\partial t^1/\partial h^1$ and $\partial t^2/\partial h^1$. We can solve these two linear equations, (5.9a) and (5.9b), simultaneously (using the "Linear-Solve" command in Mathematica) for the unknown expressions $\partial t^1/\partial h^1$ and $\partial t^2/\partial h^1$.

In like manner, we now differentiate (5.2) and (5.3) w.r.t. h^2; this gives us two (long) equations which are linear in the unknown expressions $\partial t^1/\partial h^2$ and $\partial t^2/\partial h^2$; we solve these linear equations for $\partial t^1/\partial h^2$ and $\partial t^2/\partial h^2$.

We now have expressions for the four derivatives of the implicit functions $t^1(\cdot)$ and $t^2(\cdot)$ entirely in terms of the primitives of the model, the derivatives of the functions π and v.

The next step is to expand equations (5.7) and (5.8)—that is, to write out those equations with all their implicit derivatives $\partial t^1/\partial h^2$, and so on. We now substitute the four explicit expressions we have for the implicit derivatives of t^1 and t^2 into these expanded equations. We finally can replace $t^1(h^1, h^2)$ with t^1, wherever it appears, and $t^2(h^1, h^2)$, wherever it appears, with t^2.

The new equations (5.7) and (5.8) are now quite complicated expressions, but they no longer involve any explicit reference to the implicit functions. They are equations in the various derivatives of the functions π and v. Hence we can in principle solve these seven equations for the seven unknowns.

To compute an actual solution, I calibrated the model as follows. Let $T = H = [0, \infty)$, and let v be Euclidean, $v(t, h) = -\frac{1}{2}(t - h)^2$. For the Euclidean utility function, the set of types who prefer t^1 to t^2, for $t^1 < t^2$, is $\Omega(t^1, t^2) = \{h < (t^1 + t^2)/2\}$. I use the error-distribution model of uncertainty, and so

$$\pi(t^1, t^2) = \frac{F\left(\frac{t^1+t^2}{2}\right) + \beta - \frac{1}{2}}{2\beta}, \qquad \text{for } t^1 < t^2.$$

I chose **F** to be the lognormal distribution with mean 40 and median 30—again an attempt to represent the U.S. distribution of income. I chose $\beta = .2$. This completely specifies the model.

We solved for the Condorcet-Nash equilibrium:

$$(t^1, t^2, h^1, h^2, h^{1^*}, h^{2^*}, h^*) = (27.34, 33.43, 21.98, 43.19, 24.91, 36.72, 30.39).$$

Thus the "left" party is represented by a citizen with income $21,980, who lies at the 14th centile of the income distribution, while the "right" party is represented by a citizen with income $43,190, who lies at the 90th centile of the income distribution. The equilibrium policies are the ideal policies of citizens whose incomes are $27,340 and $33,430. The probability of "left" victory is .54. The left party consists of all citizens with incomes smaller than $30,390, who make up 51.18% of the population.

It is interesting to note how the median party member *abdicates to the radicals* in this equilibrium. Given that the right party has chosen a citizen-candidate with income $43,000, the decisive "median voter" in the left party, who has income $24,900 ($h^{1^*}$), chooses a candidate for the left party who has income less than his own—namely, $h^1 = \$21,980$. Similarly, the decisive median type in the right party, who has income \$36,720 (h^{2^*}), chooses a citizen-candidate for her party who has income more than her own. Thus it is in the interest of the decisive members of the two parties not to choose themselves as candidates, but to abdicate to voters more radical than they.

The intuition behind why the median types abdicate to the radicals is as follows. Of course Ms. h^{1^*} would prefer to offer her best response—call it $\tilde{t}$— to t^{2^*}; that would give her a higher expected utility than the the pair (t^{1^*}, t^{2^*}). The problem is that t^{2^*} would not be the best response of h^2 to $\tilde{t}$, which is to say, $(\tilde{t}, t^{2^*})$ would not be a Wittman equilibrium of the game played between h^{1^*} and h^2. When two types play the Wittman game, the equilibrium consists in each of them compromising to a policy between his ideal point and the median voter's ideal point. The median member of each party, if he were the party's candidate, would like to "play tough," thus compromising less than otherwise. Choosing a more radical candidate than oneself is the only way to play tough in this game. Put another way, the Wittman game is evidently one in which a candidate would like to misrepresent his type: the mechanism for doing so is to choose a candidate of a different type than one's own.

We thus see that in a perfectly representative democracy, modeled à la Condorcet-Nash, the two parties would have preferences of citizens at the opposite far ends of the income distribution, but that, nevertheless, the equilibrium policies would each be not too far from the median voter's ideal policy, which is $t = 30$.

We also calculated the average-member Nash equilibrium for the environment of this section; denoting the equilibrium policies by (t^1, t^2), the party representatives by (h^1, h^2), and the h^* as the type defining the membership in the two parties, we found:

$$(t^1, t^2, h^1, h^2, h^*) = (28.13, 34.13, 24.78, 31.13, 58.70),$$

and the probability of Left victory was .628. Although the equilibrium policies here look similar to the ones found for the Condorcet-Nash equilibrium, the party structure is quite different. Note the right party is much smaller here than in the Condorcet-Nash equilibrium (h^* here is much larger). Furthermore, the probability of left victory here is (consequently) significantly larger. Finally, the party representatives here are less polarized than in the Condorcet-Nash equilibrium. We are not prepared to make general statements comparing these two equilibrium concepts, but it does appear as if they may well, in general, deliver fairly different results.

We finally return to the promised remark about the citizen-candidate models of Osborne-Slivinski and Besley-Coate. In those models, there are no parties; rather, each citizen decides whether he/she should announce as a candidate (there is a personal cost to running in the election). Furthermore, candidates cannot commit to policies, as they are assumed to be able to do in the models of this book, and so it is simply supposed that voters know that a candidate, if elected, will implement his/her ideal policy. The authors are then able to derive equilibria in which a small number of citizens have chosen to stand in the election.

The virtue of the model is that it provides a theory of endogenous candidates—even without any limitation on the number of candidates that enter. But the two assumptions which make the analysis tractable—that there are no parties, and that candidates cannot commit to policies—are both historically unrealistic. It is, indeed, the existence of parties that makes commitment possible, for the party lives on after the candidate has served her term, and the voters will presumably punish it if the officeholder has clearly failed to implement a policy on which she ran. Parties are long-lived actors, unlike candidates, and for them reputation matters.

5.4 Conclusion

We have presented two models of endogenous parties for an ideal we have called a perfectly representative democracy. These models are "complete" in the sense that the Downs model is complete: they derive the outcome of political competition from knowledge only of voter preferences. We showed that our complete model of political competition is importantly different from the Downs model, in the sense that at least one significant conclusion concerning the political economy of growth that holds with the Downs model fails to hold in our model (the putative positive relationship between skewness in the income distribution and the rate of taxation).

Our second model modifies the citizen-candidate approach, of recent vintage, to an environment with parties. We find, in an example, that parties emerge as highly polarized in their preferences. In particular, although the median type in each party is decisive in selecting the party's candidate, each selects candidates to represent the party who are more radical than they. We called this abdication to the radicals. Here is a testable hypothesis of the Condorcet-Nash model: does a party in a country where private campaign financing is not prevalent (hence approximating "perfectly representative democracy") tend to choose a candidate with preferences that are more radical than the preferences of the median type that votes for it? There is, indeed, an empirical regularity claimed, at least for multiparty systems, the "systematic tendency for parties in multi-party systems to be more extreme than their *own* electorates" (Iversen 1994). It would be incautious to claim this as evidence, however, for the empirical accuracy of our model.

6

Political Competition over Several Issues: The Case of Certainty

6.1 Introduction

This chapter weakens just one premise of the models in Chapter 1: we now assume that the policy space T is a compact, convex set in $\mathbf{R}^n$—that is, there are n issues where $n > 1$. We will study the existence question for Downs and Wittman equilibria in the case of certainty. The simple answer is that these equilibria fail to exist—except in singular (extraordinary) cases.

6.2 The Downs Model

To repeat, there are two parties or candidates whose payoff functions are given by

$$\Pi^1(t^1, t^2) = \pi(t^1, t^2)$$

$$\Pi^2(t^1, t^2) = 1 - \pi(t^1, t^2),$$

where π is defined in (1.5). The set of traits is H, the distribution of traits is given by $\mathbf{F}$, and the voters' preferences on T are represented by functions $v(\cdot, h) : T \to \mathbf{R}$.

We continue to assume that A1 and A2 hold, and we shall now also generally suppose differentiability (A8).

Define the gradient ∇v as the vector of partial derivatives with respect to the policy dimensions

$$\nabla v = \left(\frac{\partial v}{\partial t_1}, \ldots, \frac{\partial v}{\partial t_n} \right),$$

where a typical policy is $t = (t_1, \ldots, t_n)$.

We shall further stipulate a nonsingularity condition:

A10 $(\forall t \in T)(\forall d \neq 0, d \in \mathbf{R}^n)$, $\mathbf{F}(\{h \mid \nabla v(t, h) \cdot d = 0\}) = 0.$

Let us interpret A10 in the case where $n = 2$. It says that

$$\left\{ h \mid \frac{\partial v}{\partial t_1} \middle/ \frac{\partial v}{\partial t_2} = -\frac{d_1}{d_2} \right\}$$

is a null set: that is, the set of types whose indifference curves are tangent at a given point $\bar{t} \in T$ is a null set. (For the slope of h's indifference curve at $\bar{t} = (\bar{t}_1, \bar{t}_2)$ is

$$-\frac{\partial v(\cdot, h)}{\partial t_2} \middle/ \frac{\partial v(\cdot, h)}{\partial t_1}$$

evaluated at $(\bar{t}_1, \bar{t}_2)$.) As we shall see later, this condition will almost always be true in applications.

For the rest of this section, we will assume $n = 2$, for presentational simplicity. The results generalize in a straightforward manner to $n > 2$.

Given a point $(t_1, t_2) \in T$, consider the one-dimensional functions $v(\cdot, t_2; h)$ with t_2 and h fixed. These functions inherit the single-peakedness of v in their argument t_1: define $t_1(t_2, h)$ to be the ideal point of $v(\cdot, t_2; h)$. Formally, let $T_1(t_2) = \{t \in \mathbf{R} \mid (t, t_2) \in T\}$, and $T_2(t_1) = \{t \in \mathbf{R} \mid (t_1, t) \in T\}$. Define

$$t_1(t_2, h) = \arg \max_{t \in T_1(t_2)} v(t, t_2; h).$$

Now define $t_1^*(t_2)$ to be the "median policy" associated with these functions: $t_1^*(t_2)$ is the number t^* for which

$$\mathbf{F}(\{h \mid t_1(t_2, h) \leq t^*\}) = \tfrac{1}{2}.$$

Holding t_2 fixed, $t_1^*(t_2)$ is the one-dimensional policy such that exactly half the population has its ideal (one-dimensional) policy at that value or less.

Similarly, fix t_1, and define

$$t_2(t_1, h) = \arg \max_{t \in T_2(t_1)} v(t_1, t; h).$$

and define $t_2^*(t_1)$ as that value t^* such that

$$\mathbf{F}(\{h \mid t_2(t_1, h) \leq t^*\}) = \tfrac{1}{2}.$$

Now define a mapping $\Phi : T \to T$ by

(6.1) $\Phi(t_1, t_2) = (t_1^*(t_2), t_2^*(t_1)).$

Since T is compact and convex and Φ is continuous, by Brouwer's fixed-point theorem, Φ has at least one fixed point.[1] Denote the set of Φ's fixed points by Γ. We have:

Proposition 6.1 *Assume A1, A2. Let (t^1, t^2) be an equilibrium of the Downs game with certainty. Then $t^1, t^2 \in \Gamma$.*

Note: t^1 and t^2 are policies in T. We write $t^1 = (t_1^1, t_1^2)$, $t^2 = (t_1^2, t_2^2)$. Subscripts refer to components of policies; superscripts to policies.

Proof:

1. If $t^1 \neq t^2$, then each of $\{t^1, t^2\}$ must receive exactly one-half the vote; that is,

$$\mathbf{F}(\{h \mid v(t^1, h) > v(t^2, h)\}) = \tfrac{1}{2}.$$

If $t^1 = t^2$, then obviously each party receives one-half the vote.

2. Let $t^1 = (t_1^1, t_2^1)$, $t^2 = (t_1^2, t_2^2)$. Suppose $t^1 \notin \Gamma$—say $t_1^1 \neq t_1^*(t_2^1)$. Then if party 2 plays $(t_1^*(t_2^1), t_2^1)$ it defeats party 1 for sure. For a majority prefer $(t_1^*(t_2^1), t_2^1)$ to (t_1^1, t_2^1)—just note that this is a single-issue comparison, and $t_1^*(t_2^1)$ is the median ideal policy at $t_2 = t_2^1$. Therefore party 2 should deviate from t^2, and (t^1, t^2) is not a Downs equilibrium. ∎

Proposition 6.2 *Let $T = A \times B$, where $A \subseteq \mathbf{R}$, $B \subseteq \mathbf{R}$. If the functions $v(\cdot, h)$ are separable[2] in t_1 and t_2, then Γ is a singleton.*

(*Note:* We say that T is a *rectangle* in this case; its graph is a rectangle in $\mathbf{R}^2$.)

---

1. A fixed point of Φ is a policy (t_1, t_2) such that $t_1 = t_1^*(t_2)$ and $t_2 = t_2^*(t_1)$.

2. That v is separable in t_1 and t_2 means there are functions w_1 and w_2 such that $v(t_1, t_2, h) = w_1(t_1, h) + w_2(t_2, h)$.

Proof:

Denote $v(t_1, t_2, h) = w_1(t_1, h) + w(t_2, h)$. We have

$$t_1^*(t_2) = \arg \max_{t_1 \in T_1(t_2)} w_1(t_1) = \arg \max_{t_1 \in A} w_1(t_1),$$

which is independent of t_2; thus we may denote $t_1^*(t_2) = t_1^*$, a constant. Similarly, $t_2^*(t_1)$ is independent of t_1; thus $t_2^*(t_1) = t_2^*$. Therefore the function Φ is a constant function and has a unique fixed point—$t^* = (t_1^*, t_2^*)$. ∎

Thus $\Gamma = \{t^*\}$ in this case.

Corollary 6.1 *If $T = A \times B$, and v is separable in t_1 and t_2, then the only possible Downs equilibrium is (t^*, t^*).*

Proof:

Immediate from Propositions 6.1 and 6.2. ∎

Example 6.1 The standard example of two-dimensional preferences are the Euclidean preferences

$$v(t_1, t_2; a, b) = -\tfrac{1}{2}(t_1 - a)^2 - \tfrac{1}{2}(t_2 - b)^2.$$

Type (a, b)'s utility is decreasing in the distance of the policy to his ideal point, (a, b). Euclidean preferences are separable. It follows that the only candidate for a Downs equilibrium in the Euclidean model is (t^*, t^*).

In words, t^*, in the separable case, can be described as follows. Let t_1^* be the median ideal policy (in $\mathbf{R}$) of the types whose utility functions are $w_1(t_1, h)$. Let t_2^* be the median ideal policy (in $\mathbf{R}$) of types whose utility functions are $w_2(t_2, h)$. (See note 2.) Then $t^* = (t_1^*, t_2^*)$. Thus t^* is the pair of "one-dimensional" median ideal policies. When v is not separable, there is no such simple description: rather, we must resort to fixed-point language.

We now prove our first result that says that Downsian equilibrium almost never exists in multidimensional issue space models.

Theorem 6.1 *Suppose A1, A2, A8, and A10. Let $t^* \in \Gamma$, suppose t^* is interior in T, and suppose (t^*, t^*) is a Downs equilibrium. Then*

(6.2) $(\forall d \in \mathbf{R}^n, d \neq 0)$ $F(\{h \mid \nabla v(t^*, h) \cdot d > 0\}) = \tfrac{1}{2}.$

Recall that $\nabla v(t, h) \cdot d$ is the directional derivative of $v(\cdot, h)$ in the direction d, at t. Condition (6.2) says that at t^*, moving in any direction in policy space, *exactly half* the population will experience an increase in utility. Clearly this is singular condition. We shall examine it in an example below.

Proof of Theorem 6.1:

1. Suppose there is a direction $d \neq 0$ such that

$$\mathbf{F}(\{h \mid \nabla(v(t^*, h) \cdot d > 0\}) > \tfrac{1}{2}.$$

Then for small $\delta > 0$, the set of h such that

$$\frac{v(t^* + \delta d, h) - v(t^*, h)}{\delta} > 0$$

is a majority coalition. (We know it is feasible to move in any direction because t^* is interior in T.) Therefore $t^* + \delta d$ would defeat t^*, contradicting the premise that (t^*, t^*) is a Downs equilibrium.

2. Therefore for all $d \neq 0$,

$$\mathbf{F}(\{h \mid \nabla v(t^*, h) \cdot d > 0\}) \leq \tfrac{1}{2}.$$

Suppose there is a $d \neq 0$ such that

$$\mathbf{F}(\{h \mid \nabla v(t^*, h) \cdot d > 0\}) < \tfrac{1}{2}.$$

Then by A10,

$$\mathbf{F}(\{h \mid \nabla v(t^*, h) \cdot d < 0\}) > \tfrac{1}{2},$$

from which it follows that

$$\mathbf{F}(\{h \mid \nabla v(t^*, h) \cdot (-d) > 0\}) > \tfrac{1}{2},$$

contradicting paragraph 1.

3. It therefore follows that $d \neq 0$ implies

$$\mathbf{F}(\{h \mid \nabla v(t^*, h) \cdot d > 0\}) = \tfrac{1}{2}. \quad \blacksquare$$

The first version of Theorem 6.1 is due to Plott (1967).

Example 6.2 Assume again Euclidean preferences

$$v(t_1, t_2; a, b) = -\tfrac{1}{2}(t_1 - a)^2 - \tfrac{1}{2}(t_2 - b)^2$$

where $(a, b) \in H$. Let $\mathbf{F}$ be equivalent to Lebesgue measure on H. First we compute whether A10 holds. We have

$$\nabla v(t_1, t_2; a, b) = (a - t_1, b - t_2).$$

Thus $\nabla v(\bar{t}; a, b) \cdot d = 0$ means

(6.3) $(a - \bar{t}_1)d_1 + (b - \bar{t}_2)d_2 = 0$

The set of types (a, b) for which (6.3) holds is a line in the (a, b) plane. Hence it has Lebesgue measure zero and therefore $\mathbf{F}$-measure zero.

Consequently the axioms of Theorem 6.1 apply. Condition (6.2) says that for any $(d_1, d_2) \neq (0, 0)$ the set of types (a, b) for which

$$(a - t_1^*)d_1 + (b - t_2^*)d_2 > 0$$

has $\mathbf{F}$-measure one-half. We rewrite this condition as

(6.4) $ad_1 + bd_2 > t_1^* d_1 + t_2^* d_2.$

Inequality (6.4) says that the set of types (a, b) that lie above the line passing through t^* and perpendicular to d comprises exactly one-half the citizens. But since this holds for every $d \neq 0$, it says that *every line through t^* partitions the citizenry into two sets of equal mass.* This condition has been known for some time (see Davis, De Groot, and Hinich 1972 and Enelow and Hinich 1983).

Theorem 6.1 is all we need in the case that v is separable, for then we know Γ is a singleton and the only possible equilibrium is (t^*, t^*) where $\Gamma = \{t^*\}$. What about the nonseparable case, where Γ may have more than one element? We have

Theorem 6.2 *Let A1, A2, A3, and A8 hold. If $(\bar{t}^1, \bar{t}^2)$ is an interior Downs equilibrium where $\bar{t}^1 \neq \bar{t}^2$, it is nongeneric.*

An equilibrium is *nongeneric* if it exists only under singular conditions. For instance, if an equilibrium can be characterized as the solution of m independent equations in n unknowns, where $m > n$, then it is nongeneric.

Proof:

1. For concreteness only, we shall assume that $\dim T = \dim H = 2$.

2. We know each party wins exactly one-half the vote at $(\bar{t}^1, \bar{t}^2)$.

3. For any pair $t^1, t^2 \in T$, and for any $x \in \mathbf{R}^2$, define the function $G(x; t^1, t^2; h) = v(t^1 + x, h) - v(t^2, h)$.

4. Let $d \in \mathbf{R}^2$, $d \neq 0$ be arbitrary. Define the function Φ by

$$\Phi(\delta, d) = \mathbf{F}(\{h \in H \mid G(\delta d; \bar{t}^1, \bar{t}^2; h) \geq 0\}),$$

or

$$\Phi(\delta, d) = \iint\limits_{G(\delta d; \bar{t}^1 \bar{t}^2; h) \geq 0} d\mathbf{F}(h).$$

$\Phi(\delta, d)$ is the fraction of the polity who prefer $\bar{t}^1 + \delta d$ to $\bar{t}^2$. Since $(\bar{t}^1, \bar{t}^2)$ is a Downs equilibrium, we know that zero is a maximum of Φ in its δ argument, for every vector $d \neq 0$: otherwise, party 1 could deviate in some direction and defeat $\bar{t}^2$ for sure. (According to step 2, $\Phi(0, d) = \frac{1}{2}$.)

5. By A3, $\mathbf{F}$ possesses a density function, f; by A8, v is differentiable. It follows that the function Φ is differentiable in its argument δ. Thus the fact that zero is a maximum of Φ implies:

(6.5) $\forall d \in \mathbf{R}^n, \quad d \neq 0 \qquad \dfrac{\partial \Phi}{\partial \delta}(0, d) = 0.$

6. We now expand (6.5). For fixed $(x, \bar{t}^1, \bar{t}^2)$, the equation

(6.6) $G(x; \bar{t}^1, \bar{t}^2; h) = 0$

defines a curve in H. By the implicit function theorem, there is a differentiable function $R(h_1, x)$ such that

(6.7) $h_2 = R(h_1, x)$

for points $(h_1, h_2) \in H$ satisfying (6.6). (Here I suppress $\bar{t}^1$ and $\bar{t}^2$ as parameters of R.) Although the situation may be more complicated than what follows, a standard case is that

$$G(x; \bar{t}^1, \bar{t}^2; h_1, h_2) > 0 \qquad \text{iff } h_2 > R(h_1, x).$$

In this case, we can write Φ as follows:

(6.8) $$\Phi(\delta, d) = \int\int_{R(h_1, \delta d)}^{h_2(h_1)} f(h_1, h_2) dh_2 dh_1.$$

In (6.8), $h_2(h_1)$ is the maximum value of h_2 such that $(h_1, h_2) \in H$, for given h_1.

We can now differentiate Φ w.r.t. δ, using the fundamental theorem of calculus:

$$\frac{\partial \Phi}{\partial \delta}(\delta; d) = -\int f(h_1, R(h_1, \delta d))(\nabla_x R(h_1, \delta d) \cdot d) dh_1,$$

where $\nabla_x R$ is the vector of first partials of the function $R(h_1, x)$ w.r.t. x.

Hence condition (6.5) becomes

(6.9) $$\forall d \in \mathbf{R}^2, \quad d \neq 0 \qquad \int f(h_1, R(h_1, 0))(\nabla_x R(h_1, 0) \cdot d) dh_1 = 0.$$

Now define the vector $w \in \mathbf{R}^n$ (which depends on $(\bar{t}^1, \bar{t}^2)$), whose ith component is

$$w_i = \int f(h_1, R(h_1, 0))(\nabla_x R(h_1, 0))_i dh_1.$$

Then (6.9) can be expressed:

(6.10) $$\forall d \in \mathbf{R}^2, \quad d \neq 0 \qquad w \cdot d = 0.$$

But this implies that

(6.11) $$w = 0.$$

Note that (6.11) is a system of two equations, with parameters $\bar{t}^1$ and $\bar{t}^2$.

7. In addition, we know from Proposition 6.1 that $\bar{t}^1, \bar{t}^2 \in \Gamma$. This means

(6.12a) $\bar{t}_1^1 = t_1^*(\bar{t}_2^1)$

(6.12b) $\bar{t}_2^1 = t_1^*(\bar{t}_1^1)$

(6.12c) $\bar{t}_1^2 = t_1^*(\bar{t}_2^2)$

(6.12d) $\bar{t}_2^2 = t_1^*(\bar{t}_1^2)$

where $t_i^*(\cdot)$ are the functions of equation (6.1), for $i = 1, 2$. Equations (6.11) and (6.12) thus constitute six equations in four unknowns—the components of $\bar{t}^1$ and $\bar{t}^2$. It follows that any solution of these equations is nongeneric, as was to be shown. ∎

Remark As indicated in step 6, the expression of $\Phi(\delta; d)$ as an integral may be more complex than (6.8) but the general point remains true, that equation (6.5) entails two first-order conditions.

Thus under reasonable assumptions (the premises of Theorem 6.2), interior Downs equilibria do not exist in multidimensional issue-space models, except in singular cases.

The nonexistence of Downs equilibrium is commonly known by the term "cycling," which simply means that there is no pair of policies each of which is a best response to the other (that is, a Nash equilibrium in the policy competition game). Hence at any pair (t^1, t^2), at least one party can do better, and this leads to a series of never-ending alternative moves by the parties—the "cycle."

If $t \in T$ were a Condorcet winner, then (t, t) would be a Downs equilibrium—this statement is independent of T's dimension. So the basic fact is that, generically, there are no interior Condorcet winners when the game has a policy space of dimension greater than one.

Example 6.3 Here is an economic example. Let H be an interval in $\mathbf{R}_+$, where h is the income of a type. Suppose all types have the same utility function as in Example 1.1 over income, x, and public good G:

$$u(x, G) = x + 2\alpha G^{1/2}.$$

We assume that $\alpha^2 > \mu$, where μ is mean income, and $\mu > m$, where m is median income. The policy space is the set of affine tax schemes $cx + r$, where $0 \le c \le 1$. Thus the indirect utility function of type h over policies (c, r) is

$$v(c, r, h) = (1 - c)h - r + 2\alpha(c\mu + r)^{1/2}.$$

We further assume that:

(i) $0 \le c \le 1$ (marginal tax rates are positive and no greater than one);
(ii) $ch_{\min} + r \le h_{\min}$ (no one pays more taxes than her income);   (6.13)
(iii) $c\mu + r \ge 0$ (total taxes are non-negative).

(Note that it follows from (i) and (ii) that $c\mu + r \le \mu$.)

The policy space in the c-r plane is the trapezoid illustrated in Figure 6.1.

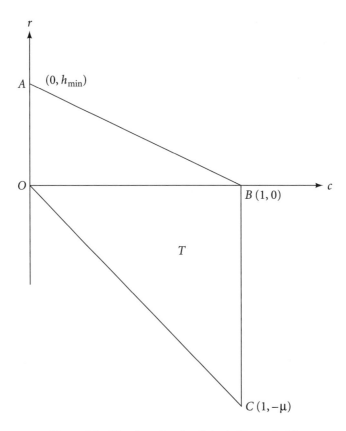

Figure 6.1   The domain of policies in Example 6.3

Theorem 6.2 tells us that there is, generically, no interior Downs equilibrium where the two parties play different policies. (Note that v is not separable.) We now check whether there can be an interior Downs equilibrium where both parties play the same policy. This requires checking the premises of Theorem 6.1. Only A10 requires checking. We have

$$(6.14) \qquad \nabla v(\bar{c}, \bar{r}, h) = \left(-h + \alpha(\bar{c}\mu + \bar{r})^{-1/2}\mu, \, -1 + \alpha(\bar{c}\mu + \bar{r})^{-1/2}\right).$$

The condition $\nabla v(\bar{c}, \bar{r}, h) \cdot d = 0$ becomes

$$(6.15) \qquad hd_1 = \alpha(\bar{c}\mu + \bar{r})^{-1/2}(\mu d_1 + d_2) - d_2.$$

If $d_1 \neq 0$, then there is a unique value of h satisfying (6.15), and so A10 is true. If $d_1 = 0$, then the left-hand side of (6.15) is zero, and so either there are no h satisfying (6.15), or *all* h satisfy (6.15). The latter happens precisely when the right-hand side of (6.15) is zero, which occurs exactly when

$$(6.16) \qquad \alpha^2 = \bar{c}\mu + \bar{r};$$

but since the r.h.s. of (6.16) is no larger than μ, (6.16) is impossible, because $\alpha^2 > \mu$.

Therefore A10 holds, and there is no interior Downs equilibrium in this economic game.

The theorems of this chapter do not exclude the possibility that there is a Downs equilibrium where at least one party plays a policy on the boundary of T. Checking whether this can occur is a painstaking process. We shall study whether there is a Downs equilibrium of the form (t, t) where t is on the boundary of T.

We must study a number of cases, corresponding to the four segments of T's boundary, and the vertices of T, at which t might be located (see Figure 6.1).

Case (1) $t \in$ int $\overline{OA}$. ("int" means "interior.")

Here, the generic policy is of the form $(0, r)$, where $0 < r < h_{\min}$. The gradient of v for h at $(0, r)$ is

$$\nabla v = (-h + \alpha r^{-1/2}\mu, \, -1 + \alpha r^{-1/2}).$$

Any direction $d = (1, \delta)$, $\delta \in \mathbf{R}$ is feasible. Now $\nabla v \cdot (1, \delta) > 0$ reduces to

$$(6.17) \qquad h < \alpha\mu r^{-1/2} + \delta(\alpha r^{-1/2} - 1).$$

As long as $(\alpha r^{-1/2} - 1) \neq 0$, we can make the r.h.s. of (6.17) as large as we please by suitable choice of δ; consequently, the set of h satisfying (6.17) can be made as large as we please, and thus a deviation in direction $(1, \delta)$ would be attractive to either party.

Now $(\alpha r^{-1/2} - 1) = 0$ implies that $\alpha^2 = r \leq h_{min}$, which is impossible, since $\alpha^2 > \mu$; so we are finished with this case.

Case (2) $t \in \text{int } \overline{BC}$.

Here, policies are of the form $(1, r)$, for $0 > r > -\mu$. In this case, any direction $d = (-1, \delta)$, for δ in $\mathbf{R}$, is feasible. We have

$$\nabla v \cdot (-1, \delta) = h - \alpha(\mu + r)^{-1/2} + \delta(-1 + \alpha(\mu + r)^{-1/2}),$$

and so $\nabla v \cdot (-1, \delta) > 0$ precisely when

(6.18) $h > \alpha(\mu + r)^{-1/2} - \delta(-1 + \alpha(\mu + r)^{-1/2}).$

We can make the r.h.s. of (6.18) arbitrarily small by suitable choice of δ (and hence guarantee that a majority of h satisfy the inequality) as long as

(6.19) $-1 + \alpha(\mu + r)^{-1/2} \neq 0.$

Now (6.19) fails only when $\alpha^2 = \mu + r$; but $\mu + r \leq \mu$ for all admissible r, which again contradicts our assumption that $\alpha^2 > \mu$.

Case (3) $t \in \text{int } \overline{AB}$.

On this segment, the policy takes the form $t = (c, (1 - c)h_{min})$, for $0 < c < 1$. Admissible directions at t are $d = (\delta_1, \delta_2)$, where $(\delta_1, \delta_2) \cdot (-1, -(1/h_{min})) \geq 0$. We shall limit ourselves to directions of the form $(-1, \delta_2)$, where $-\infty < \delta_2 \leq h_{min}$, which are admissible. In this case, $\nabla v \cdot (-1, \delta_2) > 0$ reduces to

(6.20) $h > \alpha(c\mu + (1 - c)h_{min})^{1/2}\mu + \delta_2(\alpha(c\mu + (1 - c)h_{min})^{-1/2} - 1).$

We can make the r.h.s. of (6.20) arbitrarily small (and hence guarantee that a majority of h satisfy the inequality) as long as

$$\alpha(c\mu + (1 - c)h_{min})^{-1/2} - 1 > 0;$$

we then choose δ_2 large and negative. This last inequality says

(6.21) $\alpha^2 > c\mu + (1 - c)h_{min};$

but the r.h.s. of (6.21) is no larger than μ, and so (6.21) is true by our hypothesis on α.

Case (4) $t \in \text{int } \overline{OC}$.

Here, $t = (c, -c\mu)$, for $0 < c < 1$. We compute that $\nabla v = (\infty, \infty)$, and so a move in the feasible direction $(0, 1)$ will increase every type's utility.

We must finally check whether a Downs equilibrium could consist in each party's playing a vertex of T.

Case (5) $t = (0, h_{\min})$; this is the vertex A in Figure 6.1.

To show (t, t) cannot be a Downs equilibrium, we shall show that a majority of the polity prefers $B = (1, 0)$ to t. We compute that h prefers $(1, 0)$ to $(0, h_{\min})$ exactly when

$$(6.22) \qquad 2\alpha(\mu^{1/2} - h_{\min}^{1/2}) + h_{\min} > h.$$

Hence a majority will prefer B to t if the l.h.s. of (6.22) is greater than median income:

$$2\alpha(\mu^{1/2} - h_{\min}^{1/2}) + h_{\min} > m,$$

which will be true (invoke $\alpha^2 > \mu$) if

$$(6.23) \qquad \mu - 2\mu^{1/2}h_{\min}^{1/2} + h_{\min} > m - \mu.$$

Now the r.h.s. of (6.23) is negative by hypothesis, and the l.h.s. is positive, since it is the square of $(\mu^{1/2} - h_{\min}^{1/2})$. Consequently (6.23) is true, and we are finished.

However, it turns out that (B, B) is a Downs equilibrium. To show this, we will demonstrate that B is the ideal policy in T for every $h \leq h^*$, where h^* is a greater than median income. Thus, a majority have B as their ideal point, and therefore there is no profitable deviation for either party from B.

Let $h^* = h_{\min}(1 - \alpha\mu^{-1/2}) + \alpha\mu^{1/2}$. I claim that $h^* > m$; that is,

$$(6.24) \qquad h_{\min}(1 - \alpha\mu^{-1/2}) + \alpha\mu^{1/2} > m.$$

The reader can verifty that (6.24) reduces to the inequality

$$\left(\frac{m - h_{\min}}{\mu - h_{\min}}\right)^2 \mu < \alpha^2,$$

which is true, because the term in parentheses on the l.h.s. of the inequality is less than one, and we know $\alpha^2 > \mu$.

Next observe that the admissible directions of deviation at B are of the form $(-1, \delta)$, for $-\infty < \delta < h_{\min}$. The directional derivative at $(1,0)$ for h in direction $(-1, \delta)$ is $h - \alpha\mu^{1/2} - \delta + \alpha\delta\mu^{-1/2}$. Thus h's utility increases at B in the direction $(-1, \delta)$ when

$$(6.25) \quad h > \alpha\mu^{1/2} + \delta - \alpha\delta\mu^{-1/2} = \alpha\mu^{1/2} + \delta(1 - \alpha\mu^{-1/2}).$$

Since $1 - \alpha\mu^{-1/2} < 0$, the above inequality is true for h, for some admissible δ, if and only if it is true when $\delta = h_{\min}$. But when $\delta = h_{\min}$, the r.h.s. of (6.25) is equal to h^*, and hence we have shown that there is an admissible direction at B which increases h's utility only if $h > h^*$. Thus B locally maximizes utility for a strict majority of the polity. It is indeed the ideal policy for this majority, because v is concave and T is convex.

The lesson of this example is that one must pay careful attention to the boundary of the policy space, for in economic examples, that is sometimes where a Condorcet winner, and hence a Downs equilibrium, can be found.

6.3 The Wittman Model

When dim $T > 1$, nontrivial Wittman equilibria (see Definition 3.2) generically fail to exist in the case of certainty.

Theorem 6.3 *Let $(v, v^1, v^2, T, H, \mathbf{F})$ be a game with certainty where v is continuously differentiable, the v^i are differentiable, and $\mathbf{F}$ is equivalent to Lebesgue measure. If (t^{1^*}, t^{2^*}) is an interior Wittman equilibrium with $t^{1^*} \neq t^{2^*}$ and $\pi(t^{1^*}, t^{2^*}) = \frac{1}{2}$, then it is nongeneric.*

Proof:

1. There are three cases.

Case (1) $v^1(t^{1^*}) > v^1(t^{2^*})$ and $v^2(t^{2^*}) > v^2(t^{1^*})$.
Define the function $\Psi(t^1, t^2) = \mathbf{F}(\Omega(t^1, t^2))$. Since v is continuously differentiable, and $\mathbf{F}$ possesses a density, Ψ is differentiable. Denote the n-vector of first derivatives of Ψ w.r.t. its t^1 coordinates by $\nabla_1 \Psi$ and the n-vector of first derivatives of Ψ w.r.t. its t^2 coordinates by $\nabla_2 \Psi$.

It must be that t^{1^*} is a local maximum of $\Psi(t, t^{2^*})$, for otherwise party 1 could deviate a small amount in some direction, win with probability 1, and therefore increase its payoff (this uses the fact that $v^1(t^{1^*}) > v^1(t^{2^*})$ and the continuity of v^1). Therefore

(6.26) $\nabla_1 \Psi(t^{1^*}, t^{2^*}) = 0.$

In like manner, t^{2^*} must be a local minimum of $\Psi(t^{1^*}, t)$, and so

(6.27) $\nabla_2 \Psi(t^{1^*}, t^{2^*}) = 0.$

These two equations, and the equation

$$\pi(t^{1^*}, t^{2^*}) = \tfrac{1}{2}$$

constitute $2n + 1$ equations in $2n$ unknowns; hence the existence of a solution is a singularity.

2. *Case (2)* $v^i(t^{1^*}) = v^i(t^{2^*})$, for $i = 1, 2$.
We know there is no direction at t^{1^*} in which party 1 can move that will increase both the fraction of the vote it gets and its utility; therefore the gradients of v^1 and of $\Psi(\cdot, t^{2^*})$ must point in opposite directions at t^{1^*}:

(6.28a) $\nabla v^1(t^{1^*}) = -\lambda_1 \nabla_1 \Psi(t^{1^*}, t^{2^*}),$

for some non-negative number λ_1. In like manner, there is no direction that party 2 can move in at t^{2^*} that will increase its fraction of the vote and its utility, and so

(6.28b) $\nabla v^2(t^{2^*}) = \lambda_2 \nabla_2 \Psi(t^{1^*}, t^{2^*}),$

where λ_2 is non-negative. Furthermore we have

(6.29a) $v^i(t^{1^*}) = v^i(t^{2^*}),$ for $i = 1, 2.$

and

(6.29b) $\pi(t^{1^*}, t^{2^*}) = \tfrac{1}{2}.$

The equations (6.28) and (6.29) constitute $2n + 3$ equations in $2n + 2$ unknowns, and so any solution is nongeneric.

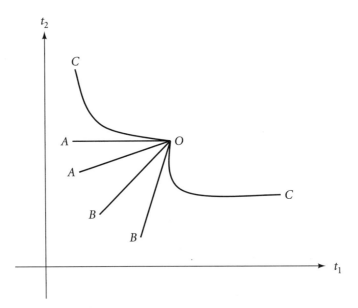

Figure 6.2 Example 6.4

3. *Case 3.* $v^1(t^{1*}) > v^1(t^{2*})$ and $v^2(t^{2*}) = v^2(t^{1*})$.
This case leads to the equations (6.26), (6.28b), (6.29b), and $v^2(t^{1*}) = v^2(t^{2*})$,
which constitute $2n + 2$ equations in $2n + 1$ unknowns. ■

There are, however, two kinds of case in which Wittman equilibrium does
exist. First, it is a Wittman equilibrium for both parties to play any strict
Condorcet winner (see Definition 1.2). (The easy proof is left to the reader.)
The second kind is of the form (t^*, t^*), but t^* is not a Condorcet winner. We
illustrate this kind in the next example.

Example 6.4 A Wittman equilibrium of the form (t^*, t^*).
Let T be the plane. Consult Figure 6.2. Let $M \subset H$ be a majority of the polity,
and let the indifference curves through the policy O of all types in M lie above
the curve COC. (In other words, let COC be the lower envelope of the set of
indifference curves through O of all types in M. Let the indifference curve of
party 1 through O be the curve AOA, and let the indifference curve of party 2
through O be BOB. I claim (O, O) is a Wittman equilibrium. The only attractive
deviation for party 1 at (O, O) is to a policy in the cone AOA, which is its upper
contour set at O: but all types in M prefer O to any such point, and so such

a deviation is defeated for sure. Similarly, party 2 has no attractive deviation, and so (O, O) is a Wittman equilibrium.

Furthermore, we can easily specify the preferences of types in M so that a point very close to O and above the curve COC defeats O, and so O is not a Condorcet winner.

The next example illustrates a case where there exists a strict Condorcet winner; it is (of course) a Wittman equilibrium, and indeed the only Wittman equilibrium.

Example 6.5   Preferences are Euclidean, where type (a, b)'s utility function is

$$v(t_1, t_2; a, b) = -\tfrac{1}{2}(t_1 - a)^2 - \tfrac{1}{2}(t_2 - b)^2.$$

We assume H is a disc in the plane with center at the origin, O, and that $\mathbf{F}$ is the uniform distribution on H. Thus any diameter of H partitions the population into two sets of equal mass. The reader should verify that (O, O) is a strict Condorcet equilibrium.

The two parties have preferences of distinct types (a_1, b_1) and (a_2, b_2), respectively.

We first dispose of the possibility that a Wittman equilibrium exists in which one party wins with probability 1. Suppose (t^1, t^2) were such an equilibrium, and suppose t^1 wins with probability one. The citizens who prefer t^1 to t^2 are all those types lying on t^1's side of the perpendicular bisector of the line segment connecting t^1 and t^2. (For these types, t^1 is closer to their ideal point than t^2 is.) Call this bisector ℓ. If t^1 wins for sure, this coalition is a majority, which means that the origin lies above ℓ. See Figure 6.3.

If $t^1 \neq (a_1, b_1)$, then party 1 can move closer to (a_1, b_1)—to some point $t^1 + \Delta$—and still preserve the fact that the perpendicular bisector of the line segment connecting $t^1 + \Delta$ and t^2 has the origin and $t^1 + \Delta$ on its same side, meaning party 1 should deviate. This implies that $t^1 = (a_1, b_1)$. Consequently, party 1 is playing its ideal point and winning for sure. This cannot be an equilibrium as long as party 2 can choose a point that it prefers to (a_1, b_1) and allows it to win with probability at least one-half.

Draw the circle C with center at the origin passing through (a_1, b_1): see Figure 6.4. If party 2 plays any point on or inside this circle, it wins with probability $\tfrac{1}{2}$ or 1, respectively. Hence it must be that (a_1, b_1) is closer to (a_2, b_2) than to any point on or inside C. This can only be true if (a_2, b_2) lies on the radius from

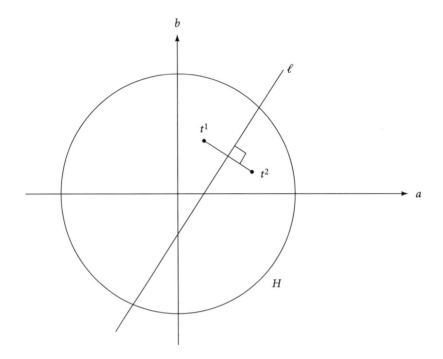

Figure 6.3

O through (a_1, b_1), as illustrated in Figure 6.4. But the case that (a_1, b_1) *and* (a_2, b_2) *lie on the same radius of H* is a singular one, which we may eliminate from consideration.

Therefore, at any nonsingular Wittman equilibrium (t^1, t^2), each party wins with probability one-half. We now examine this possibility. Suppose $\pi(t^1, t^2) = \frac{1}{2}$. It therefore must be the case that the perpendicular bisector of the line segment connecting t^1 and t^2 passes through the origin, that is, is a diameter of H. See Figure 6.5.

We claim that only in a singular case can we have $v^i(t^1) = v^i(t^2)$ for $i = 1, 2$, assuming $t^1 \neq t^2$. For if $v^i(t^1) = v^i(t^2)$ for $i = 1, 2$, then the ideal points of the parties are each equidistant from t^1 and t^2, which implies that they both lie on diameter ℓ. We disregard this singular case. Therefore, for some i, say 1, $v^1(t^1) > v^1(t^2)$. But then party 1 can deviate a small distance toward t^2 along the segment $\overline{t^1 t^2}$, win for sure, and increase its payoff.

Consequently, the only possibility is that $t^1 = t^2 = t^*$. Suppose that $t* \neq O$. Consider the diameter ℓ' through t^*, illustrated in Figure 6.6. If either party deviates toward O along diameter ℓ', it wins for sure. So such a deviation must

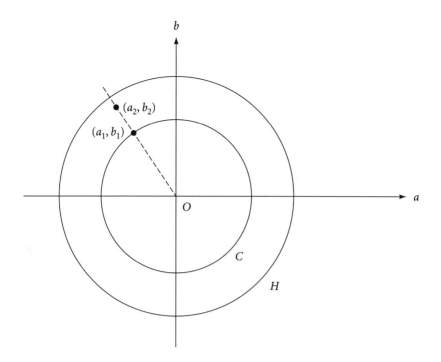

Figure 6.4

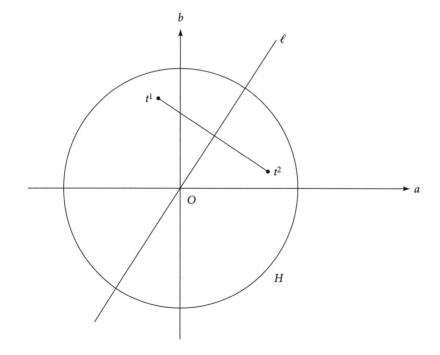

Figure 6.5

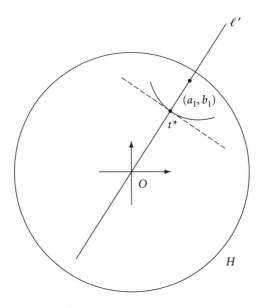

Figure 6.6

decrease utility for both parties—that is, any point between t^* and O must be farther from (a_i, b_i) than t^*, for $i = 1, 2$. This means that the circle with center (a_i, b_i) passing through t^* is tangent to the perpendicular of ℓ' through t^*. But this means that (a_i, b_i) lies on ℓ', as pictured in Figure 6.6. Since this is true for both i, we have the same singularity as before.

We have proved:

Proposition 6.3 *In the Euclidean model with $n = 2$, where types are uniformly distributed on a disc H, the unique Wittman equilibrium is (O, O), unless the ideal points of both parties lie on the same diameter of H.*

6.4 Conclusion

In this chapter we have shown that an interior Downs equilibrium exists only nongenerically when dim $T > 1$. We have also shown that only trivial interior Wittman equilibria exist generically in the multidimensional case: either one party wins for sure or, if not, then both parties play the same policy. There is, however, a difference between Downs and Wittman here: for there are examples of Wittman equilibria where parties do not play a Condorcet winner, and this is not true of Downs equilibrium.

We also noted, by example, that it is not unusual for a Downs equilibrium to exist on the boundary of the policy space: this can happen because on the boundary, and in particular at a vertex of a polygonal (or polyhedral) policy space, there are relatively few directions of admissible deviation. Thus realistic problems, in which policy spaces are compact, can support Downs equilibria. This makes the Downs tool somewhat more useful than one might have inferred from the pessimistic theorems about the singularity of interior equilibria.

On the other hand, in many natural problems, we should expect the equilibrium to be interior, if there is one. (We do not expect tax rates, for instance, to be zero or one.) And surely most, if not all, *party* competition is multi-issue. In this case, one might well worry about the fragility of the two equilibrium concepts that have been the object of our study.

That worry is, however, still premature, because parties never operate in an environment of certainty. The next move, then, is to introduce uncertainty into the multidimensional model, and to investigate the existence of political equilibrium.

7

Multidimensional Issue Spaces and Uncertainty: The Downs Model

7.1 Introduction

We have seen, in Chapter 6, that in models with multidimensional issue spaces and party certainty about voter behavior, neither Downs nor nontrivial Wittman equilibria typically exist. In this chapter we will show that Downs equilibrium fails to exist when there is party uncertainty about voter behavior, in the multidimensional framework, with the state-space and error-distribution models of uncertainty (section 7.2).

In sections 7.3 and 7.4 we introduce the models of Coughlin (1992) and Lindbeck and Weibull (1987), which are multidimensional-issue-space models in which Downs equilibrium does exist. We argue, however, that the uncertainty in the models is ephemeral, in the sense that it vanishes when the polity becomes large. Finally, we show in section 7.5 that if the "probabilistic voting" feature of the Coughlin and Lindbeck-Weibull models is grafted on to a model with party uncertainty and large polities, via our finite-type model of uncertainty, then Downs equilibrium does exist in an interesting class of models.

7.2 The State-Space and Error-Distribution Models of Uncertainty

Let us consider Downs equilibrium with the error-distribution model of uncertainty. Thus T, the policy space, is multidimensional, H is the set of types, and $\mathbf{F}$ is the distribution of types. We have

$$\pi(t, t') = \frac{\mathbf{F}(\Omega(t, t')) + \beta - 0.5}{2\beta}.$$

Suppose there is an interior Downs equilibrium (t, t') with $t \neq t'$. At a Downs equilibrium, we must have $\pi = \frac{1}{2}$. Therefore $\mathbf{F}(\Omega(t, t')) = \frac{1}{2}$. In particular, we know

$$
(7.1) \qquad \left. \begin{array}{l} \forall x \in T, \quad \mathbf{F}(\Omega(x, t')) \leq \dfrac{1}{2} \\[2em] \forall y \in T, \quad \mathbf{F}(\Omega(x, y)) \geq \dfrac{1}{2} \end{array} \right\}
$$

But (7.1) means that (t, t') is a Downs equilibrium in the *model with certainty*. It follows that we are in the case of Theorem 6.2, and under the assumptions of that theorem, Downs equilibrium exists only in singular cases.

On the other hand, suppose (t^*, t^*) is an interior Downs equilibrium for some $t^* \in T$. Then

$$
(7.2) \qquad \left. \begin{array}{l} \forall t \neq t^*, \quad \dfrac{\mathbf{F}(\Omega(t, t^*)) + \beta - 0.5}{2\beta} \leq \dfrac{1}{2} \\[2em] \forall t \neq t^*, \quad \dfrac{\mathbf{F}(\Omega(t^*, t)) + \beta - 0.5}{2\beta} \geq \dfrac{1}{2} \end{array} \right\}
$$

Expression (7.2) implies that $\mathbf{F}(\Omega(t, t^*)) \leq \frac{1}{2}$ and $\mathbf{F}(\Omega(t^*, t)) \geq \frac{1}{2}$ and so, again, (t^*, t^*) is an equilibrium of the model with certainty. Now Theorem 6.1 informs us that this is an impossibility.

Thus under the error-distribution model of uncertainty, Downs equilibria generically fail to exist, with multidimensional issue spaces. We summarize:

Theorem 7.1 *Let A1, A2, A8, and A10 hold. Let T be multidimensional, and let the error-distribution model of uncertainty hold. Then an interior Downs equilibrium exists only when condition (6.2) holds.*

In addition, Downs equilibria under the state-space model of uncertainty generically fail to exist. Here we introduce the analogue of A10.

A10′ $(\forall s \in S)(\forall \bar{t} \in T)(\forall d \neq 0, d \in \mathbf{R}^n) \qquad \mathbf{F}_s(\{h \mid \nabla v(\bar{t}, h) \cdot d = 0\}) = 0.$

A10′ is simply the statement of A10 for the entire family of probability distributions $\{F_s\}$. Let s be distributed according to distribution $\mathbf{G}$ on $[0, 1]$. We have

Theorem 7.2 *Let A1, A2, A8, and A10′ hold, and suppose the state-space model of uncertainty. Then an interior Downs equilibrium exists only in singular cases.*

Proof:

1. *Case (1)* Suppose there is a Downs equilibrium (t^*, t^*). Then, for all $d \neq 0$:

$$(7.3) \qquad \mathbf{G}(\{s \mid \mathbf{F}_s(\{h \mid \nabla v(t^*, h) \cdot d > 0\}) > \tfrac{1}{2}\}) \leq \tfrac{1}{2}.$$

Inequality (7.3) says that the set of states in which a majority of voters would prefer a policy slightly perturbed from t^* in some direction d, can never be a set with mass greater than $\tfrac{1}{2}$. Failing (7.3), there is a policy $t^* + \delta d$, for some $d \in \mathbf{R}^n$, and $\delta \in \mathbf{R}$, that defeats t^* with probability greater than $\tfrac{1}{2}$.

Now A10′ and (7.3) imply

$$(7.4) \qquad \forall d \neq 0, \qquad \mathbf{G}(\{s \mid \mathbf{F}_s(\{h \mid \nabla v(t^*, h) \cdot d < 0\}) > \tfrac{1}{2}\}) \geq \tfrac{1}{2}.$$

But (7.4) can be rewritten:

$$(7.5) \qquad \forall d \neq 0, \qquad \mathbf{G}(\{s \mid \mathbf{F}_s(\{h \mid \nabla v(t^*, h) \cdot (-d) > 0\}) > \tfrac{1}{2}\}) \geq \tfrac{1}{2}.$$

If the inequality in (7.3) were strict for some d, then the inequality in (7.5) would be strict for that d, which would contradict the supposition that (t^*, t^*) is a Downs equilibrium.

Therefore, (7.3) is an equation for all $d \neq 0$. This is a singular condition, as has been discussed in Chapter 6, with reference to the similar condition (6.2) in Theorem 6.1.

2. *Case (2)* There is an interior Downs equilibrium (t^1, t^2), $t^1 \neq t^2$.

The reader should notice that the proof of Case(1) follows the proof of Theorem 6.1. It will therefore come as no surprise that the proof of this case follows the proof of Theorem 6.2. The details are left as an exercise for the tireless reader.

∎

7.3 The Coughlin Model

Peter Coughlin (1992) proposes a "probabilistic voting model" in which Downs equilibrium exists for multidimensional issue spaces. In this section we present Coughlin's model, adapting the notation to conform with the models in this book.

Let H be the set of types, distributed according to the probability distribution **F**. Let T be a compact convex set in $\mathbf{R}^n$. The utility function is, as usual, $v(t, h)$, which we now assume is non-negative, and is concave in t. There is a function $\phi : \mathbf{R}_+ \to [0, 1]$ with these properties:

(1) $\phi(x) + \phi(\frac{1}{x}) = 1$,
(2) ϕ is continuous and increasing in x, and
(3) ϕ is concave.

Coughlin postulates that, when facing a pair of policies (t^1, t^2), a citizen of type h votes for t^1 with probability $\phi\left(\frac{v(t^1,h)}{v(t^2,h)}\right)$. Furthermore, the draws on this individual variable are independent across citizens.

Because we are interested in large polities, we will assume (as usual) that there is a continuum of individuals of each type. Because the draws of the random variable are i.i.d., and there is a continuum of citizens in each type, the *fraction* of citizens of type h who vote for t^1 is $\phi\left(\frac{v(t^1,h)}{v(t^2,h)}\right)$, and so the fraction of polity who vote for t^1 is

$$(7.6) \qquad \Phi^C(t^1, t^2) \equiv \int \phi\left(\frac{v(t^1, h)}{v(t^2, h)}\right) d\mathbf{F}(h).$$

Coughlin postulates that each candidate (party) desires to maximize his (expected) vote fraction. Thus, party 1 seeks to maximize Φ^C, and party 2 to maximize $1 - \Phi^C$.

We first note:

Proposition 7.1 *A Nash equilibrium of the Coughlin game is a Downs equilibrium, and conversely.*

Proof:

1. In a Nash equilibrium of the Coughlin game each party receives one-half the vote. For if one party received less than one-half, it could immediately

increase its vote fraction by imitating the other party. (Notice that $\phi(1) = \frac{1}{2}$, so $\Phi^C(t, t) = \frac{1}{2}$ for all t.)

2. Therefore, in a Nash equilibrium of the Coughlin game, each player wins with probability one-half. This is a Downs equilibrium, since if either player could increase its probability of victory (to 1) by deviating, we would not be in Nash equilibrium of Coughlin's game. ∎

We now observe:

Theorem 7.3 *A Downs equilibrium of the Coughlin game exists.*

Proof:
Since ϕ is concave and v is concave in t, it follows that $\Phi^C(\cdot, t^2)$ is a concave function (in t^1). Note that

$$\Phi^C(t^1, t^2) = \int \left(1 - \phi\left(\frac{v(t^2, h)}{v(t^1, h)}\right)\right) d\mathbf{F}(h) = 1 - \int \phi\left(\frac{v(t^2, h)}{v(t^1, h)}\right) d\mathbf{F}(h),$$

and so

$$1 - \Phi^C(t^1, t^2) = \int \phi\left(\frac{v(t^2, h)}{v(t^1, h)}\right) d\mathbf{F}(h);$$

therefore, $1 - \Phi^C(t^1, \cdot)$ is a concave function of t^2. The best-reply correspondences are nonempty (since T is compact). We are therefore in a situation where all the premises needed to apply Kakutani's fixed-point theorem hold, and so a Nash equilibrium of the Coughlin game exists. By Proposition 7.1, this is a Downs equilibrium. ∎

Thus Coughlin has proposed a model with a multidimensional issue space in which a Downs equilibrium exists.

We must first understand that, although Coughlin presents his model as one of "probabilistic voting," in the continuum-of-citizens version, it is what we call, in this book, a model with certainty. The only case in which there is uncertainty concerning which party will win is when each policy receives exactly one-half of the vote. In Coughlin (1992), the author often assumes a finite polity, and so uncertainty exists. But that uncertainty is uninteresting for us, because we are interested only in large-polity politics.

Therefore Coughlin's model is appropriately compared with the models of Chapter 6. The question is: why does a Downs equilibrium generically exist

in Coughlin's model, and generically not exist in our models in Chapter 6
(Theorems 6.1 and 6.2)? The answer lies in the introduction of probabilistic
voting at the individual level, as embodied in the function ϕ.

To see the contrast, let us suppose our usual framework, in which type h votes
for policy t^1 over t^2 if and only if $v(t^1, h) - v(t^2, h) > 0$ (unless he is indifferent
between the policies). The fraction who vote for t^1 is

$$\Phi(t^1, t^2) = \int_{h \in \Omega(t^1, t^2)} d\mathbf{F}(h).$$

Letting $\mathbf{1}_X$ be the indicator function,[1] we may write

$$(7.7) \qquad \Phi(t^1, t^2) = \int \mathbf{1}_{\Omega(t^1, t^2)} d\mathbf{F}(h)$$

The essential fact is that, while Φ^C is a concave function of t^1, Φ *is not even
a quasi-concave function of* t^1, in general. Therefore, Kakutani's theorem does
not apply, and we have no a priori reason to hope that a Downs equilibrium
will exist in the game with payoff functions Φ and $1 - \Phi$. Nor, should I add, is
Φ continuous on the line (t, t), while Φ^C is continuous.

We demonstrate that Φ is not (generally) quasi-concave with an example,
illustrated in Figure 7.1. Let T be a compact, convex set in $\mathbf{R}^2$. Likewise, $H \subset \mathbf{R}^2$.
Let

$$v(t_1, t_2; h_1, h_2) = -\tfrac{1}{2}(t_1 - h_1)^2 - \tfrac{1}{2}(t_2 - h_2)^2;$$

that is, h prefers t^1 to t^2 if and only if the distance from t^1 to h is smaller than the
distance from t^2 to h. Let the policies t^2, t and t' be given, as illustrated in Figure
7.1, let $\hat{t}$ be on the line segment $\overline{tt'}$ and let the lines ℓ, ℓ', and $\hat{\ell}$ be perpendicular
bisectors of the line segments $\overline{tt^2}$, $\overline{t't^2}$, and $\overline{\hat{t}t^2}$, respectively. Finally, assume that
almost all of H's mass lies in shaded half-plane, above $\hat{\ell}$.

If Φ is quasi-concave, then it must be that

$$(7.8) \qquad \Phi(\hat{t}, t^2) \geq \min(\Phi(t, t^2), \Phi(t', t^2)).$$

We shall show that (7.6) is false. Note that $\Omega(t, t^2)$ consists of all types
that lie below the line ℓ—these are the points closer to t than to t^2. This

---

1. See the Mathematical Appendix.

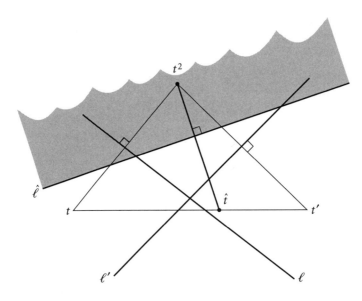

Figure 7.1

includes a substantial part of H. Therefore $\Phi(t, t^2) \cong \frac{1}{3}$, let us say. Similarly, $\Omega(t', t^2)$ consists of all points on the same side of ℓ' as t': this also includes as substantiated part of H, so we write $\Phi(t', t^2) \cong \frac{1}{3}$. $\Omega(\hat{t}, t^2)$ consist of all points below $\hat{\ell}$, which includes almost no mass of H, and so $\Phi(\hat{t}, t^2) \approx 0$; hence (7.6) is false.

This example shows that even if **F** and v are nonpathological, the function Φ is generally neither quasi-concave nor continuous. Thus the substitution of the function

$$\phi \left(\frac{v(t^1, h)}{v(t^2, h)} \right)$$

for the function $\mathbf{1}_{\Omega(t^1, t^2)}$ in the integrand of (7.7) changes the badly behaved function Φ into the well-behaved function Φ^C.

7.4 The Lindbeck-Weibull Model

Assar Lindbeck and Jorgen Weibull (1987) propose a model that shares this feature with Coughlin's model: voting at the level of the individual is probabilistic, but with a continuum of voters, the uncertainty disappears. A Downs equilibrium exists. Their model, however, has somewhat more micro-foundations than Coughlin's, as it endeavors to make precise *why* a voter's behavior appears to be probabilistic. Essentially the same model is studied by James Enelow and Melvin Hinich (1989).

Lindbeck and Weibull propose that there be two candidates, A and B. As usual, we have a set of types H, and a distribution of types, $\mathbf{F}$. The policy space T is of dimension n. But now it is assumed that candidates A and B have particular characteristics, which differentiate them, beyond the policies they propose: this could, for example, be their positions on issues that are not focal in the election. Because of this, each voter types receives a different utility, depending on which candidate is elected. In particular,

(7.9)
$$\begin{cases} v(t, A; h) = u(t, h) + a^h, \\ v(t, B; h) = u(t, h) + b^h, \end{cases}$$

where (t, A) is the event "candidate A is elected with policy t."

Now the candidates are assumed to know the function u, but they only have a probability distribution over the pairs (a^h, b^h). In particular, assume that both candidates believe that $b^h - a^h$ is distributed according to a probability measure whose distribution function is $G^h(\cdot)$.

If the candidates propose policies t^A and t^B, then type h votes for t^A when

$$u(t^A, h) + a^h > u(t^B, h) + b^h,$$

or when

$$b^h - a^h < u(t^A, h) - u(t^B, h).$$

The candidates evaluate the probability of this event as $G^h(u(t^A, h) - u(t^B, h))$. Therefore the expected fraction of the vote going to candidate A is

(7.10) $$\Phi^{LW}(t^A, t^B) = \int G^h(u(t^A, h) - u(t^B, h))d\mathbf{F}(h).$$

We note, again, that if $\mathbf{F}$ is a continuous distribution, then Φ^{LW} is the *exact* fraction of the vote which t^A receives; only if there is a finite number of individuals of all types will the *expected* vote fraction differ from the exact vote fraction. Therefore if we continue to be interested only in large polities, the Lindbeck-Weibull model is what we have called a model with certainty. Uncertainty as to the electoral outcome only exists when $\Phi^{LW} = \frac{1}{2}$, and a coin is flipped to decide the victor.

We next assume that the probability distributions $\mathbf{G}^h$ are each symmetric: that is, for all x and h,

(7.11) $G^h(x) = 1 - G^h(-x).$

Now the expected vote share for candidate B is $1 - \Phi^{LW}(t^A, t^B)$, which, by (7.11), is equal to

$$\int G^h(u(t^B, h) - u(t^A, h))d\mathbf{F}(h).$$

If Φ^{LW} is concave in t^A and $1 - \Phi^{LW}$ is concave in t^B, then, by Kakutani's fixed-point theorem, a Downs equilibrium exists for this model. (Note that Proposition 7.1 holds when we substitute "Lindbeck-Weibull" for "Coughlin" in the statement.) Since the probabilistic distributions G^h are symmetric, we have seen, in the paragraph above, that it suffices to prove concavity of Φ^{LW} in t^A, for the concavity of $1 - \Phi^{LW}$ in t^B is mathematically equivalent.

Let g^h be the (positive) density function of G^h, let $\nabla u(\cdot, h)$ be the gradient of the function $u(\cdot, h)$ at t, and let $\mathcal{H}(u(t, h))$ be the Hessian matrix of the function $u(\cdot, h)$ evaluated at t. If z is a (column) vector, denote its transpose by z^T.

Define the $n \times n$ matrix

$$M(t^A, t^B, h) = \frac{g^{h'}(u(t^A, h) - u(t^B, h))}{g^h(u(t^A, h) - u(t^B, h))} \nabla u(t^A, h) \cdot (\nabla u(t^A, h))^T + \mathcal{H}(u(t^A, h)),$$

where $g^{h'}$ is the derivative of g^h.

We have

Theorem 7.4 *Suppose $M(t^A, t^B, h)$ is a negative semi-definite matrix for all (t^A, t^B, h), where $t^A, t^B \in T$. Then there exists a Downs equilibrium in the Lindbeck-Weibull model.*

Proof:

To show that Φ^{LW} is concave in t^A, we show its Hessian matrix w.r.t. t^A is negative semi-definite for all vectors t^B. Define $\Phi^{hLW}(t^A, t^B) = G^h(u(t^A, h) -$

$u(t^B, h)$). It suffices to show that Φ^{hLW} has a negative–semi-definite Hessian matrix (w.r.t. t^A) for all t^B, evaluated at t^A. The reader may compute that this Hessian matrix is

$$\mathcal{H}(\Phi^{hLW}) = g^{h'}(u(t^A, h) - u(t^B, h))\nabla u(t^A, h) \cdot (\nabla u(t^A, h))^T$$

$$+ g^h(u(t^A, h) - u(t^B, h))\mathcal{H}(u(t^A, h)).$$

Since g^h is always positive, it is equivalent to show the negative semi-definiteness for the matrix

$$\frac{g^{h'}(u(t^A, h) - u(t^B, h))}{g^h(u(t^A, h) - u(t^B, h))}\nabla u(t^A, h) \cdot (\nabla u(t^A, h))^T + \mathcal{H}(u(t^A, h)).$$

But this requirement is the theorem's premise. ∎

Remark The condition that $M(t^A, t^B; h)$ be n.s.d. is not a "nice" condition. If u is concave, then $\mathcal{H}(u(t^A, h))$ is negative semi-definite. But the matrix $\nabla u(t^A, h) \cdot (\nabla u(t^A, h))^T$ is always positive semi-definite, so if the $g^{h'}/g^h$ term is positive, then the condition is delicate: it must be that the negativeness of the $\mathcal{H}(u)$ matrix overwhelms the positiveness of the matrix $g'/g\nabla u \cdot (\nabla u)^T$. See Lindbeck and Weibull (1987, 281) for further discussion.

The negative–semi-definiteness of $M(t^A, t^B, h)$ is exactly "Condition 1" of Enelow and Hinich (1989); "condition C1" of Lindbeck and Weibull (1987) is the unidimensional version of our condition.

When I wrote that the Lindbeck-Weibull model has micro-foundations that the Coughlin model lacks, I meant that Coughlin assumes that an individual votes for policy t^A over t^B probabilistically, while Lindbeck and Weibull base that random behavior on an unknown element of the voter's preferences over specific candidate characteristics. It should be noted, however, that the key condition for the existence of a Downs equilibrium in the latter model—that $M(t^A, t^B, h)$ be negative semi-definite—is not an attractive condition, in the sense that it involves an assumption on the pairs of objects $\{G^h, u(\cdot, h)\}$. We have no elementary (primitive) condition on voter preferences and behavior that implies the condition in question. Nevertheless, the existence of Downs equilibrium in Theorem 7.4 is a nonsingular event, in the sense that there is a generic set of models where the matrix M is indeed negative semi-definite.

7.5 Adapting the Coughlin Model to the Case of Aggregate Uncertainty

Section 7.3 and 7.4 have shown two methods for "concavifying" the payoff functions of parties (or candidates) in the Downs political game, when T is multidimensional. But the existence theorems which then hold are twice removed from the existence theorem we would like to have: first, there is true (aggregate) uncertainty in these models only when the polity is finite, and second, we are mainly interested in the (realistic) case that parties have policy preferences. In this section we shall investigate whether the concavifying methods of the earlier sections will continue to work when we introduce aggregate uncertainty. (Parties with policy preferences will be introduced in the multidimensional model in Chapter 8.)

We shall introduce aggregate uncertainty into the Coughlin model by employing the finite-type probability model of section 2.4. Upon review, the reader will recognize that that model is exactly the Coughlin model adapted to generate aggregate uncertainty.

Using the notation of section 2.4, $(\frac{1}{2} + \frac{1}{4}f(x(t^1, t^2, h^i)))$ is the *expected* fraction of voters of type h^i who vote for t^1 over t^2, where $x(t^1, t^2, h^i) = v(t^2, h)/v(t^1, h)$. However, the *actual* fraction of type h^i citizens who vote for t^1 over t^2 is $1/2 + \epsilon^i/2 f(x(t^1, t^2, h^i))$, where ϵ^i is a random variable (with mean $1/2$).

Since there is aggregate uncertainty in the model of section 2.4, maximizing the expected vote there and maximizing the probability of victory are different objectives, and the rational (Downsian) candidate will maximize the latter. We shall analyze this model in a moment. But first let us observe that, were our parties to (mistakenly) maximize expected vote share with the probabilistic structure of section 2.4, then a Nash equilibrium would exist.

Proposition 7.2 *Given the assumptions of section 2.4, suppose party 1 maximizes its expected vote share,*

$$\sum_i \frac{\omega_i}{2}\left(1 + f\left(\frac{v(t^2, h^i)}{v(t^i, h^i)}\right)\right),$$

and party 2 maximizes its expected vote share. If v is concave in t, then a Nash equilibrium exists.

Proof:

To show that expected vote share is concave in t^1, it suffices to show that

$$\Psi(t^1, t^2, h) = f\left(\frac{v(t^2, h)}{v(t^1, h)}\right)$$

is concave in t^1. The gradient of Ψ w.r.t. t^1 is

$$-f'\left(\frac{v(t^2, h)}{v(t^1, h)}\right)\frac{v(t^2, h)}{(v(t^1, h))^2}\nabla v(t^1, h);$$

the Hessian of Ψ w.r.t. t^1 is equal to

$$\left(f''(x)\frac{x^2}{(v(t^1, h))^2} + 2f'(x)\frac{x}{(v(t^1, h))^3}\right)\nabla v(t^1, h) \cdot (\nabla v(t^1, h))^T$$

$$- f'(x)\frac{x}{v(t^1, h)}\mathcal{H}(v(t^1, h)),$$

where $x = v(t^2, h)/v(t^1, h)$. Using the definition of f and the fact that v is everywhere non-negative, we compute that this matrix is negative semi-definite if and only if the matrix

(7.12) $2\nabla v(t^1) \cdot (\nabla v(t^1))^T - (v(t^1) + v(t^2))\mathcal{H}(v(t^1))$

is positive semi-definite. The matrix $-(v(t^1) + v(t^2))\mathcal{H}(v(t^1))$ is positive semi-definite because $\mathcal{H}(v(t^1))$ is negative semi-definite (v is concave), and the matrix $\nabla v(t^1) \cdot (\nabla v(t^1))^T$ is positive semi-definite since, for any $x \in \mathbf{R}^n$,

$$x\nabla v(t^1) \cdot (\nabla v(t^1))^T x^T = (\nabla v(t^1) \cdot x)^2 \geq 0.$$

Therefore Ψ is concave in t^1. The symmetric properties of f assure us that Ψ is convex in t^2, and so, by Kakutani's fixed-point theorem, a Nash equilibrium exists. ∎

Proposition 7.2 is the analogue of Theorem 7.3. Next we introduce aggregate uncertainty and show that concavity (more strongly, quasi-concavity) of the probability function π generally does not hold.

We shall illustrate this in a nonpathological example. Consider the following income distribution problem. There are three types, h^1, h^2, and h^3, each constituting one-third of the polity. A policy is an income distribution (x^1, x^2, x^3) such that $\frac{1}{3}x_1 + \frac{1}{3}x_2 + \frac{1}{3}x_3 = 1$. Thus, we may represent the policy space, T, as two-dimensional: $T = \{(x_2, x_3) \mid 0 \le x_2, 0 \le x_3, x_2 + x_3 \le 3\}$, with the understanding that $x_1 = 3 - (x_3 + x_2)$. The utility function of each type is just its income, x_i.

Let x and y be two policies. Suppose that the fraction of type 1 voters who vote for x over y is $1/2 + (\epsilon^1/2) f(\frac{y_1}{x_1})$ and the fraction of voters of type j voters, for $j = 2, 3$, who vote for x over y is $1/2 + (\epsilon^2/2) f(\frac{y_j}{x_j})$, $j = 1, 2$, where $f(x) = (1 - x)/(1 + x)$. We assume (as in section 2.4) that the $\mathbf{R}^2$-valued random variable (ϵ^1, ϵ^2) is uniformly distributed on the non-negative quadrant of the unit circle.

Let $a^1 = (1/3) f(y_1/x_1)$, $a^2 = (1/3) f(y_2/x_2) + (1/3) f(y_3/x_3)$. Then $\pi(x, y) = \text{Prob}(a^1 \epsilon^1 + a^2 \epsilon^2 \ge 0)$. Thus, referring to our analysis in section 2.4, we have

$$(7.13) \quad \pi(x, y) = \begin{cases} 1 & \text{if } a^1 > 0 \text{ and } a^2 > 0 \\ 1 - \frac{2}{\pi} \arctan\left(\frac{-a^2}{a^1}\right), & \text{if } a^1 > 0 \text{ and } a^2 < 0 \\ \frac{2}{\pi} \arctan\left(\frac{-a^2}{a^1}\right), & \text{if } a^1 < 0 \text{ and } a^2 > 0 \\ 0 & \text{if } a^1 < 0 \text{ and } a^2 < 0 \end{cases}$$

The values a^1 and a^2 are determined by the policies x and y. Fix y. Now consider the four sets of policies $(x_1, x_2) \in T$ which are associated with each of the four regions described in (7.13):

$$A^1 = \left\{(x_2, x_3) \in T \mid f\left(\frac{y_1}{x_1}\right) > 0 \text{ and } f\left(\frac{y_2}{x_2}\right) + f\left(\frac{y_3}{x_3}\right) > 0\right\},$$

$$A^2 = \left\{(x_2, x_3) \in T \mid f\left(\frac{y_1}{x_1}\right) > 0 \text{ and } f\left(\frac{y_2}{x_2}\right) + f\left(\frac{y_3}{x_3}\right) < 0\right\},$$

$$A^3 = \left\{(x_2, x_3) \in T \mid f\left(\frac{y_1}{x_1}\right) < 0 \text{ and } f\left(\frac{y_2}{x_2}\right) + f\left(\frac{y_3}{x_3}\right) > 0\right\},$$

$$A^4 = \left\{(x_2, x_3) \in T \mid f\left(\frac{y_1}{x_1}\right) < 0 \text{ and } f\left(\frac{y_2}{x_2}\right) + f\left(\frac{y_3}{x_3}\right) < 0\right\}.$$

From the definition of f, we compute that these regions are:

$$A^1 = \{(x_1, x_2) \in T \mid x_2 + x_3 < 3 - y_1, \quad \text{and} \quad x_2 x_3 > y_2 y_3\},$$

$$A^2 = \{(x_1, x_2) \in T \mid x_1 + x_3 < 3 - y_1, \quad \text{and} \quad x_2 x_3 < y_2 y_3\},$$

$$A^3 = \{(x_1, x_2) \in T \mid x_1 + x_3 > 3 - y_1, \quad \text{and} \quad x_2 x_3 > y_2 y_3\}, \text{ and}$$

$$A^4 = \{(x_1, x_2) \in T \mid x_1 + x_3 > 3 - y_1, \quad \text{and} \quad x_2 x_3 < y_2 y_3\}.$$

We display these four sets in Figure 7.2.

Now consider two potential policies by party 1, denoted x and x' in Figure 7.2. Since $\hat{x}$ is on the line segment $\overline{xx'}$, the quasi-concavity of $\pi(\cdot, y)$ requires that

$$(7.14) \qquad \pi(\hat{x}, y) \geq \min(\pi(x, y), \pi(x', y)).$$

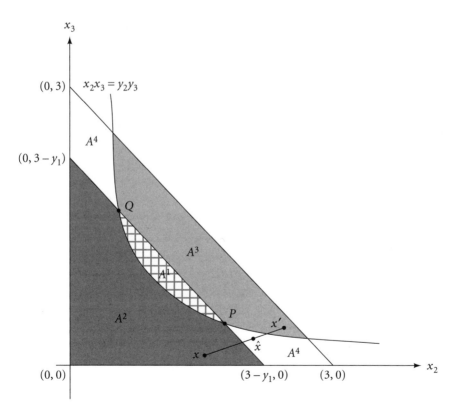

Figure 7.2

But $x \in A^2$ and $x' \in A^3$ imply that $\pi(x, y)$ and $\pi(x', y)$ are both positive (see (7.13)), while $\hat{x} \in A^4$ means that $\pi(\hat{x}, y) = 0$. Thus (7.14) is false, and so π is not quasi-concave in x.

Figure 7.2 also shows us that π is discontinuous at the two points P and Q. For if we approach P from a sequence of points in A^1, π is constantly one, while if we approach P from a sequence of points in A^4, π is constantly zero.

This example shows that with an entirely nonpathological model (the function v and the distribution $\mathbf{F}$ are well behaved), the payoff functions of the players in the Downs game with the finite-type model of uncertainty are not quasi-concave. Thus, the concavification of the payoff functions achieved in the Coughlin model fails to generalize when we introduce aggregate uncertainty.

Despite the failure of quasi-concavity, we will show that Downs equilibrium exists in a class of models of which the one studied above is an instance.

For simplicity of exposition, we continue to suppose that there are three types, where type i constitutes fraction ω^i of the citizenry. A policy is an income distribution (x_1, x_2, x_3) such that

$$(7.15) \qquad \sum \omega^i x_i = 1.$$

Type i citizens have a strictly concave, positive, differentiable utility function v^i of income. Facing policies x and y, the fraction who vote for x is

$$(7.16) \qquad \omega^1 \left(\frac{1}{2} + \frac{\epsilon^1}{2} f \left(\frac{v^1(y)}{v^1(x)} \right) \right) + \sum_{i=2}^{3} \omega^i \left(\frac{1}{2} + \frac{\epsilon^2}{2} f \left(\frac{v^i(y)}{v^i(x)} \right) \right),$$

where (ϵ^1, ϵ^2) is uniformly distributed on the non-negative quadrant of the unit disc in $\mathbf{R}^2$ and $f(X) = (1 - X)/(1 + X)$.

We have

Proposition 7.3 *Let $(\hat{y}, \lambda)$, where $\hat{y} \in \mathbf{R}^3$, be a non-negative solution of the equations*

$$(7.17) \qquad \lambda = \frac{v^{i\prime}(\hat{y}^i)}{4 v^i(\hat{y}^i)}, \qquad i = 1, 2, 3,$$

$$(7.15') \qquad \sum \omega^i \hat{y}^i = 1.$$

Then $(\hat{y}, \hat{y})$ is a Downs equilibrium of the above model.

Proof:
We know that the probability of victory of x against y is given by (7.13), where now

$$a^1 = \omega^1 f\left(\frac{v^1(y_1)}{v^1(x_1)}\right) \quad \text{and} \quad a^2 = \omega^2 f\left(\frac{v^2(y_2)}{v^2(x_2)}\right) + \omega^3 f\left(\frac{v^3(y_3)}{v^3(x_3)}\right).$$

Suppose (y, y) is a Nash equilibrium. Then for all policies x, we must have

(7.18) $a^1 + a^2 \leq 0,$

for (7.18) just says that the probability that x defeats y is at most $\frac{1}{2}$. We demonstrate this fact for the second case of (7.13). The inequality

$$1 - \frac{2}{\pi} \arctan\left(\frac{-a^2}{a^1}\right) \leq \frac{1}{2}$$

is equivalent to

$$\frac{\pi}{4} \leq \arctan\left(\frac{-a^2}{a^1}\right);$$

applying "tan" to both sides of this inequality gives

$$1 \leq \frac{-a^2}{a^1},$$

which is equivalent to (7.18), since $a^1 \geq 0$ in this case. The reader may verify the other cases.

Now we expand (7.18), which says

$$\sum \omega^i \left(\frac{v^i(x_i) - v^i(y_i)}{v^i(x_i) - v^i(y_i)}\right) \leq 0,$$

which is equivalent to

(7.19) $\displaystyle\sum \omega^i \left(\frac{v^i(x_i)}{v^i(x_i) + v^i(y_i)}\right) \leq \sum \omega^i \left(\frac{v^i(y_i)}{v^i(x_i) + v^i(y_i)}\right);$

noting that,

$$\frac{v^i(x_i)}{v^i(x_i) + v^i(y_i)} = 1 - \frac{v^i(y_i)}{v^i(x_i) + v^i(y_i)},$$

we can write (7.19) as

(7.20) $\quad \dfrac{1}{2} \leq \sum \omega^i \left(\dfrac{v^i(y_i)}{v^i(x_i) + v^i(y_i)} \right).$

Define the right-hand side of (7.20) to be the function $\Phi(x; y)$. We have just shown that (y, y) is a Downs equilibrium if and only if for all non-negative x satisfying (7.15),

$$\frac{1}{2} \leq \Phi(x; y).$$

We next note that Φ is a differentiable and convex function of x. (Convexity of Φ in x follows from the fact that the reciprocal of a positive concave function is convex.)

To show that a pair of policies (y, y) is a Downs equilibrium, it suffices to show that y is a local minimum of the function $\Phi(\cdot; y)$. Note that $\Phi(y; y) = \frac{1}{2}$, and employ the fact that a local minimum of a convex function on a convex domain is a global minimum.

Thus (y, y) is a Downs equilibrium if and only if y is a local minimum of $\Phi(\cdot; y)$. Define the constraint function

$$g(x) = 1 - \sum \omega^i x_i.$$

Then y is a local minimum of $\Phi(\cdot; y)$ iff

(7.21a) $\quad \nabla d \neq 0, \quad d \in \mathbf{R}^3, \quad \nabla \Phi(y; y) \cdot d < 0 \Rightarrow \nabla g \cdot d < 0,$

where $\nabla \Phi$ is the gradient of $\Phi(x; y)$ w.r.t. x. (7.21a) says that

(7.22b) $\quad \nabla \Phi(y; y) = \lambda \nabla g(y)$

for some $\lambda \geq 0$, which in turn reduces to

$$\frac{v^i(y_i)}{(2v^i(y_i))^2} v^i(y_i) = \lambda, \qquad \text{for all } i,$$

which in turn reduces to (7.17). ∎

Let us now apply Proposition 7.3 to the specific example we studied earlier in this section. There $v^i(x_i) = x_i$, and $\omega^1 = \omega^2 = \omega^3 = \frac{1}{3}$, and so (7.17) and (7.15′) reduce to

$$\frac{1}{4y_i} = \lambda, \qquad \sum y_i = 3,$$

which together imply that $y_1 = y_2 = y_3 = 1$, $\lambda = \frac{1}{2}$. Consequently $((1, 1, 1), (1, 1, 1))$ is a Downs equilibrium of that model despite the non-quasi-concavity of π.

The proof of Proposition 7.3 has shown more than its statement claims: namely, that any Downs equilibrium of the form (y, y) must satisfy equations (7.15′) and (7.17). We further observe that there is at most one solution for these equations. Note that the function $v^{i'}(y_i)/4v^i(y_i)$ is strictly decreasing in y^i. Thus, for given λ, there is at most one solution $y_i(\lambda)$ to (7.17), for each i. Furthermore, $\{y_i, (\lambda)\}$ are strictly decreasing in λ. Therefore there is at most one λ for which the equation

$$\sum \omega^i y_i(\lambda) = 1$$

holds. We may summarize: there is at most one simultaneous solution of the equations (7.15′) and (7.17), and that solution is the unique Downs equilibrium where both parties play the same policy.

What about the possibility of a Downs equilibrium where the parties play different policies? This cannot occur, as we show next.

Theorem 7.5 *In the above model, there is at most one Downs equilibrium. Both parties play the policy $\hat{y}$, where $\hat{y}$ is the unique solution (7.15′) and (7.17), if such exists.*

Proof:

1. Suppose that $(\hat{x}, \hat{y})$ were a Downs equilibrium where $\hat{x} \neq \hat{y}$. As usual, each party must win with probability $\frac{1}{2}$. Therefore we have

$$\hat{x} = \operatorname{argmin}_x \Phi(x; \hat{y})$$

and

$$\hat{y} = \operatorname{argmin}_y \Phi(y; \hat{x}).$$

(This follows from the analysis given in the proof of Proposition 7.3.)

2. Therefore, there exist positive numbers λ and μ such that

$$\nabla \Phi(\hat{x}; \hat{y}) = \lambda \nabla g(\hat{x})$$

and

$$\nabla \Phi(\hat{y}; \hat{x}) = \mu \nabla g(\hat{y})$$

which reduces to

$$\frac{v^i(\hat{y}_i)v^{i'}(\hat{x}_i)}{(v^i(\hat{x}_i) + v^i(\hat{y}_i))^2} = \lambda, \qquad \text{for all } i,$$

$$\frac{v^i(\hat{x}_i)v^{i'}(\hat{y}_i)}{(v^i(\hat{x}_i) + v^i(\hat{y}_i))^2} = \mu, \qquad \text{for all } i,$$

which in turn imply

$$\frac{v^{i'}(\hat{x}_i)}{v^i(\hat{x}_i)} = \frac{\lambda}{\mu} \frac{v^{i'}(\hat{y}_i)}{v^i(\hat{y}_i)}, \qquad \text{for all } i.$$

Since the function $v^{i'}/v^i$ is strictly decreasing, it follows that

$$\frac{\lambda}{\mu} > 1 \Rightarrow \hat{y}_i > \hat{x}_i, \qquad \text{for all } i,$$

$$\frac{\lambda}{\mu} < 1 \Rightarrow \hat{y}_i < \hat{x}_i, \qquad \text{for all } i,$$

$$\frac{\lambda}{\mu} = 1 \Rightarrow \hat{y}_i = \hat{x}_i, \qquad \text{for all } i.$$

If either of the first two cases of the above three cases holds, then (7.15′) is violated for one of $\{x, y\}$, a contradiction. Therefore it must be that $\hat{x} = \hat{y}$, again a contradiction. ∎

Remark   The condition (7.17), which may be written

$$\frac{d}{dy^i} \log v^i(y_i) = 4\lambda, \qquad \text{for all } i,$$

characterizes the solution to the program

$$\max_{y} \sum \omega^i \log v^i(y_i)$$

$$\text{s.t.} \quad \sum \omega^i y_i = 1.$$

Thus the policy parties play at Downs equilibrium solves the program

$$\max_{y} \prod_{i=1}^{3} (v^i(y_i))^{\omega^i}, \qquad \text{s.t.} \quad \sum \omega^i y^i = 1.$$

Actually, this product of utilities is a well-defined social-welfare function in the present model, by which I mean the following. We may choose various profiles of utility functions (v^1, v^2, v^3) to represent the preferences of types in this model, but it must be the case that the *ratios* $v^i(y_i)/v^i(x_i)$ are invariant (for fixed x_i and y_i), for otherwise the numbers $f(v^i(y_i)/v^i(x_i))$ would not be meaningful. Therefore, utility is implicitly assumed to be *cardinally measurable and ratio-scale comparable* in this model, which means that each utility function is defined up to a positive multiplicative constant; call the constant γ^i. Now note that the solution of

$$\hat{y} = \text{argmax}_{y} \prod_{i=1}^{3} (\gamma^i v^i(y_i^i))^{\omega^i}$$

is invariant as we change the (positive) numbers γ^i. Therefore, $\prod (v^i)^{\omega^i}$ is a well-defined social welfare function in our model. For clarification of this social-choice-theoretic remark, the reader may consult Roemer (1996, chap. 1).

Suppose $v^i(0) = 0$ for all i. Then the solution of

$$\max_y \prod_{i=1}^{3} (v^i(y_i))^{\omega^i}$$

is exactly the *Nash bargaining solution* of the game among the three types, where each type has "bargaining power" proportional to its numbers and the disagreement point entails no income for anyone. (See Roemer 1996, chap. 2, for a discussion of the Nash bargaining solution.)

If one believes that the "fair" income distribution is characterized as the outcome of this bargaining problem—some may, but I do not—then our theorem displays a pleasant conclusion, that democracy, here viewed as political competition à la Downs, engenders a fair outcome.

This curiosum may be contrasted with the situation in the Coughlin and Lindbeck-Weibull models. Those authors show that the respective Downs equilibria in their models maximize a utilitarian social-welfare function.

7.6 Conclusion

We have shown that, with the state-space and error-distribution models of uncertainty, (interior) Downs equilibrium generically fails to exist when the policy space is multidimensional. Coughlin and Lindbeck-Weibull proved the existence of a Downs equilibrium in multidimensional policy spaces for an "income distribution" model. In their model, however, aggregate uncertainty disappears when the polity is large. We modified the Coughlin model to endow it with aggregate uncertainty for large polities, which required using the finite-type model of uncertainty, and we showed that, in a (generic) class of income-distribution models, a Downs equilibrium does exist, despite the fact that the objective functions of the parties are not quasi-concave. The unique Downs equilibrium of those models has both parties playing the same policy.

8

Party Factions and Nash Equilibrium

8.1 Introduction

We have shown that, with two of our three models of uncertainty, Downs equilibrium fails to exist when the issue space is multidimensional. And as we will see in section 8.5, with multidimensional issue spaces, Wittman equilibrium often fails to exist. Researchers have responded to the nonexistence of Nash equilibrium in pure strategies in the multidimensional game in five ways:

• The mixed-strategy approach
• The sequential game approach
• The institutional approach
• The uncovered set approach
• The cycling approach

I shall briefly discuss each of these in turn.

It is often the case that, even if pure strategy Nash equilibria fail to exist, mixed strategy equilibria do exist in the multidimensional game. If one adopts the mixed strategy approach, then one must argue that, in the real world, parties play mixed strategies—that is, flip a complex coin to decide what policy to announce. No one seriously argues that parties literally do this, but some game theorists argue that parties nevertheless can be viewed as playing mixed strategies, as follows. Suppose that each party does not know for certain the *type* of the other party—that is, the other party's preferences. Each party has only a probability distribution over the other party's type. Each party can compute how the other party will respond to its own policy, for every type that it may be, and this induces a "mixed strategy"—that is, party 1 views party 2 as responding with a probability distribution over strategies, induced by the probability distribution that party 1 has over party 2's type. The appropriate concept of equilibrium, in this case, is a mixed-strategy equilibrium.

The problem with this approach, I think, is that it flies in the face of reality. Parties are *public institutions*, which is to say their preferences are known—at least this is a good first approximation. In my view, the mixed-strategy approach distorts reality for the sake of achieving existence of equilibrium.

The second approach is to change the game played between parties to a sequential game, and to use subgame perfect Nash equilibrium, or one of its refinements, as the equilibrium concept. The simplest such game is a two-stage game, where, let's say, the challenger moves first and the incumbent party moves second. Here subgame perfect Nash equilibrium is called Stackelberg equilibrium—the second player plays its best response to the first player, who takes this into account in proposing his policy. Stackelberg equilibrium generally exists in the multidimensional, two-party game.

But perhaps it is the incumbent who should move first and the challenger second? Indeed, is there a natural order for the two parties to move in? I think not. Those who have studied party manifestos argue that policies that parties announce in elections are close to their manifestos—indeed, that the party manifesto can be taken to be the policy of the party. (See Klingermann, Hofferbert, and Budge 1994.) And manifestos are written approximately simultaneously. (Recall that we have previously explained the uncertainty that parties have about the outcome of the election as uncertainty at the time manifestos are written, some time prior to the election.) If this is so, then it is more appropriate to model the game as one of simultaneous moves.

The third approach, which has become important in political science, is to recognize that political decisions are made in a complex institutional framework. This approach has been applied especially to decision making, and political competition, in legislatures. I conjecture that this approach is (almost) always a special case of the sequential-game approach; the set of players may, for instance, consist of committees, which move in an established sequence. Although this approach may solve the problem of legislative behavior, it is not clear that it solves the problem of competitive, popular elections. Of course, the existence of legislatures means that it is incorrect, strictly speaking, to assume that the policy of the winning party in an election will be implemented, for legislation is a process that occurs after the election. Nevertheless, if elections are "the central act of democracy" (Riker 1982, 5), then the modeler should not abdicate from modeling them as they appear to be, namely, as simultaneous-move games between parties.

The fourth approach generalizes the set of Condorcet winners in a policy space. A policy t is said to *cover* a policy r if a majority of voters prefer t to

r, and for any policy z, if a majority prefer z to t, then a majority prefer z to r. The _uncovered set_ is the set of policies that are covered by no policy. If the set of Condorcet winners is nonempty, then it coincides with the uncovered set. But the uncovered set is nonempty even if Condorcet winners fail to exist. Advocates of using the uncovered set as a solution concept in the Downs game argue that a rational player would only play a strategy in the uncovered set. For suppose a player plays a policy r which is covered by a policy t. Then r is "dominated" by t, in the sense that t defeats r _and_ any policy that defeats t defeats r. If all covered elements are thus dominated, then a player should restrict itself to playing uncovered elements.

But this argument fails to hold water, because even uncovered elements can be defeated by other policies, if the Condorcet set is empty. The argument actually says, "_If_ a party plays any policy, it might as well play an uncovered one," but it fails to show that there is _any_ policy the party _should_ play. In any case, one should observe that the uncovered set only generalizes the set of Downs equilibria, not the set of Wittman equilibria, so it is of no help if we believe that parties are of the Wittman variety. (There may be a version of uncoveredness for the Wittman game, but it would suffer as well from the criticism just enunciated.)

Finally, it has been fairly common for researchers to take the nonexistence of Downs equilibrium in the multidimensional game as the end of the matter, and content themselves with studying cycling.[1] Cycling is what presumably occurs if there is no Nash equilibrium in a game: parties enter an unending sequence of moves in which each party plays a best response to the other party's last move.

If, however, one believes that electoral competition is reasonably thought of as a simultaneous-move game by "public" parties, then one should not settle for any of these solutions. The methodological premise of the equilibrium theorist is that if a model produces no equilibrium, while the real situation it attempts to describe involves a pair of stable moves by the two actors, then the model is misconceived. I must underscore (for those skeptical of the equilibrium method) that this methodological premise does not exhibit a blind attachment to equilibrium theory: the "while" clause in the previous sentence is key in justifying the search for an equilibrium explanation of the phenomenon.

---

1. For a concise history of how analysts have responded to cycling, see Hinich and Munger (1997), 64–71.

We are thus directed back to reformulating the party-competition game, somehow, so that a Nash equilibrium in pure strategies exists. One avenue that remains potentially open is to alter the preferences of the parties (from Wittman or Downs payoff functions to something else) so that Nash equilibrium exists. This is the tack we shall pursue.

8.2 Party Factions

We begin by observing that, in reality, parties rarely act as unitary actors—they are composed of factions, which struggle internally over the line of the party. More specifically, we shall argue that parties typically consist of three factions: the reformists, the opportunists, and the militants. (In particular cases, there may be fewer or more factions, but these three seem almost ubiquitous.) The opportunists are those who use the party only as a vehicle for a career; their objective is to maximize the probability of the party's victory in the election. Reformists are the political actors of the Wittman model: they wish to maximize the expected utility of the party. If the utility function of the party is, for example, the utility function of the constituency of the party, or of an interest group whom the party represents, then the reformists are the perfect agents of that constituency or interest group, in the sense that they maximize its expected utility. The militants are those who wish to announce a policy as close as possible to the ideal policy of the interest group. If you will, they are not focused upon the outcome of the election at hand; rather, they wish to use the election as a pulpit for advertising the party's views. To summarize, the opportunists are interested in *winning;* the reformists are interested in *policies;* and the militants are interested in *publicity.*

We formalize this as follows. Let T be the policy space, and let v^1 and v^2 be the vNM utility functions of the parties defined on T, as in the Wittman model. Let $\pi : T \times T \to \mathbf{R}$ be the probability that t^1 defeats t^2. Each of the three factions of each party is endowed with a preference order on $T \times T$, denoted respectively by $\succeq_R$, $\succeq_O$, and $\succeq_M$. These orders, for the factions of party 1, are given by

$$(t^1, t^2) \succeq_R (s^1, s^2) \quad \text{iff}$$

$$\pi(t^1, t^2)v^1(t^1) + (1 - \pi(t^1, t^2))v^1(t^2) \geq \pi(s^1, s^2)v^1(s^1) + (1 - \pi(s^1, s^2))v^1(s^2);$$

$$(t^1, t^2) \succeq_O (s^1, s^2) \quad \text{iff} \quad \pi(t^1, t^2) \geq \pi(s^1, s^2); \quad \text{and}$$

$$(t^1, t^2) \succeq_M (s^1, s^2) \quad \text{iff} \quad v^1(t^1) \geq v^1(s^1).$$

Each of these orders is a binary relation on $T \times T$: that is, it is associated with a set of points in $(T \times T)^2$. (For example, we say that $((t^1, t^2), (s^1, s^2)) \in O$ iff $\pi(t^1, t^2) \geq \pi(s^1, s^2)$.)

We now define the preference relation of party 1 as the intersection of these three binary relations. This will be a quasi-order on $T \times T$, that is, an *incomplete* preference relation. Informally, this amounts to saying that the *party* weakly prefers (t^1, t^2) to (s^1, s^2) iff all three of its factions weakly prefer (t^1, t^2) to (s^1, s^2), and it (strictly) prefers (t^1, t^2) to (s^1, s^2) iff all three of its factions weakly prefer (t^1, t^2) to (s^1, s^2) and at least one faction (strictly) prefers (t^1, t^2) to (s^1, s^2). Denote party i's quasi-preference order on $T \times T$ by Π^i; now, Π^i is not a function, as in our earlier theories, but a binary relation , that is, a set in $(T \times T)^2$. Conventionally, we denote the fact that party i weakly prefers (t^1, t^2) to (s^1, s^2) by $(t^1, t^2)\Pi^i(s^1, s^2)$.

The reason the party's preferences are incomplete is that there will be (many) pairs of points in $T \times T$—(t^1, t^2) and (s^1, s^2)—such that two factions prefer (t^1, t^2) to (s^1, s^2) and one prefers (s^1, s^2) to (t^1, t^2), and so the *party* has no order on these two pairs.

We now have two parties with preference relations on $T \times T$. We define:

Definition 8.1   A policy pair (t^1, t^2) is a *party-unanimity Nash equilibrium (PUNE)* iff it is a Nash equilibrium of the game (Π^1, Π^2, T); that is, for all $s \in T$,

$$(t^1, t^2)\Pi^1(s, t^2) \quad \text{and} \quad (t^1, t^2)\Pi^2(t^1, s).$$

In English, this says that a policy pair is a PUNE iff neither party's factions can unanimously agree to alter their party's proposal, given the policy played by the opposition party. For factions to unanimously agree to deviate from their party's proposed policy, it must be that all three factions weakly prefer the proposed deviation, and at least one (strongly) prefers it, given the play by the opposition.

Note that deviations are much less likely to occur in this game than in the game played between two parties where the *sole faction* is the reformist faction—for in this game, three different preference orders have to be satisfied for the deviation to be implemented, whereas in the Wittman game, only the reformists have to be satisfied. So we should expect that there will be more Nash equilibria in this game than in the Wittman game played on the same policy space. Similarly, the Downs game is one played between two parties whose sole factions are opportunists, and so we should expect more equilibria in this game than in the Downs game.

In fact, we have the following.

Definition 8.2 A Downs equilibrium (t^1, t^2) is *strict* iff for all $s \in T, s \neq t^1, \pi(s, t^2) < \frac{1}{2}$ and for all $s \in T, s \neq t^2, \pi(t^1, s) > \frac{1}{2}$. A Wittman equilibrium (t^1, t^2) is *regular* if $0 < \pi(t^1, t^2) < 1$ and $v^1(t^1) > v^1(t^2)$ and $v^2(t^2) > v^2(t^1)$.

Let the Downs game, the Wittman game, and the three-faction game be denoted by G^D, G^W, and G^{ROM}. Let the Nash equilibria of the *ROM* game be denoted $N(G^{ROM})$. Further, denote by G^{OM} the game where unanimity of factions is required for deviation, but there are only two internal factions in each party, the militants and the opportunists, and denote its Nash equilibria by $N(G^{OM})$. Denote by $SN(G^D)$ the strict Nash equilibria of the Downs game, and by $RN(G^W)$ the regular Wittman equilibria. Then we have

Theorem 8.1

(1) $RN(G^W) \subset N(G^{ROM})$;
(2) $SN(G^D) \subset N(G^{ROM})$;
(3) $N(G^{ROM}) = N(G^{OM})$.

Proof:

1. Proof of (1). Let (t^1, t^2) be a regular Nash equilibrium of the Wittman game. Now consider the *ROM* game. By definition, there is no policy s to which the reformists in party 1 would like to deviate. Therefore, if party 1 can find a deviation s agreeable to all three of its factions, it must be that the opportunists and the militants in party 1 both weakly prefer (s, t^2) to (t^1, t^2), and at least one of them (strictly) prefers (s, t^2) to (t^1, t^2). This means that

$$\pi(s, t^2) \geq \pi(t^1, t^2) \quad \text{and} \quad v^1(s) \geq v^1(t^1),$$

and at least one of these inequalities is strict. But this implies, since $\pi(t^1, t^2) > 0$ and $v^1(t^1) - v^1(t^2) > 0$ (by regularity), that

(8.1) $$\pi(s, t^2)(v^1(s) - v^1(t^2)) > \pi(t^1, t^2)(v^1(t^1) - v^1(t^2)).$$

But (8.1) is equivalent to saying that the reformist faction of party 1 strictly prefers (s, t^2) to (t^1, t^2), which contradicts the supposition that (t^1, t^2) is a Wittman equilibrium.

This proves that there is no policy s to which all three of party 1's factions can agree to deviate. A similar argument shows that there is no policy to which all three of party 2's factions can agree to deviate from t^2, while facing t^1. Hence (t^1, t^2) is a *PUNE*.

2. Proof of (2). If (t^1, t^2) is a strict Downs equilibrium, then there is no policy s that the opportunist faction in either party will agree to deviate to. Hence (t^1, t^2) is a *PUNE*.

3. Proof of (3). First, we show that $N(G^{ROM}) \supset N(G^{OM})$. Let $(t^1, t^2) \in N(G^{OM})$, but suppose there is a policy s that the three factions of party 1 can agree to deviate to. Then it must be that the R faction in party 1 strictly prefers (s, t^2) to (t^1, t^2) and both the O and the M factions in 1 are indifferent between (s, t^2) and (t^1, t^2). But if O and M are indifferent between (s, t^2) and (t^1, t^2), it is easy to compute that the R faction must also be indifferent. This is a contradiction, which proves this direction.

We now show that that $N(G^{ROM}) \subset N(G^{OM})$. Let $(t^1, t^2) \in N(G^{ROM})$, but suppose there is a policy s that factions O and M, in party 1, can agree to deviate to (that is, both weakly prefer (s, t^2) to (t^1, t^2) and one strictly prefers the former to the latter). Then it is immediate to see that the R faction strictly prefers (s, t^2) to (t^1, t^2), contradicting the assumption that $(t^1, t^2) \in N(G^{ROM})$. This proves the claim. ∎

The first two statements in this proposition say, in English, that "strict Downs" is a refinement of PUNE, and "regular Wittman" is a refinement of PUNE—or equivalently, that PUNE is an extension of those two equilibrium concepts. Therefore, even if strict Downs and regular Wittman equilibria should fail to exist, the door is still open for PUNE to exist.

The third statement says that, as far as the concept of PUNE is concerned, the reformist faction is gratuitous. Mathematically, we can forget about the reformists as far as characterization of PUNE is concerned. This does not mean that reformists do not exist in actual politics: rather, that *if* PUNE is the appropriate characterization of political equilibrium, then the existence of reformists will not narrow the set of equilibria over what would have occurred with only militants and opportunists in the parties. As we shall see, the fact that reformists are "gratuitous" in the game G^{ROM} allows us to simplify the mathematical characterization of equilibrium.

Another interesting consequence follows from statement (3) of the theorem. The concept of Wittman equilibrium is a *cardinal concept*, by which is meant the following. The Wittman game presupposes as data, preferences over lotteries on T for each party—that is, vNM utility functions v^1 and v^2 defined on T. Now consider a Wittman game with vNM utility functions u^1 and u^2 on T, where u^i is some *nonlinear* strictly increasing transformation of v^i. That is, each party, in these two games has *different* preferences over the lotteries on T, although its induced preferences on sure policies in T are identical in the two games. It will (generically) be the case that the Wittman equilibria of the games (v^1, v^2, T) and (u^1, u^2, T) are different.

But the PUNEs associated with these two games are identical. For to compute the PUNEs of a game, we can discard the reformist factions, and the militants (in each party) in the games (v^1, v^2, T) and (u^1, u^2, T) have the *same* preferences—militants do not evaluate lotteries, they only evaluate utility on single policies in T! In other words, PUNE is an *ordinal concept*; to compute PUNEs, we need only the ordinal preferences of the militants on T (and the ordinal preferences of the opportunists on $T \times T$).

It is time to consider a criticism of the party-unanimity idea, the idea that all three factions must agree when considering whether to deviate from a proposed policy to an alternative, facing a given proposal by the opposition party. The criticism maintains that the unanimity requirement is too strong; rather, one should substitute a weaker condition sufficient for deviation, such as "two out of three factions agree to deviate," or "the factions bargain to a compromise position when facing the opposition's policy."

The first of these alternative formulations again lands us in the undesirable situation that Nash equilibrium fails to exist. Let us suppose that a party will deviate from a proposed policy, facing a fixed policy from the opposition, if two out of three of its factions can find a preferable alternative (always meaning that two factions weakly prefer the alternative, and one strictly prefers it). We then can define a *two-faction Nash equilibrium* as a pair (t^1, t^2) such that no pair of factions in either party can find an agreeable deviation. I claim that a two-faction Nash equilibrium (t^1, t^2) is a Wittman equilibrium. For suppose not, which means that the reformists in, say, party 1, strictly prefer the pair (s, t^2) to the pair (t^1, t^2), for some s. We also know that *both* the opportunists and the militants in party 1 strictly prefer (t^1, t^2) to (s, t^2), for if not, then the reformists and one other faction would agree to deviate to s from t^1, which contradicts the premise that (t^1, t^2) is a two-faction equilibrium. But if both the opportunists and the militants strictly prefer (t^1, t^2) to (s, t^2), then algebra quickly shows that the reformists cannot prefer (s, t^2) to (t^1, t^2): a contradiction.

Thus a two-faction equilibrium is a Wittman equilibrium, and as Wittman equilibria often fail to exist (see section 8.5), two-faction equilibrium does not solve our existence problem.

We briefly postpone the discussion of bargaining among factions.

There is, as well, a completely different story that leads precisely to the concept of PUNE, although the name "party unanimity" does not describe this story. Suppose the party is a unitary actor, of the Wittman variety: it would like to maximize its expected utility. The party, however, is boundedly rational, in the following sense. Neither party, i, can write down the function π or the function v^i. However, given a policy t^2, for any pair of policies t and s, party 1 can say which of s or t has the greater probability of defeating t^2. (And a symmetric statement holds for party 2.) Further, given any two policies s and t, party i can say which of the two it prefers. Therefore, the party is limited to comparisons of the following kind. Given any policies s, t, and t^2, party 1 says it prefers the electoral situation (s, t^2) to the electoral situation (t, t^2) when (1) s has a higher probability than t of defeating t^2, and (2) it prefers policy s to t. Failing either condition (1) or (2), the party then considers whether it prefers the situation (t, t^2) to (s, t^2). If not, then it cannot rank s and t, as responses to t^2.

We now define Nash equilibrium in the usual way: a policy pair (t^1, t^2) is a *boundedly rational* Nash equilibrium iff there is no electoral situation (s, t^2) that party 1 prefers to (t^1, t^2), and there is no situation (t^1, s) that party 2 prefers to (t^1, t^2). The reader will immediately observe that such an equilibrium is exactly a PUNE: for the two tests that bounded rationality permits are precisely the tests for deviation by the opportunists and the militants, in our first story. By Theorem 8.1, statement (3), it follows that boundedly rational equilibria are precisely PUNEs.

Finally, a brief historical excursus. In describing the internal struggles in the German Social Democratic Party during the first twenty years of the twentieth century, Carl Schorske ([1955] 1993) refers to the party bureaucracy, the trade union leadership, and the radicals (Karl Kautsky, Rosa Luxemburg). His description of the goals of these three factions fits the description given here for the opportunists, the reformists, and the militants, respectively. The bureaucracy was primarily interested in winning elections, the trade union leadership was interested in winning reforms for workers, and the radicals were interested in propagating the line. Regarding the radicals, Schorske writes, " 'No new taxes, but reduction of armaments!' They [the radicals] saw it as the duty of the party to carry this message to the people, to make them understand that the fight against imperialism came first and foremost" (161).

James Schlesinger (1991) describes political parties as organizations formed by benefit seekers (party members) and office seekers (candidates). The party organization is characterized by tensions between those two groups. He concludes, however, that in general parties are ruled by office seekers, and a "principal-agent" relationship characterizes the connection between benefit seekers and officeholders. Schlesinger writes: "In democratic politics, no party consists solely of office seekers or benefit seekers. Rather, conflicts arise within parties because the two goals can impose conflicting views of how to win elections and, ultimately, conflicting views of how parties should be organized" (148).

Aaron Wildavsky (1965) describes the 1964 U.S. presidential election and, specifically, why Republicans chose Goldwater as their candidate despite the belief that he had no chance to win. His conclusion is that, because of the particular circumstances, "purists" were able to control the party and impose their candidate. There are many quotations that describe purists' behavior and present them as militants. For example: "The distinguishing characteristics of the purists: their emphasis on internal criteria for decision, on what they believe 'deep down inside'; their rejection of compromise; their lack of orientation toward winning; their stress on the style and purity of decision—integrity, consistency, adherence to internal norms" (395).

In contrast with purists, "politicians" are characterized by "the belief in compromise and bargaining; the sense that public policy is made in small steps rather than big leaps; the concern with conciliating the opposition and broadening public appeal; and the willingness to bend a little to capture public support" (396). This sounds like the behavior of reformists, although Wildavsky does not characterize politicians as behaving strategically with respect to the opposition party.

Although we can readily understand the psychology of opportunists and reformists—they are, after all, the creatures of the Downs and Wittman models—what explains the modus vivendi of militants? I think militants can only be understood in a dynamic context. Their goal is to change the preferences of some voters, and to do this, they argue for putting forth a position close to the ideal point of the preference order represented by v^i, for in so doing they will have to argue why that policy is correct. According to this view, the difference between the reformists and the militants is one of time rates of discount: reformists want to do the best they can for their constituency today, while militants adopt the strategy of changing the preferences of voters, so that when they win at some future date, it can be with a better policy.

8.3 PUNE as a Bargaining Equilibrium

In the literature to date, and thus far in this book, a Wittman equilibrium has been conceived of as a Nash equilibrium between two parties each of which is a unitary actor: each party maximizes its expected utility. But we now demonstrate that Wittman equilibrium can be viewed, equally well, as an equilibrium between parties with factions that bargain with one another.

Think of two parties, each composed of the three factions we have introduced. Each faction has preferences on $T \times T$. Party 1's opportunists have von Neumann–Morgenstern preferences represented by the (vNM) utility function $O^1(t^1, t^2) = \pi(t^1, t^2)$, its militants have von Neumann–Morgenstern preferences represented by the (vNM) utility function $M^1(t^1, t^2) = v^1(t^1)$, and its reformists have von Neumann–Morgenstern preferences represented by the (vNM) utility function $R^1(t^1, t^2) = \pi(t^1, t^2)v^1(t^1) + (1 - \pi(t^1, t^2))v^1(t^2)$. We do not write down the analogous utility functions for party 2's factions.

Suppose that party 2 proposes policy t^2. The three factions of party 1 now bargain to an equilibrium: we take Nash bargaining as the procedure. What are the impasse utilities, the utilities of the various factions should party 1 fail to come to an agreement? In that case, party 2 wins the election by default; hence the probability of victory for party 1 is zero. Since policy t^2 would be the only policy in the field, only it will be publicized; hence party 1's militants receive a utility of $v^1(t^2)$. The Nash bargaining solution[2] between these two factions is the policy t that maximizes the "Nash product":

$$(8.2a) \quad \max_{t \in T}(\pi(t, t^2) - 0)(v^1(t) - v^1(t^2)).$$

The solution to this problem also maximizes $\pi(t, t^2)v^1(t) + (1 - \pi(t, t^2))v^1(t^2)$, which is the payoff of the reformists in party 1, given the opposition policy t^2— so they are completely satisfied with the bargain reached between the militants and the opportunists.

---

2. For discussion of the Nash bargaining solution, see, for instance, Roemer (1996, section 2.2).

Similarly, facing a policy t^1 from party 1, party 2's opportunists and militants Nash-bargain to a policy t that solves

(8.2b) $\max_{t \in T}((1 - \pi(t^1, t)) - 0)(v^2(t) - v^2(t^1)))$.

The solution of (8.2b) also maximizes the utility of party 2's reformists, facing t^1 from the opposition.

We now define an *unweighted Nash-bargaining equilibrium* in the two-party game as a pair of policies (t^1, t^2) such that, facing t^2, party 1's factions Nash-bargain to t^1, and facing t^1, party 2's factions Nash-bargain to t^2. We have just demonstrated that *an unweighted Nash-bargaining equilibrium is precisely a Wittman equilibrium.*

Thus we may interpret Wittman equilibrium, when it exists—as in the unidimensional model—as a faction bargaining solution. But as Wittman equilibrium may not exist when policy spaces are multidimensional, so we *weaken* the concept of bargaining from Nash bargaining to the mere requirement that, facing the policy of the opposition party, there is no policy that all factions of our party prefer to the one on the table. This is the definition of PUNE.

Thus PUNE can be regarded as a generalization of Wittman equilibrium. In other words, we do not introduce party factions only in the multidimensional problem: they exist as well in the unidimensional problem and engender, there, the Wittman equilibrium.

Indeed, we can go further, and view PUNE as a *weighted* Nash bargaining solution. Suppose that the bargaining process between party 1's opportunists and militants, facing a proposal t^2, resolves to

(8.3a) $t^1 = \underset{t}{\operatorname{argmax}}(\pi(t, t^2) - 0)^{\alpha^1}(v^1(t) - v^1(t^2))^{\beta^1}$,

and that, facing t^1, party 2's bargaining process resolves to

(8.3b) $t^2 = \underset{t}{\operatorname{argmax}}(1 - \pi(t^1, t))^{\alpha^2}(v^2(t) - v^2(t^1))^{\beta^2}$,

where $\alpha^1, \beta^1, \alpha^2$, and β^2 are positive numbers. Define a policy pair (t^1, t^2) satisfying (8.3a,b) to be a *Nash bargaining solution with weights* $((\alpha^1, \beta^1), (\alpha^2, \beta^2))$. It is obvious that if the products in (8.3a,b) are both positive at the solution, then (t^1, t^2) is a regular PUNE, for it is impossible to make either the opportunists or the militants in either party better off without reducing the utility of the other faction. The interesting question is the converse: when can we say that a PUNE is a weighted Nash bargaining solution?

Let us first note that we can view the bargaining process modeled in (8.3a,b) as including the reformist factions. If all three factions in party 1, say, participate in the bargaining process, then the weighted Nash solution would maximize

$$\pi(t, t^2)^\alpha (v^1(t) - v^1(t^2))^\beta (\pi(t, t^2)(v^1(t) - v^1(t^2)))^\gamma,$$

which reduces to the representation (8.3a), with $\alpha^1 = \alpha + \gamma$ and $\beta^1 = \beta + \gamma$.

Define

$$\Delta^1(t^2) = \{t \mid \pi(t, t^2) > 0 \quad \text{and} \quad v^1(t) - v^1(t^2) > 0\},$$

$$\Delta^2(t^1) = \{t \mid 1 - \pi(t^1, t) > 0 \quad \text{and} \quad v^2(t) - v^2(t^1) > 0\}.$$

These sets were called the *decent responses* by parties 1 and 2, respectively, in Chapter 3.

Assumption A $\text{Log}(\pi(\cdot), t^2)$ *and* $\text{Log}(v^1(\cdot) - v^1(t^2))$ *are concave functions on* T; $\text{Log}(1 - \pi(t^1, \cdot))$ *and* $\text{Log}(v^2(\cdot) - v^2(t^1))$ *are concave functions on* T.

Note that the assumption of log concavity of π has been used before—see Corollary 3.2.

Theorem 8.2   *Let* $(t^1, t^2) \in T \times T$ *be a regular PUNE at which Assumption A holds. Then* (t^1, t^2) *is a weighted Nash bargaining solution.*

Proof:
Let

$$U^1(t^2) = \{(\text{Log } \pi(t, t^2), \text{Log}(v^1(t) - v^1(t^2))) \mid t \in \Delta^1(t^2)\},$$

and

$$U^2(t^1) = \{(\text{Log}(1 - \pi(t^1, t)), \text{Log}(v^2(t) - v^2(t^1))) \mid t \in \Delta^2(t^1)\}.$$

By Assumption A, these two sets in $\mathbf{R}^2$ are convex. Because (t^1, t^2) is a PUNE, the point $P = (\text{Log } \pi(t^1, t^2), v^1(t^1) - v^1(t^2))$ lies on the boundary of $U^1(t^2)$, as

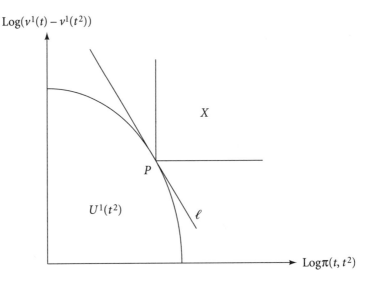

Figure 8.1   The proof of Theorem 8.2

shown in Figure 8.1. Let the set X, as depicted in the figure, consist of all points to the northeast of P. There is a line, ℓ, separating these two convex sets: let its equation be $\alpha^1 x + \beta^1 y = k$. Then it is clear from the figure that t^1 maximizes

$$\alpha^1 \operatorname{Log} \pi(t, t^2) + \beta^1 \operatorname{Log}(v^1(t) - v^1(t^2))$$

on $\Delta^1(t^2)$. Taking anti-logs, we have

$$t^1 = \operatorname*{argmax}_{t \in \Delta^1(t^2)} \pi(t, t^2)^{\alpha^1} (v^1(t) - v^1(t^2))^{\beta^1}.$$

In like manner, we deduce:

$$t^2 = \operatorname*{argmax}_{t \in \Delta^2(t^1)} (1 - \pi(t^1, t))^{\alpha^2} (v^2(t) - v^2(t^1))^{\beta^2}.$$

Thus (t^1, t^2) is a weighted Nash bargaining solution.   ■

Thus, at least when Assumption A holds, we can say that PUNEs are exactly equilibria in which the factions in each party are engaging in a Nash bargaining game.

8.4 A Differential Characterization of PUNE

There is a simple differential characterization of PUNE using Farkas' lemma (see the Mathematical Appendix), which is a version of the "separating hyperplane theorem." We shall use this characterization of PUNE in much of the rest of the book.

We suppose the data (v^1, v^2, π, T), where $T \subset \mathbf{R}^n$. We suppose that (t^1, t^2) is a PUNE which is interior in $T \times T$, and in which neither the militant nor the opportunist faction of either party is at an ideal point. Suppose further that v^i are differentiable and that π is differentiable at (t^1, t^2). Denote by ∇v^i the gradient vector of v^i, a vector in $\mathbf{R}^n$, by $\nabla_1 \pi$ the gradient vector of π with respect to t^1, and by $\nabla_2 \pi$ the gradient vector of π with respect to t^2. Let $d \in \mathbf{R}^n$ be any direction. (So $d \neq 0$.) Then it follows that

(8.4a) $\quad \nabla v^1(t^1) \cdot d > 0 \quad$ implies $\quad \nabla_1 \pi(t^1, t^2) \cdot d \leq 0, \quad$ and

(8.4b) $\quad \nabla v^2(t^2) \cdot d > 0 \quad$ implies $\quad \nabla_2 \pi(t^1, t^2) \cdot d \geq 0.$

Statement (8.4a) says that if a move in direction d from t^1 increases the utility of party 1's militants, then it must decrease the utility of party 1's opportunists, and statement (8.4b) says exactly the same thing for party 2. If either (8.4a) or (8.4b) failed for some direction d, then (t^1, t^2) would not be a PUNE, for both the militants and the opportunists in some party could find an agreeable, small deviation in that direction.

Now (8.4a) can be rewritten:

(8.5) $\quad \forall d \neq 0, \quad d \in \mathbf{R}^n, \quad \nabla v^1(t^1) \cdot d > 0 \quad$ implies $\quad -\nabla_1 \pi(t^1, t^2) \cdot d \geq 0.$

Statements (8.5) and (8.4b) imply, by Farkas' lemma, that $\nabla v^1(t^1)$ is a non-negative multiple of $-\nabla_1 \pi(t^1, t^2)$ and that $\nabla v^2(t^2)$ is a non-negative multiple of $\nabla_2 \pi(t^1, t^2)$; in other words, there are non-negative numbers λ and μ such that

(8.6a) $\quad \nabla v^1(t^1) = \lambda \nabla_1 \pi(t^1, t^2)$

and

(8.6b) $\quad \nabla v^2(t^2) = \mu \nabla_2 \pi(t^1, t^2).$

These are thus necessary conditions for (t^1, t^2) to be a PUNE of the stated type.[3]

Figure 8.2 illustrates. Here, the policy space is a simplex, T, in the three-dimensional space with coordinates (w, m, l). Point L is the policy of party 1 at a PUNE; it is interior in T. Equations (8.6a) and (8.6b) say that the indifference curves of v^1 and $\pi(\cdot, t^2)$ through t^1 are tangent: this is precisely the condition that there is no mutually attractive deviation to the two factions in party 1 (that is, no "lens" in the upper contour sets of both factions at t^1). Tangency of the two indifference curves (more generally, indifference surfaces) is characterized by their gradients' pointing in opposite directions, which is the content of (8.6a,b). There must be a similar picture for the policy of the other party at this PUNE.

What about sufficient conditions for a PUNE? Vector equations (8.6a) and (8.6b) constitute $2n$ equations in $2n + 2$ unknowns (t^1, t^2, λ and μ). Any solution with $\lambda \geq 0$ and $\mu \geq 0$ and $t^i \in T$ satisfies the *local* conditions for a PUNE: in sufficiently small neighborhoods of t^1 and t^2, there is no deviation by either party that all three of its factions prefer.[4] We cannot be guaranteed, however, that a point satisfying these two vector equations is a (global) PUNE without further curvature assumptions on the relevant functions. In particular, if the functions v^i are strictly quasi-concave (that is, single-peaked) and π is quasi-concave in t^1 and quasi-convex in t^2, then any "local PUNE" is a PUNE. But as we have seen in Chapter 6, the function π is generally not quasi-concave in our formulations of it. In Figure 8.2, the indifference curve of the militants outlines a convex upper contour set, but not so the indifference curve of the opportunists (since π is not quasi-concave in t^1).

The fact that (8.6 a and b) constitute $2n$ equations in $2n + 2$ unknowns means that either they possess no solution with non-negative λ and μ or they possess a continuum of acceptable solutions, a two-dimensional manifold of solutions— intuitively, a two-dimensional surface in $T \times T$. (There is only a degenerate case in which these equations possess a finite number of solutions.) As we shall see, in applications, we usually find ourselves in the latter situation.

---

3. Sometimes it is useful to compute PUNEs where one party's militant faction (for example) is at its ideal point. In this case, we replace equations (8.6ab) with the equation $\nabla v^1(t^1) = 0$.

4. It is important to note that conditions (8.6a and b) are stronger than "first-order conditions," in the sense that they guarantee that the point in question is a local equilibrium. First-order conditions, in contrast, only guarantee that the point in question is a stationary point—it could be a minimum, a saddle point, or a maximum of the function in question.

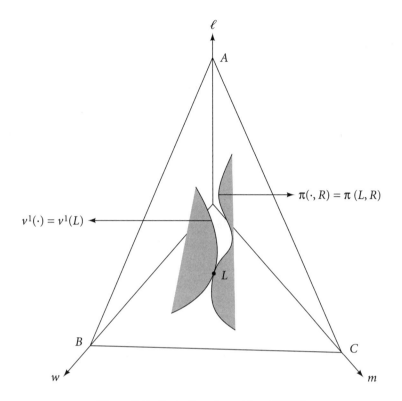

Figure 8.2 Party 1's policy at local PUNE

Finally, let us write down the separating-hyperplane condition for a policy pair (t^1, t^2) to be a PUNE, when the policy space is constrained. Suppose that the policy set T is characterized by a set of inequalities, of the form

$$g^k(t) \geq 0, k = 1, \ldots, z.$$

Furthermore, suppose the functions g^k are differentiable; we denote their gradients by ∇g^k. Suppose that at the PUNE (t^1, t^2), the following constraints are binding:

$$g^{k_1}(t^1) = g^{k_2}(t^1) = \ldots = g^{k_r}(t^1) = 0$$

and

(8.7) $g^{l_1}(t^2) = g^{l_2}(t^2) = \ldots = g^{l_s}(t^2) = 0.$

Then we have the following: if $d \neq 0$ is any direction in $\mathbf{R}^n$, then

(8.8a)
$$\nabla g^{k_1}(t^1) \cdot d > 0, \ldots, \nabla g^{k_r}(t^1) \cdot d > 0,$$
$$\nabla v^1(t^1) \cdot d > 0 \Rightarrow \nabla_1 \pi(t^1, t^2) \cdot d \leq 0.$$

and

(8.8b)
$$\nabla g^{h_1}(t^2) \cdot d > 0, \ldots, \nabla g^{h_s}(t^2) \cdot d > 0,$$
$$\nabla v^2(t^2) \cdot d > 0 \Rightarrow \nabla_2 \pi(t^1, t^2) \cdot d \geq 0.$$

Statement (8.8a) says that, if moving in direction d from t^1 keeps the policy in the feasible region (T) and increases the utility of the militants in party 1, then it must decrease the utility of the opportunists in party 1; (8.8b) says the same thing for party 2.

Now (8.8a) is equivalent to:

(8.9)
$$\forall d \in \mathbf{R}^n, \quad d \neq 0, \quad \nabla g^{k_1}(t^1) \cdot d > 0, \ldots, \nabla g^{k_r}(t^1) \cdot d > 0,$$
$$\nabla v^1(t^1) \cdot d > 0 \Rightarrow -\nabla_1 \pi(t^1, t^2) \cdot d \geq 0.$$

We now apply Farkas' lemma, as follows. Let

$$a^1 = \nabla g^{k_1}(t^1), \ldots, a^r = \nabla g^{k_r}(t^1), \quad a^{r+1} = \nabla v^1(t^1), \quad b = -\nabla \pi(t^1, t^2);$$

then (8.9) tells us that statement B of Farkas' lemma is false for this set of vectors $\{a^1, \ldots, a^{r+1}, b\}$. It therefore follows that statement A of Farkas' lemma is true for this set of vectors, which means there exist non-negative numbers $x^0, x^{h_1}, \ldots, x^{h_r}$ such that:

(8.10a) $\quad -\nabla_1 \pi(t^1, t^2) = \displaystyle\sum_{i=1}^{r} x^{k_i} \nabla g^{k_i}(t^1) + x^0 \nabla v^1(t^1).$

In like manner, (8.8b) implies that there must exist non-negative numbers $y^0, y^{h_1}, \ldots, y^{h_s}$ such that

(8.10b) $\quad \nabla_2 \pi(t^1, t^2) = \displaystyle\sum_{j=1}^{s} y^{h_j} \nabla g^{h_j}(t^2) + y^0 \nabla v^2(t^2).$

Conversely, if (t^1, t^2) satisfies equations of the form (8.10a and b), then it is, at least locally, a PUNE.

We see that equations (8.10a) and (8.10b) and the equations (8.7) constitute $2n + r + s$ equations in $2n + r + s + 2$ unknowns. Again, either there are no local PUNEs, or there is a 2-manifold of them.

We have shown that, no matter what the dimension of the policy space, there will be a 2-manifold of PUNEs, if there are any (except for singular cases). Since the dimension of $T \times T$ is $2n$, the set of PUNEs form a very small set—at least in terms of measure—in $T \times T$, for a 2-manifold is a set of measure zero in $T \times T$, which has dimension greater than two.[5]

8.5 Regular Wittman Equilibrium

Knowing that the set of PUNEs is a 2-manifold and that (when Assumption A holds) PUNEs are weighted Nash bargaining solutions, we can finally understand the existence problem for Wittman equilibrium with uncertainty in multidimensional policy spaces.

In a weighted Nash bargaining solution, all that matters are the relative weights $\gamma^i = \frac{\alpha^i}{\beta^i}$, for $i = 1, 2$; thus we may characterize a PUNE as an ordered pair (γ^1, γ^2). A regular Wittman equilibrium has $(\gamma^1, \gamma^2) = (1, 1)$. Denote the set of weights (γ^1, γ^2) associated with PUNEs for a given environment e as $\Omega(e)$. Since the set of PUNEs is a 2-manifold (when it exists), $\Omega(e)$ will typically contain an open set in $\mathbf{R}_+^2$. $\Omega(e)$ may or may not contain $(1, 1)$. If $(1, 1) \notin \Omega(e)$, then e admits no regular Wittman equilibrium. However, if $(1, 1) \in \Omega(e)$, and if $(1, 1)$ is in the interior of $\Omega(e)$, then regular Wittman equilibrium is generic: that is, if e' is a slight perturbation of e, then e' will also possess a regular Wittman equilibrium (because the set $\Omega(e)$ will move continuously with the perturbation).

We know of no interesting conditions that guarantee that $(1, 1) \in \Omega(e)$. All we can say is that there is no guarantee that Wittman equilibrium exists when $\dim T > 1$, but if one does exist, it is probably generic.

Example 8.1 We proceed to construct an example where regular Wittman equilibrium is generic. Let there be a continuum of types parameterized by w,

---

5. The dimension of the solution manifold is affected by the number of (nonredundant) factions in the parties. We shall see in Chapter 12 that when there are three nonredundant factions, the set of PUNEs is a 4-manifold.

the wage an individual is capable of earning. The proportional income tax rate, t, is used to finance the provision of two public goods, G_1, and G_2. The utility function of consumer-workers is

$$u(x, G_1, G_2) = x + 5 \text{ Log } G_1 + 7 \text{ Log } G_2,$$

where x is consumption of the private good. If the tax rate is t, then all workers supply labor in amount $1 - t$. Let w be distributed according to a probability measure **F** whose mean is denoted μ. Then the indirect utility function is:

$$v(t, G_1, w) = (1 - t)^2 w + 5 \text{ Log } G_1 + 7 \text{ Log}(t(1 - t)\mu - G_1),$$

where we have expressed the consumption of G_2 using the budget constraint. There are two parties, L and R, whose utility functions are the utility functions of two types, w_L and w_R. That is, the parties' utility functions are:

$$v_L(t, G) = v(t, G, w_L) \text{ and } v_R(t, G) = v(t, G, w_R).$$

We use the error-distribution model of uncertainty, with degree of uncertainty η. We may compute that, if $t^1 > t^2$, then all w less than the number $\Psi(t^1, G^1; t^2, G^2)$ prefer policy (t^1, G^1) to policy (t^2, G^2), where:

$$\Psi(t^1, G^1; t^2, G^2) =$$

$$\frac{[5 \text{ Log } G^2 + 7 \text{ Log}(t^2(1 - t^2)\mu - G^2) - (5 \text{ Log } G^1 + 7 \text{ Log}(t^1(1 - t^1)\mu - G^1)]}{(1 - t^1)^2 - (1 - t^2)^2}.$$

Consequently, if party L puts forth the policy with the larger tax rate, then its probability of victory is

$$\pi(t^1, G^1; t^2, G^2) = \frac{F(\psi(t^1, G^1; t^2, G^2)) + \eta - .5}{2\eta}.$$

It is easy to see that both parties will propose interior policies $(t, G) > 0$. Consequently the equations for a PUNE are:

$$\nabla v_L(t^L, G^L) = -x^L \nabla_L \pi(t^L, G^L, t^R, G^R), \quad \text{and}$$

$$\nabla v_R(t^R, G^R) = x^R \nabla_R \pi(t^L, G^L, t^R, G^R),$$

where x^L and x^R are non-negative Lagrangian multipliers. Now define:

$$\gamma^L = \frac{\pi(\tau^L, \tau^R)}{v_L(\tau^L) - v_L(t^R)} x^L \quad \text{and} \quad \gamma^R = \frac{1 - \pi(\tau^L, \tau^R)}{v_R(\tau^R) - v_L(t^L)} x^R,$$

where τ^L and τ^R are the two policies. Note that γ^L and γ^R are themselves non-negative. Then we can write the above two PUNE equations as:

(8.11)
$$\gamma^L \frac{\nabla_L \pi(t^L, G^L, t^R, G^R)}{\pi(t^L, G^L, t^R, G^R)} + \frac{\nabla v_L(t^L, G^L)}{v_L(t^L, G^L) - v_L(t^R, G^R)} = 0,$$

$$\gamma^R \frac{\nabla_R(1 - \pi(t^L, G^L, t^R, G^R))}{1 - \pi(t^L, G^L, t^R, G^R)} + \frac{\nabla v_R(t^R, G^R)}{v_R(t^R, G^R) - v_R(t^L, G^L)} = 0$$

but these are just the first-order conditions for a weighted Nash bargaining solution, where γ^L is the relative power of the factions in L, and γ^R is the relative power of the factions in R! This shows us how to calculate the relative power of the factions in a PUNE.

We now parameterize the model as follows. **F** is the lognormal distribution with median 30 and mean 40, and $(w^L, w^R, \eta) = (20, 50, .20)$. (Thus **F** is approximately the distribution of income in the United States, in thousands of dollars, the L party represents an individual with a wage capacity of \$20,000, and the R party represents an individual with a wage capacity of \$50,000.)

A Wittman equilibrium is a solution of equations (8.11) with $\gamma^L = \gamma^R = 1$. Wittman equilibrium exists: in fact, the policies are:

$$(t^L, G^L) = (.220894, 2.86833), \qquad (t^R, G^R) = (.153792, 2.169),$$

and L wins with a probability of .532. I next generated many PUNEs with (γ^L, γ^R) in a small neighborhood of (1, 1). Figure 8.3 shows a plot of these PUNEs, in (γ^L, γ^R) space. The cluster around the point (1, 1) are the PUNEs in question.

Consequently, the point (1, 1) is interior in the set of PUNEs for this model, and so any small perturbation of the parameters of the model will continue to support a Wittman equilibrium; that is, Wittman equilibrium is generic in this two-dimensional model.

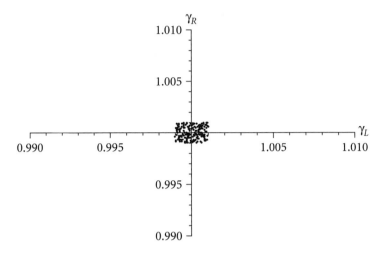

Figure 8.3   Some pairs of points (γ_L, γ_R) associated with PUNEs of Example 8.1

8.6 PUNEs in the Unidimensional Model

We have demonstrated in section 8.3 that PUNE is a generalization of Wittman equilibrium. Let us study what the set of PUNEs is if the policy space is unidimensional.

Let us suppose the error-distribution model of uncertainty. Let t^1, t^2, and $\hat{t}^m$ be the ideal points of party 1, party 2, and the "median voter," and suppose that $\hat{t}^1 < \hat{t}^m < \hat{t}^2$. Let (t^1, t^2) be any policy pair such that $\hat{t}^1 < t^1 < \hat{t}^m < t^2 < \hat{t}^2$. The opportunists in party 1 will want to deviate from t^1 in the direction of $\hat{t}^m$, while the militants in party 1 will want to deviate in the direction of $\hat{t}^1$. Similarly for the factions in party 2. Thus (t^1, t^2) is a PUNE.

As usual, there is a continuum of PUNEs, but in the unidimensional case, the continuum fills the policy space—it is a 2-manifold in $\mathbf{R}^2$. Thus PUNE has no predictive power whatsoever and is a useless equilibrium concept in this setting.

We should understand this as follows. Recall that I justified the PUNE concept as incorporating our agnosticism about the nature of intraparty bargaining. What we have shown is that, with multidimensional policy spaces, that agnosticism still allows us to make interesting predictions about equilibrium, in the sense that the set of PUNEs is a small set in the space $T \times T$. But with unidimensional politics, that agnosticism turns out to kill our predictive power.

We may still hold to our agnosticism about the nature of intraparty bargaining, but we then have very little to say about what happens in unidimensional politics. Adopting, however, the assumption of (unweighted) Nash bargaining gives us a precise prediction of the outcome in unidimensional competition.

As I believe politics are rarely, if ever, unidimensional, I am not particularly bothered by the indeterminacy of PUNE in the unidimensional model.

8.7 PUNEs in a Multidimensional Euclidean Model

In this section we compute the PUNEs in a common model, the Euclidean model with a two-dimensional issue space. Let preferences of voters be given by

$$v(x, y; h_1, h_2) = -\tfrac{1}{2}(x - h_1)^2 - \tfrac{1}{2}(y - h_2)^2,$$

where (x, y) is a policy, and the set of traits, H, is the unit disc in $\mathbf{R}^2$. Let traits be uniformly distributed on the disc. Let the parties' preferences be given by

$$v^i(x, y) = -\tfrac{1}{2}(x - a^i)^2 - \tfrac{1}{2}(y - b^i)^2, \qquad i = 1, 2,$$

where (a^i, b^i) are interior points in the disc. We use the error-distribution model of uncertainty; that is,

$$\pi(t^1, t^2) = \frac{\mathbf{U}(\Omega(t^1, t^2)) + \beta - \tfrac{1}{2}}{2\beta},$$

where $t^i = (x^i, y^i)$ are two policies and $\mathbf{U}$ is the uniform probability distribution on the disc. $\Omega(t^1, t^2)$ is, in this case, the segment of the unit disc on t^1's side of the perpendicular bisector of the line segment $\overline{t^1 t^2}$. Thus, $\mathbf{U}(\Omega(t^1, t^2))$ is just a constant times the area of this segment (the constant is $\frac{1}{\pi}$, since the area of the disc is π).

Given two policies t^1 and t^2, perform the following construction, which is illustrated in Figure 8.4. Draw the segment $\overline{t^1 t^2}$, draw its perpendicular bisector, ℓ, and draw the diameter, d, of H parallel to ℓ. Let r be the distance from the center of H to ℓ. Clearly, for a neighborhood of t^1 and t^2, the length r is a differentiable function of t^1 and t^2: we write $r = r(t^1, t^2)$. Secondly, the measure of $\Omega(s^1, s^2)$ is just a function of r, for (s^1, s^2) in a neighborhood of (t^1, t^2): this

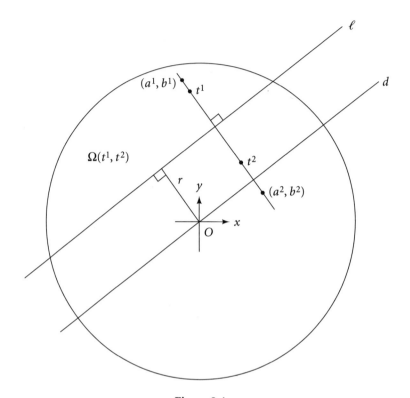

Figure 8.4

follows from the fact that **U** is the uniform distribution on the disc. We can therefore write, for (s^1, s^2) in a neighborhood of (t^1, t^2),

$$\pi(s^1, s^2) = \phi(r(s^1, s^2)),$$

where ϕ is some differentiable function of a real variable.

We now can write equations (8.6a and b) for this example, which become:

(8.12a) $a^1 - x^1 = -\lambda \dfrac{d\phi}{dr} \dfrac{\partial r}{\partial x^1}$

(8.12b) $b^1 - y^1 = -\lambda \dfrac{d\phi}{dr} \dfrac{\partial r}{\partial y^1}$

(8.12c) $a^2 - x^2 = \mu \dfrac{d\phi}{dr} \dfrac{\partial r}{\partial x^2}$

(8.12d) $b^2 - y^2 = \mu \dfrac{d\phi}{dr}\dfrac{\partial r}{\partial y^2}$

where λ and μ are positive constants. In turn, these equations imply

(8.13a) $\dfrac{x^1 - a^1}{b^1 - y^1} = -\dfrac{\frac{\partial r}{\partial x^1}}{\frac{\partial r}{\partial y^1}}$

(8.13b) $\dfrac{x^2 - a^2}{b^2 - y^2} = -\dfrac{\frac{\partial r}{\partial x^2}}{\frac{\partial r}{\partial y^2}}.$

Consider the indifference curve of $r(\cdot, t^2)$ through the point t^1. Its slope at t^1 is exactly the r.h.s. of equation (8.13a). (We are varying the first policy, keeping r constant, for t^2 fixed.) Now I claim that the tangent to this indifference curve at t^1 is parallel to d: this is clear if one observes that the fastest way to *increase* r is to move along the line $\overline{t^1 t^2}$ in Figure 8.4 away from t^1; the way to hold r constant is to move in the direction perpendicular to $\overline{t^1 t^2}$, which means parallel to d.

Now the l.h.s. of equation (8.13a) is the slope of the perpendicular to the line joining (a^1, b^1) to $t^1 = (x^1, y^1)$. Therefore, invoking the last paragraph, (8.13a) says that the line joining (a^1, b^1) to t^1 is perpendicular to d, which means that (a^1, b^1) lies on the line containing $\overline{t^1 t^2}$. In like manner, using (8.13b), we conclude that (a^2, b^2) lies on this line as well.

Hence, in any PUNE, the policies both lie on the line connecting the ideal points of the two parties.

The equations (8.12a, b, c, and d) give us some more information, namely that

(8.14a) $\operatorname{sgn}(a^1 - x^1) = -(\operatorname{sgn}\dfrac{\partial\phi}{\partial r})(\operatorname{sgn}\dfrac{\partial r}{\partial x^1})$

(8.14b) $\operatorname{sgn}(a^2 - x^2) = (\operatorname{sgn}\dfrac{\partial\phi}{\partial r})(\operatorname{sgn}\dfrac{\partial r}{\partial x^2})$

(8.14c) $\operatorname{sgn}(b^1 - y^1) = -(\operatorname{sgn}\dfrac{\partial\phi}{\partial r})(\operatorname{sgn}\dfrac{\partial r}{\partial y^1})$

(8.14d) $\operatorname{sgn}(b^2 - y^2) = (\operatorname{sgn}\dfrac{\partial\phi}{\partial r})(\operatorname{sgn}\dfrac{\partial r}{\partial y^2}).$

From these equations we can conclude that t^1 and t^2 lie *between* (a^1, b^1) and (a^2, b^2). Let us observe that this is true in Figure 8.4. Here it is the case that as r increases (locally by varying t^1 or t^2), the probability of a party 1 victory decreases, so $\partial \phi / \partial r < 0$. A little geometric experimentation will convince the reader that $\partial r / \partial x^1 < 0$ and $\partial r / \partial x^2 < 0$. Consequently, (8.14a and b) tell us that $a^1 - x^1 < 0$ and $a^2 - x^2 > 0$; a similar exercise with equations (8.14c and d tells us that $b^1 - y^1 > 0$ and $b^2 - y^2 < 0$. Consequently, t^1 and t^2 lie between (a^1, b^1) and (a^2, b^2).

The condition on policies that we have derived exhausts what the first-order conditions tell us, because the information in equations (8.12) is entirely contained in equations (8.13) and (8.14). Actually, we have only characterized the conditions for a local PUNE; because we have not shown that the function π is quasi-concave in this example, it is possible that some of these pairs of policies are not global PUNEs. We shall not pursue this dangling issue here.

While we know that the set of PUNEs is small in $T \times T$, in the sense that it is a manifold of lower dimension than $T \times T$, in this example something further can be said: that the projection of the set of PUNEs onto the strategy space of each party is also small. The fact that the projection of the set of PUNEs onto the policy space of each party is a line (a 1-manifold) is due to the singularity of this example—to wit, the uniform distribution of types. Usually, as we shall see, when parties play on a two-dimensional policy space, the set of PUNEs projects onto a 2-manifold in each party's strategy space.

8.8 Conclusion

We have proposed a concept of political Nash equilibrium that is nonvacuous when the issue space is multidimensional. We have argued that although we are agnostic about the nature of the bargaining process among intraparty factions, we are confident that actual political equilibria lie in the set of PUNEs. Indeed, if a log concavity assumption holds, then PUNEs can be viewed as equilibria where the factions in each party reach a weighted Nash bargaining solution. We have computed the set of PUNEs for a Euclidean example, and have observed that the set of policies played by a party in equilibrium is a fairly small set in the policy space. This gives us hope that, although the set of PUNEs is a continuum, it may often be fairly concentrated in the policy space.

We remind the reader that our philosophy here differs from what has been commonly practiced in political science. The generic nonexistence of Downs equilibrium in multidimensional policy spaces has induced many researchers to view political reality as one where cycling is prevalent. The existence story for Wittman equilibrium with multidimensional policy spaces is somewhat more optimistic, as we have shown; nevertheless, Wittman equilibria will not exist for many models. Our response to the nonexistence of Downs and Wittman equilibria has been to propose another equilibrium concept, for we believe that cycling is not a ubiquitous phenomenon in political competition. Our equilibrium concept can be justified in two ways: by viewing parties as consisting of factions with different goals, or by viewing them as Wittman parties that are only boundedly rational. It remains to see whether the PUNE concept is tractable in applications, and in fact delivers equilibria.

9

The Democratic Political Economy
of Progressive Taxation

9.1 Introduction

Why do both left and right parties tend to propose progressive income tax policies in democratic political competition? Some authors (for example, Young
1994) have used arguments of fairness, but such arguments are surely not in the
spirit of political economy, in which players (in this case, parties) are primarily
assumed to represent interest groups. Marhuenda and Ortuño-Ortín (1995)
note that the "the literature . . . is still very inconclusive on the connection
between progressive taxation and voting." Snyder and Kramer (1988) analyze
the problem, and reach the right conclusion, but only under a strange constraint, that parties may propose only tax functions that are ideal for some voter.
Cukierman and Meltzer (1991) study the question when a Condorcet winner
exists among quadratic income tax schemes, when voters have preferences
over income and leisure, but succeed in demonstrating such existence only
under unreasonable conditions.[1] Moreover, it is only in a Downsian framework that players necessarily propose the Condorcet winner, if there is one, in
equilibrium.

In this chapter, we assume that there are two parties, representing relatively
poor and relatively rich constituencies, and we apply the PUNE concept to
study the taxation issue. Society's problem is to choose an income tax regime.
Since we wish to study when that regime will be progressive, we work with the
family of quadratic income taxes, where *after-tax income* of an individual takes
the form $aw^2 + bw + c$, where w is the individual's income. Using a balanced
budget constraint, and assuming that taxes are purely redistributive, we may

---

1. I do not wish to imply that the analysis which follows dominates that of Cukierman and
Meltzer, for they work with a class of utility functions which include leisure as an argument,
while I do not.

view the domain of policies as two-dimensional, deriving c as a function of a and b, and hence regard a tax policy as an ordered pair (a, b). Each party must propose a tax policy (a, b) in the political contest.

Our aim is to understand why progressive taxation is ubiquitous in democracies.

9.2 The Model

Each citizen wishes to maximize her after-tax income. A type is characterized by her income, w. Individuals supply labor inelastically—they derive no welfare from leisure. The distribution of citizen types is given by a probability measure $\mathbf{F}$ on $[0, 1]$. Thus maximum income is normalized at one.

A *tax policy* is a triple (a, b, c), where the after-tax income of an individual with income w is $aw^2 + bw + c$. Taxes are purely redistributive, so the balanced-budget condition is

$$(9.1a) \qquad \int (aw^2 + bw + c)d\mathbf{F}(w) = \mu,$$

where $\mu = \int wd\mathbf{F}$ is mean income, which implies

$$(9.1b) \qquad c = -a\mu_2 - b\mu + \mu,$$

where

$$(9.1c) \qquad \mu_2 \equiv \int w^2 d\mathbf{F}.$$

Thus after-tax income is

$$a(w^2 - \mu_2) + b(w - \mu) + \mu.$$

Define type w's (ordinal) utility function on tax policies as:

$$u(a, b, w) = a(w^2 - \mu_2) + b(w - \mu) + \mu.$$

Henceforth we understand that tax policies are two-dimensional, denoted (a, b).

Let (a, b) and (a', b') be two tax policies and define

$$\Delta a \equiv a - a', \qquad \Delta b \equiv b - b'.$$

Then a voter of type w is indifferent between policies (a, b) and (a', b') iff she enjoys the same after-tax income in both, that is, iff

(9.2a) $\Delta a(w^2 - \mu_2) + \Delta b(w - \mu) = 0.$

Define the function

(9.3) $\phi(w) \equiv \dfrac{w^2 - \mu_2}{w - \mu}, \qquad \text{for } w \neq \mu.$

It follows from (9.2a) that, for $w \neq \mu$, voter w is indifferent between the two policies iff

(9.2b) $\Delta a \phi(w) + \Delta b = 0.$

This tells us that, viewing the domain of policies (a, b) as $\mathbf{R}^2$, the indifference curves of type w are straight lines of slope $-\phi(w)$. The indifference curves of type $w = \mu$ are vertical straight lines.

We have thus far restricted policies only by a budget-balancing constraint. We further assume:

B1   (i) $\forall w, \quad a(w^2 - \mu_2) + b(w - \mu) + \mu \geq 0$
     (ii) $\forall w, \quad 2aw + b \geq 0$

B1(i) says that every individual's after-tax income must be non-negative; B1(ii) says that after-tax income must be a nondecreasing function of income. Thus (i) is an individual budget constraint, and (ii) is an incentive compatibility constraint. The reader may check that the set of policies satisfying B1 is the triangular region $\mathcal{T} = OUV$ illustrated in Figure 9.1.

Policy $O = (0, 0)$ is total confiscation of income and redistribution to the mean, and policy $T = (0, 1)$ is laissez-faire (no taxation).

Define a policy (a, b) to be *progressive* iff it generates an after-tax income function which is concave in (pretax) income. This is equivalent to having $a \leq 0$. Thus progressive policies are precisely those in triangle OUT in Figure 9.1. (Strictly) progressive policies are ones for which the assessed tax is a strictly convex function of income.

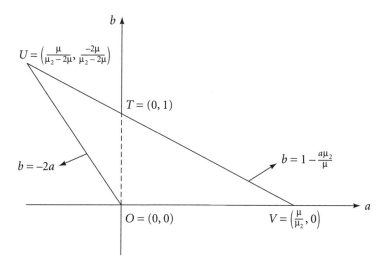

Figure 9.1

Let us study the function ϕ, illustrated in Figure 9.2.
The salient facts are

- ϕ is increasing, asymptotically to infinity, in the interval $[0, \mu)$;
- ϕ is increasing, beginning at the value $-\infty$, in the interval $(\mu, 1]$;
- $\phi(w) = 0$ iff $w = \sqrt{\mu_2}$;
- $\phi(1) > \phi(0)$ and $\phi(1) < 2$.

The only one of these facts I shall derive is the last one. Suppose, to the contrary, that $\phi(1) \geq 2$. Then, by definition of ϕ, $\mu_2 - 1 \leq 2\mu - 2$, and so $\mu_2 \leq 2\mu - 1$. But $\mu^2 < \mu_2$ (**F** has positive variance); hence $\mu^2 < 2\mu - 1$, which means $(\mu - 1)^2 < 0$, an impossibility. Because $\phi(1) > \phi(0)$, we may define a type w^* as that unique type such that $w^* > \mu$ and $\phi(w^*) = \mu_2/\mu$. Because $\phi(1) < 2$, we may define a type $\tilde{w}$ as that unique type such that $\phi(\tilde{w}) = 2$. The values w^* and $\tilde{w}$ are illustrated in Figure 9.2.

We next study the indifference curves and ideal points of the various types. An individual w prefers policy (a, b) to (a', b') iff

(9.4) $\Delta a(w^2 - \mu_2) + \Delta b(w - \mu) > 0.$

It follows that:

- if $w < \mu$, then $\Delta a \phi(w) + \Delta b$ decreases as utility increases;
- if $\mu < w$, then $\Delta a \phi(w) + \Delta b$ increases as utility increases.

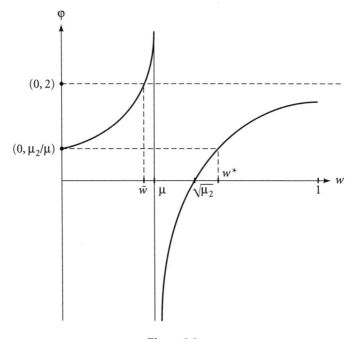

Figure 9.2

Using this observation, it immediately follows that:

Lemma 9.1

(1) O is the ideal point of $\{w \mid w < \tilde{w}\} = W_1$;
(2) U is the ideal point of $\{w \mid \tilde{w} < w < \mu\} = W_2$;
(3) U is the ideal point of $\{w \mid \mu < w < \sqrt{\mu_2}\} = W_3$;
(4) U is the ideal point of $\{w \mid \sqrt{\mu_2} < w < w^*\} = W_4$;
(5) V is the ideal point of $\{w \mid w > w^*\} = W_5$.

Proof (refer to Figure 9.1):

1. $w \in W_1$ have indifference curves which are less steep than *OU*, since $\phi(w) < 2$, and utility increases in the southwest direction, since $w < \mu$. Draw an indifference line of *w* which intersects $\mathcal{T}$; to increase utility, push the line in the southwest direction as far as possible, while still intersecting $\mathcal{T}$. One can push the line down until it intersects $\mathcal{T}$ just in the vertex *O*, because the slope of the indifference line is negatively sloped, and less steep than the side *OU* of $\mathcal{T}$. Thus *O* is the ideal point of any $w \in W_1$.

2. $w \in W_2$ have indifference curves which are steeper than OU, and utility increases in the southwest direction. The same geometric exercise as described in step 1 shows that w's ideal point is U.

3. $w \in W_3$ have positively sloped indifference curves, and utility increases in the northwest direction. U is their ideal point.

4. $w \in W_4$ have negatively sloped indifference curves that are less steep than UV, which increase in the northeast direction. U is their ideal point.

5. $w \in W_5$ have negatively sloped indifference curves, steeper than UV, and utility increases in the northeast direction. V is their ideal point. ∎

We next introduce political parties. There are two, called Left and Right. For simplicity, we assume that Left "represents" a particular citizen type w_L and Right represents a citizen type w_R. We assume:

B2 (i) $w_L < \tilde{w}$, and
     (ii) $w_R > w^*$.

Thus Left (Right) represents a relatively poor (rich) citizen.

When I say that Left "represents" a citizen type w_L, I mean that Left's militants have the (ordinal) preferences of w_L, and that Left's reformists are endowed with a von Neumann–Morgenstern utility function v_L on tax policies (a, b), which is consistent with w_L's (ordinal) after-tax income preferences—that is, v_L is an ordinal transform of $u(\cdot, w_L)$. Similarly, Right's reformists are endowed with a von Neumann–Morgenstern utility function v_R on tax policies consistent with w_R's ordinal income preferences.

According to Lemma 9.1, Left's ideal policy is the point O, and Right's is the point V (see Figure 9.1). Types in the region $(\tilde{w}, w^*)$ are the "moderates," with ideal point U. Note, as well, that B2 implies that $\phi(w_L)$ and $\phi(w_R)$ are both positive, and so both those types have negatively sloped indifference curves.

We next introduce party uncertainty about voter behavior: we shall employ the state-space model of uncertainty. There is a continuum of states $s \in [0, 1]$, and in state s, the probability measure of voter income is $\mathbf{F}_s$ on $[0, 1]$. Both parties share the prior that s is distributed according to a probability measure $\mathbf{G}$ on $[0, 1]$. It is assumed that

B3 *The measures* $\mathbf{F}$, $\mathbf{G}$, *and* $\mathbf{F}_s$, *for all s, are equivalent to Lebesgue measure on* $[0, 1]$. *The distribution function of* $\mathbf{F}_s$ *is denoted* F_s, *and is a continuous function of s as well.*

Suppose Left (Right) proposes a policy $t_L = (a, b)(t_R = (a', b'))$. A citizen w prefers t_L to t_R iff (9.4) holds. Define $\Omega(t_L, t_R)$ as the set of types for which (9.4) holds. Then Left defeats Right (by majority vote) exactly in those states s such that

$$(9.5) \qquad F_s(\Omega(t_L, t_R)) > \tfrac{1}{2}.$$

We follow the usual convention that if a voter is indifferent between t_L and t_R, she votes randomly. By the continuum assumption, it follows that distinct policies t_L and t_R tie in state s iff $F_s(\Omega(t_L, t_R)) = \tfrac{1}{2}$.

Let $S(t_L, t_R)$ be the set of s such that (9.5) holds. It follows that, from the parties' viewpoints, Left defeats Right with probability

$$(9.6) \qquad \pi(t_L, t_R) = G(S(t_L, t_R)).$$

We have now defined the preferences of all three factions of each party. For Left, for example, these are represented by the functions Π^L (reformists), π (opportunists), and $u(\cdot, w_L)$ (militants).

9.3 The Equilibrium Concepts

To review the concept of party unanimity, Left would entertain a deviation from t_L to t'_L iff

$$(9.7) \qquad (\pi(t'_L, t_R), u(t'_L, w_L)) \geq (\pi(t_L, t_R), u(t_L, w_L)),$$

with the convention on vector ordering given in this footnote.[2]

Similarly, at (t_L, t_R), Right would entertain a deviation from t_R to t'_R iff

$$(9.8) \qquad (1 - \pi(t_L, t'_R), u(t'_R, w_R)) \geq (1 - \pi(t_L, t_R), u(t_R, w_R)).$$

Thus a policy pair (t_L, t_R) is a party-unanimity Nash equilibrium (PUNE) iff there is no $t'_L \in T$ at which (9.7) holds and there is no $t'_R \in T$ at which (9.8) holds.

---

2. $(x_1, x_2) \geq (y_1, y_2)$ iff $x_i \gtreqqless y_i$ and for some i, $x_i > y_i$
   $(x_1, x_2) \gtreqqless (y_1, y_2)$ iff $x_i \gtreqqless y_i$.

We introduce next a refinement of PUNE for the problem of the present chapter.

Definition 9.1 (t_L, t_R) is a *strong party-unanimity Nash equilibrium* iff (t_L, t_R) is a PUNE and it is false that $t_L = (0, 0)$ and $\pi(t_L, t_R) = 1$.

"Strongness" is a (very) weak refinement of PUNE. If we eliminate nonstrong PUNE from consideration, we are saying something about the capacity of Right's intraparty factions to compromise in the face of almost sure calamity. Recall that policy $(a, b) = (0, 0)$ is a complete leveling of all incomes to the mean. If, in a PUNE, $t_L = (0, 0)$ and $\pi(t_L, t_R) = 1$, then facing the prospect of Left's winning almost surely with the leveling policy $(0, 0)$, Right does not deviate. Strongness says that, facing such a prospect, Right's opportunist and reformist factions will be able to persuade the militant faction to deviate to a policy with a positive probability of defeating $(0, 0)$.

Let us remark about Condorcet winners. Suppose it is the case that

$$\forall s, \mathbf{F}_s(W_2 \cup W_3 \cup W_4) > \tfrac{1}{2}.$$

(Refer to Lemma 9.1 for notation.) Then $W_2 \cup W_3 \cup W_4$ is a majority coalition in all states, all of whose members have ideal point $U \in T$. It follows that U is a Condorcet winner in T: it defeats all policies except itself, for sure. Thus it would be a Downsian equilibrium for both parties to propose U. It would as well be a PUNE for both parties to propose U, since neither opportunist faction would be willing to deviate: at (U, U), each party has probability one-half of victory, and under any unilateral deviation, the deviating party has probability zero of victory. Nevertheless, in a PUNE, it might be the case that neither party proposes U.

9.4 Analysis of Party Competition

We could analyze the PUNEs in this model using the differential character-ization of PUNEs of Chapter 8. Instead we undertake an entirely geometric analysis, made possible by the linearity of citizen indifference curves on the policy space.

Let us look at a typical strategy pair that might arise in the game between our two parties. Denote henceforth by L the policy (a, b) announced by Left, and by R the policy (a', b') announced by Right. Examine Figure 9.3, which reproduces

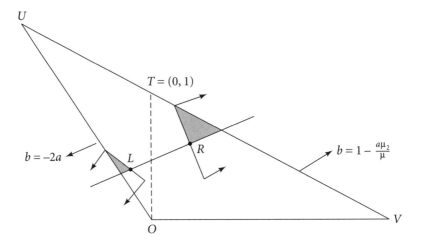

Figure 9.3

the domain $\mathcal{T}$, with the two hypothetical proposals, L and R. Assume that w_L prefers L to R, and w_R prefers R to L.

In Figure 9.3, the slope m of LR is positive. We know from section 9.2 that type $\hat{w}$ is indifferent between L and R iff $\phi(\hat{w}) = -m$. But this determines a unique $\hat{w}$, illustrated in Figure 9.4, which is an amended reproduction of Figure 9.2. It now follows, from examination of (9.4), that the set of types preferring L to R is $[0, \hat{w})$, and the set of types preferring R to L is $(\hat{w}, 1]$. These sets are illustrated by the heavy bars labeled "L" and "R" in Figure 9.4.

In Figure 9.3, I have also drawn an indifference curve for voter w_L through the point L, and an indifference curve for voter w_R through the point R. The arrows indicate the directions of increasing utility.

Now imagine, in the situation of Figure 9.3, that Left is considering deviating from L, locally, to a point in the adjacent shaded triangle, while Right is fixed at R. Any such deviation is preferred by Left's militants, since the shaded triangle lies on the preferred side of w_L's indifference curve at L. Any such deviation also would reduce the steepness of the line LR; but according to Figure 9.4, that means it would *increase* the set of types who prefer the Left policy to R, and hence must (weakly) increase the probability that Left defeats R. Hence, (L, R) cannot be a PUNE: both militant and opportunist factions of Left would agree to deviate from L into the shaded region.

Let us define the set of policies below w_L's indifference curve at L and above the line LR as the *cone of attractive policies for Left at L*. Similar analysis shows

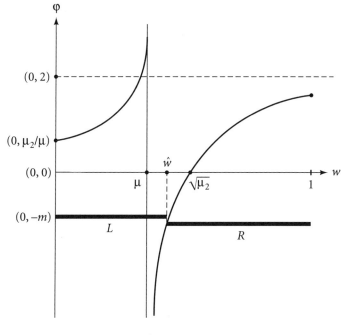

Figure 9.4

that the shaded cone at R is the cone of attractive policies for Right at R—that is, the set of policies which the factions in Right would deviate to at R, given L fixed. A pair (L, R) is a PUNE only if the intersection of each cone of attractive policies with $\mathcal{T}$ is empty.[3]

We shall use this technique in the rest of this chapter. The analysis is simple by virtue of the pleasant fact that voter indifference curves in the policy space are straight lines, and so it is easy to identify the cone of attractive policies for a party at a pair of proposals.

Before proceeding further, we state a useful general principle.

Lemma 9.2 *Let (L, R) be a policy pair in $\mathcal{T} \times \mathcal{T}$. A local deviation to one side of LR from L by Left increases Left's probability of victory iff a local deviation by Right from R on the same side of LR increases Right's probability of victory.*

---

3. This is only an "only if" statement. It is possible that, locally, neither party wants to deviate, but that there is a distant deviation that is attractive for one party.

Proof:

The key observation is that when Left or Right deviates from L or R on the same side of LR, while the other party remains fixed, they change the slope of LR in opposite ways: for example, if Left's deviation renders LR steeper, then Right's deviation renders LR less steep. The lemma now follows from a consideration of what happens to the sizes of the coalitions of types favoring each party (see, for example, Figure 9.4). ■

And an obvious fact:

Lemma 9.3 *If (L, R) is a PUNE, then w_L weakly prefers L to R and w_R weakly prefers R to L.*

Proof:

Suppose, to the contrary, that w_L strictly prefers R to L. Then Left can deviate by moving along the line LR from L toward R: this leaves the probability of victory unchanged and increases the welfare of w_L, so both opportunists and militants will support the deviation. ■

Our first task is to prove the existence of strong PUNE.[4] To this end, we assume:

B4   *There is a set S of states, with $\mathbf{G}(S) > 0$, such that*

$$s \in S \Rightarrow F_s(\tilde{w}) < \tfrac{1}{2}.$$

In particular, if B4 did not hold, the Left could win with probability one against any Right proposal by proposing its ideal point, O! It follows that B4 is a necessary condition for the existence of a strong PUNE. Theorem 9.1 says it is, as well, sufficient.

Theorem 9.1   *If B1, B2, B3 and B4 hold, then there exist strong PUNE.*

Proof:

1. Choose $L \in OU$ and $R \in UT$, such that the slope, m, of LR is negative and close in absolute value to 2, as illustrated in Figure 9.5: in particular, choose L to

---

4. It is trivial to note that $L = O$ and $R = V$ is always a PUNE, for the militants in each party will refuse to deviate from their ideal points. But in general, this pair of proposals is not a strong PUNE (that is, Left may win with probability one).

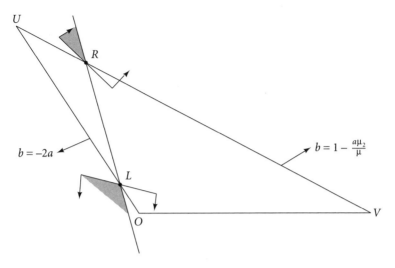

Figure 9.5

be close to O. The type $\hat{w}$ who is indifferent between L and R has $\phi(\hat{w}) = -m$; it follows from Figure 9.2 that $\hat{w} \in (\tilde{w}, \mu)$. Hence the coalition which votes Left, at these proposals, is $[0, \hat{w})$.

2. For any small $\epsilon > 0$, we can choose (L, R) so that the slope of LR is sufficiently close to -2 that the coalition who vote Left is precisely $[0, \tilde{w} + \epsilon)$. By B4 and B3 it follows that there is a set of states of positive G-measure such that $F_s(\tilde{w} + \epsilon) < \frac{1}{2}$. Therefore $\pi(L, R) < 1$.

3. From Figure 9.2, it follows that Left can increase the size of the Left coalition, and hence weakly increase the probability of victory, by deviating from L to the left of LR, for such a move increases the absolute value of the slope of LR. By Lemma 9.2, Right can weakly increase its probability of victory by deviating from R to the left of LR. Moreover, a deviation by Left from L to the right of LR, and below w_L's indifference curve through L, will decrease the size of the Left coalition, since L is close to O (again, examine Figure 9.2). Since $\pi(L, R) < 1$, it will therefore decrease π, since F_s and G are equivalent to Lebesgue measure. It follows that Left's cone of attraction at L is the lower shaded region in Figure 9.5, and further, that there are no deviations in $\mathcal{T}$ which are attractive for Left. The last clause uses the fact that L is close to O, so the points to the right of LR and below w_L's indifference curve are all close to O.

4. To calculate Right's cone of attractive policies at R, note that if Right deviates from R to any point R' on the segment RV, the slope of the line LR' is either negative and greater in absolute value than the slope of LR, or positive

and less in absolute value than μ_2/μ. It follows (consult Figure 9.2) that the type $\hat{w}$ who is indifferent between L and R' lies always in the interval $(\tilde{w}, w^*)$ and hence the Right coalition will be $(\hat{w}, 1]$, which is always smaller than it is at R. Without loss of generality, these are the only deviations from R that are above w_R's indifference curve at R and to the right of LR that we need consider (for if there is any attractive deviation in that region, there must be one on the segment RV). It follows that Right's cone of attraction at R is the upper shaded region in Figure 9.5, and there are no attractive deviations for Right in $\mathcal{T}$.

5. It follows that (L, R) is a PUNE.

6. It immediately follows that (L, R) is a strong PUNE. ∎

We next introduce the only distributional assumption of our analysis:

B5 $F_s(\mu) > \frac{1}{2}$ *almost surely.*

B5 is reasonable if median income is less than mean income, for it says that in almost all states, more than half the voters have income less than the mean.

We now state our main result:

Theorem 9.2   *If B1, B2, B3, and B5 hold, then in all strong PUNEs, both Left and Right play progressive policies.*

In other words, the distributional assumption B5 and the (weak) refinement notion enable us to deduce the ubiquity of progressive tax proposals in political competition between Left and Right.

Some readers may find the introduction of the "strong PUNE" refinement, and hence the statement of Theorem 9.2, inelegant. We can, in fact, avoid that terminology, if we wish, as follows:

Corollary 9.1   *Let B1, B2, B3, and B5 hold. Then, in any PUNE, with probability one, a progressive policy wins the election.*

Proof:

Theorem 9.2 says that the only PUNE in which a party does not propose a progressive policy is one in which Left proposes $(0, 0)$ and wins with probability one. But $(0, 0)$ is a progressive policy. The claim immediately follows.[5]

---

5. This circumlocution for avoiding the necessity of introducing the strong PUNE concept is due to Klaus Nehring.

We now prove Theorem 9.2.

Step (1)   There is no strong PUNE where Right plays a regressive policy.

Suppose Right plays a policy R in triangle OTV (see Figure 9.1), but not on the line OT (that is, R is regressive). Let Left play $L = O$. I claim Left wins with probability one. For the slope of LR is positive, and so the type, w, who is indifferent between L and R has $\phi(w)$ negative, which, by Figure 9.2, means $w > \mu$; thus, by B5, Left wins with probability one. It follows that *any* PUNE where Right plays R must have Left playing O, because O is ideal for both Left's militants and opportunists. The conclusion follows.

Therefore, the remainder of the proof shows that Left never plays a regressive policy in a strong PUNE.

Step (2)   There is no PUNE where either party plays a policy which is interior in $\mathcal{T}$.

1. If (L, R) is a PUNE and $L \in$ interior T, then slope $LR = -\phi(w_L)$.

Suppose, to the contrary, that slope $LR \neq -\phi(w_L)$. Let ℓ be w_L's indifference line containing L. Then ℓ and LR do not coincide. The militants of Left strictly prefer any policy on line LR and below ℓ (that is, on the O side of ℓ), and Left's opportunists are indifferent to such a move (moving along the line LR leaves the probability of victory constant). Hence (L, R) is not a PUNE.

2. If $L \in$ interior $\mathcal{T}$, $R \in$ boundary $\mathcal{T}$, and slope $LR = -\phi(w_L)$, then (L, R) is not a PUNE.

By step 1, $R \in \overline{OU} \cup \overline{UT}$. We know that the slope of $\overline{LR}$ lies between the slopes of $\overline{OU}$ and $\overline{UV}$, since $w_L \in [0, \tilde{w})$. Suppose that $R \in \overline{UT}$. It follows that O lies below (to the left) of $\overline{LR}$. Hence Left's militants wish to deviate below $\overline{LR}$. Therefore such a deviation must decrease Left's probability of victory (or this would not be a PUNE). Therefore, by Lemma 9.2, a deviation to the right of $\overline{LR}$ increases Right's probability of victory. But Right's militants also like this deviation, since V lies above $\overline{LR}$; so Right should deviate down the line $\overline{RV}$. Hence (L, R) is not a PUNE, a contradiction.

Next, suppose that $R \in \overline{OU}$. Then the facts about $\overline{LR}$'s slope imply that $\overline{LR}$ lies above O and below V. The reader may now replicate the reasoning of the preceding paragraph.

3. If $L, R \in$ interior T and slope $LR = -\phi(w_L)$, (L, R) is not a PUNE. This step is easier than step 2, and is left to the reader.

4. We have now disposed of the possibility of a PUNE where L is interior. Exactly symmetric arguments show there can be no PUNE where $R \in$ interior $\mathcal{T}$.

Step (3)   There is no strong PUNE where Left plays a regressive policy.

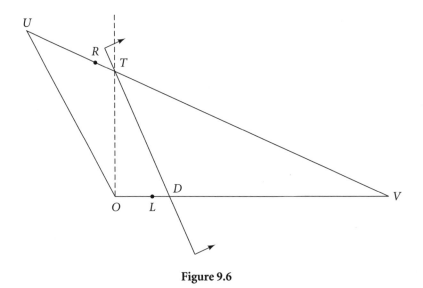

Figure 9.6

Consult Figure 9.6; the line through D and T is an indifference curve of w_R. We know that both parties play on the boundary of $\mathcal{T}$ in a PUNE. Any strong PUNE in which Left plays a regressive policy must have Left playing on the segment OD, for if Left played in the triangle DVT, then Right would be playing a regressive policy, because we know that Right weakly prefers its policy to Left's in a PUNE (Lemma 9.3). But step 1 above has shown that there is no strong PUNE in which Right plays regressive.

Consequently, any strong PUNE in which Left plays regressive looks like the pair $\{L, R\}$ in the figure. At this play, we know that the π decreases as Left deviates from L toward O—for otherwise, Left would so deviate. Therefore π increases as Left deviates from L toward D. Consequently, $1 - \pi$ increases as Right deviates from R toward T (Lemma 9.2). But this deviation is attractive to Right's militants, as well, and so $\{L, R\}$ is not a PUNE.

This completes the argument. ∎

9.5 Calibration

According to the 1990 U.S. Census, mean household income in the United States was $30,900 and the standard deviation of household income was

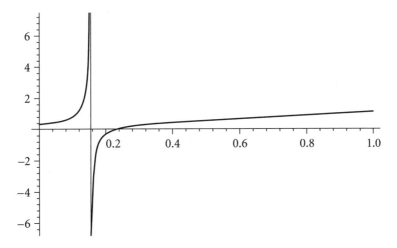

Figure 9.7 The empirical function ϕ for the United States

$34,000.[6] Let us take maximum household income, for all effective purposes, to have been $200,000 in 1990. Then, normalizing maximum income at unity, we compute that $\mu = .1545$ and $\mu_2 = .05277$. The empirical function ϕ is graphed in Figure 9.7.

We calculate that $\tilde{w} = \$27,500$ and $w^* = \$68,300$. Our assumption B2 requires that Left represent a voter whose income is not greater than $27,500, and Right a voter whose income is not less than $68,300. Given that mean income is $30,900, these are reasonable assumptions—if not for the Democrats and Republicans in the United States, then perhaps for Labour and the Conservatives in the United Kingdom.

Our assumptions B5 and B4 say that it is always the case that at least one-half the voters have an income less than $30,900, but there is positive probability that fewer than one-half the voters will have an income less than $27,500.

9.6 Conclusion

Let me summarize the model. There is a population with a distribution of income, who must vote on a redistributive tax policy, which is limited to

---

6. I thank my colleague Marianne Page for computing these statistics.

be some quadratic function of income. Voters supply labor inelastically—
so income is fixed, for each voter. There are two parties, one representing a
relatively poor voter, the other a relatively rich voter. Within each party, there
are three factions: reformists, militants, and opportunists. Parties are unsure
about the distribution of voter types.

Call the policy space $\mathcal{T}$. Each faction of each party has (complete) preferences
on $\mathcal{T} \times \mathcal{T}$, that is, on pairs of policies that it and its opposition can propose.
All three factions in a party must agree for the *party* to prefer one element in
$\mathcal{T} \times \mathcal{T}$ to another: this leads to each party's having a preference quasi-order on
$\mathcal{T} \times \mathcal{T}$—it is the intersection of the preference orders of its three factions. A
political equilibrium is a Nash equilibrium where each party maximizes with
respect to its quasi-order.

The main result says that if the majority of voters, in all states, have an income
less than the mean income, then in any political equilibrium, both parties
propose progressive tax policies.

Perhaps the assumption one would most like to weaken is the inelasticity of
labor supply. Do the results remain true if individuals experience disutility from
labor? One can prove the following. Suppose that individuals have preferences
over income and leisure, such that the labor supply elasticity with respect to the
wage is uniformly (for all incomes and all individuals) less than some number
$\delta > 0$. Consider, now, a sequence of economies, letting δ approach zero. For
δ sufficiently small, strong PUNE exist, and in all of them, the policies are
arbitrarily close to being progressive. (The proof goes by showing that, as δ
gets small, the feasible set of policies converges to the triangle OUV and the
indifference curves of individuals become arbitrarily close to being straight
lines. We then use the results established above to get the limit result.) Is there
a stronger result, saying that both parties will propose progressive policies for
δ not close to zero? I expect not. If the labor supply elasticity of the high-wage
agents is sufficiently large, it does not seem that progressive policies would
necessarily be advocated by either party.

10

Why the Poor Do Not Expropriate the Rich in Democracies

10.1 The Historical Issue and a Model Preview

The framers of the U.S. Constitution extended suffrage only to (male) property holders because they believed that, were the poor to be given the vote, they would soon expropriate the rich. Property owners, it was believed, would behave "responsibly." If all citizens have the vote, and median wealth is less than the mean (always true of actual wealth distributions), then a majority of voters (namely, those whose wealth is less than the mean) should prefer a tax rate of unity, fully redistributing all wealth to the mean.

Nevertheless, universal suffrage has not engendered the expropriation of the rich through the tax system, and a variety of reasons have been offered in explanation, including the following: (1) voters recognize that there would be adverse dynamic effects to expropriating the rich, who have scarce productive talents which would cease to be supplied were their holders taxed too harshly, and all would consequently suffer (trickle-down); (2) many voters whose wealth lies below the mean entertain the hope that they or their children will someday become richer than the mean, and they shun high tax rates for fear of hurting their future selves or children; (3) even if there would be few dynamic effects from high taxation, as described in (1), the rich convince the citizenry that there would be, with propaganda disseminated through the media, which they control; (4) the citizenry believe that the rich person—and indeed everyone—deserves the wealth he/she receives, and hence high tax rates would be unethical. Marxists have called explanations (3) and (4) instances of "false consciousness." Putterman (1997) has recently tried to assign degrees of importance to the explanations here suggested, and some others.

In this chapter, I propose another possible explanation for the nonexpropriation of the rich in democracies, which depends upon there being party competition on a policy space with two dimensions, the first being taxation, the second some noneconomic issue such as race, religion, nationalism, or "values." The proposal I shall offer has nothing to do with incentives and trickle-down: were wealth simply manna from heaven, which fell unequally on the population, but could be redistributed, the argument I present would still hold.

The model behind the view that those with wealth less than the mean would vote for a tax rate of unity on wealth presupposes that political competition is unidimensional. But, indeed, political competition, in at least the United States and Europe, is surely at least two-dimensional. Poole and Rosenthal (1991) have shown that roll-call votes in the U.S. Congress, going back to 1789, are best explained by a two-dimensional model: knowing the position of congressmen on taxation and race (slavery before the Civil War and integration/civil rights after), one can explain 85% of the variance in roll-call votes, and adding a third dimension explains very little more. Laver and Hunt (1992) present empirical evidence that democratic politics are multidimensional in a set of over twenty countries. Somewhat more schematically, Kitschelt (1994) argues that, in the main European countries, politics can be understood, in the past thirty years, as being two-dimensional, over redistribution and a "communitarian" dimension, whose poles he labels "authoritarian" and "libertarian." The authoritarian voter wants more police, more defense spending, illegalization of abortion, tough antidrug legislation, the death penalty (in the United States), and is proclerical. The libertarian voter wants the respective opposites, and is anticlerical. Kitschelt argues that the "communitarian" dimension is quite orthogonal to the economic dimension: blue-collar workers in manufacturing tend to be redistributionist and authoritarian, while some professional workers are antiredistributionist and libertarian. On the other hand, many poor, minority voters are redistributionist and libertarian, while the "petty bourgeoisie" are antiredistributionist and authoritarian. Kalyvas (1996) and Przeworski and Sprague (1986) together form a convincing argument that, in at least the period 1880–1940, both religion and redistribution were important dimensions in European politics.

Suppose, then, that voter preferences are defined over wealth and some nonwealth issue—for concreteness, let us call the second dimension "religion." The citizenry's preferences are characterized by a joint probability distribution over tax-religion policy space. Suppose there are two political parties with policy preferences: one party represents constituents who are poor and anticlerical (the Labor Party), and the other represents constituents who are rich and pro-clerical (the Christian Democratic Party).

Given this political institution, here is a rough intuition for why Labor might not optimize in the electoral contest by proposing a tax rate of unity. Suppose that many poor voters are anticlerical, but there are a significant number of proclerical poor, and that richer citizens are mostly proclerical, but there are a significant number of anticlerical voters among them. Indeed, there may be a substantial number of voters, among the poor, who are so proclerical that they will not vote Labor even if Labor proposes a tax rate of unity, as long as the Christian Democrats propose a more proclerical policy than Labor. Thus Labor would not maximize the expected welfare of its poor, anticlerical constituents if it proposes a tax rate of unity, assuming it remains "principled" on the religion issue. It may well be in the interest of Labor's constituents to propose a tax rate less than one, thereby winning the votes of some richer citizens who are quite anticlerical. This, Marx might well have said, is an instance of religion's being the opium of the people—that is, the poor, proclerical voters are acting against their "real" interests. (If one thinks of the noneconomic issue as race, which is perhaps the most appropriate one for the United States, one might paraphrase Marx by arguing that racism is the opiate of the (white) masses.) But we are not here inquiring into why citizens have these preferences. The essential point is that, if voters care deeply about some noneconomic issue, and have widely disparate views on that issue, it does not follow that all those whose wealth is less than the mean will necessarily support a party which proposes a tax rate of unity.

We shall, in this chapter, study party-unanimity Nash equilibrium in the game between these two parties. The substantive question is: is there a reasonable condition on the distribution of voter preferences (or traits), such that the equilibrium in the electoral contest between a Labor Party that represents a poor anticlerical voter and a Christian Democratic Party that represents a rich, clerical voter entails Labor's proposing a tax rate which is significantly less than one?

In the process of answering the posed question, we answer another question as well. Kitschelt has argued that the noneconomic dimension (what he calls the "communitarian" issue) has increased in importance in Western democracies in the postwar period. Clearly, in a two-dimensional model, as the noneconomic issue becomes more salient for voters, we can expect both components of the equilibrium policies to change. Is there any reason to believe that, as

the importance of the noneconomic issue increases, the equilibrium tax policies proposed by the Labor Party should decrease, as opposed to increasing, or
moving around nonmonotonically? We can interpret the main results as answering this question affirmatively, assuming that a stipulated condition on the
distribution of voter traits holds.

We finally investigate whether the stipulated condition holds for the distribution of traits in the U.S. and British electorates, where we take the noneconomic
issue to be, in one case, racial attitudes, and in another, communitarian attitudes. Some tentative predictions about U.S. and British political behavior are
drawn from the model.

10.2 The Politico-Economic Environment

Let the space of citizen traits be $H = W \times \mathbf{R}$, with generic element (w, a), where
$W = [\underline{w}, \overline{w}]$ is the set of wealth (or income) levels, and $\mathbf{R}$ is the set of religious
views, taken to be the real number line. The (indirect) utility function of a
citizen with traits (w, a) over *policies* (t, z), where t is a uniform tax rate on
wealth or income, and z is a religious position of the government, is given by
$v(t, z; w, a)$. The population is characterized by a probability distribution on
H. There are two parties: Labor, or Left, represents a constituent with traits
(w_L, a_L) and the Christian Democratic Party, or Right, represents a constituent
with traits (w_R, a_R). We assume that $w_L < \mu < w_R$, where μ is mean population
income. Each party, i, proposes a policy pair $\tau^i = (t^i, z^i)$. We suppose there is
a stochastic element in these elections, so that, given a pair of policies (τ^1, τ^2),
there is a probability that Left will win, denoted $\pi(\tau^1, \tau^2)$. The function π is
known to both parties. Then the payoff functions of the reformists in the Left
and Right parties are:

$$\Pi^1(\tau^1, \tau^2) = \pi(\tau^1, \tau^2)v(\tau^1; w_L, a_L) + (1 - \pi(\tau^1, \tau^2))v(\tau^2; w_L, a_L)$$

(10.1)

$$\Pi^2(\tau^1, \tau^2) = \pi(\tau^1, \tau^2)v(\tau^1; w_R, a_R) + (1 - \pi(\tau^1, \tau^2))v(\tau^2; w_R, a_R).$$

We derive the function v from the direct utility function. A citizen with religious view a has a von Neumann–Morgenstern utility function $u(x, z; a) =
(1 - \alpha)x - \alpha/2(z - a)^2$, where x is after-tax wealth and z is the government's
religious policy. The number α in the interval $[0, 1]$ shall be called the *salience*
of the religious issue; it has the same value for all citizens. The indirect util-

ity function of voter (w, a) at policy (t, z), where t is a proportional tax rate, is

(10.2) $v(t, z; w, a) = (1 - \alpha)((1 - t)w + t\mu) - \alpha/2(z - a)^2,$

where μ is mean wealth.

Before proceeding with the two dimensional analysis, let us study the uni-dimensional case, which is induced when $\alpha = 0$. This is exactly the model of Example 2.1, which was further pursued in section 4.1. Proposition 4.1 showed that the unique Wittman equilibrium consists in Left's proposing a tax rate of unity and Right's proposing a tax rate of zero. Moreover, $(0, 1)$ is the *unique* PUNE when $\alpha = 0$, because the probability of victory is invariant with respect to policies in this game, as long as $t_L > t_R$. Thus in the unidimensional model, where the salience of religion is zero, we get polarized tax policies.

We proceed to the two-dimensional analysis. From (10.2), we may compute that voter (w, a) prefers policy $\tau_L = (t_L, z_L)$ to $\tau_R = (t_R, z_R)$, iff

(10.3a) $\bar{z} + \dfrac{(1 - \alpha)\Delta t(w - \mu)}{\alpha \Delta z} > a$ if $\Delta z > 0,$

(10.3b) $\bar{z} + \dfrac{(1 - \alpha)\Delta t(w - \mu)}{\alpha \Delta z} < a$ if $\Delta z < 0,$

(10.3c) $w < \mu$ if $\Delta z = 0$ and $\Delta t < 0,$

(10.3d) $w > \mu$ if $\Delta z = 0$ and $\Delta t > 0,$

where $\Delta z \equiv z_R - z_L$, $\Delta t \equiv t_R - t_L$, and $\bar{z} \equiv (z_L + z_R)/2$.

We shall assume that the population distribution of traits is given by a density function $h(w, a) = g(w)r(a, w)$ on H, where $g(w)$ is a density on W and, for each w, $r(a, w)$ is a density on $\mathbf{R}$. The interpretation is that the wealth distribution of the population is given by g, and the distribution of religious views at wealth w is given by $r(a, w)$. It will be important that wealth and religious views are not independently distributed.

We employ the state-space model of uncertainty. A random variable, s, which is uniformly distributed on $[0, 1]$, determines the distribution of traits among voters on election day. We assume that, in state s, the probability distribution of voters is $\mathbf{H}_s$, with a density function given by

(10.4) $h_s(w, a) = g_s(w)r(a, w);$

the interpretation is that s affects only the wealth distribution of the active electorate, but a representative sample of religious views shows up at each wealth level at the polls in every state of the world.

The coalition of voters $\Omega(\tau_L, \tau_R)$ who prefer τ_L to τ_R is given by (10.3). Thus the measure of voters who prefer τ_L to τ_R if, for instance, $\Delta z > 0$, is, from (10.3a):

$$(10.5) \quad H_s(\Omega(\tau_L, \tau_R)) = \int_W \int_{-\infty}^{\bar{z}+\frac{(1-\alpha)\Delta t(w-\mu)}{\alpha \Delta z}} g_s(w)r(a, w)da\,dw.$$

Let $\Phi(z, s)$ be the distribution function for religious views in state s; that is,

$$\Phi(z, s) = \int_W \int_{-\infty}^{z} g_s(w)r(a, w)da\,dw.$$

We assume:

C1   For any z, $\Phi(z, s)$ is strictly decreasing in s.[1]

If the rich tend to be more religious than the poor, and the fraction of rich voters increases with s (as when high s means foul weather on election day), then C1 will surely hold.

Policy τ_L defeats τ_R in just those states s that $H_s(\Omega(\tau_L, \tau_R)) > \frac{1}{2}$. (We needn't worry about what happens if $H_s(\Omega(\tau_L, \tau_R)) = \frac{1}{2}$, an event with zero probability.) It follows from C1 and (10.5) that $H_s(\Omega(\tau_L, \tau_R)) > \frac{1}{2}$ just in case $s < s^*(\tau_L, \tau_R)$, where $s^*(\tau_L, \tau_R)$ is defined uniquely by

$$(10.6) \quad \int_W \int_{-\infty}^{\bar{z}+\frac{(1-\alpha)\Delta t(w-\mu)}{\alpha \Delta z}} g_{s^*}(w)r(a, w)da\,dw = \frac{1}{2}.$$

Thus the probability that τ_1 defeats τ_2 is the probability of the event $\{s < s^*\}$, which is $s^*(\tau_1, \tau_2)$, since s is uniformly distributed on $[0, 1]$.

---

1. C1 plays the role that the assumption "m_s is a strictly decreasing function of s" played in Example 2.1.

Letting $\pi(\tau_L, \tau_R)$ be the probability that τ_L defeats τ_R where $z_R > z_L$, we have

$$(10.7) \quad \pi(\tau_L, \tau_R) = \begin{cases} 1 & \text{if } \mathbf{H}_1(\Omega(\tau_L, \tau_R)) > \frac{1}{2} \\ s^*(\tau_L, \tau_R) & \text{if } \mathbf{H}_{s^*}(\Omega(\tau_L, \tau_R)) = \frac{1}{2} \\ 0 & \text{if } \mathbf{H}_0(\Omega(\tau_L, \tau_R)) < \frac{1}{2} \end{cases}$$

More completely, we may write the function $\pi(\tau_L, \tau_R)$ for all possible cases, using (10.3), as follows. Let λ be Lebesgue (uniform) measure on $[0, 1]$. Then

$$\pi(\tau_L, \tau_R) = \begin{cases} \lambda(\{s \mid \int_W \int_{-\infty}^{\bar{z} + \frac{(1-\alpha)\Delta t(w-\mu)}{\alpha \Delta z}} g_s(w) r(a, w) da\, dw > \frac{1}{2}\}) & \text{if } \Delta z > 0, \\ \lambda(\{s \mid \int_W \int_{\bar{z} + \frac{(1-\alpha)\Delta t(w-\mu)}{\alpha \Delta z}}^{\infty} g_s(w) r(a, w) da\, dw > \frac{1}{2}\}) & \text{if } \Delta z < 0, \\ \lambda(\{s \mid \int_{\underline{w}}^{\mu} g_s(w) dw > \frac{1}{2}\}) & \text{if } \Delta z = 0 \text{ and } \Delta t < 0, \\ \lambda(\{s \mid \int_{\mu}^{\overline{w}} g_s(w) dw > \frac{1}{2}\}) & \text{if } \Delta z = 0 \text{ and } \Delta t > 0, \\ \frac{1}{2} & \text{if } \Delta z = \Delta t = 0. \end{cases}$$

It may be verified that, since $g_s(w)$ is continuous in s and w, and $r(a, w)$ is continuous, the function π is continuous except on the subset $V \equiv \{\Delta z = 0 = \Delta t\}$ of the domain $T \times T$, where $T = [0, 1] \times \mathbf{R}$ is the policy space.

It is easily verified that the functions Π^R and Π^L are everywhere continuous on $T \times T$; the discontinuity of π on the subspace V of the domain, defined above, turns out not to matter, since on V, $v(\tau_R; w, a) = v(\tau_L; w, a)$ for any (w, a).

10.3 Analysis of PUNEs

For each positive value of the salience α, we can define a political game $\mathcal{G}_\alpha = \langle \alpha, (a_L, w_L), (a_R, w_R), g, r, \{g_s\}, v \rangle$ between the two parties. Importantly, in game $\mathcal{G}_\alpha$, all citizens have the religious issue salience α. Our strategy will be to study the PUNEs of this game as α approaches one. Denote a typical PUNE for the game $\mathcal{G}_\alpha$ by $((t_L(\alpha), z_L(\alpha)), (t_R(\alpha), z_R(\alpha)))$. $\mathcal{G}_1$ is the unidimensional game where citizens care only about the religious issue.

We introduce a condition:

C2 The mean wealth of the cohort of voters with the median religious view in all states is greater than mean wealth, μ, of the population.

We next introduce two definitions:

Definition 10.1   Let $a(s)$ be the median religious view in state s. For any $\delta > 0$, we say *uncertainty is less than* δ iff there is a number v such that, for all s, $a(s)$ lies in a δ interval around v.

The second definition is a refinement of PUNE.

Definition 10.2   Let ϵ be a (small) positive number. A policy pair $((t_L, z_L),$ $(t_R, z_R))$ is an ϵ-*PUNE* in the game $\mathcal{G}$ if it is a PUNE and there is no deviation by either party at which the party would win with probability one, and that would cost its militants less than ϵ in utility. (For party L, for example, there exists no (t, z) such that $\pi(t, z, t_R, z_R) = 1$ and $v^L(t_L, z_L) - v^L(t, z) < \epsilon$.)

Restricting our gaze to ϵ-PUNEs, for small ϵ, is saying that militants will not be able to hold out with extreme positions if a very small change in policy can guarantee the party's victory. If a policy is very close to the militants' ideal point, then small changes will not cause the militants to lose much utility.

Finally, we call a PUNE *nontrivial* if neither party wins with probability one.

We shall show that if C2 holds, then for α sufficiently close to one, party L proposes a zero tax rate in all nontrivial ϵ-PUNEs of $\mathcal{G}_\alpha$, for ϵ sufficiently small. Thus if religion is sufficiently salient, then the L party plays the least redistributive economic policy. Finally, we show that nontrivial ϵ-PUNEs exist in these games, so that the result is not vacuous.

Let $(z_L(1), z_R(1))$ be any PUNE in the unidimensional game $\mathcal{G}_1$, and let $\overline{\mu}_{s^*}$ be the mean income of the citizen cohort who have precisely the median value of the religious trait in the state $s^*(z_L(1), z_R(1))$. We state:

 C2*   For all nontrivial PUNEs in the game $\mathcal{G}_1$, we have

(10.8) $$\overline{\mu}_{s^*} - \mu > \frac{(\mu - w_L)\Delta z(1)}{2(z_L(1) - a_L)},$$

where $\Delta z(1) = z_R(1) - z_L(1)$.

Our line of argument is as follows. All proofs of propositions in this section are presented in section 10.5.

Proposition 10.1 *Let v be in the interval (a_L, a_R). Suppose that for all s, $| a(s) - v | < \delta$. Let $\gamma > 0$. Then for all ϵ sufficiently close to zero, if (z_L, z_R) is a nontrivial ϵ-PUNE of the game $\mathcal{G}_1$ and if δ is sufficiently small, then $z_R - z_L = \Delta z < \gamma$.*

This proposition says that if uncertainty is small, then for arbitrarily small $\epsilon > 0$, ϵ-PUNEs of the one-dimensional game $\mathcal{G}_1$ must have the two parties' playing (religious) policies very close to each other.

Proposition 10.2 *Fix $\epsilon > 0$, and let $\{((t_L(\alpha), z_L(\alpha)), (t_R(\alpha), z_R(\alpha)))\}$ be a sequence of nontrivial ϵ-PUNEs in the games $\mathcal{G}_\alpha$, and let $\lim_{\alpha \to 1} z_L(\alpha) = z_L(1)$ and $\lim_{\alpha \to 1} z_R(\alpha) = z_R(1)$. Then $(z_L(1), z_R(1))$ is a nontrivial ϵ-PUNE in the game $\mathcal{G}_1$.*[2]

Proposition 10.3 *If uncertainty is small and C2* holds, then for all α sufficiently close to one, $t_L(\alpha) = 0$.*

Finally, we have:

Theorem 10.1 *If uncertainty is small, condition C2 holds, and α is sufficiently close to one, then for ϵ small, in any nontrivial ϵ-PUNE of the game $\mathcal{G}_\alpha$, $t_L(\alpha) = 0$.*

Finally, we prove that Theorem 10.1 is not vacuous:

Theorem 10.2 *Let uncertainty be small and condition C2 hold. Then, for all α close to one, and for ϵ small, ϵ-PUNEs exist in the game $\mathcal{G}_\alpha$.*

If we prove these propositions, we will have shown that, if there is a noneconomic issue which is sufficiently important to voters, if parties represent constituents who have preferences over taxation and the noneconomic issue, and if assumption C2 holds and uncertainty is small, then in all ϵ-PUNEs, the tax policy of the Left party will be significantly less than unity. (We remarked earlier that when $\alpha = 0$, the Left always proposes a tax rate of one in equilibrium: so as α increases, the tax rate eventually decreases to zero.) The result is striking because it may simultaneously be true that the ideal tax rate for the majority of the population, in all states, is unity. This "paradox" is due to the structure of political competition, which is party competition, in which the different

---

2. We can ignore tax rates in the game $\mathcal{G}_1$, since they are irrelevant there.

dimensions of policy cannot be unbundled. Although the ideal tax rate for the majority of a population may be unity, that tax rate will not be observed in equilibrium, even when one party represents (a subconstituency of) that expropriation-desiring majority.

I will try to give some intuition for how condition C2 drives our result. If α is close to one, then the game $\mathcal{G}_\alpha$ is essentially a one-dimensional game over religious policy. If uncertainty is small, then the median religious view varies little across states. In an equilibrium where both parties win with positive probability, both parties must therefore play a religious policy close to that approximately constant median religious view. We may even say that the cohort of the population who hold approximately the median religious view comprise the decisive voters. But if that cohort's wealth is greater than mean population wealth, as condition C2 states, then their ideal tax rate is zero. Competition forces Left (and Right) to propose a tax rate of zero, to attract the decisive cohort. Those who may object to some slippage in this argument should read the proofs.

We may apply exactly the same analysis to determine when Right parties (who represent rich, religious voters) will propose *high* tax rates. The key condition now turns out to be

$$(\text{C.3*}) \qquad \overline{\mu}_{s*} - \mu < \frac{(w_R - \mu)\Delta z(1)}{2(z_R(1) - a_R)}.$$

Note that the r.h.s. of (C3*) is negative, so (C3*) will be satisfied if:

C3 Uncertainty is small, and for all states, the mean wealth of the cohort of voters with the median religious view is *less* than mean population wealth.

Under these conditions, when α is sufficiently close to one and ϵ is small, Right will propose a tax rate of unity in all nontrivial ϵ-PUNEs.

10.4 Empirical Tests [3]

For the United States, I suggest that "race" is the prominent noneconomic issue. Using the National Election Surveys (NES), we computed whether the

---

3. I thank research assistants Woojin Lee and Humberto Llavador for carrying out the data analysis in this section.

average income of voters who hold the median view on the race issue is greater than mean population income—to see whether condition C2 holds. Among the many questions asked in these surveys is a "thermometer" question on "Blacks." Respondents are asked to choose a number between 0 and 100 telling how "warmly" or "favorably" they feel about the issue with 100 the warmest possible. In the question we used, the issue was simply stated as "Blacks." The results for 1974–1994 are presented in Table 10.1.

Not all respondents in the NES are voters; in particular, the respondent is asked if he voted. We took the mean population income (μ) to be the mean reported income of all respondents in the survey (column 1 of Table 10.1). Column 2 of the table gives the mean income of voters (which we do not use in our statistical test). Column 4 gives the median thermometer value of all voter responses on the "Black" issue, and column 3 gives the mean income of this median cohort ($\bar{\mu}$). It is evident that $\bar{\mu} > \mu$: in fact, using a central-limit-theorem test, we computed that for the four election years from 1988 on), $\bar{\mu} > \mu$ at the .999 significance level.

Table 10.1 Black issue (1974–1994)

Year	Mean income population	Mean income voters	Mean income cohort	Value of black issue for median voter[a]	Std. dev. income population	Std. dev. income voters	Std. dev. income cohort
1974	$12,730	$14,296	$15,043	65.07	$9,745	$10,104	$10,572
1976	$14,628	$15,929	$17,964	61.08	$10,719	$11,051	$11,774
1980	$20,955	$22,729	$23,357	64.46	$15,041	$15,236	$15,792
1982	$22,734	$24,482	$25,054	63.7	$15,959	$15,905	$12,937
1984	$25,402	$27,911	$29,458	65.01	$18,806	$19,375	$19,715
1986	$28,412	$31,896	$33,089	67.37	$20,439	$21,143	$20,860
1988	$29,927	$33,828	$37,597	62.92	$22,350	$23,170	$24,157
1990	$31,262	$35,977	$38,233	71.31	$23,980	$24,575	$24,810
1992	$35,751	$39,567	$40,277	65.57	$26,836	$27,209	$26,479
1994	$37,727	$43,263	$46,087	64.33	$27,864	$28,713	$31,733

a. Range [0, 100], where the higher the number the more favorable the agent feels toward black issues.

Table 10.2 Salience of values issue, U.S. electorate

Year	Salience
1974	0.312
1976	0.331
1980	0.397
1982	0.539
1984	0.605
1986	0.921
1988	1.236
1990	0.929
1992	0.595
1994	2.109

It is not surprising (compare columns 3 and 2 of Table 10.1) that the mean income of voters is greater than the population mean income. But it is not this fact alone which explains our result, since we note that, in every year, the mean income of the median cohort of voters is greater than the mean income of *voters*, as well.

Regarding the salience of noneconomic issues for the American electorate, George Gallup (of the Gallup Poll) says: "[Americans in 1995] are more concerned about the state of morality and ethics in their nation than at any time in the six decades of scientific polling."[4] We attempted to test whether the salience of noneconomic issues has been increasing, as follows. The National Election Survey asks each respondent to list the three most important issues, in his view. There are hundreds of acceptable answers to this question, coded in the NES. We coded these issues as "economic issues," "values issues," or "other issues," and defined the *salience of values*, for a cohort, as the number of values issues mentioned divided by the number of economic issues mentioned in the answer to this question. Table 10.2 gives the salience rate, so computed, for the election years 1974–1994.

Evidently Gallup's view is borne out: never, in the preceding twenty years, was the salience of values issues higher than in 1994. In fact, the salience of values

---

4. *The Economist*, November 11–17, 1995, 29.

issues had been rising steadily during this period in the United States, except for a decline in the period 1988–1992, roughly corresponding to a recession.

The British Social Attitudes Survey is the annual counterpart, in the United Kingdom, of the U.S. General Social Survey. In 1993, the BSAS asked a series of questions designed to ascertain the respondents' views on the authoritarian-libertarian dimension. The respondent was asked to mark his degree of agreement, on a scale of one to five (strongly agree, agree, neither agree nor disagree, disagree, strongly disagree) with the following statements:

(a) It is right that young people should question traditional British values;
(b) British courts generally give sentences that are too harsh;
(c) The death penalty is never an appropriate penalty;
(d) Schools should teach children to question authority;
(e) There are times when people should follow their conscience, even if it means breaking the law.

It is important to note that we do not have information on voters in the British data, only on the general population.

We coded the answers one to five, and assigned each respondent an average value, including in the sample only respondents who answered at least three of the five questions. We then computed the median cohort, whose response was 2.67, lying between "agree" and "neither agree nor disagree." We computed the mean income of the median cohort, and the mean income of the sample.

In Table 10.3, I report the statistical features of the answers to these questions that are relevant for us. This time, the mean income of the median cohort appears to be *less* than the mean income of the sample; the central-limit-theorem test says that this order of the two means is correct with probability

Table 10.3 British social attitudes survey, 1993: Authoritarian versus libertarian preferences

Sample size	2,100
Mean income of sample (μ)	£15,194
Median view on issue	2.667
Mean income of median cohort (m)	£14,691
Size of median cohort (n)	219
S.D. of median cohort's income (σ)	9,777
$\Pr\{m < \mu\}$	0.78

.78—not a very high confidence level. One must note, however, that we do not have the mean income of the median *voter* cohort, which may be greater than mean population income. If, however, we assume that "$\bar{\mu} - \mu < 0$" is true, then, from the discussion of section 10.3, the relevant hypothesis is about the behavior of not the Labour Party but rather the Conservative Party. The inference is that, with probability .78, inequality C3* holds, and the model, in that case, implies that a Conservative Party in power would move to the *left* in its economic policy as the salience of the authoritarian-libertarian issue increased.

From these tests the model suggests that, if the salience of the noneconomic issue of race increases in the United States, Democrats will propose increasingly conservative tax policies, while we have no reason to believe that Republicans will propose increasingly liberal tax policies. We have somewhat weaker reason to believe that, as the salience of the authoritarian-libertarian issue increases in Britain, the Conservative Party will move to the left in its economic policies.

10.5 Proofs of Theorems

Proof of Proposition 10.1:

Let $a^{\text{inf}} = \inf_s a(s)$ and $a^{\text{sup}} = \sup a(s)$. Since (z_L, z_R) is a nontrivial PUNE of the game $\mathcal{G}_1$, it follows that $(z_L + z_R)/2 \in (a^{\text{inf}}, a^{\text{sup}})$, for otherwise one party would win with probability one. As well, we know that $a_L \leq z_L \leq z_R \leq a_R$. Now suppose that z_L is less than a^{inf}, and suppose that δ is small. If L deviates to $z_L + 4\delta$, this costs L's militants very little in utility, but L now wins with probability one, because $(z_L + 4\delta + z_R)/2 > a^{\text{inf}} + 2\delta > a^{\text{sup}}$. (If $a(s)$ is less than the average of the two policies for all s, then L wins in every state.) Hence for any $\epsilon > 0$, if (z_L, z_R) is an ϵ-PUNE, and δ is small enough, we must have $z_L \geq a^{\text{inf}}$. An exactly parallel argument shows that $z_R \leq a^{\text{sup}}$. Therefore, $\Delta z \leq 2\delta$. Consequently, if uncertainty is small enough, we know that Δz is as small as we please. ∎

Proof of Proposition 10.2:

We first observe that $(z_L(1), z_R(1))$ must be a PUNE in $\mathcal{G}_1$. Suppose this were not so. Then one party—say L—could profitably deviate. This means L's militants would gain in the deviation. If L's opportunists also gained in the deviation, then for α close to one, L's militants and opportunists would also strictly gain in a similar deviation from $(t_L(\alpha), z_L(\alpha))$, which is impossible. It follows that L's opportunists do not gain in the postulated deviation in $\mathcal{G}_1$, which means the probability of L victory at $(z_L(1), z_R(1))$ is already one, and stays at one under the deviation. (This remark relies upon understanding the simple structure of PUNEs in the unidimensional Euclidean game $\mathcal{G}_1$.) But this means that $\lim_{\alpha \to 1} \pi(t_L(\alpha), z_L(\alpha), t_R(\alpha), z_R(\alpha)) = 1$. That is, the probability of L victory becomes arbitrarily close to one for α close to one in the sequence of PUNEs under consideration. But it then follows that, for α close enough to one, a very small deviation by L could render the probability of L victory one, which means that the PUNE in question is not an ϵ-PUNE. This contradiction establishes that $(z_L(1), z_R(1))$ is a PUNE of $\mathcal{G}_1$.

It now follows that $(z_L(1), z_R(1))$ is a nontrivial PUNE in $\mathcal{G}_1$, for if the probability of victory for one party were one, then the argument above would show that for α close to 1, $(t_l(\alpha), z_L(\alpha))$ would not be an ϵ-PUNE in $\mathcal{G}_\alpha$.

Finally, suppose that there was a deviation by party L, say, from $(z_L(1), z_R(1))$ at which the probability of L victory became one and L's militants lost utility less than ϵ. Then for α close enough to one, a similar deviation would give L an almost sure victory in $\mathcal{G}_\alpha$, at a cost of less than ϵ to L's militants, contradicting the fact that $(t_L(\alpha), z_L(\alpha), t_R(\alpha), z_R(\alpha))$ is an ϵ-PUNE in $\mathcal{G}_\alpha$. ∎

We next differentiate (10.6) with respect to the two components of Left's policy, which gives

$$
(10.9a) \quad \frac{\partial s^*}{\partial t_L} = \frac{\int\limits_W g_{s*}(w) r(\bar{z} + \frac{(1-\alpha)\Delta t}{\alpha \Delta z}(w - \mu), w) \frac{(1-\alpha)(w-\mu)}{\alpha \Delta z} dw}{\int\limits_W \int_{-\infty}^{\bar{z} + \frac{(1-\alpha)\Delta t}{\alpha \Delta z}(w-\mu)} \frac{\partial g_{s*}(w)}{\partial s} r(a, w) da\, dw},
$$

and

$$
(10.9b) \quad \frac{\partial s^*}{\partial t_L} = \frac{-\int\limits_W g_{s*}(w) r(\bar{z} + \frac{(1-\alpha)\Delta t}{\alpha \Delta z}(w - \mu), w) \left(\frac{1}{2} + \frac{(1-\alpha)\Delta t(w-\mu)}{\alpha(\Delta z)^2}\right) dw}{\int\limits_W \int_{-\infty}^{\bar{z} + \frac{(1-\alpha)\Delta t}{\alpha \Delta z}(w-\mu)} \frac{\partial g_{s*}(w)}{\partial s} r(a, w) da\, dw}.
$$

Proof of Proposition 10.3:

This proposition does not use the fact that the PUNEs in question are ϵ-PUNEs.

Suppose there is a sequence of α's tending to one, with an associated sequence of nontrivial PUNEs, in which $t_L(\alpha) > 0$. We shall show that, at each α sufficiently close to one, there is a direction in which Left's militants and opportunists will agree to deviate, which contradicts the assumption that we are at a PUNE.

To be specific, we shall show the existence, for α near one, of a direction $(-1, \delta(\alpha))$ such that

(10.10) $\nabla v_L \cdot (-1, \delta(\alpha)) > 0,$

and

(10.11) $\nabla_L s^* \cdot (-1, \delta(\alpha)) > 0,$

which means that both the militants and the opportunists in Left can increase their utility by moving in the direction $(-1, \delta(\alpha))$.

The components of the gradient $\nabla_L s^* = (\partial s^*/\partial t_L, \partial s^*/\partial z_L)$ are given by equations (10.9ab). Since $t_L(\alpha) > 0$, the direction $(-1, \delta(\alpha))$ is feasible at τ_L, for any number $\delta(\alpha)$.

Inequality (10.10) expands to

$$\delta(\alpha) < \frac{(1-\alpha)(w_L - \mu)}{\alpha(z_L(\alpha) - a_L)}.$$

For the moment, let us choose $\delta(\alpha) = ((1-\alpha)(w_L - \mu))/(\alpha(z_L(\alpha) - a_L))$. Substituting this value into the inequality (10.11), using the formulae for the components of $\nabla_L s^*$, and taking the limit of the derived expression as α goes to one, we may compute that (10.11) holds for α close to one if:

$$\int g_{s^*}(w) r(\bar{z}(1), w) \frac{w - \mu}{\Delta z(1)} dw + \frac{w_L - \mu}{2(z_L(1) - a_L)} \int g_{s^*}(w) r(\bar{z}(1), w) dw > 0.$$

(10.12)

Recall that $\bar{\mu}_{s^*}$ denotes the mean income in state s^* of the cohort of citizens with the median religious view. Then we have, by definition:

$$\bar{\mu}_{s^*} = \frac{\int w g_{s^*}(w) r(a(s^*), w) dw}{\int g_{s^*}(w) r(a(s^*), w) dw}.$$

Now divide inequality (10.12) by $\int g_{s^*}(w) r(\bar{z}(1), w) dw$, which gives us

$$\frac{\int w g_{s^*}(w) r(\bar{z}(1), w) dw}{\int g_{s^*}(w) r(\bar{z}(1), w) dw} - \mu > \frac{(\mu - w_L)\Delta z(1)}{2(z_L(1) - a_L)}.$$

But if uncertainty is small, then

$$\overline{\mu}_{s^*} \approx \frac{\int w g_{s^*}(w) r(\overline{z}(1), w) dw}{\int g_{s^*}(w) r(\overline{z}(1), w) dw}.$$

(We are here invoking Proposition 10.2, which tells us that $(z_L(1), z_R(1))$ is an ϵ-PUNE in $\mathcal{G}_1$, and so $\overline{z}(1)$ is close to $a(s^*)$.) It therefore follows that (10.12) is implied by C2*; hence (10.11) is true for this choice of $\delta(\alpha)$.

It follows that if we choose $\delta(\alpha) = \frac{(1-\alpha)(w_L - \mu)}{\alpha(z_L(\alpha) - a_L)} - \gamma$, for γ sufficiently small, then both (10.10) and (10.11) hold, which is the desired contradiction. ∎

Proof of Theorem 10.1:

Proposition 10.1 has shown that if $(z_L(1), z_R(1))$ is an ϵ-PUNE of $\mathcal{G}_1$ for all $\epsilon > 0$, then $\Delta z(1)$ is very close to zero, and $(z_L(1) - a_L)$ is bounded away from zero, since $z_L(1)$ is very close to the number ν in the interior of the interval (a_L, a_R). It follows that the r.h.s. of inequality (10.8) can be made arbitrarily close to zero. Now C2 implies that (10.8) is true. Now invoke Proposition 10.3. ∎

Proof of Theorem 10.2:

Let (z_L^*, z_R^*) be a nontrivial ϵ-PUNE in the game $\mathcal{G}_1$. (It is easy to see that, for small $\epsilon > 0$, these exist.) I shall argue that $((0, z_L^*), (0, z_R^*))$ is a PUNE in the game $\mathcal{G}_\alpha$, for α close to one. It is immediate that, for α close to one, neither party wins with probability one at this policy pair, which establishes the claim of nontriviality. The claim that $((0, z_L^*), (0, z_R^*))$ is indeed an ϵ-PUNE in $\mathcal{G}_\alpha$ also follows from its being an ϵ-PUNE in $\mathcal{G}_1$.

Suppose to the contrary, that for a sequence of α's approaching one, $((0, z_L^*), (0, z_R^*))$ is not a PUNE in $\mathcal{G}_\alpha$. There are two possibilities.

Case (1) There is a subsequence of α's such that Left's militant and opportunist factions would agree to deviate from $(0, z_L^*)$ in the game $\mathcal{G}_\alpha$.

Let, then, $(t_L(\alpha), z_L(\alpha))$ be a policy that Left's militants and opportunists would agree to deviate to from $(0, z_L^*)$ and that is a best response by Left to $(0, z_R^*)$, in the game $\mathcal{G}_\alpha$. It follows that $z_L(\alpha)$ must be close to z_R^* for α close to one, or else the probability of Left victory would be zero, contradicting the supposition that Left's opportunists agreed to deviate to this point from $(0, z_L^*)$. It therefore follows, by condition C2, that, for large α:

(10.13) $\overline{\mu}_{s^*} - \mu > \dfrac{(z_R^* - z_L(\alpha))(\mu - w_L)}{2(z_L(\alpha) - a_L)}.$

But (10.13) plays exactly the role of C2*: we can invoke the argument in the proof of Proposition 10.3 to conclude that, for large α, $t_L(\alpha) = 0$, in any Left best response to $(0, z_R^*)$.

Hence Left agrees to deviate to $(0, z_L(\alpha))$ from $(0, z_L^*)$ when facing $(0, z_R^*)$ in $\mathcal{G}_\alpha$. But, since both tax rates are zero, this means that Left would agree to deviate from $(0, z_L^*)$ to $(0, z_L(\alpha))$ *in the game* $\mathcal{G}_1$ when facing $(0, z_R^*)$—which is impossible, since $((0, z_L^*), (0, z_R^*))$ is a PUNE in $\mathcal{G}_1$. The contradiction shows that, for large α, $(0, z_L^*)$ is indeed a best response by Left to $(0, z_R^*)$ in $\mathcal{G}_1$.

Case (2) There is a subsequence of α's such that $(0, z_R^*)$ is not a Right best response to $(0, z_L^*)$ in $\mathcal{G}_\alpha$.

Let, then, $(t_R(\alpha), z_R(\alpha))$ be a Right best response in $\mathcal{G}_\alpha$ to $(0, z_L^*)$ to which Right's militants and opportunists agree to deviate, from $(0, z_R^*)$. We shall similarly prove that, for large α, it must be that $t_R(\alpha) = 0$, and a contradiction will then follow, just as above. This time, however, we cannot invoke the argument of Proposition 10.3, for we did not study Right's strategy in that proof. We therefore must prove independently that $t_R(\alpha) = 0$.

We know, by condition C2, that, for large α:

$$(10.14) \quad \overline{\mu}_{s^*} - \mu > \frac{(z_R(\alpha) - z_L^*)(\mu - w_R)}{2(z_R(\alpha) - a_R)},$$

because if $z_R(\alpha) - z_L^*$ did not become small, then Left would eventually win with probability one, and $(t_R(\alpha), z_R(\alpha))$ would not be an attractive deviation to Right's opportunists from $(0, z_R^*)$ in $\mathcal{G}_\alpha$.

Suppose $t_R(\alpha) > 0$. We shall construct a direction $(-1, \delta(\alpha))$ such that

$$(10.15a) \quad \nabla_R s^* \cdot (-1, \delta(\alpha)) < 0$$

and

$$(10.15b) \quad \nabla v_R \cdot (-1, \delta(\alpha)) > 0,$$

where the gradients are evaluated at $((t_R(\alpha), z_R(\alpha)), (0, z_L^*))$, which means that Right would agree to deviate in that direction, in $\mathcal{G}_\alpha$.

By differentiating (10.6), we compute that the components of the gradient $\nabla_R s^*$ are given by

$$\frac{\partial s^*}{\partial t_R} = \frac{\int\limits_W g_{s^*}(w) r(\bar{z} + \frac{(1-\alpha)\Delta t}{\alpha \Delta z}(w - \mu), w) \frac{(1-\alpha)(w-\mu)}{\alpha \Delta z} dw}{D},$$

and

$$\frac{\partial s^*}{\partial z_R} = \frac{- \int_W g_{s^*}(w) r(\bar{z} + \frac{(1-\alpha)\Delta t}{\alpha \Delta z}(w - \mu), w) \left(\frac{1}{2} - \frac{(1-\alpha)\Delta t(w-\mu)}{\alpha(\Delta z)^2} \right) dw}{D},$$

where D is the denominator in equation (10.9a). Using these formulae to expand (10.15a), and letting α tend to one, we observe that (10.15a) holds for α close to one iff

(10.16) $\delta(\alpha) < \dfrac{2(1-\alpha)(\mu - \overline{\mu}_{s^*})}{\alpha \Delta z},$

recalling here that $\Delta z = z_R(\alpha) - z_L^*$.

Let $\hat{\delta}(\alpha) = (2(1-\alpha)(\mu - \overline{\mu}_{s^*})/\alpha \Delta z$. Now suppose, contrary to (10.15b), that

(10.17) $\nabla v_R \cdot (-1, \hat{\delta}(\alpha)) \leq 0.$

Expanding (10.17) yields

$$\overline{\mu}_{s^*} - \mu \leq \frac{(z_R(\alpha) - z_L^*)(\mu - w_R)}{2(z_R(\alpha) - a_R)},$$

which contradicts (10.14). Hence (10.15b) holds at the above choice for $\hat{\delta}(\alpha)$. Consequently, for sufficiently small γ, (10.15b) holds for the direction $(-1, \hat{\delta}(\alpha) - \gamma)$.

But inequality (10.15a) holds as well for the direction $(-1, \hat{\delta}(\alpha) - \gamma)$, for any positive γ, since (10.16) is true. Hence this case is impossible as well. ∎

10.6 Concluding Remark

We may finally reflect upon a view, which has often been held in Left circles, that the Right deliberately "creates" a certain noneconomic issue—or tries to increase the salience of some such issue for voters—as a means of pulling working-class voters away from Left parties, thereby driving economic policies to the right. In this view, the Right party pretends to care about, say, the "religious" issue, while in fact being interested only in lowering tax rates (or rolling back nationalization and so on). Right may implement this masquerade by attracting political candidates who do, indeed, feel strongly on the "religious" issue.

Our analysis certainly indicates that this can be a strategy to achieve more conservative economic policy. Of course, Left can play the same game, and attempt to increase the salience of an issue for which C3 holds, thus forcing Right to move to the left on economic policy. Our analysis, then, suggests a new way to read the history of the emergence of noneconomic issues in electoral politics. Have Left and Right parties "chosen" which noneconomic issues to emphasize (that is, increase the salience of) with an eye toward pushing electoral equilibrium on the economic dimension in a desired direction?

Whatever the verdict on that historical issue, our analysis suggests that emerging new dimensions of citizen concern, which are addressed in competitive, party politics, can change the positions of parties on classical issues in surprising ways.

11

Distributive Class Politics and the Political Geography of Interwar Europe

11.1 Introduction

Since European socialist parties decided to participate in elections, around the turn of the twentieth century, many scholars have viewed European politics as the expression of the "democratic class struggle." That phrase was apparently first used in the title of a book by Dewey Anderson and Percy Davidson (1943), *Ballots and the Democratic Class Struggle,* with reference to the American experience, and the idea continues to resonate. Seymour Martin Lipset's (1959) classic *Political Man* is organized around the theme, with a chapter entitled "Elections: The Expression of Democratic Class Struggle," and the title of Adam Przeworski and John Sprague's (1986) *Paper Stones* is a phrase that early German socialists used to describe ballots: like real stones, casting them against the bourgeoisie could topple them from power.[1] The class analysis of elections is the hallmark of almost countless other studies: the best include Tingsten (1941), Abraham (1981), and Hamilton (1982).

These studies are written in the main by historians and political scientists; as is to be expected, the latter tend to abstract, somewhat more than the former, from thick historical particularity in favor of general explanation. Among the best of these is Gregory Luebbert's (1991) *Liberalism, Fascism, or Social Democracy: Social Classes and the Political Origins of Regimes in Interwar Europe,* in which the author attempts to explain what determined the choice of regime in countries in interwar Europe. Luebbert proposes that liberals failed to win, in this period, because they were not willing to use state power to intervene against what citizenries saw as the heartless effects of the unrestricted market,

---

1. Other indicative titles are Walter Korpi, *The Democratic Class Struggle* (1983), and Paul Nieuwbeerta, *The Democratic Class Struggle in Twenty Countries* (1995).

while both the socialists and the fascists were willing to do so. What, then, determined social democratic victories in some states and fascist victories in others? Luebbert proposes that the decisive factor was the status of class struggle in the countryside.

Luebbert says that the electorate was composed of four numerically significant classes: the urban working class, the urban middle class, the rural peasantry (family farmers who own land), and the rural proletariat (landless laborers). The classes of large capitalists and large landowners may, of course, have been important in their influence on parties,[2] but they were trivial as far as direct voting was concerned. The key to electoral victory, Luebbert claims, was the formation of an electoral alliance between the landed peasantry and one of the urban classes. *If* class struggle in the countryside was quiescent, then, he says, the social democrats were able to appeal to the landed peasantry and to construct an alliance between them and the urban workers, usually sufficient for electoral victory over the Right. In the cases where rural class struggle was active, however, the socialists always took the side of the rural proletariat, alienating the landed peasantry (their employers), thus leaving the latter class open to appeals from the fascists, who were then able to construct an alliance between them and the urban middle class. The three countries in which this second scenario transpired (says Luebbert) were Germany, Italy, and Spain.

It is worth reproducing Luebbert's prose on this point, as it is central to the present study.

> As we see, however, their [the German Social Democrats'] inability to make an effective alliance with the countryside had much more to do with their involvement in agrarian class conflict than it did with the burdens of membership in the initial Weimar coalition per se. The polarization of peasant-worker relations that ensued militated against an alliance that would have embraced measures to address the peasants' grievances as producers. (Luebbert 1991, 285)

> When socialist parties did succeed in making regime-stabilizing coalitions with the peasantry, it was not because they had a superior grasp of the strategic requirements of the moment, but because they did not attempt to organize the rural proletariat. (287)

---

2. As Abraham (1981) strongly argues.

Hence, the Spanish Socialists' campaign for land reform in the south of Spain antagonized peasants even in the north. (286)

Socialists succeeded in making a coalition with family peasants wherever the agrarian proletariat had been mobilized by others before socialists had an opportunity to do so. (288)

It was this entanglement [in rural class conflict] rather than conflicts between urban consumers and rural producers that distinguished socialist movements in Germany, Italy, and Spain from socialist movements in Norway, Sweden, Denmark, and Czechoslovakia. (300)

Whatever the quibbles about precisely who voted for the Nazis in Germany, it is clear that the social core of that support came from the urban middle classes and the Protestant peasantry of the west. (301)

Given the impuissance of liberal movements . . . the precondition of fascism was a working-class movement engaged in a defense of the rural proletariat. The coalitions of urban and rural middle classes that took shape in Spain, Italy, and Germany were premised on a common ambition to extirpate the socialist working-class menace. (303)

My aim in this chapter is to construct a model of party competition which can test Luebbert's theory. The model will consist of two parties, to be thought of as Socialists and Fascists, or Left and Right, each of which proposes a policy to voters. A *policy* will be a distribution of the national income among the four classes named above. If national income is fixed, as I shall assume, then the policy space is three-dimensional, since there are four classes. Giving each party the freedom to choose any income distribution (among the four classes) models the idea that both Left and Right parties were willing to intervene in the market: while the allocations of income that the market can deliver arguably constitute a small subset of the relevant three-dimensional simplex, these parties, according to Luebbert, did not restrict themselves to that subset. I will examine equilibria of the model under two conditions: first, that class conflict between the two rural classes is quiescent—has been resolved—and second, that it has not been resolved. The hypothesis I test is that the probability of a Left victory is greater in the first case than in the second case.

We shall use the concept of PUNE to model political competition between the Left and the Right. In the first part of the chapter, we assume that there are only two parties. Later we shall introduce a third party—the Communists—as well.

11.2 The Luebbert Model

According to Luebbert, interwar European politics were class politics: each party appealed to distinct classes by proposing policies which possessed clear consequences for the class distribution of income. Whether the Left or the Right won was, he wrote, critically determined by whether class struggle in the countryside was settled or contested.

11.2.1 THE FOUR-CLASS MODEL

The four relevant classes are the workers (W), the middle class (M), the landed peasantry (L), and the agricultural proletariat (A) or landless laborers. I shall telescope political behavior by assuming that each party proposes a division of national income among the four classes, that is, a vector (w, m, ℓ, a), where $\omega w + \mu m + \lambda \ell + \alpha a = 1$, all components of which are non-negative, and $(\omega, \mu, \lambda, \alpha)$, are the population proportions of the four classes. w is the income a worker will receive at this *policy,* and so on. The three-dimensional policy simplex is denoted by S_3.

This formulation of the policy space is, clearly, a vast simplification. In point of fact, parties proposed complex policies—involving nationalization, taxation, tariff policy, and land reform, to name several. I am assuming that voters interpret each policy as implying some distribution of income, (w, m, ℓ, a). That process of interpretation is here eclipsed. Furthermore, I am assuming that national income is fixed, and does not respond to different policies, and that no other constraints (except being in S_3) limit policies.

There are two parties, here called Left (L) and Right (R). The Left party "represents" primarily the workers, and secondarily the agricultural proletariat; the Right "represents" mainly the middle class and secondarily the landed peasantry. The (von Neumann–Morgenstern) utility functions of the parties are given by

(11.1a) $v_L(w, m, \ell, a) = \text{Log } w + \beta_L \text{ Log } a$

(11.1b) $v_R(w, m, \ell, a) = \text{Log } m + \beta_R \text{ Log } \ell$

where β_L and β_R are in the interval $[0, 1]$.

We assume that each party consists of opportunist, militant, and reformist factions, as usual. Since we may dispense with the reformist factions, we may view v_L and v_R as representing the ordinal preferences on S_3 of the two militant factions. Thus equations (11.1) say that the militant faction in each party has Cobb-Douglas preferences over the distribution of income within a pair of classes—the Left's militants caring about the two propertyless classes, and the Right's caring about the two propertied classes.

We employ, in this application, the finite-type model of probability (see section 2.4). The function π is defined on $S_3 \times S_3$. Denote a policy proposed by Left as $L = (w, m, \ell, a)$ and by the Right as $R = (w', m', \ell', a')$.

Let $f(x) = (1 - x)/(1 + x)$. Define

(11.2)
$$
\phi(L, R) = \omega \left(\frac{1}{2} + \frac{\epsilon_1}{2} f \left(\frac{w'}{w} \right) \right) + \mu \left(\frac{1}{2} + \frac{\epsilon_1}{2} f \left(\frac{m'}{m} \right) \right)
$$
$$
+ \lambda \left(\frac{1}{2} + \frac{\epsilon_2}{2} f \left(\frac{\ell'}{\ell} \right) \right) + \alpha \left(\frac{1}{2} + \frac{\epsilon_2}{2} f \left(\frac{a'}{a} \right) \right)
$$

ϵ_1 and ϵ_2 are i.i.d. random variables, uniformly distributed on $[0, 1]$. I shall assume that $\phi(L, R)$ is the fraction of the population who vote for L against R, which depends upon the realization of ϵ_1 and ϵ_2. To recall, note that if $L = R$, then $\phi = \frac{1}{2}$. If $w > w'$, then more than one-half the worker vote for L, but there is a random element in exactly what fraction vote for L. The term $f(w'/w)$ will be close to one if w is much bigger than w', and close to -1 if w' is much bigger than w. The random element can be interpreted in various ways: perhaps there is some indeterminacy in how the workers will vote because they care about issues other than economic ones, such as religion; perhaps there is indeterminacy because different voters transform (or interpret) the actual policies into income distributions in different ways.

Similarly, the other terms in the expression (11.2) express the fractions of the other three classes that vote for Left. Ideally, one would include four random variables in this expression, one for each class; I have settled for two, because having two already generates a sufficiently complex probability function.

It follows from (11.2) that the probability that L defeats R is

(11.3) $\quad \pi(L, R) = \text{Prob}[\phi(L, R) > \frac{1}{2}].$

Letting $a_1 = f(w'/w)\omega + f(m'/m)\mu$, and

$$a_2 = f\left(\frac{\ell'}{\ell}\right)\lambda + f\left(\frac{a'}{a}\right)\alpha,$$

we must compute

(11.4) $\pi(L, R) = \text{Prob}[a_1\epsilon_1 + a_2\epsilon_2 > 0].$

There are six cases.[3]

  Case (1) $a_1 > 0, a_2 < 0, -a_2/a_1 < 1$. Here we have

$$\pi = \text{Prob}\left[\epsilon_1 > \frac{-a_2\epsilon_2}{a_1}\right].$$

Clearly,

$$\pi = \int_0^1 \int_{\frac{-a_2\epsilon_2}{a_1}}^1 d\epsilon_1 d\epsilon_2.$$

Integrating (draw a picture of the unit square—see Figure 2.1), we have

$$\pi = 1 + \frac{a_2}{2a_1}.$$

In like manner, we can compute the probability of Left victory in the other five cases.

  Case (2) $a_1 > 0, a_2 < 0, -a_2/a_1 > 1$. Here,

$$\pi = \frac{-a_1}{2a_2}.$$

  Case (3) $a_1 < 0, a_2 > 0, -a_2/a_1 < 1$. Here,

$$\pi = -\frac{1}{2}\frac{a_2}{a_1}.$$

---

3. The model of probability used here corresponds to one illustrated by Figure 2.1. Had I used instead the model associated with Figure 2.2, there would be only one formula for the function π—much simpler. Unfortunately, I had not thought of the second approach when the research for this chapter was carried out.

Case (4) $a_1 < 0, a_2 > 0, -a_2/a_1 > 1$. Here,

$$\pi = 1 + \frac{a_1}{2a_2}.$$

Finally, we have obviously:

Case (5) $a_1 > 0, a_2 > 0 \Rightarrow \pi = 1$.
Case (6) $a_1 < 0, a_2 < 0 \Rightarrow \pi = 0$.

Thus we have defined the function π.

We now have all the information needed to define PUNE.

We next characterize the local conditions for a pair of policies' constituting a PUNE. Define $g(w, m, \ell, a) = 1 - (\omega w + \mu m + \lambda \ell + \alpha a)$. The "budget constraint" for each party is

$$g(L) \geq 0, \qquad g(R) \geq 0.$$

Define the gradients

$$\nabla_L \pi = \left(\frac{\partial \pi}{\partial w}, \frac{\partial \pi}{\partial m}, \frac{\partial \pi}{\partial \ell}, \frac{\partial \pi}{\partial a} \right)$$

$$\nabla_R \pi = \left(\frac{\partial \pi}{\partial w'}, \frac{\partial \pi}{\partial m'}, \frac{\partial \pi}{\partial \ell'}, \frac{\partial \pi}{\partial a'} \right)$$

$$\nabla v_L = \left(\frac{1}{w}, 0, 0, \frac{\beta_L}{a} \right)$$

$$\nabla v_R = \left(0, \frac{1}{m}, \frac{\beta_R}{\ell}, 0 \right).$$

Our conditions for a PUNE , via Farkas' lemma, are

(11.5a) $-\nabla g(L) = x_L \nabla v_L(L) + y_L \nabla_L \pi(L, R),$

(11.5b) $-\nabla g(R) = x_R \nabla v_R(R) - y_L \nabla_L \pi(L, R),$

(11.5c) $g(L) = 0, \quad \text{and} \quad g(R) = 0.$

These equations would suffice to characterize (global) PUNE if the function π were quasi-concave—but, in fact, it is not. We shall be content with locating local PUNEs.

Equations (11.5 a–c) constitute ten equations in twelve unknowns (w, m, ℓ, a, $w', m', \ell', a', x_L, y_L, x_R, y_R$). Thus they possess either no solution satisfying the non-negativity conditions or a continuum of such solutions.

11.2.2 THE MODEL WHEN AGRICULTURAL CLASS STRUGGLE IS RESOLVED

We must now model the idea that in some countries, class struggle between the landed peasantry and the agricultural worker was not an issue. To do this simply, I propose to say that, when class struggle in the countryside is resolved, a division of the agricultural product had been agreed upon; specifically, there exists a number $\gamma > 0$ such that all policies are constrained by

(11.6) $\ell = \gamma a.$

(One can interpret $\gamma/(1 + \gamma)$ and $1/(1 + \gamma)$ as the shares of the agricultural product going to landlord and tenant, respectively.) Thus each party proposes a policy subject to two constraints: the "budget" constraint (11.5c) and (11.6). We may reformulate this by saying that each party proposes a policy (w, m, ℓ) subject to

(11.7) $\omega w + \mu m + \left(\lambda + \dfrac{\alpha}{\gamma}\right) \ell = 1,$

leaving a, the agricultural workers' share, implicit. Thus policies are drawn for the simplex S_2 defined by (11.7).

Assumption (11.6) is equivalent to saying that each party will propose how much to give the rural sector, but it will leave the division of rural income to already existing contracts between family farmers and landless laborers.

The Right's utility function is defined on S_2 as

$$\hat{v}_R(w, m, \ell) = \text{Log } m + \beta_R \text{ Log } \ell,$$

as in (11.1b). The utility of Left on S_2 is, according to (11.1a), Log w + β_L Log ℓ/γ: but these preferences can be equally well represented by

$$\hat{v}_L(w, m, \ell) = \text{Log } w + \beta_L \text{ Log } \ell,$$

because γ is a constant.

By consulting (11.2), and using the constraint (11.6), we observe that the fraction of voters who vote Left is

$$\hat{\phi}(w, m, \ell, w', m', \ell') = \omega \left(\frac{1}{2} + \frac{\epsilon_1}{2} f \left(\frac{w'}{w} \right) \right) + \mu \left(\frac{1}{2} + \frac{\epsilon_1}{2} f \left(\frac{m'}{m} \right) \right)$$
$$+ (\lambda + \alpha) \left(\frac{1}{2} + \frac{\epsilon_2}{2} f \left(\frac{\ell'}{\ell} \right) \right);$$

hence the probability of victory is given by

$$\hat{\pi}(w, m, \ell, w', m', \ell') = \text{Prob}[\hat{\phi} > \tfrac{1}{2}].$$

The formulae defining $\hat{\pi}$ are hence given by the six cases discussed earlier, where now we define a_1 as previously, but newly define

$$a_2 = (\lambda + \alpha) f \left(\frac{\ell'}{\ell} \right).$$

Now define the budget equation as

$$\hat{g}(w, m, \ell) = 1 - \left(\omega w + \mu m + \left(\lambda + \frac{\alpha}{\gamma} \right) \ell \right).$$

Then a pair of policies $L = (w, m, \ell)$ and $R = (w', m', \ell')$ constitute a (local) interior PUNE iff there exist positive numbers x_L, y_L, x_R, y_R such that

(11.8a) $-\nabla \hat{g}(L) = x_L \nabla \hat{v}_L(L) + y_L \nabla_L \hat{\pi}(L, R)$

(11.8b) $-\nabla \hat{g}(R) = x_R \nabla \hat{v}_R(R) + y_R \nabla_R \hat{\pi}(L, R)$

(11.8c) $\hat{g}(L) = 0,$

and

(11.8d) $\hat{g}(R) = 0.$

This is a system of eight equations in ten unknowns; either there is no solution satisfying the non-negativity conditions, or there is a continuum of such solutions.

I call this model the *three-class model.*

11.3 Testing Luebbert's Theory

My method for testing Luebbert's theory is simple. I first describe the skeleton of the method, and then fill in the flesh. We study two countries, Germany and Sweden. In Germany, class struggle in the countryside was unresolved. Therefore we model Germany with the four-class model. We compute the (average) probability of Left victory in PUNEs of this model. Then we compute, counterfactually, the average probability of Left victory, had the three-class model described Germany. If the three-class-model probability of Left victory is greater than the four-class-model probability, Luebbert's theory is supported.

Sweden was a country in which, according to Luebbert, class struggle in the countryside was resolved. We compute the average probability of Left victory in PUNEs of the three-class model. Counterfactually, we also compute the average probability of victory in PUNEs of the four-class model, with Swedish parameters. Again, Luebbert predicts the first number is greater than the second. Now for some details.

11.3.1 DATA

The data of the models are the sets $\{\omega, \mu, \lambda, \alpha, \beta_L, \beta_R, \gamma\}$. The vectors $(\omega, \mu, \lambda, \alpha)$ are computed from Przeworski, Underhill, and Wallerstein (1978), who assembled them from census data.[4] They are

For Germany in 1933: $\{\omega, \mu, \lambda, \alpha, \} = (.4242, .3501, .1584, .0673)$,
For Sweden in 1930: $\{\omega, \mu, \lambda, \alpha, \} = (.4225, .2385, .2149, .1244)$.

Thus the propertied classes constitute 51% of the adult population in Germany and 45% in Sweden. Germany is more urbanized than Sweden: 77% of the population live in cities, versus 66% in Sweden. In sum, Sweden is less urbanized but more proletarianized than Germany.

---

4. Przeworski, Underhill, and Wallerstein (1978) report the detailed occupational distribution of the population of various European countries for various years. We partitioned the occupations into our four classes.

We chose various values for the remaining data $(\beta_L, \beta_R, \gamma)$ in our calculations.

11.3.2 THE CALCULATIONS OF PUNE

First, I describe the four-class model. Our problem is to find non-negative solutions of equations (11.5 a–c) in the twelve unknowns. These equations cannot be solved analytically. We first reduce the ten equations in twelve unknowns to four equations in six unknowns, as follows. Solve the first two equations of (11.5a) for (x_L, y_L)—this is easy, as the equations are linear in (x_L, y_L). Likewise, solve the first two equations of (11.5b) for (x_R, y_R). Solve the two budget equations for one Left policy variable and for one Right policy variable. This leaves four equations in six unknowns.

We now generate values for two of these six unknowns randomly, and solve the four-equation system in the remaining four unknowns, via Newton's method (we used Mathematica). We then check the values of all twelve variables: if they are non-negative, we have found a local PUNE. This and the previous paragraph describe one *iteration*.

Because we have two free variables to choose, we have a 2-manifold of solutions, and it will generically be the case that (if solutions exist) they will project onto a set of positive measure in the coordinate plane associated with two of the policy components.

A slight complication is introduced because there are six possible formulae for the function π, and hence for the gradients $\nabla_L \pi$ and $\nabla_R \pi$. We therefore in fact investigated four *cases,* corresponding to the four cases listed above in which $0 < \pi < 1$. For instance, we carried out the above procedure letting π be defined by Case 1 $\left(\pi(L, R) = 1 + \frac{a_2(L,R)}{2a_1(L,R)} \right)$. Consequently, when we generated a solution to the equations, we had to check whether, in fact, the solution is in the region of the simplex S_3 where the "Case 1" definition of π applies.

Our procedure was to compute 500 iterations for each case: thus 2,000 iterations for each experiment.

The method for solving the three-class model is analogous. First, solve two equations of the system (11.8a) for (x_L, y_L), then solve two equations of (11.8b) for (x_R, y_R), then solve (11.8c) for one Left policy variable and (11.8d) for a Right policy variable. This leaves two equations in four unknowns. We generate two of these unknowns randomly, and solve for the remaining two. We check the "case" constraint on π, and the non-negativity of the solution. We performed 2,000 iterations for each experiment.

Tables 11.1 and 11.2 (Tables 11.3 and 11.4) report the average probability of Left victory (π) in the PUNEs we found for Sweden (Germany), and the standard deviation of these probabilities (σ_1). They also report the *average expected vote* for Left, which is defined as

$$v = E(\phi(L, R)) = \frac{1}{2} + \frac{1}{4}\left(\omega f\left(\frac{w'}{w}\right) + \mu f\left(\frac{m'}{m}\right) + \lambda f\left(\frac{\ell'}{\ell}\right) + \alpha f\left(\frac{a'}{a}\right)\right).$$

We report as well the standard derivation of v for the PUNEs found (σ_2).

Table 11.1 Sweden, 1930

Run	β_L	β_R	γ	No. of classes	π	σ_1	v	σ_2	No. of PUNEs /2000
1	0.5	0.5	1.5	3	.638	.096	.5008	.0012	120
2	0.5	0.5	1.3	3	.644	.136	—	—	128
3	0.5	0.5	N.A.*	4	.435	.071	.5006	1.9×10^{-6}	9
4	0.5	0.5	N.A.	4	.452	.059	.5004	10^{-6}	9
5	0.5	1	1.5	3	.624	.150	.5042	.0036	51
6	0.5	1	N.A.	4	.318	.009	.498	3×10^{-6}	20
7	0.5	1	N.A.	4	.337	.022	.499	8×10^{-6}	36
8	0.1	0.5	1.5	3	.597	.185	.5044	.0061	281/4000
9	0.1	0.5	1.3	3	.589	.186	.5099	4.6×10^{-8}	152
10	0.1	0.5	1.5	3	.594	.184	.5042	.006	146
11	0.1	0.5	N.A.	4	.667	.023	.506	3×10^{-5}	58
12	0.1	0.5	N.A.	4	.634	.034	.5053	4×10^{-4}	111
13	0.5	0.1	1.5	3	.475	.170	.500	.0017	103
14	0.5	0.1	N.A.	4	.394	—	.500	—	1
15	1	1	1.5	3	.800	.064	.5004	.002	19
16	1	1	N.A.	4	.387	.023	.4998	1.3×10^{-6}	85

Note: N.A. indicates not applicable; a dash indicates not computed.
* There is no parameter γ in the four-class model.

Table 11.2 Sweden, 1930

Run	β_L	β_R	γ	No. of classes	w	m	ℓ	a	w'	m'	ℓ'	a'	π	No. of PUNEs /2000
1	0.5	0.5	1.5	3	1.16	0.62	1.22	0.81	0.76	1.30	1.25	0.83	.638	120
2	0.5	0.5	1.3	3	1.18	0.67	1.11	0.85	0.79	1.30	1.15	0.88	.644	128
3	0.5	0.5	N.A.*	4	1.23	0.74	0.65	1.32	0.83	1.45	1.06	0.62	.435	9
4	0.5	0.5	N.A.	4	1.21	0.77	0.68	1.30	0.84	1.41	1.05	0.67	.452	9
5	0.5	1	1.5	3	1.20	0.37	1.36	0.91	0.50	1.28	1.63	1.09	.624	51
6	0.5	1	N.A.	4	1.27	0.90	0.51	1.10	0.95	1.35	1.00	0.51	.318	20
7	0.5	1	N.A.	4	1.29	0.85	0.49	1.17	0.90	1.38	1.06	0.49	.337	36
8	0.1	0.5	1.5	3	1.21	0.60	1.17	0.78	0.64	1.34	1.38	0.92	.597	281/4000
9	0.1	0.5	1.3	3	1.22	0.63	1.08	0.83	0.69	1.33	1.26	0.97	.589	152
10	0.1	0.5	1.5	3	1.22	0.59	1.15	0.77	0.64	1.36	1.37	0.91	.594	146
11	0.1	0.5	N.A.	4	1.19	0.51	1.01	1.25	0.56	1.33	1.46	1.04	.667	58
12	0.1	0.5	N.A.	4	1.20	0.55	0.98	1.21	0.60	1.33	1.41	1.01	.634	111
13	0.5	0.1	1.5	3	1.16	0.65	1.20	0.80	1.13	1.33	1.11	0.74	.475	103
14	0.5	0.1	N.A.	4	1.02	0.76	1.39	1.00	0.86	1.18	1.05	1.11	.394	1
15	1	1	1.5	3	1.25	1.09	0.72	0.48	0.83	1.30	0.71	0.47	.800	19
16	1	1	N.A.	4	1.17	0.83	1.48	0.56	0.83	1.37	0.45	1.17	.386	85

Note: N.A. indicates not applicable.
* There is no parameter γ in the four-class model.

Figures 11.1a, 11.1b, and 11.1c graph the set of PUNEs found, for run 8, Sweden, the data being {country, year, β_L, β_R, γ}={Sweden, 1930, 0.5, 0.5, 1.5}. Figure 11.1a graphs the projection of the simplex S_2 onto the (w, ℓ) plane of Left policies, and Figure 11.1b shows the projection of S_2 onto the (m', ℓ') plane of Right policies. Figure 11.1c displays the PUNEs on S_2. When each PUNE, consisting of two policies, is color coded, as on the back cover of this book, the Left and Right policies of a PUNE appear in the same shade. Then the PUNEs appear to be symmetrical around a line in S_2, so that the Left and Right policies are approximately equidistant from that line, although the distance changes with the PUNE.

Table 11.3 Germany, 1930

Run	β_L	β_R	γ	No. of classes	π	σ_1	ν	σ_2	No. of PUNEs /2000
1	0.5	0.5	2	3	.727	.175	.501	.00097	35
2	0.5	0.5	1.5	3	.739	.165	.501	6×10^{-4}	25
3	0.5	0.5	N.A.	4	.408	.055	.500	3.6×10^{-6}	29
4	0.5	0.5	N.A.	4	.344	.026	.499	10^{-6}	17
5	0.5	1	1.5	3	.222	.182	.497	.0022	30
6	0.5	1	N.A.	4	.412	.096	.503	7×10^{-5}	21
7	0.1	0.5	1.5	3	.717	.175	.509	.0073	62
8	0.1	0.5	1.5	3	.712	.208	.510	.0079	56
9	0.1	0.5	N.A.	4	.445	.116	.504	7×10^{-5}	26
10	0.1	0.5	N.A.	4	.424	.111	.503	7×10^{-5}	30
11	0.5	0.1	1.5	3	.418	.190	.498	.004	29
12	0.5	0.1	N.A.	4	.105	—	.490	—	1
13	1	1	1.5	3	.767	.071	.500	8×10^{-5}	11
14	1	1	N.A.	4	.344	.026	.499	10^{-6}	17

Note: N.A. indicates not applicable; a dash indicates not computed.
* There is no parameter γ in the four-class model.

Table 11.4 Germany, 1933

Run	β_L	β_R	γ	No. of classes	w	m	ℓ	a	w'	m'	ℓ'	a'	π	No. of PUNEs /2000
1	0.5	0.5	2	3	1.13	0.33	2.11	1.06	0.40	1.20	2.14	1.07	.727	35
2	0.5	0.5	1.5	3	1.10	0.34	2.04	1.36	0.41	1.16	2.07	1.38	.739	25
3	0.5	0.5	N.A.*	4	1.21	0.79	0.60	1.71	0.77	1.31	1.18	0.38	.408	29
4	0.5	0.5	N.A.	4	1.13	0.95	0.54	1.50	0.91	1.18	1.10	0.35	.344	17
5	0.5	1	1.5	3	1.35	0.56	1.12	1.07	0.68	1.24	1.37	0.91	.222	30
6	0.5	1	N.A.	4	1.17	0.82	0.66	1.68	0.80	1.16	1.40	0.50	.412	21
7	0.1	0.5	1.5	3	1.30	0.41	1.49	1.00	0.35	1.29	1.96	1.31	.717	62
8	0.1	0.5	1.5	3	1.29	0.41	1.51	1.01	0.35	1.29	1.97	1.32	.712	56
9	0.1	0.5	N.A.	4	1.21	0.78	0.86	1.14	0.77	1.20	1.26	0.81	.445	26
10	0.1	0.5	N.A.	4	1.19	0.82	0.86	1.11	0.81	1.18	1.21	0.82	.424	30
11	0.5	0.5	1.5	3	1.10	0.65	1.49	1.00	0.75	1.20	1.29	0.86	.418	29
12	0.5	0.1	N.A.	4	1.03	0.09	3.91	1.71	0.26	1.27	1.56	2.15	.105	1
13	1	1	1.5	3	1.15	0.90	0.97	0.65	0.91	1.19	0.96	0.64	.767	11
14	1	1	N.A.	4	1.13	0.95	0.54	1.50	0.91	1.18	1.10	0.35	.344	17

Note: N.A. indicates not applicable.
* There is no parameter γ in the four-class model.

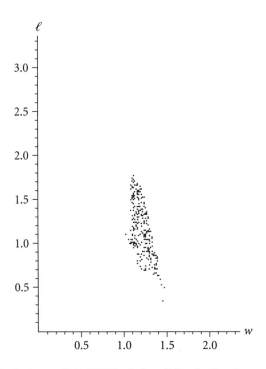

Figure 11.1a Projections of 281 PUNEs, Left policies, for Sweden onto the (w, ℓ) plane

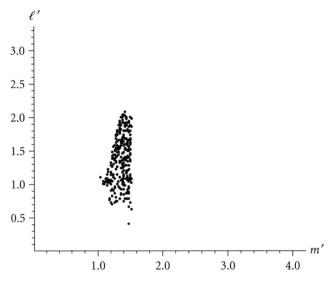

Figure 11.1b Projections of 281 PUNEs, Right policies, for Sweden onto the (m', ℓ') plane

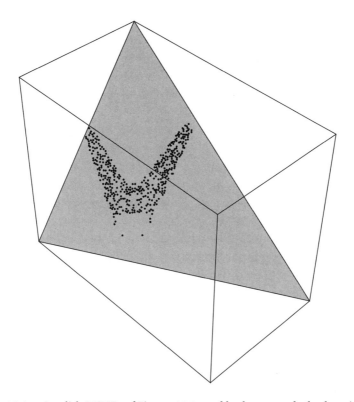

Figure 11.1c Swedish PUNEs of Figures 11.1a and b, shown on the budget simplex

11.3.3 OBSERVATIONS

(1) From Figures 11.1a and 11.1b, we see that, although we are dealing with a continuum of equilibria, they appear to be quite localized in the domain simplices. So the *average* values of the policies given in Tables 11.2 and 11.4 are quite indicative of what the *typical* equilibrium looks like.

(2) In all PUNEs, the expected vote (v) is very close to 0.5; note how small the standard deviations (σ_2) are. In fact, in all PUNEs we found, $0.48 < v < 0.52$. Contrast this with the probability of Left victory, which varies a great deal across experiments. As we have pointed out in Chapter 2, it is not inconsistent to say that Left has a high probability of victory *and* that we expect approximately one-half the population to vote for Left. The expectation that the vote will be close is different from the expectation that each party has an even chance of winning.

(3) To test Luebbert, we compare the average probability of Left victory in the three-class and four-class models. For Sweden (see Table 11.1), all experiments are consistent with Luebbert's theory except for the case $(\beta_L, \beta_R) = (0.1, 0.5)$ [see runs 8–12]. In that exceptional case, the Left has a higher probability of victory if there is class struggle in the countryside. I suggest that the explanation can be gleaned from looking at Table 11.2. Note that, unlike the other cases, the Left offers the landed peasantry more than one unit of per capita national income when class struggle is active in the countryside. This is because the Left essentially does not care about the rural proletariat in this case ($\beta_L = 0.1$), and so the Left militants allow the opportunists to determine the allocation of income in the rural sector. Hence Luebbert's explanation of Left defeat does not apply.

Turning to Germany (see Table 11.3), we see that all experiments are consistent with Luebbert's theory, except $(\beta_L, \beta_R) = (0.5, 1)$ [see runs 5 and 6], although the case $(\beta_L, \beta_R) = (0.5, 0.1)$ [see runs 11 and 12] is inconclusive as we found only one local PUNE in the four-class model for that parameter vector.

(4) When $\beta_L = \beta_R$, we should expect $\pi > \frac{1}{2}$ in the three-class model (see runs 1, 2, and 15 of Table 11.1 and 1, 2, and 13 of Table 11.3). This is because the utility functions of the two militant factions are in this case the same, except that the Left cares about workers primarily, and the Right cares about the middle class primarily, and $\omega > \mu$. This expectation is borne out in the observations.

(5) When there is class struggle in the countryside (four-class model, Sweden and Germany, in the cases $(\beta_L, \beta_R) = (0.5, 0.5)$ [see runs 3 and 4 of Tables 11.2 and 11.4] and $(\beta_L, \beta_R) = (0.5, 1)$ [see runs 6 and 7 of Table 11.2 and run 6 of Table 11.4]), the two parties polarize in opposite ways vis-à-vis the rural population: the Left dramatically favors the agricultural workers over the small farmers, and the Right dramatically favors the landed peasantry over the agricultural workers. In these two cases, $\pi < \frac{1}{2}$. These are the clearest illustrations of Luebbert's mechanism. The Left champions the cause of the agricultural proletariat, while the Right favors the small farmers, which increases the Right's probability of victory, because $\lambda > \alpha$, over what it would be in the three-class model.

(6) The case $(\beta_L, \beta_R) = (0.1, 0.5)$ is ambiguous. For Germany (see runs 9 and 10 of Table 11.4), the same intuition holds as in observation (5): in the four-class model the Left and Right polarize in opposite ways vis-à-vis the rural classes, and the probability of Left victory falls, in comparison with the three-class model. But in Sweden (see runs 11 and 12 of Table 11.2), although there is

some polarization in what the parties offer the rural classes, the probability of Left victory remains high—in fact, higher than in the three-class model. This is inconsistent with Luebbert's theory.

(7) With the exception of the case $(\beta_L, \beta_R) = (1, 1)$ in both Sweden and Germany, both parties offer the small farmers income greater than their per capita share (one) in the three-class model. The irony is that, in the one case where parties do count the welfare of the peasantry as heavily as the welfare of their primary class ($\beta = 1$), the peasantry get less. I have no intuition for this.

(8) The middle class is 50% larger in Germany than in Sweden. One might expect that this would cause the Left to offer them more in Germany than in Sweden: there is, however, no such pattern observed. The agricultural proletariat is twice as large in Sweden as in Germany. One might expect that, in the four-class model, this would cause the Right to offer them more in Sweden than in Germany, an expectation that is borne out by our observations.

(9) I next summarize the observations in a different way. Define

$$a_{LU} = \frac{\omega w + \mu m}{\omega + \mu}, \qquad a_{RU} = \frac{\omega w' + \mu m'}{\omega + \mu},$$

$$a_{LW} = \frac{\omega w + \alpha a}{\omega + \alpha}, \qquad a_{RW} = \frac{\omega w' + \alpha a'}{\omega + \alpha},$$

for two policies (w, m, ℓ, a) and (w', m', ℓ', a'). a_{LU} is the fraction of per capita national income that Left proposes to give to the urban classes, a_{LW} is the fraction of per capita national income that Left proposes to give to the working classes, and so on. Table 11.5 presents mini-tables of the form

	Urban	Workers
Left	a_{LU}	a_{LW}
Right	a_{RU}	a_{RW}

for every run reported in Table 11.2 (Sweden), and Table 11.6 presents the mini-tables for every run in Table 11.4 (Germany).

The second columns of all the mini-tables in Tables 11.5 and 11.6 offer no surprises: the Left (Right) always proposes to give the working (propertied) classes more than their share of national income. But the first columns of the mini-tables are not so intuitive. After all, both parties in all cases (at least weakly) favor "their" urban class over "their" rural class, and so one might conjecture that all the column-one entries in the mini-tables would be greater than one: but this is not the case. The main reason seems to be that, when class struggle has been resolved in the countryside, the parties are effectively competing directly for the votes of landed peasantry—see their utility functions—which raises what they offer the landed peasantry. Consider runs 1–4 for Sweden, in which $(\beta_L, \beta_R) = (0.5, 0.5)$. In runs 1 and 2, corresponding to the three-class model, the rural sector receives more than its share of national income, but

Table 11.5 Sweden, 1930

	Urban	Workers		Urban	Workers
Run 1			Run 9		
Left	0.965263	1.08039	Left	1.00723	1.13129
Right	0.954737	0.775922	Right	0.920799	0.75369
Run 2			Run 10		
Left	0.996082	1.10494	Left	0.992807	1.11764
Right	0.973918	0.810472	Right	0.899649	0.701415
Run 3			Run 11		
Left	1.05329	1.25047	Left	0.944776	1.20365
Right	1.05359	0.782233	Right	0.83768	0.669183
Run 4			Run 12		
Left	1.05133	1.23047	Left	0.965595	1.20227
Right	1.04556	0.801331	Right	0.863255	0.69326
Run 5			Run 13		
Left	0.900683	1.13404	Left	0.976082	1.07811
Right	0.781286	0.634204	Right	1.01031	0.809528
Run 6			Run 14		
Left	1.13657	1.23133	Left	0.926238	1.01545
Right	1.09425	0.849916	Right	0.956218	0.89369
Run 7			Run 15		
Left	1.13133	1.2627	Left	1.1923	1.07485
Right	1.0731	0.80674	Right	1.19131	0.979874
Run 8			Run 16		
Left	0.99002	1.11219	Left	1.04739	1.03125
Right	0.892436	0.70369	Right	1.04392	0.930514

in runs 3 and 4, the four-class model, they receive less—as it "should be." The same pattern holds in runs 5–7. However, the pattern breaks down in runs 8–12—here, the rural sector does not receive more in the three class model than in the four-class model, although it does receive more than its share of national income in all five runs (except for the marginal run 9, Left). In runs 15 and 16, where each party weights the welfare of "its" urban and rural classes equally, the urbanites receive more than their share of national income. Here, the aforementioned pattern reverses: in run 16 (four-class model), the rural sector receives a larger share of national income than in run 15 (three-class model).

Table 11.6 Germany, 1933

	Urban	Workers		Urban	Workers
Run 1			Run 8		
Left	0.76828	1.12042	Left	0.892108	1.25166
Right	0.76172	0.491742	Right	0.775021	0.48282
Run 2			Run 9		
Left	0.756366	1.1356	Left	1.01558	1.20042
Right	0.749113	0.54282	Right	0.964425	0.775477
Run 3			Run 10		
Left	1.0201	1.27846	Left	1.0227	1.17905
Right	1.01416	0.716598	Right	0.977296	0.811369
Run 4			Run 11		
Left	1.04861	1.18066	Left	0.896532	1.08631
Right	1.03208	0.83332	Right	0.953468	0.765062
Run 5			Run 12		
Left	0.992801	1.31166	Left	0.604979	1.12311
Right	0.933204	0.711493	Right	0.716672	0.518793
Run 6			Run 13		
Left	1.01175	1.23983	Left	1.03696	1.08154
Right	0.962774	0.758922	Right	1.0366	0.87303
Run 7			Run 14		
Left	0.897586	1.25892	Left	1.04861	1.18066
Right	0.775021	0.481451	Right	1.03208	0.83332

Next consider the German story (Table 11.6). How well does the conjecture, that the rural sector does better when class struggle is resolved than when it isn't, hold? It holds in runs 1–4, and in runs 7–10. In runs 5–6 it also holds, but perhaps not with statistical significance; runs 13 and 14 appear to show no significant difference in what the peasants are offered, and the small sample of run 12 eliminates runs 11–12 from consideration.[5]

The lesson we might cautiously draw from Tables 11.5 and 11.6 is that the rural population should receive, from both parties, a larger share of the national income when the class struggle among them is resolved. The political logic here seems clear. I do not know whether the conjecture is borne out historically.

11.4 Introducing the Communists: A Three-Party Model[6]

We now assume there are three parties, the Communists (C), the Socialists (L), and the Right (R). The utility functions of the militants in the three parties, on the domain S_3, are v_C, v_L, and v_R, where

$$v_C(w, m, \ell, a) = \text{Log } w.$$

Thus the Communists care only about the urban working class—this is a reasonable representation of the historical reality.

We now face a decision concerning how to model opportunists. We shall represent the opportunists in Left and Right as wanting to win the plurality of votes, but the opportunists in the Communist Party as wanting to defeat the Socialists. I propose that this is a reasonable representation of historical reality, for during the period 1926–1934, the Communists argued that Socialist parties were "social fascists," representing the bourgeoisie in hidden garb (see Claudin 1975). It therefore seems reasonable that an opportunist in the Communist Party would further his career by working to defeat the Social Democrats. Indeed, some historical commentators (cf. Claudin) argue that, had Communists not viewed the Social Democrats as their enemy, the cooperating left parties could have defeated fascism.

---

5. Recall that our runs are sampling from the full set of PUNEs, so statistical analysis is, in principle, possible.

6. This section is not for the computationally faint-hearted. There is, I believe, a value in showing that sometimes one must plunge one's hands in the mud.

Letting C, L, and R represent policies proposed by the three parties, define $\pi_{CL}(C, L, R)$ as the probability that C defeats L, $\pi_L(C, L, R)$ as the probability that L defeats both C and R, and $\pi_R(C, L, R)$ as the probability that R defeats C and L. I propose that the opportunists in these three parties have the utility functions π_{CL}, π_L, and π_R, respectively.

The most precise analysis of the competition between Socialists and Communists in this period is that of Przeworski and Sprague (1986), who compute statistically the vote trade-off that Socialist parties, in the various European countries, faced, defined as the number of working-class votes a Socialist party would lose for each middle-class vote it gained as it altered its policy to the right. In these authors' conception, Socialist Party leaders were concerned not just to increase their total vote, but to preserve their working-class vote. Thus even a positive vote trade-off (more middle-class votes gained than working-class votes lost) would not be sufficient to guarantee the mooted policy move. In our model, these concerns are embodied not in a unified party leadership but in different factions: the Socialist militants want to hew closely to a working-class line, while opportunists pursue (middle-class and peasant) votes.

11.4.1 FORMULATION OF THE STOCHASTIC ELEMENT IN VOTING

We shall assume that all voters are sincere, although this is not a good assumption when more than two parties compete if a coalition government is a possible outcome of the election. We consider coalition government in Chapter 14 below.

It is possible to generalize the stochastic voting formulation of equation (11.2) to the three-party model, but it turns out that the associated formulae for π_{CL}, π_L, and π_R are complex: the simplex S_2 (for I shall model the three-class case) is partitioned into approximately sixteen elements, with different (differentiable) expressions for the probability functions on each element. This renders computation of equilibria virtually impossible.

I therefore adopted the following, simpler formulation. Denote $C = (w_C, m_C, \ell_C, a_C)$, $L = (w_L, m_L, \ell_L, a_L)$, and $R = (w_R, m_R, \ell_R, a_R)$ as three policy proposals. Define

$$W_i = \frac{w_i}{w_C + w_L + w_R}, \qquad M_i = \frac{m_i}{m_C + m_L + m_R},$$

$$L_i = \frac{\ell_i}{\ell_C + \ell_L + \ell_R}, \qquad A_i = \frac{a_i}{a_C + a_L + a_R},$$

for $i = C, L$, and R. I propose to assume that the fractions of workers who vote for C, L, and R are, respectively,

$$W_C + x, \qquad W_L - x, \qquad \text{and} \qquad W_R,$$

where x is a random variable with zero mean, governed by a probability measure $\mathbf{F}_x$. I propose that the fractions of the middle class that vote for C, L, and R, are, respectively,

$$M_C, \qquad M_L + y, \qquad \text{and} \qquad M_R - y,$$

where y is a random variable with zero mean, governed by a probability measure $\mathbf{F}_y$. The random variables x and y are independent. Finally, I propose that the landed peasantry vote (with no stochastic element) for the three policies in proportions L_C, L_L, and L_R, and that the agricultural workers also vote non-stochastically for the three policies in proportions A_C, A_L, and A_R.[7]

I shall assume the case of the three-class model—that is, class struggle in the countryside is quiescent—because I am principally interested in whether the high probability of Left victory in the three-class model falls when Communists participate actively in elections.

We can now formulate the three probability functions. The event that C defeats L (that is, C receives more votes than L receives) is the event

$$\omega(W_C + x) + \mu M_C + (\lambda + \alpha)L_C > \omega(W_L - x) + \mu(M_L + y)$$

(11.9)

$$+ (\lambda + \alpha)L_L$$

(To see this, recall that $L_i = \gamma A_i$ for $i = C, L$, and R.) Define

$$\Delta_{CL} = \omega(W_C - W_L) + \mu(M_C - M_L) + (\lambda + \alpha)(L_C - L_L),$$

with $\Delta_{RL}, \Delta_{RC}, \Delta_{LC}$, and so on, defined in like manner. Then (11.9) can be rewritten

(11.10) $\quad y < \dfrac{2\omega x}{\mu} + \dfrac{\Delta_{CL}}{\mu} \equiv N_2(x).$

---

7. Why not insert more random perturbations in these vote fractions? For simplicity's sake.

It follows that

$$(11.11) \quad \pi_{CL} = \int_{-\infty}^{\infty} \int_{-\infty}^{N_2(x)} dF_y(y) dF_x(x).$$

(Note, of course, that π_{CL}'s dependence on the three policies is captured in Δ_{CL}.)

In like manner, the event that L wins is the union of the two events "L defeats C defeats R" and "L defeats R defeats C." Each of these events can be expressed as an inequality analogous to (11.10). After simplifying, we may express

$$(11.12) \quad \pi_L = \int_{-\infty}^{D} \int_{A_2(x)}^{\infty} dF_y(y) dF_x(x) + \int_{D}^{\infty} \int_{N_2(x)}^{\infty} dF_y(y) dF_x(x),$$

where

$$D = \frac{\Delta_{RC} - \Delta_{CL}}{3\omega}, \qquad A_2(x) = \frac{\omega}{2\mu}x + \frac{\Delta_{RL}}{2\mu}.$$

In like manner, the event "R wins" is the union of the two events "R defeats L defeats C" and "R defeats C defeats L"; the probability of this event is

$$(11.13) \quad \pi_R = \int_{-\infty}^{D} \int_{-\infty}^{A_2(x)} dF_y(y) dF_x(x) + \int_{D}^{\infty} \int_{-\infty}^{A_1(x)} dF_y(y) dF_x(x),$$

where $A_1(x) = -\omega x/\mu + \Delta_{RC}/\mu$.[8]

Note that, because of the stochastic formulation of voting I have assumed, we can express the three functions π_{CL}, π_L, and π_R as functions solely of the vectors (w_C, m_C, ℓ_C), (w_L, m_L, ℓ_L), and (w_R, m_R, ℓ_R)—that is, we can define them on the domain $S_2 \times S_2 \times S_2$. (This is because the fractions $a_i/(a_C + a_L + a_R)$ are identical to the fractions $\ell_i/(\ell_C + \ell_L + \ell_R)$.) Thus under the supposition that class struggle in the countryside is resolved, we can use the utility functions $\hat{v}_C$, $\hat{v}_L$, and $\hat{v}_R$, defined on the domain S_2 and the probability functions $\hat{\pi}_{LC}$, $\hat{\pi}_L$, and $\hat{\pi}_R$, defined on the domain $S_2 \times S_2 \times S_2$.

---

8. See the appendix to this chapter for the derivation of formulae (11.12) and (11.13).

11.4.2 EQUILIBRIUM

In this three-party model it is no longer true that the reformists are gratuitous in the mathematical characterization of PUNE. Nevertheless, to simplify our analysis, we shall continue to suppose that the militants and opportunists are the only active factions. (Otherwise, we would have to add two more Lagrange multipliers, associated with gradients of the reformist factions, to the set of unknowns.) A PUNE is therefore a policy for each party such that no party, given the policies of the other two, can find another policy to which both its militants and opportunists agree to deviate. The necessary conditions are: there exist policies C, L, and R and non-negative numbers x_C, y_C, x_L, y_L, x_R, and y_R such that

(11.14a) $-\nabla \hat{g}(C) = x_C \nabla \hat{v}_C(C) + y_C \nabla_C \hat{\pi}_{CL}(C, L, R),$

(11.14b) $-\nabla \hat{g}(L) = x_L \nabla \hat{v}_L(L) + y_L \nabla_L \hat{\pi}_L(C, L, R),$

(11.14c) $-\nabla \hat{g}(R) = x_R \nabla \hat{v}_R(R) + y_R \nabla_R \hat{\pi}_R(C, L, R),$

and

(11.14d) $\hat{g}(C) = 0, \quad\quad \hat{g}(L) = 0, \quad\quad \hat{g}(R) = 0.$

Here

$$\nabla_C \hat{\pi}_{CL} = \left(\frac{\partial \hat{\pi}_{CL}}{\partial w_C}, \frac{\partial \hat{\pi}_{CL}}{\partial m_C}, \frac{\partial \hat{\pi}_{CL}}{\partial \ell_C} \right),$$

with similar expressions for $\nabla \pi_L$ and $\nabla_R \pi_R$.

    These constitute twelve equations in fifteen unknowns. Consequently, we can expect to find a 3-manifold of PUNEs.

11.4.3 THE CHOICE OF F_x AND F_y

Since $W_C + x$, $W_L - x$, $M_L + y$, and $M_R - y$ are supposed to be numbers in the interval $[0, 1]$, we should choose the probability measures which govern the behavior of the random variables x and y to have finite support—more precisely, support consisting of some proper subinterval of $[-1, 1]$. Unfortunately, if we do so, the formulae (11.11–11.13) become very complex: for example, regarding (11.12), the precise analytical representation of π_L depends upon the relationship of the numbers D, $A_2(x)$, and $N_2(x)$ to the boundaries of the supports of F_x and F_y. Even choosing F_x and F_y to be uniform distributions causes there to be approximately a dozen different cases for the (differentiable) functional form of π_L, on a dozen elements of a partition of the domain. This renders calculation of equilibria impractical, to say the least.

The way to circumvent the problem is to choose probability distributions with support on the whole real line. Then there will be a single differentiable expression for each of π_{CL}, π_L, and π_R. This is what I have done. To be specific I chose F_x and F_y, the distribution functions, to be logistic distributions on the real line:

$$(11.15a) \quad F_x(x; a, b) = \frac{1}{1 + \exp\left(\frac{-(x-a)}{b}\right)}, \quad \text{and}$$

$$(11.15b) \quad F_y(y; c, d) = \frac{1}{1 + \exp\left(\frac{-(y-c)}{d}\right)}.$$

Discussion of the choice of the parameters a, b, c, and d is briefly postponed.

Substituting into (11.11), (11.12), and (11.13) from (11.15a,b) gives explicit formulae for the probability functions. There is, however, a problem of complexity. For careless choices of the parameters a, b, c, and d, the derivatives of the expressions for π_{CL}, π_L, and π_R have no closed-form representations—and these derivatives enter the equations (11.14a,b,c) that we must solve. Moreover, solving these equations by Newton's method requires taking derivatives of these derivatives—an impossibly time-consuming task, if the gradients themselves have no closed-form representations.

This problem can, however, be resolved by careful choice of (a, b, c, d). The first step is to introduce the following change of variable in equations (11.11), (11.12), and (11.13):

$$v = e^{-\left(\frac{x-a}{b}\right)}.$$

We may then write[9]

$$(11.16a) \quad \pi_{CL} = \int_0^{\infty} \frac{1}{(1 + y_{CL}v^K)(1 + v)^2} dv,$$

---

9. See the appendix to this chapter for the derivation of formulae (11.16a,b,c).

$$\text{(11.16b)} \quad \pi_L = 1 - \int_{e^{\frac{-(D-a)}{b}}}^{\infty} \frac{1}{(1 + y_{RL} v^{K/4})(1 + v)^2} dv - \int_0^{e^{\frac{-(D-a)}{b}}} \frac{1}{(1 + y_{CL} v^{K})(1 + v)^2} dv,$$

and

$$\text{(11.16c)} \quad \pi_R = \int_0^{e^{\frac{-(D-a)}{b}}} \frac{1}{(1 + y_{RC} v^{-K/2})(1 + v)^2} dv + \int_{e^{\frac{-(D-a)}{b}}}^{\infty} \frac{1}{(1 + y_{RL} v^{K/4})(1 + v)^2} dv,$$

where

$$\text{(11.17)} \quad \begin{cases} y_{CL} = \exp\left(\dfrac{-\Delta_{CL} - 2a\omega}{\mu d} + \dfrac{c}{d}\right) \\[2mm] y_{RL} = \exp\left(\dfrac{-\Delta_{RL} - a\omega}{2\mu d} + \dfrac{c}{d}\right) \\[2mm] y_{RC} = \exp\left(\dfrac{-\Delta_{RC} + a\omega}{\mu d} + \dfrac{c}{d}\right) \\[2mm] K = \dfrac{2\omega}{\mu} \dfrac{b}{d}. \end{cases}$$

Notice that if $K = 4$, then all the integrands in formulae (11.16a,b,c) become rational functions of v, and hence can be integrated in closed form, thus allowing us to compute closed-form expressions for the required gradients of π_{CL}, π_L, and π_R.

We now choose $a = c = 0$. This sets the means of $\mathbf{F}_x$ and $\mathbf{F}_y$ equal to zero. What remains is the choice of (b, d). I chose (b, d) to satisfy, along with a third variable, z, the following three equations:

$$\text{(11.18)} \quad \begin{cases} F_x(\tfrac{1}{3}; 0, b) - F_x(\tfrac{-1}{3}; 0, b,) = z \\[2mm] F_y(\tfrac{1}{3}; 0, d) - F_y(\tfrac{-1}{5}; 0, d,) = z \\[2mm] \left(\dfrac{2\omega}{\mu}\right) \dfrac{b}{d} = 4. \end{cases}$$

For the 1933 German values of (ω, μ), the solution is

$$b = 0.00893, \qquad d = 0.0542, \qquad z = 1 - 10^{-16}.$$

If the computer is indeed accurate to sixteen places, then with these choices of the parameters (a, b) and (c, d), x will lie outside the interval $(-\frac{1}{3}, \frac{1}{3})$ only with probability 10^{-16}, and y will lie outside the interval $(-\frac{1}{5}, \frac{1}{3})$ with the same probability. This means that the numbers $W_C + x$, $W_L + y$, $M_L - y$, and $M_R - y$ will essentially always be "legitimate" population shares.[10] The third equation in (11.18) sets K equal to four.

11.4.4 COMPUTATIONAL PROCEDURE

We solve the equations for a PUNE as follows. Solve two equations of (11.14a) for (x_C, y_C); solve two equations of (11.14b) for (x_L, y_L); solve two equations of (11.14c) for (x_R, y_R). Solve the three equations of (11.14d) for m_C, m_L, and w_R, respectively. This leaves three equations in the six unknowns w_C, ℓ_C, w_L, ℓ_L, m_R, and ℓ_R. My procedure was to choose values of w_C, w_L, and m_R randomly in the interval $[1, 1.5]$, and then solve the three remaining equations for the three remaining unknowns. We then check the values of the $(x_L, y_L, x_C, y_C, x_R, y_R)$: if they are non-negative, we have a PUNE. This calculation constitutes one iteration of the program.[11]

Tables 11.7 and 11.8 summarize the results for Sweden and Germany. The central observation from Table 11.7 is unsurprising: the presence of the Communist Party dramatically reduces the advantage that the Socialists have over the Right. In both Sweden and Germany, the probability that the Socialists win is about 8%, contrasted with probabilities of greater than one-half in the two-party, three-class model. In the three-party case, the probability that some left party wins a plurality $[1 - \pi_R]$ is less than 20% in both Sweden and Germany, much smaller than the probability of Left's winning in the analogous two-party

---

10. Indeed, graphing the density functions of $\mathbf{F}_x$ and $\mathbf{F}_y$ shows that, for all practical purposes, x and y lie in the interval $(-0.1, 0.1)$.

11. Even with the efforts I made to produce simple expressions for the probability functions, it takes a work station (vintage 1998) approximately four hours to perform 100 iterations of this program, written in Mathematica 3.0. I supply the Jacobian of the system to the FindRoot subroutine. The three-party problem is much more complex than the two-party problem.

Table 11.7 The three-party probabilities

	β_L	β_R	γ	π_{CL}	σ_{CL}	π_L	σ_L	π_R	σ_R	v_C	v_L	v_R	PUNEs /100
Germany	.5	.5	1.5	.768	.208	.082	.123	.809	.239	.333	.317	.349	31
Sweden	.5	.5	1.5	.725	.240	.080	.136	.831	.256	.331	.321	.348	70

Table 11.8 The three-party PUNE policies

	β_L	β_R	γ	w_C	m_C	ℓ_C	w_L	m_L	ℓ_L	w_R	m_R	ℓ_R
Germany	.5	.5	1.5	1.34	0.77	0.80	1.25	0.48	1.49	0.69	1.19	1.43
Sweden	.5	.5	1.5	1.29	0.74	0.93	1.25	0.44	1.22	0.76	1.22	1.30

model.[12] With a caveat concerning my change in the formulation of uncertainty between the two-party and three-party models, the conclusion is that the presence of a Communist party dramatically increases the probability of a Right victory.

The expected vote fractions of the three parties are, however, almost equal. Although I do not report standard deviations on the v variables, they are very small. No party, in any PUNE, has an expected vote fraction outside the interval (0.30, 0.36). As in the two-party model, probabilities of victory vary much more than expected vote fractions.

Finally, what is the probability that the two left parties together win a majority of the vote? This is the probability that Right wins a minority, which is

$$\text{Prob}\left[\frac{\omega W_R + \mu M_R + (\lambda + \alpha)L_R - 0.5}{\mu} < y\right] =$$

$$1 - F_y\left[\frac{\omega W_R + \mu M_R + (\lambda + \alpha)L_R - 0.5}{\mu}; c, d\right].$$

It turns out that in all PUNEs, the left parties together win a majority with a probability that is indistinguishably less than one. This is not a surprise, given that in expectation each party wins about one-third of the vote. Counter-

---

12. Analogous in the sense of sharing the parameter values (β_L, β_R, γ).

theoretically, in Germany the Nazi Party won 43.9% of the vote in the 1933 Reichstag elections, while the Communists and Socialists together won only 30.6% (Hamilton 1982, 476). However, there were more than three parties in that election.

Table 11.8 presents the average values of the policies in the PUNEs found. Here there are no surprises. As would be expected, the Communists offer more on average to the workers than the other two parties do, the Right offers more to the middle class than the other two parties do, and the Communists offer least to the peasantry. The model bears out our intuitions.

Although I do not report the standard deviations of the parties' policies over the PUNE that I found, I present, in Figures 11.2a, 11.2b, and 11.2c, the projections of the 70 PUNEs, for the Swedish run, onto the (w, ℓ) plane. We observe that the PUNEs are quite concentrated in the policy simplices, and so the average policy values reported in Table 11.8 are reflective of the typical PUNE.

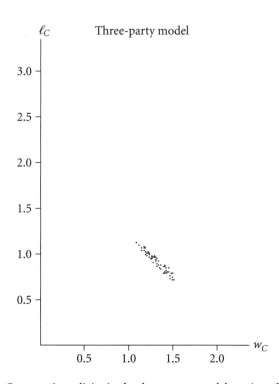

Figure 11.2a Communist policies in the three-party model, projected onto the (w, ℓ) plane

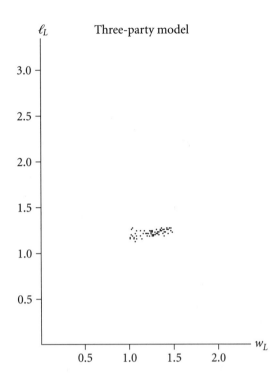

Figure 11.2b
Socialist policies in the
three-party model, projected
onto the (w, ℓ) plane

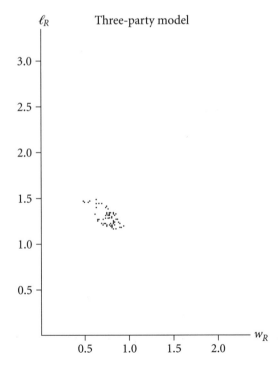

Figure 11.2c
Right policies in the three-
party model, projected onto
the (w, ℓ) plane

11.5 Conclusion

Our analysis provides strong but not conclusive support for Luebbert's theory of regime choice in European countries during the interwar period. The support is strong because Luebbert's claim is true for most parameter vectors of our model, and moreover, Luebbert's mechanism appears also to hold (that is, the Left sustained lower probabilities of victory when class struggle in the countryside was active *because* it proposed to give a lot to the agricultural proletariat and only a little to the landed peasantry). The support is not conclusive, because there are parameter values of our model for which Luebbert's claim is false. Finally, we undertook some three-party analysis. Although the results were not surprising, they show that the PUNE concept yields a tractable model with many parties as well as with many issue dimensions.

We assumed that voters were interested only in their economic fortunes: we have relegated noneconomic interests to their influence on an unstudied random variable that affects the fractions of classes that vote for policies. Perhaps this assumption is not so disturbing to some, although it surely is not uncontestable. When voters chose between Socialists and Communists in Germany, there was surely more at issue than the policies those parties announced concerning income distribution. A vote for the Communists was implicitly a statement of sympathy with the USSR—that is, a statement with ideological as well as economic content. Thus, in reality, I do not believe that the Communists had a .77 probability of defeating the Socialists in Germany, as Table 11.7 says.[13] That is because many citizens voted against the Communists for reasons other than economic ones. To model this would require adding another dimension to the policy space—say, the party's posture toward the USSR. Doing so would certainly be tractable, in our model, but I have not pursued this tack for lack of data that would enable me to calibrate citizen preferences on the issue.

Finally, I must remark that the Right has been modeled, here, as a conservative party which represents the propertied classes. There is nothing in the model that captures the fascist nature of the victorious parties in Germany, Italy, and Spain. This analysis, therefore, has nothing to say about why fascism, rather than traditional conservatism, became the scourge of Europe in the interwar period.

---

13. In the four Reichstag elections held between 1930 and 1933 in Germany, the Communists (KPD) received between 53% and 83% of the Socialist (SPD) vote. (See Hamilton 1982, 476.)

11.6 Methodological Coda 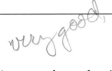 *very good!*

It is fitting to ponder, at the end of a chapter like this one, what value is added, or can be added, by a social science approach to a complex historical question. First, do we learn anything from Luebbert that we did not learn from a more classic historical analysis, and second, do we learn anything from the formalization of Luebbert's theory that I have proposed, using the concept of party-unanimity Nash equilibrium, that we did not learn from Luebbert's informal analysis?

Luebbert abstracts from much historical detail. He characterizes the democratic struggle as one vying for the support of four classes, and he argues that the Left lost to the Right when it made a certain strategic error. That error was to support a very small class, the agricultural proletariat, thus alienating itself from the natural enemy of the small class, the larger class of landed farmers. However, this error was only made under a certain contingency—namely, when the two agricultural classes were locked in struggle over division of the pie. In countries where the relationship between the two agricultural classes was relatively harmonious, the Left did not stir things up, and consequently it was able to appeal to the landed peasantry as effectively as the Right was. Since the urban working class was larger than the urban middle class, the Left then stood a good chance of defeating the Right.

Naturally this cannot constitute a complete explanation for why Germany became fascist and Sweden did not, because in each actual historical situation, there were many other variables which are ignored by the analysis, and even if Luebbert has located the most important *general* mechanism—more important, say, than the role of religion or of anti-Semitism—it is always possible that a particular variable in a particular country—say, the nature of the armistice at Versailles—was of overwhelming importance. The claim of the abstract argument can be at best the following: that if we observe a large sample of countries, then we should observe Left victories more often in the subsample where the agricultural class struggle was quiescent than where it was active. The justification of this claim is that, on average, the idiosyncratic characteristics of countries, which is to say the characteristics that have not been modeled, will "average out."

What does the formal analysis with PUNE add to Luebbert's abstraction? I think, principally, it shows that it was not a coincidence that the Left supported the agricultural workers, thus alienating the peasantry, when agricultural class struggle was active. This was, if you will, a consequence of the factional intraparty struggle and, in particular, the role of the militants in the Left. The opportunists in the Left would, presumably, have been happy not to have supported land reform, but the militants would not settle for that. The equilibrium analysis shows that, given parties with factions guided by rather simple and clear motivations, the Left will win with smaller probability in a country where agricultural class struggle is active than where it is passive, ceteris paribus. In this sense, the analysis instructs us not to view Left support for land reform as a tactical error: it was part and parcel of the historical development of social democratic parties, which emerged in every case with militant factions— factions in the absence of which these parties might well have lost their socialist character. Thus, imagining a social democratic party without a militant faction may well be equivalent to imagining a nonsocialist party.

That ceteris paribus phrase is, to be sure, what distinguishes the methodology of the social scientist from that of the historian: the social scientist wants, above all, a controlled experiment where aspects of the environment which he or she deems secondary to the main explanation are held constant; while for the historian, the interest lies in the distinguishing details between situations. Neither method dominates the other: each, that is, adds value to the explanation provided by the other.

How correct is Luebbert's explanation? Has he found the best explanation of the genesis of highly differentiated political regimes in the interwar period, or does his explanation simply predict, fortuitously, what actually occurred? The final verdict, I think, must lie with the historian. For the social scientist begins by excluding much information which is available about the historical events in question, before her story commences. Abstraction is, in other words, a process of the destruction of information, a process embarked upon in the hopes of revealing an underlying skeleton not otherwise perceptible. And what guides the social scientist in deciding what information to destroy or ignore is not theorized—it is, simply, intuition. That intuition is, one hopes, based on inductive reasoning from many other modeling exercises deemed to have been successful. I believe that the historian must have the final word, because he, at least in principle, begins by not ignoring anything. (Whether any practicing historian actually works this way is unknown to me; historians, too, doubtless have their theories which serve to restrict the information they must examine.) Nevertheless, the adjudicating historian must be one who is not averse to the abstract method as such, one, that is, who assents to the view that at least in principle social science can shed light on the evolution of society.

Appendix 11A

I. The Derivation of Formulae (11.12) and (11.13)

(1) The event that "L wins" is the union of the two events "L defeats R defeats C" and "L defeats C defeats R." Accordingly, the probability that "L wins," π_L, is the sum of the probability that "L defeats R defeats C," $\pi_L^{(1)}$, and the probability that "L defeats C defeats R," $\pi_L^{(2)}$.

(i) We compute $\pi_L^{(1)}$ first. The event "L defeats R defeats C" is the intersection of the event "L defeats R" and the event "R defeats C." A simple computation shows that the event "L defeats R" is $\{y : y > A_2(x) \equiv (\omega/2\mu)x + \Delta_{RL}/2\mu\}$, and the event "$R$ defeats C" is $\{y : y < A_1(x) \equiv -(\omega/\mu)x + \Delta_{RC}/\mu\}$. Therefore the event "$L$ defeats R defeats C" is $\{y : A_2(x) < y < A_1(x)\}$, and this event is nonvacuous iff $A_2(x) < A_1(x)$, or equivalently iff $x < D \equiv (\Delta_{RC} - \Delta_{CL})/3\omega$. Hence the probability that "L defeats R defeats C" is

$$\pi_L^{(1)} = \int_{-\infty}^{D} \int_{A_2(x)}^{A_1(x)} d\mathbf{F}_y(y) d\mathbf{F}_x(x).$$

(ii) The probability that "L defeats C defeats R" is computed in a similar manner. Note that the event "L defeats C defeats R" is the intersection of two events, "L defeats C" and "C defeats R." A simple computation shows that the event "L defeats C" is given by $\{y : y > N_2(x) \equiv (2\omega/\mu)x + \Delta_{CL}/\mu\}$, and the event "$C$ defeats R" is $\{y : y > A_1(x) \equiv -(\omega/\mu)x + \Delta_{RC}/\mu\}$. Hence the event "$L$ defeats C defeats R" is $\{y : y > \max\{A_1(x), N_2(x)\}\}$. Note that $N_2(x) > A_1(x)$ iff $x > D \equiv (\Delta_{RC} - \Delta_{CL})/3\omega$. Hence the probability that "L defeats C defeats R" is

---

This appendix was prepared by Woojin Lee.

$$\pi_L^{(2)} = \int\limits_D^\infty \int\limits_{N_2(x)}^\infty dF_y(y)dF_x(x) + \int\limits_{-\infty}^D \int\limits_{A_1(x)}^\infty dF_y(y)dF_x(x).$$

Now, by combining (i) and (ii) and using the fact that

$$\int\limits_{-\infty}^D \int\limits_{A_2(x)}^{A_1(x)} dF_y(y)dF_x(x) + \int\limits_{-\infty}^D \int\limits_{A_1(x)}^\infty dF_y(y)dF_x(x) = \int\limits_{-\infty}^D \int\limits_{A_2(x)}^\infty dF_y(y)dF_x(x),$$

we have the probability that "L wins":

$$\pi_L = \pi_L^{(1)} + \pi_L^{(2)} = \int\limits_{-\infty}^D \int\limits_{A_2(x)}^\infty dF_y(y)dF_x(x) + \int\limits_D^\infty \int\limits_{N_2(x)}^\infty dF_y(y)dF_x(x),$$

which is the formula (11.12).

(2) The event "R wins" is the union of the two events "R defeats L defeats C" and "R defeats C defeats L." Accordingly, the probability that "R wins," π_R, is the sum of the probability that "R defeats L defeats C," $\pi_R^{(1)}$, and the probability that "R defeats C defeats L," $\pi_R^{(2)}$.

(i) The event "R defeats L defeats C" is the intersection of the event "R defeats L" and the event "L defeats C." A simple computation shows that the event "R defeats L" is $\{y : y < A_2(x) \equiv (\omega/2\mu)x + \Delta_{RL}/2\mu\}$, and the event "$L$ defeats C" is $\{y : y > N_2(x) \equiv (2\omega/\mu)x + \Delta_{CL}/\mu\}$. Therefore the event "$R$ defeats L defeats C" is $\{y : N_2(x) < y < A_2(x)\}$ and this event is nonvacuous iff $N_2(x) < A_2(x)$, which is equivalent to the condition that $x < D \equiv (\Delta_{RC} - \Delta_{CL})/3\omega$. Hence the probability that "R defeats L defeats C" is

$$\pi_R^{(1)} = \int\limits_{-\infty}^D \int\limits_{N_2(x)}^{A_2(x)} dF_y(y)dF_x(x).$$

(ii) The probability that "R defeats C defeats L" is computed in a similar manner. A simple computation shows that the event "R defeats C" is given by $\{y : y < A_1(x) \equiv (-\omega/\mu)x + \Delta_{RC}/\mu\}$, and the event "$C$ defeats R" is $\{y : y < N_2(x) \equiv (2\omega/\mu)x + \Delta_{CL}/\mu\}$. Hence the event "$R$ defeats C defeats

L" is $\{y : y < \min\{A_1(x), N_2(x)\}\}$. Since $N_2(x) > A_1(x)$ iff $x > D \equiv (\Delta_{RC} - \Delta_{CL})/3\omega$, the probability that "$R$ defeats C defeats L" is

$$\pi_R^{(2)} = \int_D^\infty \int_{-\infty}^{A_1(x)} d\mathbf{F}_y(y)d\mathbf{F}_x(x) + \int_{-\infty}^D \int_{-\infty}^{N_2(x)} d\mathbf{F}_y(y)d\mathbf{F}_x(x).$$

Now, by combining (i) and (ii) and using the fact that

$$\int_{-\infty}^D \int_{N_2(x)}^{A_2(x)} d\mathbf{F}_y(y)d\mathbf{F}_x(x) + \int_{-\infty}^D \int_{-\infty}^{N_2(x)} d\mathbf{F}_y(y)d\mathbf{F}_x(x)$$

$$= \int_{-\infty}^D \int_{-\infty}^{A_2(x)} d\mathbf{F}_y(y)d\mathbf{F}_x(x)$$

we have the probability that "R wins":

$$\pi_R = \pi_R^{(1)} + \pi_R^{(2)} = \int_D^\infty \int_{-\infty}^{A_1(x)} d\mathbf{F}_y(y)d\mathbf{F}_x(x) + \int_{-\infty}^D \int_{-\infty}^{A_2(x)} d\mathbf{F}_y(y)d\mathbf{F}_x(x),$$

which is the formula (11.13).

II. The Derivation of Formulae (11.16a, b, c)

We chose the logistic distribution functions on the line. The distributions are

$$F_x(x; a, b) = \frac{1}{1 + \exp(-\frac{x-a}{b})} \quad \text{and} \quad F_y(y; c, d) = \frac{1}{1 + \exp(-\frac{y-c}{d})}.$$

The corresponding density functions are

$$f_x(x; a, b) = \frac{\exp(-\frac{x-a}{b})}{b(1 + \exp(-\frac{x-a}{b}))^2} \quad \text{and} \quad f_y(y; c, d) = \frac{\exp(-\frac{x-c}{d})}{d(1 + \exp(-\frac{x-c}{d}))^2}.$$

(1) The probability that "C defeats L" is

$$\pi_{CL} = \int_{-\infty}^{\infty} \int_{-\infty}^{N_2(x)} d\mathbf{F}_y(y) d\mathbf{F}_x(x)$$

$$= \int_{-\infty}^{\infty} \frac{1}{1 + \exp(-\frac{N_2(x) - c}{d})} \frac{\exp(-\frac{x-a}{b})}{b(1 + \exp(-\frac{x-a}{b}))^2} dx.$$

Let $v = \exp(-(x - a)/b)$. Then $dv/dx = \exp(-(x - a)/b(-1/b)) = -v/b$, and $v \in (\infty, 0)$ as $x \in (-\infty, \infty)$. Using the fact that $\exp(-x) = \exp(-a)v^b$, we have

$$\exp\left(-\frac{N_2(x) - c}{d}\right) = \exp\left(-\frac{\Delta_{CL}}{\mu d} + \frac{c}{d}\right) \exp\left(-x\frac{2\omega}{\mu d}\right)$$

$$= \exp\left(-\frac{\Delta_{CL}}{\mu d} + \frac{c}{d} - \frac{2a\omega}{\mu d}\right) v^{b\frac{2\omega}{\mu d}}.$$

Letting

$$y_{CL} \equiv \exp\left(-\frac{\Delta_{CL}}{\mu d} + \frac{c}{d} - \frac{2a\omega}{\mu d}\right) \quad \text{and} \quad K \equiv b\frac{2\omega}{\mu d},$$

we have

$$\exp\left(-\frac{N_2(x) - c}{d}\right) = y_{CL}v^K.$$

Now

$$\pi_{CL} = \int_{-\infty}^{\infty} \frac{1}{1 + \exp(-\frac{N_2(x) - c}{d})} \frac{\exp(-\frac{x-a}{b})}{b(1 + \exp(-\frac{x-a}{b}))^2} dx$$

$$= \int_{\infty}^{0} \frac{1}{1 + y_{CL}v^K} \frac{v}{b(1 + v)^2} \left(-\frac{b}{v}dv\right)$$

$$= \int_{0}^{\infty} \frac{1}{1 + y_{CL}v^K} \frac{v}{(1 + v)^2} dv.$$

(2) The probability that "L wins" is

$$
\pi_L = \int_{-\infty}^{D} \int_{A_2(x)}^{\infty} dF_y(y)dF_x(x) + \int_{D}^{\infty} \int_{N_2(x)}^{\infty} dF_y(y)dF_x(x)
$$

$$
= 1 - \int_{-\infty}^{D} \frac{1}{1 + \exp(-\frac{A_2(x)-c}{d})} \frac{\exp(-\frac{x-a}{b})}{b(1 + \exp(-\frac{x-a}{b}))^2} dx
$$

$$
- \int_{D}^{\infty} \frac{1}{1 + \exp(-\frac{N_2(x)-c}{d})} \frac{\exp(-\frac{x-a}{b})}{b(1 + \exp(-\frac{x-a}{b}))^2} dx.
$$

Let $v = \exp(-(x - a)/b)$. Then $dv/dx = -v/b$, and $v \in (\infty, \exp(-(D - a)/b))$ as $x \in (-\infty, D)$. Using the fact that $\exp(-x) = \exp(-a)v^b$, we have

$$
\exp\left(-\frac{A_2(x) - c}{d}\right) = \exp\left(-\frac{\Delta_{RL}}{2\mu d} + \frac{c}{d} - \frac{a\omega}{2\mu d}\right) v^{b\frac{\omega}{2\mu d}}.
$$

Letting

$$
y_{RL} \equiv \exp\left(-\frac{\Delta_{RL}}{2\mu d} + \frac{c}{d} - \frac{a\omega}{2\mu d}\right) \quad \text{and} \quad K \equiv b\frac{2\omega}{\mu d},
$$

we have

$$
\exp\left(-\frac{A_2(x) - c}{d}\right) = y_{RL}v^{K/4}.
$$

Hence

$$
\int_{-\infty}^{D} \frac{1}{1 + \exp(-\frac{A_2(x)-c}{d})} \frac{\exp(-\frac{x-a}{b})}{b(1 + \exp(-\frac{x-a}{b}))^2} dx
$$

$$
= \int_{e^{-\left(\frac{D-a}{b}\right)}}^{\infty} \frac{1}{1 + y_{RL}v^{K/4}} \frac{1}{(1 + v)^2} dv.
$$

Similarly, using the fact that $\exp(-(N_2(x) - c)/d) = y_{CL}v^K$, we have

$$\int_D^\infty \frac{1}{1 + \exp(-\frac{N_2(x)-c}{d})} \frac{\exp(-\frac{x-a}{b})}{b(1 + \exp(-\frac{x-a}{b}))^2} dx = \int_\infty^{e^{-\left(\frac{D-a}{b}\right)}} \frac{1}{1 + y_{CL}v^K} \frac{1}{(1 + v)^2} dv.$$

Hence the probability that "L wins" is

$$\pi_L = 1 - \int_{e^{-\left(\frac{D-a}{b}\right)}}^\infty \frac{1}{1 + y_{RL}v^{K/4}} \frac{1}{(1 + v)^2} dv - \int_0^{e^{-\left(\frac{D-a}{b}\right)}} \frac{1}{1 + y_{CL}v^K} \frac{1}{(1 + v)^2} dv.$$

(3) The probability that "R wins" is

$$\pi_R = \int_D^\infty \int_{-\infty}^{A_1(x)} d\mathbf{F}_y(y)d\mathbf{F}_x(x) + \int_{-\infty}^D \int_{-\infty}^{A_2(x)} d\mathbf{F}_y(y)d\mathbf{F}_x(x)$$

$$= \int_D^\infty \frac{1}{1 + \exp(-\frac{A_1(x)-c}{d})} \frac{\exp(-\frac{x-a}{b})}{b(1 + \exp(-\frac{x-a}{b}))^2} dx$$

$$+ \int_{-\infty}^D \frac{1}{1 + \exp(-\frac{A_2(x)-c}{d})} \frac{\exp(-\frac{x-a}{b})}{b(1 + \exp(-\frac{x-a}{b}))^2} dx.$$

Letting $v = \exp(-(x - a)/b)$ and $K \equiv b(2\omega/\mu d)$ as before, we have

$$\exp\left(-\frac{A_1(x) - c}{d}\right) = y_{RC}v^{-K/2},$$

where

$$y_{RC} = \exp\left(-\frac{\Delta_{RC}}{\mu d} + \frac{c}{d} + \frac{a\omega}{\mu d}\right).$$

Hence

$$\int_{D}^{\infty} \frac{1}{1 + \exp(-\frac{A_1(x)-c}{d})} \frac{\exp(-\frac{x-a}{b})}{b(1 + \exp(-\frac{x-a}{b}))^2} dx$$

$$= \int_{0}^{e^{-\left(\frac{D-a}{b}\right)}} \frac{1}{1 + y_{RC} v^{-K/2}} \frac{1}{(1 + v)^2} dv,$$

and

$$\int_{-\infty}^{D} \frac{1}{1 + \exp(-\frac{A_2(x)-c}{d})} \frac{\exp(-\frac{x-a}{b})}{b(1 + \exp(-\frac{x-a}{b}))^2} dx$$

$$= \int_{e^{-\left(\frac{D-a}{b}\right)}}^{\infty} \frac{1}{1 + y_{RL} v^{K/4}} \frac{1}{(1 + v)^2} dv.$$

12

A Three-Class Model of American Politics

12.1 Introduction

There is no labor or social democratic party in the United States. In this chapter we offer a partial explanation for why this is so, based upon a simple class model of politics.

We assume that the polity is partitioned into three classes: large capitalists and their agents, workers, and petite bourgeoisie. The large capitalists and their agents own and/or run a large firm, which uses as inputs labor and infrastructure, the latter being provided by the government. All workers work for this firm. The petite bourgeoisie are small shopkeepers, who work for themselves and do not hire outside labor. The only input in their production function is their own labor (no government infrastructure).

The policy space is two-dimensional. The polity must decide upon a uniform tax rate levied on all incomes, and on the division of tax revenues between spending on infrastructure and a lump-sum transfer payment to all citizens.

Per capita incomes of the three classes are arranged as follows: the capitalists have the largest per capita income, and the workers the smallest. Both the capitalists and the petite bourgeoisie have income greater than mean income. The capitalists and their agents each receive an equal share of the profits of the firm.

The policy preferences of the three classes are, roughly, as follows. Workers want taxes, and in general they desire both spending on infrastructure, and transfer payments. They benefit from infrastructural spending, which raises their marginal productivity in the firm and hence their wage. Capitalists want taxes and infrastructural spending, since without infrastructure there is no production and no profits. They do not want transfer payments. The petite bourgeoisie want no taxation—they do not benefit from infrastructure and since their income is above the mean, they lose from the financing of transfer payments.

251

There are two political parties, the Democrats and the Republicans. Both capitalists and petite bourgeoisie belong to the Republican Party. What we shall be concerned with is the composition of the Democratic Party. We assume that workers belong to the Democrats, and we shall model two scenarios: (1) that *only* workers belong to the Democratic Party, that is, that it is a labor party, and (2) that both workers and capitalists belong to the Democratic Party.

More precisely, we will model the Republican Party as containing five factions: capitalist militants, capitalist reformists, petite bourgeois militants, petite bourgeois reformists, and opportunists. In Scenario One, the Democrats contain three factions—worker militants, worker reformists, and opportunists, and in Scenario Two, the Democrats contain five factions—the three just named, plus capitalist reformists and capitalist militants.

In each scenario, we model political equilibrium as PUNE, where, of course, all factions of a party have to agree for a deviation to occur. As the reformists are again gratuitous, we can model the Republicans as containing three important factions, and the Democrats as containing either two or three, depending upon the scenario.

I believe that, in American reality, the Republican Party is a coalition of petite bourgeois and large capitalist elements, and the Democratic Party is a coalition of worker and capitalist elements. (Of course, this is an approximate statement, whose validity is in large part constrained by the stylization of a three-class characterization of society.) The concept of infrastructure is meant to capture the fact that large firms depend upon government investment more than small business does. (This could be challenged.) Our modeling exercise intends to show that the capitalists are better off in the political equilibrium in which they are represented in the Democratic and Republican parties than in the political equilibrium where they are represented only in the Republican Party. If there is free entry of classes into parties, this will explain why the Democratic Party is not a labor party in the United States.

We shall discover that the capitalists do indeed fare better when they are represented in the Democratic Party. Why, then, do capitalists not join labor parties in all countries? The answer must be that there is not, in general, free entry of representatives of classes into parties.[1]

---

1. Michael Wallerstein comments that capitalists *are* represented in European social democratic parties.

12.2 The Model

The population distribution of workers, petite bourgeoisie, and capitalists is given by $(\omega, \rho, 1 - (\omega + \rho))$, where ω is the fraction of workers and ρ is the fraction of petite bourgeoisie; the remainder are capitalists and their agents. There is one good, produced both by the petite bourgeoisie and by the large firm. The production function of the large firm is

$$g(G, L) = \beta G^\gamma L^\delta,$$

where G is units of government infrastructure per capita, L is the amount of labor per capita, and g is level of production per capita. Each petite bourgeois produces an amount α in his own shop. At full-employment economic equilibrium, workers earn their marginal product, which is $\delta \beta G^\gamma \omega^{\delta-1}$, and each capitalist receives as income his per capita share of profits, which is $(1 - \delta) \beta G^\gamma \omega^\delta)/(1 - (\omega + \rho))$.

The policy vector is (a, G, T), where a is the uniform income tax rate, G is infrastructural spending per capita, and T is the lump-sum transfer payment per capita. The policy space is in fact two-dimensional, since there is a budget constraint:

(12.1) $\quad a(g(G, \omega) + \rho \alpha) = T + G.$

Each individual desires to maximize his after-tax income. Thus we may write the utility functions of typical members of the three classes as:

$$v^W(a, G) = (1 - a)\delta \beta G^\gamma \omega^{\delta-1} + T,$$

(12.2) $\quad v^{PB}(a, G) = (1 - a)\alpha + T,$

$$v^C(a, G) = (1 - a)\frac{(1 - \delta)\beta G^\gamma \omega^\delta}{1 - (\omega + \rho)} + T,$$

where it is understood that we express T as a function of a and G, using (12.1).

We next describe the probability function π. We use the finite-type model of uncertainty. Let τ^D and τ^R be the platforms of the two parties. Define the numbers a^1 and a^2 by

$$a^1 = \omega f\left(\frac{v^W(\tau^R)}{v^W(\tau^L)}\right), \quad \text{and} \quad a^2 = \rho f\left(\frac{v^{PB}(\tau^R)}{v^{PB}(\tau^L)}\right) + (1 - (\omega + \rho))f\left(\frac{v^C(\tau^R)}{v^C(\tau^L)}\right),$$

where f is the function defined in equation (2.14). As in section 2.4, we now define $\pi(\tau^L, \tau^R)$ as the probability that $a^1\epsilon^1 + a^2\epsilon^2$ is positive, where (ϵ^1, ϵ^2) is uniformly distributed on the positive quadrant of the unit disc in $\mathbf{R}^2$ (see Figure 2.2 and equation (2.18)).

12.3 Characterization of PUNEs

We shall take the two-dimensional policy vector to be (a, G), and express the budget constraint as $h^1(a, G) \geq 0$, where

(12.3) $h^1(a, G) = a(g(G, \omega) + \rho\alpha) - G,$

which says that the transfer payment must be non-negative. In addition, we have the constraints on tax rates:

$$0 \leq a \leq 1.$$

This may be expressed as $h^2(a) \geq 0$ and $h^3(a) \geq 0$, where

$$h^2(a) = a \quad \text{and} \quad h^3(a) = 1 - a.$$

We first characterize PUNEs under Scenario One, where the Democratic Party is a labor party. The equations (8.10a) and (8.10b), modified to admit the additional factions to the parties when appropriate, take the form

(12.4)
$$-\nabla_D\pi = x^0\nabla v^W + x^1\nabla h^1 + x^2\nabla h^2 + x^3\nabla h^3,$$
$$\nabla_R\pi = y^0\nabla v^C + z^0\nabla v^{PB} + y^1\nabla h^1 + y^2\nabla h^2 + y^3\nabla h^3.$$

A PUNE occurs when we have a solution to these equations, where the Lagrangian multipliers are all non-negative, and the "complementary slackness" conditions hold (that is, $x^1 > 0$ iff $T^D = 0$, $x^2 > 0$ iff $a^D = 0$, $x^3 > 0$ iff $a^D = 1$, $y^1 > 0$ iff $T^R = 0$, and so on).

Similarly, at a PUNE under Scenario Two, we have the following equations:

(12.5)
$$-\nabla_D\pi = x^0\nabla v^W + w^0\nabla v^C + x^1\nabla h^1 + x^2\nabla h^2 + x^3\nabla h^3,$$
$$\nabla_R\pi = y^0\nabla v^C + z^0\nabla v^{PB} + y^1\nabla h^1 + y^2\nabla h^2 + y^3\nabla h^3.$$

A PUNE of this type occurs when the Lagrangian multipliers are all non-negative, and the complementary slackness conditions hold.

Solving (12.4) and (12.5) requires investigating a number of cases. We reason as follows. The constraint h^2 will never be binding for either party at a PUNE—both parties, that is, will propose positive tax rates, for a zero tax rate means zero income for both workers and capitalists. We thus have the following possible cases for *each* party, $J = D, R$:

(i) $a^J < 1$ and $T^J > 0$;
(ii) $a^J = 1$ and $T^J > 0$;
(iii) $a^J < 1$ and $T^J = 0$;
(iv) $a^J = 1$ and $T^J = 0$.

We now eliminate (iv) as unlikely for both D and R, (ii) as unlikely for R, and (iii) as unlikely for D. Thus we are assuming that a solution for the D policy is of either case (i) or case (ii), and a solution for the R policy is of either case (i) or case (iii). This gives us four types of equilibria to search for.

Suppose we are looking for a PUNE in Scenario One where D has a policy of case (ii) and R has a policy of case (iii). Then (12.4) reduces to

(12.6a)
$$-\nabla_D \pi = x^0 \nabla v^W + x^3 \nabla h^3,$$
$$\nabla_R \pi = y^0 \nabla v^C + z^0 \nabla v^{PB} + y^1 \nabla h^1.$$

In addition we have the two equations:

(12.6b) $a^D = 1, \quad h^1(a^R, G^R) = 0.$

These constitute six equations in nine unknowns (the four policy variables plus the five Lagrangian multipliers). Indeed, in every case, under Scenario One, we will have three more unknowns than equations.

We search for solutions of this system of equations as follows. We can solve for the variables x^0, x^3, y^0, and z^0 from the four equations making up (12.6a), in terms of the other unknowns. (This is easy, because the equations are linear in the Lagrange multipliers.) a^D is already specified by (12.6b). We solve the second equation in (12.6b) for G^R in terms of a^R. We now specify a^R, G^D, and y^1 randomly where a^R is chosen less than one, G^D is feasible given a^D, and y^1 is chosen to be positive. We check whether x^0, x^3, y^0, and z^0 are positive: if so, we have found a PUNE. What has been described is one *iteration* of our search. We then repeat this process many times.

A similar procedure is used for solving equations (12.5).

12.4 Results

We specified the data of the model as follows:

$$(\omega, \rho, \delta, \gamma, \beta, \alpha) = (.55, .40, .6875, .15625, 8940.72, 50000).$$

Thus the capitalists and their agents (firm managers, corporation lawyers, accountants, and so on) make up 5% of the polity. The data vector is justified by the observation that it delivers equilibria in which the income distribution seems reasonable (see below).

As we discussed earlier, we search for PUNEs, under each party-membership scenario, in four different cases. In fact we found PUNEs, under Scenario One, in only one case, and PUNEs under Scenario Two in only two cases. We report the characteristics of these solutions in Tables 12.1 and 12.2. In each case where PUNEs exist, there is a continuum of them. We performed 2,000 iterations for each type of equilibrium; we report the number of PUNEs we found. The policy values reported are averages of the policy values in the PUNEs we found; similarly, the reported value of π is the average probability of Democratic victory, and the reported values of v^W, v^{PB}, and v^C are the average *expected* post-tax incomes, that is, averages of the values $\pi v^J(a^D, G^D) + (1 - \pi)v^J(a^R, G^R)$ for $J = W$, PB, and C, in the PUNEs found.

Table 12.1 reports the one type of PUNE that exists under both membership scenarios. The salient observation is that when the capitalists join the

Table 12.1   PUNEs where $T^D > 0$, $a^D < 1$, $T^R = 0$, and $a^R < 1$

Scenario	No. of PUNEs	a^D	G^D	a^R	G^R	π	v^W	v^{PB}	v^C
$D = \{W\}$	617	.375	2739.	.062	2543.	.81	27,172	44,428	96,951
$D = \{W, C\}$	149	.215	4145.	.057	2306.	.77	25,388	44,741	111,963

Table 12.2   PUNEs where $T^D > 0$, $a^D < 1$, $T^R > 0$, and $a^R < 1$

Scenario	No. of PUNEs	a^D	G^D	a^R	G^R	π	v^W	v^{PB}	v^C
$D = \{W, C\}$	25	.230	4834.	.139	2794.	.55	25,773	44,529	111,455

Democratic Party, the tax rate the Democrats propose in equilibrium falls significantly, the amount of government expenditures on infrastructure increases significantly, and the post-tax income of the capitalists increases significantly. Table 12.2 reports the other type of PUNE that exists, but it only occurs in the scenario when the capitalists are in both parties.

The one-line summary of these exercises is that the expected income of capitalists is approximately 15% higher, on average, in political equilibria in which capitalists are represented in both parties than in political equilibria in which they are represented only in the Republican Party. If there is free entry into parties and capitalists can organize, they should join the Democratic Party.

We can compute other characteristics of these equilibria. In the equilibria of the first row of Table 12.1, national income per capita is $40,382 while the government lump-sum transfer, which might be viewed as the model counterpart of government expenditures on social services and transfer payments, is $10,048 per capita, constituting about 25% of national income.[2] In the equilibria of the second row of Table 12.1, national income per capita rises to $41,344, while government expenditures on social services fall to $3,718 per capita, or only 9% of national income. Capitalist participation in the Democratic Party raises national income but results in drastic cuts in social services.

It is furthermore noteworthy that even when the Democrats are a labor party, the tax rate they propose, on average, in PUNE, is 37.5%—surely not expropriationary—and this is despite the fact that there is no deadweight loss from taxation in the model. (Neither capitalists nor workers abstain from participating in production when the tax rate rises.) Moreover, workers constitute an absolute majority of the citizenry in the parameterization in question. The nonexpropriationary policy is ultimately due to the fact that not all workers vote for the policy that is in their interest (recall our finite-type model of voting, used here), and to the presence of opportunists in the Democratic Party.

12.5 Conclusion

We have analyzed a stylized three-class model of the U.S. politico-economy. Assuming that capitalists and petite bourgeoisie are represented in the Republican Party, we have shown that capitalists do significantly better (in terms of

---

2. In thinking about the real U.S. economy, recall that the per capita income figure derived in the model should be compared with income per labor-force participant in actuality.

income) if they belong to the Democratic Party as well, in contrast to the scenario in which the Democratic Party is a labor party. If there is free entry into parties, this may explain why the Democrats are not a labor party in the United States.

Methodologically, this chapter shows that we can insert more factions into parties, representing different interest groups in the population, and the PUNE concept remains tractable.

13

Endogenous Parties with Multidimensional Competition

13.1 Introduction

With the exception of Chapter 5, we have taken the preferences of parties to be exogenous. In this chapter we apply the method of Chapter 5 to derive the preferences of parties endogenously from the distribution of types and the political institution of elections, in the multidimensional model.

We shall, however, derive not parties as they actually are in capitalist democracies, but parties which might arise in an ideal of *perfectly representative democracy*. The distinction between these two kinds of party is due, in large part, to the institution of private financing of political parties. In real-world democracies, the political positions of parties are strongly influenced by the policy preferences of major financial supporters. The perfectly representative democracy is, for present purposes, defined as one in which every citizen belongs to one party, and each member has an equal influence on the preferences of the party to which he belongs.

This chapter presents our most complete theory of political competition, as it derives from the data of citizen preferences and endowments the two parties that will come to be, and the political equilibria that will be observed, all in a multidimensional context. Therefore this theory can be seen as replacing the "median-voter" model, which also derives from those primitives a predicted political equilibrium. The advantage of our theory, to belabor the point, is that it provides a complete explanation of political competition while taking the institutions of parties seriously, and when competition concerns more than one dimension of policy.

After presenting the theory, we shall derive perfectly representative parties for two examples. The first uses the National Election Surveys to parameterize the preferences of the U.S. polity, where we take the issue space to consist of two dimensions—taxation and race. We compute parties endogenously, and

259

political equilibrium. The second example is based on the model of progressive taxation developed in Chapter 9: here, we endogenize the parties of the model of that chapter.

13.2 Endogenous Parties

The idea is a generalization of that presented in Chapter 5. Let the set of types be H, the policy space be T, and the utility function of type h over policies be $v(\cdot, h)$. Let the probability distribution of types be $\mathbf{F}$. If (τ^1, τ^2) is a pair of policies, then the set of types that prefer τ^1 to τ^2 is denoted $\Omega(\tau^1, \tau^2)$. We adopt the error-distribution model of uncertainty, so that the probability that τ^1 defeats τ^2 is

$$\pi(\tau^1, \tau^2) = \frac{\mathbf{F}(\Omega(\tau^1, \tau^2) + \beta - 0.5}{2\beta},$$

where β is a datum of the problem. Of course different definitions of π could equally well be used.

A *party-unanimity Nash equilibrium with endogenous parties* (PUNEEP) is a partition of the space of types into two elements that we denote L and R, a utility function v^L for the "party L," a utility function v^R for the "party R," a PUNE (τ^L, τ^R) for the model of party competition with parties having those two utility functions, such that every type in L weakly prefers τ^L to τ^R and every type in R weakly prefers τ^R to τ^L. Finally, v^L is the average of utility functions $v(\cdot, h)$ for h in L, and v^R is the average of utility functions $v(\cdot, h)$ for h in R.

It should be remarked that we use the average of members' utility functions as the parties' utility, instead of the utility function of the median member, because with multidimensional policy spaces there is in general no median ideal policy. Of course averaging utility functions means that those functions must be to some degree interpersonally comparable (to be precise, they must be cardinally unit comparable). An alternate definition of PUNEEP replaces the last sentence of the above paragraph with "$v^L = v(\cdot, h^L)$, where h^L is the average type of L, and $v^R = v(\cdot, h^R)$, where h^R is the average type of R." We will use this formulation in the examples below. This definition of party representative is not fully satisfactory, for it does not model the process of intraparty competition for the preferences of the party's militants and reformists, but we claim it engenders a tractable theory of political equilibrium.

In practice, there are two difficulties encountered in computing PUNEEP. The first is that the set $\Omega(\tau^1, \tau^2)$ should have a fairly simple structure, or else computation of the function π and its derivatives is difficult. We must be able to write π as a differentiable function so that the computer can solve the Farkas' lemma conditions, which involve its derivatives. The second difficulty is that, as before, it is generically the case that a 2-manifold of equilibria exist, and some art must be employed in choosing the two parameters to randomize in order to solve for equilibrium.

We illustrate the computation of PUNEEP with the two examples that follow.

13.3 Taxation and Race

A voter's type is a pair (w, r), where w is her income and r is her racial view. Preferences of voters over policy pairs (t, ρ), where t is a uniform tax rate and ρ is the government's racial position, are given by:

$$(13.1) \quad v(t, \rho; w, r) = (1 - t)(1 - \gamma t)w + t(1 - \gamma t)\mu - \frac{\alpha}{2}(r - \rho)^2,$$

where γ is a fraction less than one and μ is mean income. The term $(1 - \gamma t)$ is a simple way of capturing the fact that labor supply is somewhat elastic with respect to the tax rate; thus w is here interpreted as full-time income of the individual, and γt is the fraction of full-time GNP which is lost due to workers' reducing their labor supply in the presence of taxation. This is a short-cut to a fuller model in which preferences for leisure would be represented in the utility function. Thus representing those preferences, and giving micro-foundations to the effect captured above by γ, would complicate the model in a way that might obscure the computation we wish to elucidate.

We shall calibrate, in what follows, a distribution of types, F, a probability measure on the type set $H = [0, \infty) \times [0, \infty)$.

Let $\tau^L = (t^L, \rho^L)$ and $\tau^R = (t^R, \rho^R)$ be policies put forth by two parties, and let σ_1 and σ_2 be the following functions of these policies:

$$(13.2) \quad \sigma_1(\tau^L, \tau^R) = \frac{\rho^L - \rho^R}{(t^R - t^L)(1 + \gamma - \gamma(t^L + t^R))},$$

$$\sigma_2(\tau^L, \tau^R) = \frac{\mu(1 - \gamma(t^L + t^R))}{(1 + \gamma - \gamma(t^L + t^R))}.$$

We may compute that, if $t^L > t^R$, a type (w, r) prefers τ^L to τ^R iff $r < \Psi(w; \tau^L, \tau^R)$, where

$$(13.3a) \quad \Psi(w; \tau^L, \tau^R) = \frac{\rho^L + \rho^R}{2} + \frac{\sigma_2}{\alpha\sigma_1} - \frac{w}{\alpha\sigma_1},$$

a function that is linear in w. Thus $\Omega(\tau^L, \tau^R)$ is the set of all types that lie beneath a straight line in the (w, r)-type plane. This is a set with a simple structure, and hence we shall have a tractable form for the function π.

For a given pair of policies $\tau^L = (t^L, \rho^L)$ and $\tau^R = (t^R, \rho^R)$ let

$$(13.3b) \quad b = \frac{\rho^L + \rho^R}{2} + \frac{\sigma_2}{\alpha\sigma_1}, \qquad m = \frac{1}{\alpha\sigma_1}.$$

Then the set of types who prefer τ^L to τ^R is precisely the set of types beneath the line $r = b - mw$. The average type of that set has components:

$$(13.4a) \quad w^L = \frac{\underset{W}{\int} \underset{r<\Psi(w)}{\int} wf(w, r)dr\,dw}{\underset{W}{\int} \underset{r<\Psi(w)}{\int} f(w, r)dr\,dw}, \qquad r^L = \frac{\underset{W}{\int} \underset{r<\Psi(w)}{\int} rf(w, r)dr\,dw}{\underset{W}{\int} \underset{r<\Psi(w)}{\int} f(w, r)dr\,dw},$$

where $\Psi(w) = b - mw$, while the average type of the set who prefer τ^R to τ^L has components:

$$(13.4b) \quad w^R = \frac{\underset{W}{\int} \underset{r>\Psi(w)}{\int} wf(w, r)dr\,dw}{\underset{W}{\int} \underset{r>\Psi(w)}{\int} f(w, r)dr\,dw}, \qquad r^R = \frac{\underset{W}{\int} \underset{r>\Psi(w)}{\int} rf(w, r)dr\,dw}{\underset{W}{\int} \underset{r>\Psi(w)}{\int} f(w, r)dr\,dw}.$$

Here f is the density function of the probability measure $\mathbf{F}$.

We shall below fit this model to U.S. data. In that fit, it turns out that the endogenous party PUNEs we find all have the Right playing a tax rate of zero. We therefore now write explicitly the equations for PUNEEP with that constraint binding. Such a PUNEEP is a pair of numbers (b, m), a pair of policies (τ^L, τ^R), a pair of types $((w^L, r^L), (w^R, r^R))$ such that:

(R1) b and m satisfy equations (13.3b);
(R2) v^L is the utility function of type (w^L, r^L) and v^R is the utility function of type (w^R, r^R), where (w^L, r^L) and (w^R, r^R) are given by (13.4a and b);

(R3) $t^R = 0$; and

(R4) there are non-negative numbers x_1, y_1, and y_2 such that:

$$x_1 \nabla v^L(\tau^L) = -\nabla_L \pi(\tau^L, \tau^R)$$

$$y_1 \nabla v^R(\tau^R) + y_2 \begin{pmatrix} 1 \\ 0 \end{pmatrix} = \nabla_R \pi(\tau^L, \tau^R).$$

The reader will observe, by thinking through the definition of PUNEEP, that conditions (R1)–(R4) characterize a PUNEEP where party R, which consists of all types above the line $r = b - mw$, plays a tax rate of zero. The key requirement is (R1), which tells us that every member of coalition L votes for (w^L, r^L) and every member of coalition R votes for (w^R, r^R).

13.4 Fitting the Model to U.S. Data[1]

We shall fit a bivariate lognormal distribution to U.S. data for our probability measure **F**. A bivariate lognormal distribution is characterized by five parameters $(m_w, m_r, v_w, v_r, v_{wr})$, since its density is given by

$$f(w, r; m, \Sigma) = \frac{1}{2\pi \sqrt{|\Sigma|} wr} \exp[-\tfrac{1}{2}((\log w, \log r) - m)'$$
$$\Sigma^{-1}((\log w, \log r) - m),$$

where

$$m = (m_w, m_r) \quad \text{and} \quad \Sigma = \begin{bmatrix} v_w & v_{wr} \\ v_{wr} & v_r \end{bmatrix}.$$

We estimated these parameters for a series of years by using the empirical distributions obtained from the data set of the National Election Surveys (NES), compiled by the Institute for Social Research at the University of Michigan. We chose "Family Income" (variable number 114) as the proxy for w, and "Respondent's Position on Aid to Minorities" (variable number 830) as the proxy for r. The NES categorizes five different income groups according to percentiles,[2] and

---

1. The bivariate lognormal distribution in this section was estimated by Woojin Lee.

2. That is, (1) 0–16 percentile, (2) 17–33 percentile, (3) 34–67 percentile, (4) 68–95 percentile, and (5) 96–100 percentile.

also provides the nominal income intervals corresponding to these percentiles. We transform the nominal incomes into the real incomes using the GDP deflators (chain-type price indexes for GDP with the base year of 1990) obtained from *Economic Report of the President,* and represent an income interval as its midpoint. In the NES, the racial position of each respondent is coded from 1 (government should help minority groups) to 7 (minority groups should help themselves).[3]

We obtain the empirical distribution of traits by counting the number of respondents for the 35 different pairs of (w, r) and dividing each number by the total number of respondents. We learn from the empirical distributions that there is a positive correlation between real incomes and high values of the racial variable. We calculated, but do not report here, that the correlation coefficient between w and r is positive each year, although its magnitude is not large.

For the bivariate lognormal distribution, it is well known that:

$$(13.5) \quad \begin{cases} \mu_w = \exp[m_w + \tfrac{1}{2}v_w], \\[4pt] \mu_r = \exp[m_r + \tfrac{1}{2}v_r], \\[4pt] \sigma_w^2 = \exp[2m_w + v_w](\exp[v_w] - 1), \\[4pt] \sigma_r^2 = \exp[2m_r + v_r](\exp[v_r] - 1), \\[4pt] \mathrm{cov}\,(w, r) = \exp[\mu_w + \mu_r + \tfrac{1}{2}(v_w + v_r)](\exp[v_{wr}] - 1). \end{cases}$$

The maximum likelihood estimators (MLE) of the bivariate lognormal distribution are used to estimate $(\mu_w, \mu_r, \sigma_w^2, \sigma_r^2, \mathrm{cov}\,(w, r))$, and then we solve the above five equations for five unknown parameters, $(\hat{m}_w, \hat{m}_r, \hat{v}_w, \hat{v}_r, \hat{v}_{wr})$. These estimates together with $\hat{\rho}_{wr} = \hat{v}_{wr}/(\hat{v}_w \hat{v}_r)$ are summarized in Table 13.1.

We calibrate our model with the 1984 data.

We take $(\alpha, \beta, \gamma) = (10, 0.1, 0.1)$ in the calculations that follow. The model is now completely specified.

As I remarked, this model possesses PUNEEP in which both parties play interior racial policies, the Left plays an interior tax policy, and the Right plays a

---

3. The NES question is as follows. "Some people feel that the government should make every effort to improve the social and economic position of blacks. Others feel that the government should not make any special effort to help blacks because they should help themselves. Where would you place yourself on the following scale? 1. Government should help blacks . . . 7. Blacks should help themselves." (No descriptive statements are associated with the intermediate numbers.)

tax policy of zero. We now indicate how we find a solution satisfying conditions (R1)–(R4) of the last section. We choose a pair of positive numbers (b, m) randomly. This defines a line in (w, r) space, as we have described. We next compute the average types of the partition of H defined by this line, via (13.4a) and (13.4b). This defines the two utility functions v^L and v^R, as required by condition (R2). The first vector equation in (R4) (which is the condition that says the factions of Party L cannot agree on an improving deviation) consists of two scalar equations: solve the first one for x_1. This leaves the second equation: call it "eqnL." Next solve the second vector equation in (R4) for y_1 and y_2 (this equation system is linear in the Lagrange multipliers). We now have left three equations—eqnL and the two equations of (13.3b): solve these simultaneously for t^L, ρ^L, and ρ^R. Now the Lagrange multipliers become numbers: check that they are non-negative, and check that t^L is in $(0, 1)$. If so, we have found a PUNEEP.

I have omitted, in this description, explanation of the computation of the derivatives $\nabla \pi$. This is an exercise in calculus that need not detain us here.

Table 13.1 Bivariate lognormal parameters

Year	m_w	m_r	v_w	v_r	v_{wr}	ρ_{wr}
1970	3.29357	1.36013	.379272	.198197	.013936	.050831
1972	3.26156	1.34936	.360523	.193763	.003107	.011757
1974	3.32864	1.37051	.405046	.190215	.030641	.110389
1976	3.31863	1.36295	.363150	.189987	.029640	.112841
1978	3.33480	1.40374	.307867	.165845	.034380	.152150
1980	3.37475	1.45160	.353716	.114527	.021443	.106539
1982	3.29339	1.41568	.343194	.133671	.016471	.076901
1984	3.37094	1.33077	.326918	.147457	.029046	.132294
1986	3.38109	1.41755	.402292	.132781	.004473	.019355
1988	3.37616	1.42167	.417288	.156757	.032214	.125953
1990	3.35139	1.42184	.415514	.149531	.027464	.110181
1992	3.40018	1.47562	.375699	.130346	.020154	.091074

We know that the set of types who prefer Left to Right has measure $F(\{(w, r) \mid r < b - mw\})$. This number is given by a messy double integral; it must be differentiated with respect to the policies. Once we compute the form of this derivative, Mathematica can compute it numerically for any set of policies.

Of course, we do not know a priori which, if any, of the policy constraints will bind. Therefore, the author programmed six different versions of sets of conditions analogous to (R1)–(R4), each corresponding to a particular set of binding policy constraints. It turned out that only solutions of this type were found. Although we have no proof, we suspect that all endogenous party PUNEs for this problem are of this form.

Table 13.2 presents a set of 50 PUNEEPs that were found in a run with 75 iterations. This high density of PUNEs was due to our choosing the random elements (b, m) artfully, and that was possible only after locating the region of (b, m) space where PUNEEP reside with a much coarser paving of the (b, m) plane. The averages of the relevant magnitudes in this set of PUNEEPs are

$$(t^L, \rho^L) = (.297, 3.44),$$
$$(t^R, \rho^R) = (0, 4.72),$$
$$\pi = .626,$$
$$(w^L, w^R) = (27.92, 42.1197),$$
average expected tax rate $= 0.209$, and

average expected race position $= 3.82$.

The median values of w and r in the population are 29.10 and 3.78, respectively.

It bears noting that, although the Left almost always, in the set of PUNEEPs, wins with probability greater than one-half, it is the Right that does not compromise on tax policy. (It can be computed that the ideal tax policy of every member of Right is zero, while the ideal tax policy of most members of Left is one. Only a very small fraction of types, in this model, have an ideal tax policy that is greater than zero and less than one.) That the Left wins with probability greater than one-half means that, in those PUNEs, more than half of the voters belong to Left. So why does Left compromise and not Right? Could we attribute this to the analysis of the model in Chapter 10; that is, does the critical condition C2 of section 10.3 hold? We compute, for our bivariate lognormal measure F, mean income is 34.2727, while mean income of those who have the median value of the race trait is 34.1748. Thus C2 is false, but by a very small amount. Indeed, these two numbers are close enough that our Chapter 10 analysis does not yield any predictions in this example.

Table 13.2   Endogenous party PUNEs in the tax-race model of section 13.3

t^L	ρ^L	t^R	ρ^R	π	w^L	w^R
.278473	3.42484	0	4.70675	.62798	28.1008	41.8526
.495909	3.40968	0	5.70585	.897914	29.4701	43.5609
.308556	3.46601	0	4.73978	.644001	27.823	42.4019
.152177	3.39752	0	4.15032	.450298	27.4459	40.5774
.350091	3.37865	0	5.18172	.757974	29.0817	42.1635
.308922	3.41397	0	4.87176	.674624	28.4139	42.0343
.0566689	3.40592	0	3.67896	.29876	26.5602	39.8463
.344392	3.39761	0	5.086	.733561	28.8206	42.2305
.206995	3.45646	0	4.34143	.523662	27.3115	41.5026
.555808	3.45223	0	5.70924	.90019	29.1154	44.2874
.566787	3.50239	0	5.52209	.855491	28.4886	44.6543
.190344	3.4877	0	4.24522	.500939	26.9318	41.6247
.505109	3.4669	0	5.46856	.841385	28.7333	43.9748
.390141	3.43055	0	5.17198	.761088	28.6759	42.8248
.354133	3.48796	0	4.86201	.681705	27.8154	42.9267
.427003	3.45601	0	5.22763	.778366	28.5413	43.2882
.465263	3.46501	0	5.33545	.807302	28.5963	43.65
.310051	3.46877	0	4.73901	.64416	27.7983	42.4352
.384391	3.51735	0	4.89546	.69425	27.6174	43.3771
.460548	3.48403	0	5.24974	.786181	28.337	43.7333
.19373	3.50782	0	4.24091	.503859	26.7621	41.8299
.414214	3.4371	0	5.24637	.781788	28.7156	43.0646
.400241	3.40665	0	5.30462	.794634	29.0224	42.7614
.281123	3.42828	0	4.71068	.629704	28.0799	41.8995
.124686	3.52241	0	3.98462	.429173	26.2686	41.4185

Table 13.2 *(continued)*

t^L	ρ^L	t^R	ρ^R	π	w^L	w^R
.14601	3.412	0	4.11037	.441119	27.2802	40.6361
.195529	3.49879	0	4.25711	.506977	26.8697	41.7588
.0779044	3.42905	0	3.78269	.340872	26.5986	40.2136
.290259	3.39222	0	4.84498	.663504	28.5421	41.7282
.404896	3.45354	0	5.1518	.757814	28.4681	43.0939
.446194	3.48005	0	5.2137	.776476	28.327	43.5956
.325883	3.50949	0	4.70813	.640843	27.4121	42.8758
.163665	3.52112	0	4.12414	.471437	26.4823	41.7151
.168984	3.37248	0	4.26582	.481425	27.8284	40.5283
.0349273	3.35044	0	3.54123	.235378	26.6958	39.2021
.615623	3.47835	0	3.77833	.916566	28.9652	44.886
.303223	3.40647	0	4.86654	.671999	28.464	41.9351
.311197	3.51271	0	4.66338	.629224	27.366	42.7721
.325215	3.42183	0	4.92234	.690303	28.4217	42.2253
.192404	3.36919	0	4.39117	.520406	28.0351	40.7174
.323733	3.37083	0	5.07946	.728171	29.0103	41.8853
.382128	3.38942	0	5.29193	.789481	29.1366	42.5048
.20018	3.37946	0	4.41692	.530819	28.0055	40.8569
.0142047	3.36092	0	3.43625	.20332	26.4079	39.1203
.179865	3.41798	0	4.26255	.490725	27.4703	40.975
.169577	3.50876	0	4.15251	.477317	26.6274	41.6455
.403549	3.43594	0	5.20766	.771281	28.6775	42.9697
.0937643	3.35999	0	3.86792	.348054	27.2472	39.7754
.279335	3.47855	0	4.60325	.606369	27.539	42.2591
.264147	3.48566	0	4.5361	.587994	27.3975	42.1892

13.5 Quadratic Taxation

In this section we calculate parties endogenously for the quadratic taxation model of Chapter 9. We employ the model of that chapter, with one amendment: we now substitute the error-distribution model of uncertainty for the state-space model used there. We replace axiom B5 with:

B5' $F(\mu) > \frac{1}{2}$.

If $L = (a_L, b_L)$ and $R = (a_R, b_R)$ are two tax policies, and $\Omega(L, R)$ is the set of two types who prefer L to R, we write the probability of Left victory as

$$(13.6) \quad \pi(L, R) = \frac{F(\Omega(L, R)) + \beta - \frac{1}{2}}{2\beta}.$$

The reader can verify that the arguments of Chapter 9 go through with the error-distribution model of uncertainty and assumption B5'. (Although this sounds potentially tedious to verify, in fact it is very simple. All we have to note is that deviations that increase the fraction of voters who prefer one policy to another also increase the probability that the first policy defeats the second.)

Recall that both policies must be progressive in a strong PUNE: Figures 13.1 and 13.2 illustrate the two possible types of (strong) PUNE. Let us first analyze the PUNE of Figure 13.1. The policy $L = (a_L, b_L)$ satisfies the constraint $h_2(a, b) = 0$, where $h_2(a, b) = b + 2a$, and the policy $R = (a_R, b_R)$ satisfies the constraint $h_1(a, b) = 0$, where $h_1(a, b) = 1 - a\mu_2/\mu - b$. These two constraint equations have been written so that the region of policy feasibility is $h_i(a, b) \geq 0$ (see Figure 9.1).

Recall that if Left moves along the line $\overline{LR}$ from L the probability of victory remains constant. Either party can increase its probability of victory (assuming $\pi < 1$) by moving into the half-plane indicated by the normal vectors drawn at L and R in the figure. Defining $\Delta a = a_L - a_R$ and $\Delta b = b_L - b_R$, the normal vector, denoted n, is given by

$$n = (\Delta b, -\Delta a)^T.$$

(The superscript T denotes the transpose of a vector.) (The slope of $\overline{LR}$ is $\Delta b / \Delta a$.)

Recall that the utility function of type w is $v(a, b; w) = a(w^2 - \mu_2) + b(w - \mu)$. Let the parties represent types w^L and w^R. (That is, the reformists and

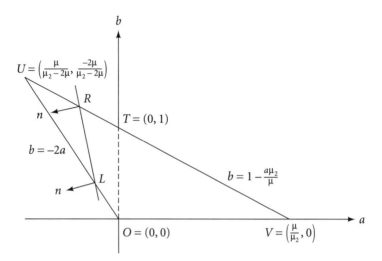

Figure 13.1

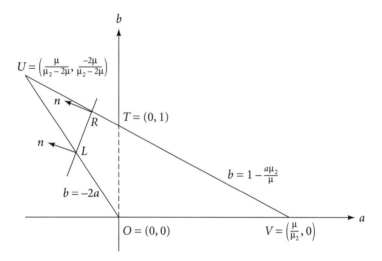

Figure 13.2

militants of the Left party have utility function $v(\cdot; w^L)$.) Then the condition for (L, R)'s being a (local) PUNE is

$$\forall d \in \mathbf{R}^2, d \neq 0 \quad \nabla v(a_L, b_L; w^L) \cdot d > 0 \quad \text{and} \quad \nabla h_2 \cdot d > 0 \Rightarrow n \cdot d < 0$$

$$\text{and} \quad \nabla v(a_R, b_R; w^R) \cdot d > 0 \quad \text{and} \quad \nabla h_1 \cdot d > 0 \Rightarrow n \cdot d < 0.$$

Hence, by Farkas' lemma, (L, R) is a local PUNE if the following equations hold:

(13.7a) $-n = x_L \nabla v(L; w^L) + y_L \nabla h_2,$

(13.7b) $-n = x_R \nabla v(R; w^R) + y_R \nabla h_1,$

(13.7c) $h_2(L) = 0,$

(13.7d) $h_1(R) = 0,$

where x_L, y_L, x_R, and y_R are non-negative numbers. We may conveniently rewrite (13.7a) and (13.7b) as follows. Define the matrices

$$M_L = (\nabla v(a_L, b_L; w^L), \nabla h_2), \qquad M_R = (\nabla v(a_R, b_R; w^R), \nabla h_1).$$

Then the Lagrangian multipliers are non-negative iff

(13.8a) $M_L^{-1} n \leq 0 \quad \text{and} \quad M_R^{-1} n \leq 0,$

where "0" in these inequalities is the zero vector in $\mathbf{R}^2$, and A^{-1} is the inverse of matrix A.

Next, we append the equations that determine w^L and w^R in a PUNE with endogenous parties. We shall assume that a party is represented by its average type (wage). Let $w^*(L, R)$ be the type that is indifferent between policies L and R (that type is unique in either of the two types of PUNE illustrated in Figures 13.1 and 13.2—to see this, check the graph of ϕ in Figure 9.2). Then we have:

(13.8b) $w^* = w^*(a_L, b_L, a_R, b_R),$

(13.8c) $w^L = \dfrac{\int\limits_0^{w^*} w d\mathbf{F}(w)}{\mathbf{F}(w^*)},$

(13.8d) $w^R = \dfrac{\int\limits_{w^*}^{1} w d\mathbf{F}(w)}{1 - \mathbf{F}(w^*)}.$

Equation (13.8b) says that the pivotal type which separates the two parties must be indifferent between the two policies (so that all types $w < w^*$ will prefer policy L to policy R and all types $w > w^*$ will prefer policy R to policy L), and (13.8c and d) stipulate that each party is "represented" by its average member.

Equations (13.7 c–d) and (13.8 b–d) constitute five equations in the seven unknowns $a_L, b_L, a_R, b_R, w^*, w^L, w^R$. This determines (in general) a 2-manifold of solutions; when we find a candidate solution, we must check that inequalities (13.8a) hold. The function $w^*(\cdot)$ depends on the type of PUNE, as we shall see below.

Our search strategy for PUNEs is now as follows. For PUNEs of the Figure 13.1 variety:

(1) Randomly choose a_L and a_R to satisfy $0 > a_L > a_R > \mu/(\mu_2 - 2\mu)$;
(2) Solve equations (13.7 c–d) and (13.8 b–d) ;
(3) If inequalities (13.8a) hold, we have found a local PUNE of the Figure 13.1 variety.

In like manner, for PUNES of the Figure 13.2 variety, step 1 of the above iteration procedure now becomes:

(1′) Randomly choose a_L and a_R to satisfy $0 > a_R > a_L$
$> \max[\mu/(\mu_2 - 2\mu), a_R\mu_2/2\mu - 1/2]$.

The last inequality in this string guarantees both that a_L lies on the segment $\overline{OU}$ of $\triangle VOU$ and that $b_L \leq b_R$, as Figure 13.2 requires.

To calibrate the model, I chose **F** to be the Beta distribution on $[0, 1]$ with mean 0.1545 and second moment (μ_2) 0.05277. This corresponds to the U.S. income distribution in 1990 (see section 9.5). I chose $\beta = 0.125$: thus, at the time of writing party manifestos, uncertainty about the vote is on the order of $\pm 12.5\%$.

We next calculate the type w^* that is indifferent between two policies. We know, from the analysis of Chapter 9, that

$$(13.9) \quad \phi(w^*) = \frac{-\Delta b}{\Delta a}.$$

Equation (13.9) is a quadratic equation in w^*, which has two roots. One of these roots is the right one for PUNEs of the Figure 13.1 type and the other for PUNEs of the Figure 13.2 type. We shall skip the analysis of Figure 13.1 PUNEs, for it turns out (by computation) there are *no endogenous party equilibria of this kind*.

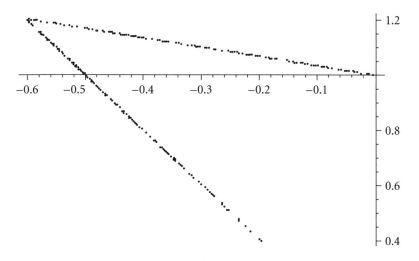

Figure 13.3

For PUNEs of the Figure 13.2 variety, we have, letting $m = \Delta b / \Delta a$ and solving (13.9),

$$(13.10) \quad w^* = \frac{-m + (m^2 + 4(m\mu + \mu_2))^{1/2}}{2}.$$

(We know this is the correct root of the quadratic, since $m > 0$ in this case, and the other root would render w^* a negative number.) The r.h.s. of (13.10) is our function $w^*(a_L, b_L, a_R, b_R)$. We are now ready to compute equilibria. We proceed by choosing a_L and a_R randomly in the appropriate intervals, then computing b_L and b_R from equations (13.7c–d), then solving (13.8b–d) for w^*, w_L, and w_R, and finally checking the negativity conditions (13.8a).

I now discuss the details of the solution. The Beta distribution of income, calibrated as explained above, has a density function

$$f(w) = \frac{(1 - w)^{\omega-1} w^{\nu-1}}{B(\nu, \omega)},$$

where B is the Beta function, $\nu = 0.543855$, and $\omega = 2.97624$.[4]

---

4. For details about the Beta distribution, see Evans, Hastings, and Peacock (1993).

I ran the program for 300 iterations, and found 172 endogenous party PUNEs. Figure 13.3 plots the projection of the Left and Right policies onto the policy triangle $\mathcal{T}$; they lie, of course, on the segments OU and TU of the policy triangle. The average values of these PUNEs are

$$a_L = -.440, \qquad b_L = .880, \qquad a_R = -.300, \qquad b_R = 1.102,$$

$$w_L = .055, \qquad w_R = .352, \qquad w^* = .172, \qquad \pi = .913.$$

After-tax income at the average L policy and the average R policy are plotted in Figure 13.4: the more progressive heavy line is after-tax income under L, the less progressive dashed line is after-tax income under R, and the light line is the diagonal (w, w). Figures 13.5a and b plot the marginal rate of taxation as a function of income for the two policies: we see that Left taxes the highest income at a marginal rate of 100%, while Right taxes the highest income at a marginal rate of less than 50%. It is noteworthy that Left wins with an average probability of over .90. Mr. w^L is at the 39th centile of the wage distribution,

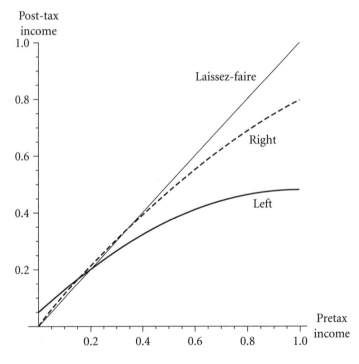

Figure 13.4 Tax policies for Left and Right, at the average endogenous party equilibrium

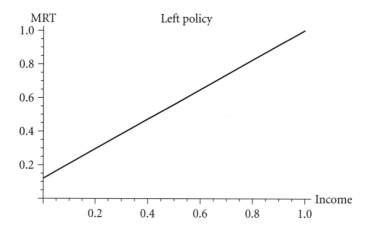

Figure 13.5a   Marginal rate of taxation as a function of income, Left policy

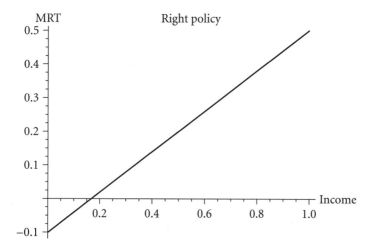

Figure 13.5b   Marginal rate of taxation as a function of income, Right policy

Ms. w^R is at the 86th centile, and Mr. w^* is at the 67th centile: thus Left, in endogenous party equilibrium, represents two-thirds of the polity. Since every member of Left prefers its policy to Right, this means that Left gives more after-tax income to the bottom 67% of the wage distribution, and Right gives more after-tax income to the top 33% (this indeed checks, although it is difficult to see in Figure 13.4).

Two other aspects of this equilibrium are noteworthy: (1) how differentiated the average PUNEs are at endogenous party equilibrium, and (2) the relative "moderation" of the Left policy (recall that the most expropriationist policy, given by $(a, b) = (0, 0)$, generates an after-tax income which is the constant $\mu = .1525)$.

In the United States, I think that the Democratic Party proposes redistributive policy much less radically redistributive than the Left tax policy in Figure 13.4; I do not know how the Republican Party's policy relates to the R policy in Figure 13.4. There may be many reasons that reality differs from this model. Among those is the fact that American democracy is not perfectly representative, in the sense that the reformists and militants in the two parties do not have the policy preferences (in terms of after-tax income) of the *average* type that supports the respective parties. In reality it is probably the case that those who finance parties have more than their per capita influence on the nature of the parties' preferences. We therefore briefly turn, in the next section, to the problem of party finance. And finally, there are issues other than after-tax income that exercise the U.S. polity (and in that vein, recall the results of Chapter 11).

13.6 Private Financing of Parties

Perfectly representative democracy, in the sense of this chapter, is a utopian ideal. In the United States (at least), the policy preferences of party donors influence the preferences of the parties. In a model with party finance, the default assumption should be that parties aggregate the preferences of their donor types according to their contributions, not according to their population frequency.

It is not conceptually difficult to introduce party finance into the model of endogenous party formation. To solve the free-rider problem, it is best to assume a finite-type polity—for example, the three-type polity of Chapter 12. We assume that each type is organized by a corporate agent (a union or a business council) that assesses its members for contributions to the parties. We shall write down a game played among types, where the strategies are ordered pairs of contributions to the two parties. The preferences of parties are determined at the Nash equilibrium of this game.

Let the policy space be T, let there be N types, let the von Neumann–Morgenstern utility function of type h be $v^h(t, x) = \tilde{v}^h(t) - x$, where $\tilde{v}^h$ represents type h's policy preferences, t is a policy, and x is the total contributions of the individual to the two parties. Let (z_L^h, z_R^h) be the contributions of a type-h individual to the L and R parties, and represent by z the profile of such contributions across types. (We assume these contributions, assessed by the "union," are the same for every individual in a given type.) The L party's policy preferences are now defined to be $v^L = \sum_h z_L^h \tilde{v}^h$, with a similar formula for the R party.[5]

With respect to these preferences, there is an average PUNE, which we denote by $(t^L(z), t^R(z))$. Thus we have defined a mapping $z \to (t^L(z), t^R(z))$ which associates to any profile of party contributions an average PUNE. We may now define the payoff function of type h as

$$\Pi^h(z) = \pi(z)\tilde{v}^h(t^L(z)) + (1 - \pi(z))\tilde{v}^h(t^R(z)) - (z_L^h + z_R^h),$$

where $\pi(z)$ is the average probability of L victory in the PUNEs at z.

We now define an *equilibrium in the party formation process with private party financing* as a Nash equilibrium of this game among types, where each type is constrained to contribute finance not to exceed its post-tax income.

In English, each type optimizes against the other types by choosing its party finance contributions to maximize its utility, where it takes account of the effect its contributions have on the preferences of the parties and hence on the PUNEs which are forthcoming, and debits contributions as a disutility.

It would be a delicate task to compute this kind of equilibrium; if there were three types, the strategy space would be six-dimensional. We would have to compute derivatives of the payoff functions, which means having a precise understanding of how changing the weights in the aggregation that defines a party's preferences influences the average PUNE. The payoff to such a computation would probably not be worth the effort expenditure (at least with the present author's low-tech programming skills).

For a review of the recent literature on the influence of interest groups on politics, the reader may consult Austen-Smith (1997).

13.7 A Technical Remark on the Existence of PUNEs

In the last several chapters we have seen a number of examples of PUNEs in multidimensional models. The reader is entitled to ask: is there an interesting

---

5. Alternatively, some other aggregation rule can be chosen. Formally, one must ensure that the kind of measurability and comparability possessed by the utility functions is respected by the aggregation rule. See Roemer (1996, chap. 1).

This model does not explain how party finance is used by the party. In a more complex model, we may introduce the party budget into the function π: ceteris paribus, richer parties have a higher probability of winning, as they spend more on informing voters about their candidate.

general existence theorem for party-unanimity Nash equilibrium? I conjecture there is not.

The problem is that we already have a very general existence theorem: there is always a PUNE where each party plays the ideal policy of its militant faction. Assuming these policies are unique, this is a PUNE, for the militants will never agree to deviate from their respective ideal points. This is, however, an uninteresting PUNE. Somewhat more interestingly, for fixed parties, let one party play the ideal point of its militants. There will be a set of "best responses" by the other party—policies which are Pareto efficient with respect to the utilities of its three factions. Any of these, along with the first party's policy, constitute a PUNE. But these PUNEs are extreme in the sense that the militants in the first party entirely dominate the party. What we really desire is a theorem asserting the existence of a PUNE in which no faction is at its ideal point. But that appears to be hard to come by.

Consider the following construction. Let T be the policy space with generic element t. For any policy t^L let $C^R(t^L)$ be the "contract curve" in T, consisting of policies at which the militants and opportunists in Party R have no agreeable deviation, given that Left is playing t^L. Now take a typical point $t \in C^R(t^L)$, and construct the contract curve $C^L(t)$—the points in T which are Pareto efficient with respect to the militants and opportunists in Left, given that Right plays t. Consider the union $\bigcup_{t \in C^R(t^L)} C^L(t)$; define the correspondence

$$\theta(t^L) = \bigcup_{t \in C^R(t^L)} C^L(t),$$

which maps T, viewed as the policy space of Left, into itself. A fixed point of θ is the left component of a PUNE.

Let t^{L*} and t^{R*} denote the ideal points of Left's and Right's militants. It is easy to verify that t^{L*} is a fixed point of θ. (Just note that t^{R*} lies on $C^R(t^{L*})$, since it lies on every contract curve for Right, and t^{L*} lies on $C^L(t^{R*})$, since it lies on every contract curve of Left.) Thus we require an existence theorem which tells us there is another fixed point. It is, however, not easy to show that θ has another fixed point.

It is probably very difficult to find interesting sufficient conditions for the existence of (nontrivial) PUNEs. The reader should recall the difficult existence proof for Wittman equilibrium in section 3.4, under not very satisfactory assumptions. It seems the wiser strategy is either to prove the existence of

PUNEs for each particular application, as we did in the models of Chapters 9 and 10, or to try to compute PUNEs, as we have often done in the past several chapters.

13.8 Conclusion

We have proposed a theory of endogenous parties for a model with a two-dimensional issue space. That theory, based on Baron (1993) and on collaborative work with Ignacio Ortuño-Ortín (see section 5.2), conceives of parties as being stable when no citizen wishes to change the party he belongs to when he sees the policies both parties play in electoral competition. In the aggregation procedure which associates citizen types to party preferences, we made the assumption of "perfect representation."

Although our model deviates from political reality, because actual party formation is not "perfectly representative," the model is theoretically satisfying because it derives political equilibrium from the usual primitives—preferences and endowments of citizens. We note that the policies recommended by parties in equilibrium are quite polarized—a far cry from Downsian convergence.

We know, in particular, that the United States is not a perfectly representative democracy. We propose that the influence of campaign contributions on party preferences is the key factor of which we have taken no account in electoral politics. Another important factor may be that, in U.S. reality, many citizens do not vote, and we cannot expect even perfectly representative parties to include the preferences of these abstaining citizens in its calculus. Work remains to be done to incorporate these phenomena into a model of endogenous parties.

We finally showed how a more realistic model of endogenous parties can be constructed, which views parties as corporations whose preferences are determined by the "One dollar one vote" rule. Computing equilibria of this model is, however, beyond our scope here. Doubtless simplifications can be proposed that would make the proposed analysis tractable.

13.9 Why the Poor Do Not Expropriate the Rich: Reprise

We have now seen a series of models addressing the issue of redistribution in democracies. In the classic unidimensional Downs model under certainty, both parties propose the ideal tax policy of the voter with median income, which is unity, assuming that mean income is greater than median income. In the unidimensional Wittman model with uncertainty of Proposition 4.1, the Left and Right parties propose tax rates of unity and zero, respectively. But in our more nuanced analysis, Left parties do not propose to expropriate the rich, even when we postulate no deadweight loss from taxation.

We can now see that this is due to the conjunction of three features of the political economy of democracy:

(1) the multidimensionality of politics,
(2) the heterogeneity of preferences, and
(3) the complex nature of party competition.

The first feature includes the fact that political competition may concern noneconomic issues as well as redistribution, as in Chapter 11, but also that, even when competition is only about redistribution, tax policy may be complex, as in the models of quadratic taxation in this chapter and Chapter 10. In Chapter 11 we showed that the Left will propose low tax rates if the mean income of the cohort of voters with the median value on the "religious" trait is greater than the population's mean income, even when the majority of voters have an ideal tax rate of unity, and in section 13.5, we observed that, even when redistribution is the only issue, the Left does not propose an expropriationary policy. Nor does it do so in the three-class model of Chapter 12.

By the second feature in the list, I mean that voters have different incomes, but also that they have different views on noneconomic issues, and by the third feature, I mean that parties are composed of factions with different goals.

I do not believe it is useful to ask what the *main* explanation of nonexpropriationary policy in democracies is. We have shown that that characteristic follows from the conjunction of the three listed features, and because they all *are* features of almost all democracies, that demonstration suffices. Moreover, it may be a correct observation that the Nordic countries are ones where politics most closely approximate unidimensionality, because of the linguistic, religious, and ethnic homogeneity of the populations; if so, our theory suggests it is not a surprise that these democracies have redistributed more pervasively than all others.

14

Toward a Model of Coalition Government

14.1 Introduction

A coalition government forms when there are more than two parties and none of them wins an electoral majority. The underlying situation may be that each party is allotted parliamentary seats in proportion to its vote, and that a majority coalition is required to pass legislation.

The literature on coalition government, or multiparty politics, is reviewed by Austen-Smith (1996) and Shepsle (1991). We shall not attempt to repeat their work, but shall propose a model of multiparty politics which flows rather naturally from the approach we have developed thus far. In the first part of the chapter we restrict ourselves to the case of a unidimensional policy space, and in the last part, to the multidimensional case. We shall throughout assume that there are three parties. The logic for n parties is the same, although the computations necessary to calculate equilibrium, for even four parties, become fierce.

We shall assume, in the first part of the chapter, that parties are of the Wittman variety, maximizing a preference order on policy space. We shall also assume that parties are uncertain about voter behavior, and we adopt the state-space approach to uncertainty. In the latter part of the chapter, when doing multidimensional analysis, we take the view that parties are composed of factions.

The natural way of thinking about party competition when there are more than two parties is in a framework with dates (see Austen-Smith and Banks 1988). To wit, there are three dates at which relevant actions occur:

Date 0.   Each party announces a policy;
Date 1.   Citizens vote;
Date 2.   A government forms, and announces its policy.

Clearly, for citizens to vote intelligently, they must understand the process by which a government forms and a policy is announced, once the vote is in.

In the two-party case, we assumed that each citizen votes for the party whose policy he prefers; that behavior, however, is not necessarily rational when there are more than two parties. In particular, if a voter predicts that her favorite party will not be in the coalition, she might view a vote for it as wasted. Such voters will be called *strategic,* while a citizen who always votes for the policy she prefers is called *sincere.*

We shall continue to assume that there is a continuum of citizens, and so no voter can ever be pivotal. Nevertheless, we shall endow voters with psychologies according to which they may be either sincere or strategic in their voting behavior. This is an attempt to capture real political behavior: in large polities with multiparty politics we observe strategic voting by at least some citizens, even though they know their votes are not pivotal.

Our game plan in this chapter will follow the instructions issued by Austen-Smith and Banks (1988), who wrote:

> Voters are interested in policy outcomes, not policy promises. And policy outcomes are determined within an elected legislature that typically comprises representatives of several districts or political parties. Rational voters, therefore, will take into account the subsequent legislative game in making their decisions at the electoral stage of the process. In turn, rational candidates will take account of such deliberations in selecting their electoral strategy and subsequent legislative behavior conditional on electoral success. So to understand more fully both electoral and legislative behavior—in the sense of being able to explain and predict policy positions, policy outcomes, and coalition structures—it is necessary to develop a theory of both political arenas simultaneously. (405)

14.2 The Payoff Function of a Wittman Party

We assume, as usual, a set of citizen types H, a set of policies T (with no restriction, in this section, on its dimension), a utility function $v(t, h)$, a set of states S, and a probability distribution $\mathbf{G}$ on S. In state s, the distribution of voter types is given by a probability measure $\mathbf{F}_s$. Parties 1, 2, and 3 have policy preferences represented by von Neumann–Morgenstern utility functions v^i, $i = 1, 2, 3$. Parties agree on the distributions $\mathbf{G}$ and $\mathbf{F}_s$.

14.2.1 COALITION FORMATION

We begin with the last stage of the game, namely, with a description of how a government forms, and a policy is selected, once the vote has occurred. Denote the *platform vector* of the three parties by $t = (t^1, t^2, t^3)$, and let the distribution of votes be $p = (p^1, p^2, p^3)$. There are two (nonsingular) possibilities: either one party has a majority, or none does, but one party has a plurality.[1] In the first case, the majority party takes power and implements its policy—this is just as in the two-party case.

In the case that party j is the plural party, we assert that it takes the lead in forming a coalition. The plural party will be called the *formateur*. It must choose one partner to form a (majority) government. We prescribe the following rule. If parties $\{i, j\}$ compose the coalition, then the *policy of the government* will be determined by a lottery over t^i and t^j, where the weights in the lottery are proportional to the vote shares of i and j. Formally, define the function

$$G^j(t, p) = \frac{p^j}{p^i + p^j} v^j(t^j) + \frac{p^i}{p^i + p^j} v^j(t^i)$$

(14.1)

$$- \left(\frac{p^j}{p^k + p^j} v^j(t^j) + \frac{p^k}{p^k + p^j} v^j(t^k) \right).$$

In writing the function G^j, we adopt the convention that the coalition partners are evaluated by j in ascending order of their index (thus, in (14.1), $i < k$). Then party j chooses to coalesce with party i if $G^j > 0$ and chooses to coalesce with party k if $G^j < 0$. $G^j(t, p)$ is just the difference in expected utilities for party j if it coalesces with i or k. If $G^j = 0$, then we must adopt some tie-breaking rule: we can say that j chooses each coalition partner with probability one-half, for instance.

This defines completely the coalition formation process.[2] In the case we have avoided, that two parties tie for the plurality, we may choose a formateur between them by flipping a coin , and the process then proceeds as above. Our

---

1. A singular possibility is that two parties tie for the plurality. Of course, we should not prejudge that this case is singular—but it turns out that it will be.

2. Austen-Smith (private communication) notes that it is unreasonable to assume that the first potential coalition partner, B, approached accepts the offer. For B may compute that its welfare is higher if a coalition is formed between A and C. Introducing such considerations would complexify our analysis considerably, although a complete theory would require their recognition. In sum, the present theory eclipses the important problem of party bargaining in the process of coalition formation.

approach in this chapter is to avoid such complicating details, however, for pedagogical reasons.

The formation of a government policy as described is not, perhaps, the first approach one thinks of. Why not just say that the government's policy is the convex combination of policies of the coalition partners, weighted by the respective vote shares of those partners? Our choice is made, frankly, to produce more credible equilibria. Suppose the coalition's policy were, indeed, the convex combination of the platforms of its members just alluded to. Then each party might propose extreme policies (one very right, the other very left), and their convex combination could be a reasonable, moderate policy. So that formulation can lead to crazy equilibria where the platform vector is composed of extreme policies—perhaps far to the left or right of *any* voter's ideal point. On the other hand, a lottery between very unattractive policies is still very unattractive, so our formulation will not (obviously) lead to parties' proposing extreme policies.

We should notice that the process we have adopted may make it attractive for a party that does not expect to be plural to decrease the fraction of the vote it gets, by becoming more extreme, for it may, thereby, make itself a more attractive coalition partner to the plural party. But recall that a party, in the present model, is reformist and not opportunist—it does not desire to become a coalition member per se, but only wishes to join the coalition if doing so improves the policy lottery produced by the coalition government (from the viewpoint of its preference order).

We may summarize as follows. Let $L(t)$ be the set of lotteries on the policies making up the platform vector t. Let P be the 2-simplex of possible distributions of the vote (3-vectors p whose non-negative components sum to one). We have defined a function $\theta : T \times P \to L(t)$, which associates any pair (t, p) to a lottery on t. We call θ the *coalition formation process*.

It need hardly be said that we have here declared by fiat a coalition formation process whose nature political scientists have studied in great historical detail (see, for example, Baron and Ferejohn 1989; Strom 1990; and Laver and Shepsle 1996). Our aim in this chapter is to construct a plausible model. Real coalition formation processes are doubtless far more complex than θ.

14.2.2 HOW CITIZENS VOTE

Each type h of citizen is further partitioned into two subtypes: those who vote sincerely and those who vote strategically. To simplify things, we shall assume that, in each type, a fraction ϵ are sincere and the fraction $(1 - \epsilon)$ are strategic. The number ϵ is a datum of our model.

Each subtype of voter has a psychology. The psychology of sincere voters is simple: they always derive maximum welfare, *in the process of voting,* from voting their true preferences. The psychology of strategic voters is different. If such a voter predicts that there will be a coalition government $\{i, j\}$, then he derives a utility of 1 from voting for the party in $\{i, j\}$ that he prefers, a utility of -1 from voting for the party in $\{i, j\}$ that he disprefers, and a utility of 0 from voting for party k. We might summarize this by saying that he thinks of his vote as productive, detrimental, and wasted, respectively, in these three cases. It is best for one's vote to be productive, and worst for it to be detrimental. If, on the other hand, he predicts that party i will be the majority party, and that party j will come in second, then he derives a utility of 1 from voting for his preferred party in $\{i, j\}$, a utility of -1 from voting for his dispreferred party in $\{i, j\}$, and a utility 0 from voting for party k. We further suppose that these utilities, defined when he knows for sure what the electoral outcome will be, obey the von Neumann–Morgenstern axioms over lotteries on electoral outcomes.

To illustrate, suppose a voter believes that with probability π there will be a coalition $\{i, j\}$, with probability $1 - \pi$ party i will win with a majority, and the voter's preferences are $t^j \succ t^k \succ t^i$. Then the voter computes her expected utility from voting for i, j, or k as follows:

$$\text{Eu(voting } i) = \pi(-1) + (1 - \pi)(-1)$$

$$\text{Eu(voting } j) = \pi(1) + (1 - \pi)(1)$$

$$\text{Eu(voting } k) = \pi(0) + (1 - \pi)(0) = 0.$$

The voter clearly maximizes utility by voting for j.

We next define the concept of a *consistent vote at platform vector t in state s.* Verbally, a consistent vote in state s is a distribution of the vote, p, at platform vector t, such that, when every voter computes the lottery induced by the coalition formation process at (t, p), and calculates, according to that belief, how he should vote, the vote (in state s) aggregates exactly to p. Thus p is a stationary point in the voting process at t in state s.

To write this down precisely, let t be given, let H^i be the set of voter types who prefer t^i to the other two policies, and let H^{ij} be the subset of H^i of types who prefer t^j to t^k. (In our quest for simplicity, we ignore cases of indifference.)

We now describe how voters react if they believe the vote distribution will be $p = (p^1, p^2, p^3)$ and the platform vector is t.

There are several cases.

Case (1) Party 2 is plural, and $G^2(t, p) > 0$.

We imagine, now, that all citizens take p to be their belief about the vote distribution. Thus the coalition formed, were p the actual vote, would be $\{2, 1\}$. Then, according to our specification of voter psychology, the fraction who will vote for party 2, in state s, is

$$(14.2a) \quad q^2 = F_s(H^2) + (1 - \epsilon)F_s(H^{32}).$$

Thus all those who prefer t^2 vote for party 2, as do the strategic voters whose preferences are $t^3 \succ t^2 \succ t^1$.

In like manner, the fraction who would vote for Party 1 is

$$(14.2b) \quad q^1 = F_s(H^1) + (1 - \epsilon)F_s(H^{31}),$$

while the fraction voting for party 3 is simply the sincere voters who prefer t^3, that is,

$$(14.2c) \quad q^3 = \epsilon F_s(H^3).$$

Clearly other cases where one party is plural are handled in the same way.

Case (2) $p^1 > 0.5$, and $p^3 > p^2$.

In this case, the reader can verify that the vote fractions in state s will be:

$$q^1 = F_s(H^1) + (1 - \epsilon)F_s(H^{21}),$$

$$q^2 = \epsilon F_s(H^2), \quad \text{and}$$

$$q^3 = F_s(H^3) + (1 - \epsilon)F_s(H^{23}).$$

We will not write down voter behavior in singular cases where there are ties, although the logic permits us to do so.

Clearly other cases where one party is major are handled in the same way.

We have defined a mapping $\Psi_{ts} : P \rightarrow P$. At any pair $(t, s) \in T \times S$, it associates a *belief* about the vote distribution (p) to an *action* by voters which aggregates to a vote distribution, $\Psi_{ts}(p)$. We now define a vote distribution p to be *consistent* (at platform vector t in state s) if it is a fixed point of Ψ_{ts}, and if, at p, the coalition formateur behaves as postulated. For instance, a vector p such that

$$p^1 = \mathbf{F}_s(H^1) + (1 - \epsilon)\mathbf{F}_s(H^{31}),$$

$$p^2 = \mathbf{F}_s(H^2) + (1 - \epsilon)\mathbf{F}_s(H^{32}), \quad \text{and}$$

$$p^3 = \epsilon\mathbf{F}_s(H^3),$$

and at p, 2 is the plural party and $G^2(t, p) > 0$ is a consistent vote.

Unfortunately, consistent vote distributions at (t, s) are neither, in general, unique, nor do they always exist. (We shall give some examples below.) For the moment, let us assume that for every $(t, s) \in T \times S$, there is a unique consistent vote distribution.

14.2.3 PARTY BEHAVIOR

We are now in a position to define the payoff functions of the parties, functions $\Pi^i : T \times T \times T \to \mathbf{R}$. For any $t \in T^3$, and in any state s, there is (by assumption) a unique consistent vote, call it $p(t, s)$. At the pair $(t, p(t, s))$, there is a lottery on t induced by the coalition formation process, $\theta(t, p(t, s))$. The expected utility of party i at this lottery is $v^i(\theta(t, p(t, s)))$. But now party i has to take its expectation over the set of possible states, and so its payoff is

$$(14.3) \quad \Pi^i(t) = \int_S v^i(\theta(t, p(t, s)))d\mathbf{G}(s).$$

Each party desires to maximize its payoff, and we define a *Wittman equilibrium for the three-party game* as a Nash equilibrium (in pure strategies) of the three-player game with payoff functions Π^i.

Wittman equilibria will often exist when the party space is unidimensional. We provide an example in section 14.3.

As we see, the subtlety in the three-party model is to define the payoff functions of the parties. Some remarks are in order.

Remark 1 On finding a consistent vote distribution at platform vector t in state s.

This is a simple process, in the sense that a finite algorithm will do the job of finding all fixed points. There are a finite number of possible cases, given t and $\mathbf{F}_s$; either party 1 is plural, or party 2 is plural, and so on. In each case, we can

deduce what the fixed point must be, if there is one, according to the formulae
provided in, for instance, equations (14.2a,b,c).

There are, as I noted, two possible problems: either nonexistence or nonuniqueness.

Remark 2   On handling nonuniqueness of a consistent vote at (t, s).

One way to do this is to suppose that parties assume each consistent vote
distribution is equally likely. I prefer, however, to introduce a *polling process*.

Assume that there is a series of opinion polls after the parties announce their
policies. Before the first poll (but after the party announcements), the state, s,
is revealed. In the first poll, everyone polled announces sincerely which policy
he prefers: this gives a vote distribution $q^1(t, s)$. When this poll is published, it
becomes the current belief of voters, who then compute how they should vote
given that belief; in the second poll, voters announce their votes, which will give
a vote distribution $\Psi_{ts}(q^1(t, s)) = q^2(t, s)$. In the third poll, voters have taken
q^2 to be their beliefs and announce, accordingly, their intentions to vote, which
aggregate to $\Psi_{ts}(q^2(t, s)) = q^3(t, s)$. It is not hard to deduce that if a consistent
vote exists, it will be arrived at by at most the third poll: that is, either q^3 is a
consistent vote, or there will be an unending cycle in this process.

Note that this procedure will always locate a particular consistent vote distribution, if there are several, for it is anchored by the initial condition that
voters announce sincerely on the first poll. This, then, is a way of solving the
nonuniqueness problem.

Moreover, I conjecture that the polling process just described reflects the
role that polls play in politics. Fresh after the party conventions, when polled,
citizens announce sincerely, and after that, if they are strategic, they react
(myopically, we would say) to the previous poll. Thus the polling process serves
an important function of locating a consistent vote distribution.[3] (The reason
that polls may not converge in real life could either be that no consistent vote
distribution exists or, more likely, that many voters are oscillating in their view
about which party they prefer. That kind of oscillation is not modeled here.)

Remark 3   On handling nonexistence of a consistent vote distribution at (t, s).

---

3. Voters think one step ahead, but not two steps ahead. Perhaps this is the simplest way of
capturing bounded rationality.

One could take lotteries over the various vote distributions that *could* be fixed points, in the sense that they are implied by equations like (14.2a,b,c), associated with the various cases, but I prefer a simpler alternative. First, note that we are only concerned with platform vectors that lack a consistent vote distribution for a set of states of positive **G**-measure—bad behavior on sets of states of zero measure will not affect the definition of the payoff function. But in that case, I would simply say the payoff functions are not defined at t. (Alternatively, we assign a payoff of $-\infty$ to all parties in the case where consistent vote distributions fail to exist for a set of states of positive measure.) Thus no party will ever deviate to a policy that renders the platform vector one of this kind.

A simple example suggests that the nonexistence of consistent vote distributions is not a major problem, as follows. T is the real line, $H = \{h^1, h^2, h^3\}$, where h^i are real numbers, each type h^i has Euclidean preferences with ideal point h^i, and there are three parties, one representing each type. We take $\epsilon = .9$, and assume that there is only one state, and **F** is the discrete distribution $(.32, .4, .28)$. Let $(h^1, h^2, h^3) = (10, 20, 50)$. We study the question: how often, on T^3, is there no consistent vote distribution? To answer this question, we generated randomly vectors $(t^1, t^2, t^3) \in [-100, 15] \times [15, 35] \times [35, 200]$. The example is constructed so that party 2 will always be plural. With 10,000 randomizations, we found 260 cases with no consistent vote—thus, in about 2.6% of the cases. (In these cases, the vote oscillates between what would occur if voters expected the coalition to be $\{2, 1\}$ and what would occur were they to expect the coalition to be $\{2, 3\}$. Thus when they expect the coalition to be $\{2, 1\}$, a vote is induced which makes it attractive for party 2 to coalesce with party 3, and so on.)

Remark 4   On postulating both sincere and strategic voters.

There are two reasons to do so. First, both types of voter surely exist in reality. Second, if we had only strategic voters in our model, endowed with the psychology described above, then *every* consistent vote will give one party the majority, and hence there will be no coalition governments. For suppose voters expect the coalition to be $\{2, 1\}$. Then all strategic voters will vote either for party 2 or for party 1, so one of these parties wins the majority (barring ties), and hence a consistent expectation can only be that there is a majority winner. Even if ties become important, and so there is a coalition between two parties each of which receives half the vote, it is uninteresting to have equilibria in which the outside party receives zero votes.

Hence, unless we alter the psychology that leads to strategic voting, the simplest way to give some hope for the existence of equilibria with coalition governments is to include sincere voters.

14.3 An Example of Coalition Government: Unidimensional Wittman Equilibrium

We study an example where there is a continuum of types, but only two states. Thus we let $S = \{1, 2\}$, $\mathbf{G}$ assigns probability one-half to each state, $H = [0, \infty)$, $T = [0, \infty)$, $v(t, h) = -(t - h)^2$, $\mathbf{F}_1$ is the lognormal distribution on H with mean 40 and median 30, and $\mathbf{F}_2$ is the lognormal distribution on H with mean 40 and median 20. We shall specify the parties and ϵ below: for the moment, represent the preferences of party i by v^i. Note that the policy space is the positive real line.

Thus think of this model as one of U.S. politics, where h is the annual income of a citizen in thousands of dollars, and t is an economic policy. We identify $t = h$ as the optimal economic policy for a citizen with income h. $\mathbf{F}_1$ is an approximation to the actual distribution of household income in the United States (in thousands of dollars) in the early 1990s, and $\mathbf{F}_2$ is a more skewed distribution with the same mean.

The parties shall be thought of as Left (1), Center (2), and Right (3); we shall calibrate the model further (which means choosing the parties' preferences and ϵ) so as to generate two kinds of equilibria: one where there is a coalition government, in both states, at equilibrium with Center as formateur, and another where in one state there is a coalition government, and in the other, Center wins a majority.

Suppose the parties propose policies $t^1 < t^2 < t^3$ (which is what we should expect, given their names). Then, in state s, all those types with $h < (t^1 + t^2)/2$ prefer t^1 to the other two policies. More generally, the fraction of the polity that prefers t^i to the other two policies in state s, which we denote $p_{is}(t)$, is given by:

$$p_{1s}(t) = \mathbf{F}_s\left(\frac{t^1 + t^2}{2}\right),$$

$$p_{3s}(t) = 1 - \mathbf{F}_s\left(\frac{t^3 + t^2}{2}\right),$$

$$p_{2s}(t) = \mathbf{F}_s\left(\frac{t^3 + t^2}{2}\right) - \mathbf{F}_s\left(\frac{t^1 + t^2}{2}\right).$$

What must a consistent vote distribution look like in state 1 if it is to be the case that party 2 is the plural party and prefers to coalesce with party 1? If voters believe that to be the case, then the distribution of the vote in state 1 will be

$$q_1 = (p_{11}(t), p_{21}(t) + (1 - \epsilon)p_{31}(t), \epsilon p_{31}(t)).$$

Thus because preferences are single-peaked, all strategic voters whose preferred policy is t^3 will cast their vote for party 2. The distribution q_1 is indeed a consistent vote distribution if, at q_1, party 2 is plural and prefers to coalesce with party 1, that is, the second component of q_1 is the largest component and is less than one-half, and $G^2(t, q_1) > 0$. In this case, the policy lottery that emerges from the coalition formation process is

$$\left(\frac{p_{21} + (1 - \epsilon)p_{31}}{1 - \epsilon p_{31}} \circ t^2, \frac{p_{11}}{1 - \epsilon p_{31}} \circ t^1 \right),$$

where the notation $(x \circ t, y \circ r)$ means the lottery that gives t with probability x and r with probability y.

What are the necessary and sufficient conditions for q_2 to be a consistent vote distribution at t in state 2 when party 2 is plural and prefers to coalesce with party 3? In that case, the vote distribution must be

$$q_2 = (\epsilon p_{12}(t), p_{22}(t) + (1 - \epsilon)p_{12}(t), p_{32}(t)),$$

and it must be the case that $G^2(t, q_2) < 0$. In this case, the coalition's policy is the lottery:

$$\left(\frac{p_{22} + (1 - \epsilon)p_{12}}{1 - \epsilon p_{12}} \circ t^2, \frac{p_{32}}{1 - \epsilon p_{12}} \circ t^3 \right).$$

Defining

$$W_1(t) = \frac{p_{11}(t)}{1 - \epsilon p_{31}(t)}, \qquad W_2(t) = \frac{p_{32}(t)}{1 - \epsilon p_{12}(t)},$$

using equation (14.3) and knowledge of what the policy lotteries are in the two cases, we can write the payoff functions of the parties in this situation as:

$$\Pi^i(t) = \left(1 - \frac{W_1(t) + W_2(t)}{2}\right) v^i(t^2) + \frac{W_1(t)}{2} v^i(t^1)$$

(14.4)

$$+ \frac{W_2(t)}{2} v^i(t^3), \qquad \text{for } i = 1, 2, 3.$$

We now can use the calculus. The local condition for a platform vector t to induce the coalition governments in the two states as described above in Nash equilibrium is that for each i, t^i maximize Π^i locally, given the other two policies, that $G^2(t, q_1(t)) > 0$ and $G^2(t, q_2(t)) > 0$, and that party 2 indeed be the plural party at q^1 and q^2. Thus we can solve the model by setting the three appropriate first derivatives of the payoff functions equal to zero and then checking that the ancillary conditions hold at the solution.

Note that, mathematically, (14.4) is just like the Wittman payoff function in the two-party model, where we now have a positive convex combination of the party's utility at *three* policies. In particular, the weights in (14.4) are the probabilities that voters (and parties) will, in the end, see the three respective policies implemented.

I further calibrated the model by taking the Left party to represent the voter type 10 (thus $v^1(t) = -(t - 10)^2$), the Center party to represent the type 25, and I then searched for values for the type h^3 whom the Right party represents in order to generate equilibria of the kind described—that in both states Center is plural, and that in state 1 it coalesces with Left and in state 2 it coalesces with Right. The results for $\epsilon = .9$ are reported in Table 14.1. The table shows that there is only a small range of values h^3 for which equilibria[4] of this kind occur—roughly, between 40 and 44. In all cases, Left proposes a policy of 0, to the left of its ideal point, Center proposes policies slightly to left of its ideal point, and Right proposes policies that are sometimes to the left and sometimes to the right of its ideal point. In the table, "Exp[s]" is the expected value of the policy in state s, and G_s^2 denotes the value of G^2 in state s.

---

4. To be sure we have genuine Nash equilibria, we must check that, globally, there are no attractive deviations for any party. The policies described below are each global maxima of their respective conditional payoff functions, but we must check more than that: for instance, would it be profitable for the right to deviate to a point at which it would become a plurality winner? There are only a finite number of possibilities, but the exercise is tedious.

It will be instructive to examine more closely why the allocations in Table 14.1 are equilibria. Let us fix attention on the case $h^3 = 40$. Why should not Left deviate above zero? After all, that might make it an even more attractive coalition partner for Center, and it would increase its vote share. The answer is tricky. If Left deviates a small amount to the right, its vote share increases, Center's vote share decreases, and Right's vote share stays the same. It remains the case that the structure of coalitions is the same in the two states, but now, in the coalition $\{2, 3\}$, Right's policy has a higher probability of winning than before, because Right's *relative* share of the vote in the Center-Right coalition has increased. This decreases Left's expected utility in state 2, and it turns out that this utility decrement dominates the utility increment that Left enjoys (in state 1) by moving toward its ideal point.

But perhaps Left should deviate a lot to, say, $t^1 = 19$. After all, Left prefers 19 to 0 (since its ideal point is 10). Then Left might be so attractive to Center that Center will coalesce with Left in *both* states. We now check this. At the policy platform (19, 21.462, 40.256), if all voters behaved sincerely, the vote distribution would be (.302, .213, .485) in state 1. It looks as if Right will now be the formateur: we indeed check that the vote shares $(.302\epsilon, .302(1 - \epsilon) + .213, .485)$ are consistent at this platform vector in state 1 with Right's being the plural party who chooses to coalesce with Center! Thus in this state we must compute Left's utility as its expected utility from the Right-Center lottery so determined.

In state 2, if all voters voted sincerely at the new platform vector, the vote distribution would be (.504, .140, .356)—Left is the majority winner. Consequently this is a consistent vote distribution in state 1 with Left's being the majority winner.

Table 14.1 Three-party equilibria, coalition governments
$\{\epsilon = 0.9, (h^1, h^2) = (10, 25)\}$

h^3	t^1	t^2	t^3	p_{11}	p_{21}	p_{31}	p_{12}	p_{22}	p_{32}	Exp[1]	Exp[2]	G_1^2	G_2^2
40	0	21.462	40.256	.088	.476	.437	.269	.375	.356	18.122	30.618	5.05	74.157
41	0	21.488	41.039	.088	.482	.43	.269	.379	.352	18.171	30.907	10.514	68.183
42	0	21.512	41.881	.088	.487	.425	.269	.383	.348	18.217	31.185	16.016	62.147
43	0	21.534	42.57	.088	.493	.419	.27	.386	.344	18.261	31.451	21.546	56.06
44	0	21.554	43.318	.089	.498	.413	.27	.39	.341	18.302	31.707	27.093	49.933

We now compute Left's expected utility over these two states (when Left has deviated to 19), which turns out to be −183.6. However, at the allocation in the first line of Table 14.1, Left's expected utility is −159.96. So the deviation to 19 is not attractive to Left.

This illustrates the complex strategic nature of party behavior in the model.

An interesting feature of these equilibria is the relationship between the degree of skewness in the income distribution and the expected policy. Recall that state 2 is the one where the income distribution is more skewed—a lower median income, with the same mean income as in state 1. The expected value of the policy in state 2, however, is considerably more right than the expected value of the policy in state 1. Thus increasing skewness of the income distribution is associated with policies which are *less* redistributive, which is exactly the opposite conclusion to what is argued in a prominent strand in the current literature (see, for example, Persson and Tabellini 1994). Of course, the political models of that literature are all Downsian, unidimensional models, and so we should not be surprised that their conclusions are not robust when more complex political mechanisms are introduced.[5] The phenomenon is easily understood by studying the table. In state 1, Left gets very few votes—only 8.8% of the polity—because the polity is relatively well-off, but in state 2, Left gets 26.9% of the votes. Therefore, Left is an attractive coalition partner for Center in state 1, since although it has a radical policy, there is only a small chance it will win the lottery in the coalition government, while in state 2, there is a significant chance that Left would win the policy lottery—so Center prefers to coalesce with Right.

We see from this example that these equilibria possess nonintuitive properties—whether they conform to empirical observation is another question. The main observations seem to be, first, that unlike Wittman equilibrium in the two-party case, here the extreme parties may propose policies more extreme than their ideal points in equilibrium, and second, that "politics make strange bedfellows" in the sense of the "pathology" just described with regard to Center's choice of coalition partner. Moreover, strategic behavior is complex, in the sense that a party must consider how its policy deviation will affect the relative strengths of the coalition partners in states where it is *not* in the coalition. Whether actual parties are *this* strategic is an open question.

---

5. In fact, we showed that the Persson-Tabellini result was not robust when two-party Wittman politics were introduced, in section 5.2, as well.

We proceed to study a second case, in which we generate equilibria where, in state 1, Center is the majority winner, and in state 2, Center is the formateur who chooses to coalesce with Right. For this case, the payoff functions become:

$$\Pi^i(t) = \tfrac{1}{2}v^i(t^2) + \tfrac{1}{2}((1 - W_2(t))v^i(t^2) + W_2(t)v^i(t^3)).$$

(In state 1, the lottery is degenerate: the policy is t^2 for sure.) We solve the three first-order conditions, and in addition, we check that Center receives a majority in state 1, that it receives a plurality in state 2, and that in the second state, $G^2 < 0$.

Here I searched for solutions where $h^1 = 20$ and $h^2 = 30$—thus parties 1 and 2 each represent the median voter in one state of the world. Table 14.2 reports results for $\epsilon = 1$, and Table 14.3 for $\epsilon = .7$.

When all voters are sincere (Table 14.2), the asserted kinds of government form for h^3 in the range 52 to 59. We note that Left always proposes a policy much more extreme than its ideal, Center policy is less than its ideal, and Right's is just slightly less than its ideal. Again a first glance at a typical row of Table 14.2 suggests that Left could profitably deviate to somewhere near its ideal point—but that turns out not to be the case. As in the last example, a deviation by Left to 20, say, so lowers the vote Center receives that it renders Right the formateur

Table 14.2 Three-party equilibria, coalition and majority governments
$\{\epsilon = 1.0, (h^1, h^2) = (20, 30)\}$

h^3	t^1	t^2	t^3	p_{11}	p_{21}	p_{31}	p_{12}	p_{22}	p_{32}	Exp[1]	Exp[2]
52	0	24.718	51.632	.121	.503	.375	.341	.367	.291	24.718	36.629
53	0	24.729	52.33	.121	.508	.371	.341	.37	.289	24.729	36.834
54	0	24.739	53.018	.121	.512	.366	.342	.372	.286	24.739	37.031
55	0	24.747	53.695	.121	.517	.362	.342	.375	.284	24.747	37.22
56	0	24.753	54.363	.122	.521	.358	.342	.377	.281	24.753	37.403
57	0	24.758	55.021	.122	.525	.354	.342	.379	.279	24.758	37.579
58	0	24.762	55.669	.122	.529	.35	.342	.382	.276	24.762	37.748
59	0	24.765	56.309	.122	.533	.346	.342	.384	.274	24.765	37.91

Table 14.3 Three-party equilibria, coalition and majority governments
$\{\epsilon = 0.7, (h^1, h^2) = (20, 30)\}$

h^3	t^1	t^2	t^3	p_{11}	p_{21}	p_{31}	p_{12}	p_{22}	p_{32}	Exp[1]	Exp[2]
52	0	25.842	50.465	.133	.604	.263	.249	.46	.292	25.842	35.401
53	0	25.868	51.195	.134	.607	.26	.249	.462	.289	25.868	35.606
54	0	25.893	51.916	.134	.61	.256	.249	.465	.286	25.893	35.805
55	0	25.916	52.627	.134	.613	.253	.249	.467	.283	25.916	35.997
56	0	25.939	53.328	.134	.616	.25	.25	.47	.281	25.939	36.182
57	0	25.961	54.02	.135	.619	.247	.25	.472	.278	25.961	36.361
58	0	25.982	54.704	.135	.621	.244	.25	.474	.276	25.982	36.535
59	0	26.001	55.378	.135	.624	.241	.25	.477	.273	26.001	36.703

in state 1. Although Left becomes the majority winner in state 2, the trade-off turns out to be deleterious to Left.

By examining Table 14.3, which has the same environment as Table 14.2 except that now $\epsilon = .7$, we see the effect that introducing strategic voters has. Strategic voters appear to cause the policies to converge to some extent.

14.4 Multidimensional Three-Party Politics

As in the two-party game, we cannot depend upon the existence of Wittman equilibria when the policy space is multidimensional. We can, however, define equilibrium with party factions in the three-party problem, just as we did in the two-party problem. As we will indicate, these equilibria will typically exist, although computing them is generally difficult because of the difficulty in computing the Wittman payoff functions, which now become the payoff functions of the reformists.

The stochastic environment is as in section 14.2. There is a set of voter types H, a set of states s, distributed according to $\mathbf{G}$, where the distribution of voter types in state s is $\mathbf{F}_s$.

We assume a multidimensional policy space, T, three parties, where the militants of party i have a (von Neumann–Morgenstern) utility function v^i on T, and the reformists of party i have utility function Π^i on T^3, given by (14.3). We face a decision on how to conceptualize opportunists. Do opportunists wish to maximize the probability of being in the government (meaning being either a majority winner or a coalition member) or the probability of being a majority or plurality winner—that is, of being a formateur? Presumably, opportunists in "large" parties wish to maximize the probability of being in the majority or plurality, while opportunists in small parties wish to maximize the probability of being in the coalition government. Let us simply define $\pi^i : T^3 \to [0, 1]$ as the particular probability that the opportunists in party i are maximizing. (We could, of course, complexify further, by postulating that there are two kinds of opportunist in each party.)

For any policy triple $t = (t^1, t^2, t^3)$ we can compute (modulo the problems of nonexistence and multiplicity of consistent votes already discussed) the set of states $S^i(t)$ in which party i is the majority winner and the set of states $S^{ij}(t)$ in which party i is the formateur of the coalition government $\{i, j\}$. It is now clear how to define the functions π^i. For instance, suppose that the opportunists in party i wish to maximize the probability that their party is either a majority or a plurality winner. Then we define

(14.5) $\pi^i(t) = \mathbf{G}(S^i(t) \cup S^{ij}(t) \cup S^{ik}(t)).$

We have now defined the utility functions of all the factions in a party. We define a party-unanimity Nash equilibrium (PUNE) as a triple of policies such that, given the policies of any two parties, the factions of the third party cannot all agree to deviate to an alternative policy for their party.

If the set of states is a continuum and $\mathbf{G}$ possesses a density, then the opportunists' utility functions will be almost everywhere differentiable, and we can then write the analytical conditions for a local PUNE using Farkas' lemma. If there are no binding constraints on policies at equilibrium then those conditions may be written

$$-\nabla v^1(t^1) = x_1 \nabla_1 \Pi^1(t) + y_1 \nabla_1 \pi^1(t),$$

(14.6) $$-\nabla v^2(t^2) = x_2 \nabla_2 \Pi^2(t) + y_2 \nabla_2 \pi^2(t),$$

$$-\nabla v^3(t^3) = x_3 \nabla_3 \Pi^3(t) + y_3 \nabla_3 \pi^3(t).$$

Any solution of these equations where the x_i and y_i are non-negative is (at least locally) a PUNE. If the dimension of the policy space is n, then (14.6) constitutes $3n$ equations in $3n + 6$ unknowns, so that there will generically exist either no solution or a 6-manifold of solutions. The smallest value for n

is two, in which case the set of PUNEs will be a set of full measure in the cross-product T^3; for any larger value of n, the set of PUNEs will be a set of measure zero in T^3. If there are binding constraints on policies, these comments do not change: each binding constraint adds one more Lagrangian multiplier and one more equation, thus not changing the dimensionality of the equilibrium manifold.

Actually solving for equilibria, from equations (14.6), is harder than solving for PUNEs in the two-party case, where typically the equilibrium manifold is of dimension two. Consider, for example, a problem where dim $T = 3$. One can solve six of the nine equations making up (14.6) for the Lagrange multipliers—this is easy, as the equations are linear in the multipliers. We are left with three equations and the nine policy variables. One must specify six variables at random, solve the three equations in three unknowns that remain, and then check that the multipliers are all non-negative at the solution. It will in general be much harder to locate (by random choice) a 6-vector that will lead to a solution than it is, to locate by random choice, a 2-vector (in the two-party case) that leads to a solution.

The reader can deduce, at this point, that if c is the number of coalitions in each party and if p is the number of parties, then the dimension of the equilibrium manifold will generally be $(c - 1)p$. In the two-party case we were lucky in being able to eliminate the reformists, and so, from the mathematical viewpoint, c was equal only to two, and hence $(c - 1)p = 2$. In proceeding with applications in the three-party case, I would probably eliminate one of the factions—say the reformists—which would reduce the dimension of the equilibrium manifold to three.

The remarks of the last several paragraphs apply to *solving* equations (14.6). But that must be preceded by *writing down* equations (14.6), which is to say, calculating the derivatives of the various utility functions. These functions are difficult to write down, even for "simple" examples. Thus, although our experience with the two-party case can lead us confidently to predict that the concept of PUNE with three parties is not vacuous, it would be wise to introduce further simplifications in the model in order to render the concept tractable.

The formulation of Baron and Diermeier (forthcoming) may be one to incorporate here. They propose that the vote proportions the parties receive in the election determine the probabilities that the respective parties are chosen to form a government: but the policy of a coalition government is always determined by *an equal-probability lottery* of the policies of its members. With this rule, the payoff functions of both the reformists and the opportunists become much simpler than in our formulation.

14.5 Coalition Government with a Multidimensional Issue Space: An Example

For the example that we shall construct, we indeed shall adopt the Baron-Diermeier (forthcoming) formulation. To be specific, we shall assume that if a party wins a majority, then it implements its platform; if no party wins a majority, then there is a lottery that determines which party shall be the formateur, where party i is chosen with probability equal to the vote share that party i received in the election. If party i chooses party j as its partner, then the policy of the government is determined by a lottery in which t^i and t^j each receive probability one-half.

Given these rules, the coalition formation process follows the same logic as in section 14.3. The formateur chooses that partner that maximizes its expected utility.

A further simplification is possible once we have adopted the Baron-Diermeier coalition formation process. Because a stochastic element has already been introduced in that process, we do not need to introduce one elsewhere in our model. Therefore, we will assume that there is a fixed probability distribution of types, **F**. That is, we can dispense with our set of states.

We shall now compute PUNEs for a modified version of the three-class model studied in Chapter 12. To wit, we now assume that there are two *basic* types in the polity, capitalists and worker-shopkeepers. Capitalists own equal shares in a firm which produces a single output from two inputs, labor (L) and infrastructure (G), according to the production function

$$g(G, L) = \beta G^\gamma L^\delta.$$

The fraction of capitalists in the polity is denoted c. Among worker-shopkeepers, there is a continuum of subtypes. A typical subtype, called λ, is capable of producing the good in her shop at a rate of α units per year, but she can only do this for fraction λ of the year; for the fraction of time $1 - \lambda$, she must sell her labor to the capitalist firm. We may interpret this by supposing that there is some capital stock necessary to run the shop, and these individuals possess different amounts of it. Let **F** be a probability distribution on the interval $[0, 1]$; we suppose that the fraction of worker-shopkeepers whose trait

λ lies in a (measurable) subset D of $[0, 1]$ is $\mathbf{F}(D)$. The mean of $\mathbf{F}$ is denoted θ, and we define

$$\rho = \theta(1 - c) \quad \text{and} \quad \omega = (1 - \theta)(1 - c).$$

Assuming that each member of the population works full time for the work year, then ρ is the fraction of labor-days expended in small shops and ω is the fraction of labor days expended by workers in factories, while c is the fraction of labor-days expended by capitalists (counting their profits and monitoring workers). Note, by definition, we have $c + \omega + \rho = 1$. It follows that the mass of worker-shopkeepers is $\omega + \rho$.

As in Chapter 12, labor is inelastically supplied. If it turns out to be the case that α is larger than the yearly wage income from factory work, then all worker-shopkeepers will work as much time as they can in their shops (that is, λ) and will work in the factory the remaining portion of the year. Thus the labor supply, per capita, to the factory will be exactly ω, and the total output of shops will be $\rho\alpha$. The reader will now recognize that we have set up the environment so that the economy, from a macro viewpoint, looks exactly like the one in Chapter 12.

We now assume that there are three parties: one representing capitalists (C), one representing the proletarianized worker (W)—that is, the worker-shopkeeper whose λ equals zero—and the third representing the pure petit bourgeois (PB)—the worker-shopkeeper whose λ is one. The policy vector is (a, G, T), as in Chapter 12, the budget constraint continues to be given by equation (12.1), and the utility functions of the three parties continue to be given by (12.2). Because we eliminate T via (12.1), we denote the policy of party J by (a^J, G^J).

We now suppose that there are two factions in each party, militants and opportunists. The militants' utility functions are given by (12.2). We suppose that the opportunists in the PB and W parties each wish to maximize the probability of being either in the majority or the formateur, while the opportunists in C wish to maximize the probability of being in the coalition government. Recall, from the discussion of the last section, that this is a substantive modeling decision, since in the three-party context, ignoring the reformists will alter the set of equilibria. We nevertheless do so in the interests of simplicity.

We proceed to calculate PUNEs with the following property: if either W or PB is chosen to be formateur, it chooses C as partner; if C is chosen to be formateur it chooses W as partner. If this is indeed the case at a PUNE, then party C will be in the coalition with probability one. Hence the opportunists in C are at their ideal point. If each of W and PB would indeed choose C as its coalition partner if C varied its policy in a small neighborhood, then (a^C, G^C) must be the ideal point of C's militants—for otherwise C's militants could increase their utility by moving toward the ideal point, while leaving C's opportunists completely satisfied (with a unit probability of being in the coalition). *Thus we shall search for PUNEs where (a^C, G^C) is the ideal point of C's militants.* Denote this policy by (a^*, G^*).

The after-tax income of a worker-shopkeeper of type λ, at the policy (a, G), which is just her utility at that policy, is

$$(14.7) \quad v(a, G; \lambda) = \lambda v^{PB}(a, G) + (1 - \lambda)v^W(a, G).$$

We therefore compute that the set of worker-shopkeepers who prefer a policy (a, G) to a policy (a', G') is the set of λ such that:

$$(14.8) \quad \begin{aligned} \lambda\{(1 - a)(\delta\beta G^\gamma\omega^{\delta-1} - \alpha) - (1 - a')(\delta\beta G'^\gamma\omega^{\delta-1} - \alpha)\} \\ < (1 - a)\delta\beta G^\gamma\omega^{\delta-1} - (1 - a')\delta\beta G'^\gamma\omega^{\delta-1} + \Delta T, \end{aligned}$$

where $\Delta a = a - a'$ and $\Delta T = T - T'$.

If we denote by (a, G) the policy of the W party and by (a', G') the policy of the PB party, and we conjecture that the term in curly brackets on the l.h.s. of (14.8) is positive at equilibrium, then we may write (14.8) as

$$(14.9) \quad \lambda < \frac{\phi^1(a, G, a', G')}{\phi^2(a, G, a', G')},$$

where $\phi^2(a, G, a', G')$ is the expression in curly brackets on the l.h.s. of (14.8), and $\phi^1(a, G, a', G')$ is the r.h.s. of (14.8). Thus the set of worker-shopkeepers who prefer W's policy (a, G) to PB's policy (a', G') has mass

$$\mathbf{F}\left[\frac{\phi^1(a, G, a', G')}{\phi^2(a, G, a', G')}\right](\omega + \rho).$$

We now discuss strategic voting. If indeed we are at an equilibrium of the type described—that formateur W chooses to coalesce with C and formateur PB chooses to coalesce with C—then C is guaranteed to be in the coalition. Hence, a strategic voter who prefers C's policy to the other two policies should vote for either W or PB, depending on whether he prefers the $\{W, C\}$ lottery or the $\{PB, C\}$ lottery. (Recall that, in any case, C's policy wins the lottery in the coalition government with probability one-half, so there is no point voting for C.) However, a strategic voter who prefers W's policy should vote for W, as that increases the probability that W is formateur, and a strategic voter who prefers PB's policy should likewise vote for PB. Hence the only strategic voters who do not vote sincerely at this kind of equilibrium are those whose favorite policy is C's. Let ϵ be the fraction of capitalists who are sincere voters.

Now suppose it is the case (as it will be!) that every capitalist prefers W's policy to PB's policy. If every worker-shopkeeper of type λ satisfying (14.9) prefers W's policy to (a^*, G^*), then these constitute exactly the fraction of the noncapitalist vote that party W receives. Since $(1 - \epsilon)$ is the fraction of capitalists that vote for W, the fraction of the vote that W receives, and hence the probability that W will be the formateur is:

$$(14.10) \quad \pi^W(a, G, a', G', a^*, G^*) = \mathbf{F}\left[\frac{\phi^1(a, G, a', G')}{\phi^2(a, G, a', G')}\right](\omega + \rho) + (1 - \epsilon)c,$$

as long as the r.h.s. of (14.10) is less than one-half. Equation (14.10) embodies the Baron-Diermeier assumption, that a party is chosen as formateur with probability equal to its fraction of the vote. It follows that

$$(14.11) \quad \pi^{PB} = 1 - \epsilon c - \pi^W,$$

as long as the r.h.s. of (14.11) is less than one-half, for according to our assumptions, the only agents who will be voting for party C are the capitalists.

Recall the constraints given by the functions h^1, h^2, and h^3 of section 12.3 (equation (12.3) and following). If we recognize only militants and the opportunists in the three parties, then a PUNE must satisfy the equations:

$$
\begin{aligned}
-\nabla_W \pi^W &= x^0 \nabla v^W + x^1 \nabla h^1 + x^2 \nabla h^2 + x^3 \nabla h^3, \\
(14.12) & \\
\nabla_{PB} \pi^W &= y^0 \nabla v^{PB} + y^1 \nabla h^1 + y^2 \nabla h^2 + y^3 \nabla h^3,
\end{aligned}
$$

where the x's and y's are non-negative, and complementary slackness holds (that is, a Lagrangian multiplier is zero if its corresponding constraint is slack at the policy). The reader is by now familiar with the reasoning that generates equations (14.12).

Let the density of **F** be denoted f. Defining $\zeta(a, G, a', G') = \frac{\phi^1(a,G,a',G')}{\phi^2(a,G,a',G')}$, we can write (examine (14.10)):

$$(14.13) \quad \nabla\pi^W(a, G, a', G') = (\omega + \rho)f(\zeta(a, G, a', G'))\nabla\zeta,$$

where the gradient in (14.13) is the vector of derivatives with respect to either (a, G) or (a', G'). Now the term $(\omega + \rho)f(\zeta(a, G, a', G'))$ is a positive number, so, in equations (14.12), we may simply absorb it into the non-negative x and y coefficients, and we may consequently rewrite (14.12) as:

$$(14.14) \quad \begin{aligned} -\nabla_W\zeta &= x^0\nabla v^W + x^1\nabla h^1 + x^2\nabla h^2 + x^3\nabla h^3, \\ \nabla_{PB}\zeta &= y^0\nabla v^{PB} + y^1\nabla h^1 + y^2\nabla h^2 + y^3\nabla h^3. \end{aligned}$$

Thus the solutions of (14.14) are independent of the distribution of λ's. It is not the case, however, that the set of PUNEs is independent of **F**, because a solution of (14.14) is only a PUNE if no party wins a majority at that policy platform, and to determine that, we need to know the distribution **F**.

Recall that in the PUNEs we are searching for, $(a^C, G^C) = (a^*, G^*)$. The equations (14.14) plus the binding constraints will always constitute a system with two more unknowns than equations, so we are searching for a 2-manifold of solutions. When we find a solution of (14.14), we must check the ancillary condition that the W party prefers an equal-probability lottery between (a^W, G^W) and (a^*, G^*) to the one between (a^W, G^W) and (a^{PB}, G^{PB}) and, similarly, that the PB party prefers to coalesce with the C party rather than with the W party. Finally, we must check that, for every λ, the worker-shopkeeper of type λ prefers either the W party or the PB party to (a^*, G^*), for we made this assumption above in calculating the fraction of the vote received by the three parties—the vote fraction received by the C party should be precisely $(1 - \epsilon)c$. We must, finally, verify that $\phi^2(a^W, G^W, a^{PB}, G^{PB}) > 0$, for we assumed this in deriving (14.9).

We proceed to the details of solving equations (14.14). Unfortunately, we did not succeed in finding solutions of the postulated type for the parameter values of the model used in Chapter 12. We finally worked with the following parameterization:

$$\{\omega, \rho, c, \delta, \gamma, \beta, \alpha, \epsilon\} = \{.43, .43, .14, .66, .15625, 8940.72, 50000, .9\}.$$

Table 14.4 PUNEs in the three-party model

Party	a	G	Vote share	Expected utility
W	.672	2477	.495	$27,585
PB	.037	1385	.379	$42,946
C	.145	5989	.126	$39,364

We chose **F** to be the normal distribution with mean 0.5 and standard deviation 0.5/3; this distribution has 99.9% of its mass on the interval [0, 1].[6]

We indeed found PUNEs (that is, solutions of (14.14) with non-negative Lagrangian multipliers, and for which the ancillary conditions assuring that coalitions of the postulated type form) where all three parties propose a positive rate of income taxation, the *PB* party proposes that all taxes be spent on infrastructure (none on transfers), and the *C* party proposes its ideal point, which also involves spending all taxes on infrastructure. The only party that proposes transfer payments is *W*. In a run with 2000 iterations, we found 16 PUNEs satisfying the conditions stipulated above. Table 14.4 presents the average values of the policies and the vote shares.

Although the transfers proposed in the *W* policy are not listed in the table, we can compute that they are on average about $25,300. There is thus a sharp contrast in the policies of the three parties (no convergence here!). It is note-worthy that in all the PUNEs we found, the vote share of the *W* party is between .492 and .499. The one disappointing characteristic of these equilibria is that the utility (that is, expected post-tax income) of the capitalists and their agents is less than that of the wealthiest members of the petite bourgeoisie. This is because we had to increase the number of capitalists (and hence decrease their average income) from their number in Chapter 12 in order to find PUNEs of the stipulated kind.

14.6 Conclusion

We have studied several models of three-party competition in both the unidimensional and the multidimensional case. Our main aim has been to show

---

6. It is convenient to use a distribution whose support is the whole real line, because then π^W is a smooth function (see (14.10)). If we use a distribution with support [0, 1], then π^W will have kinks when ζ is 0 or 1.

that Wittman equilibrium generalizes to produce political equilibria in the three-party model when the policy space is unidimensional, and that PUNE generalizes to produce equilibria when the policy space is multidimensional. The main complexity in moving from the two- to the three-party model is that a process of coalition formation occurs after the election and before the policy is implemented. We have truncated that process here, by giving all power to the plural party, in the sense that that party can name its coalition partner. (In real coalition formation, the formateur's preferred partner may reject the offer.) This was a modeling choice, made because we wanted to concentrate analysis on the process of voting. We proposed that two kinds of voter exist, sincere and strategic, and we proposed a specific psychology for the strategic voter.

We have spent some time in calculating equilibria for specific examples, because this illustrates that these equilibria do, in general, exist. Furthermore, in the model of section 14.3, there is interesting complexity in party strategy, on account of the nature of the coalition formation and policy choice process. There is less complexity in party strategy in the example of section 14.5, because the Baron-Diermeier coalition formation process is simpler than the one put forth early in the chapter.

Mathematical Appendix

References

Index

※

Mathematical Appendix

A.1 Basics of Probability Theory

A.1.1 MEASURABLE SPACES

A *measurable space* is a pair $(\Omega, \mathcal{F})$, where Ω is an abstract set, called the *sample space*, and $\mathcal{F}$ is called a σ-field, which is a set of subsets of Ω, with the following properties:

(i) $\Omega \in \mathcal{F}$;

(ii) if $A \in \mathcal{F}$ then $A^c \in \mathcal{F}$, where A^c is the complement of A in Ω;

(iii) if $\{A_1, A_2, \ldots\}$ is a countable set of subsets of Ω, each in $\mathcal{F}$, then their union is in $\mathcal{F}$.

A *measure space* is a measurable space equipped with a measure, $(\Omega, \mathcal{F}, \mu)$, where $\mu : \mathcal{F} \to \mathbf{R}_+$, the positive real numbers. The measure μ must satisfy:

(1) $\mu(\oslash) = 0$, where $\oslash$ is the empty set;

(2) if $A_1, A_2, \ldots$ is a countable sequence of pairwise disjoint sets, which are members of $\mathcal{F}$, then $\mu(\cup_i A_i) = \sum_i \mu(A_i)$. The second property is called *countable additivity.*

A *probability space* is a measure space where, in addition:

(3) $\mu(\Omega) = 1$.

In this case, we call μ a *probability measure,* and the members of $\mathcal{F}$ are called *events.*

Examples

1. Let $\Omega = \mathbf{R}$, let $\mathcal{F}$ be the Borel field on $\mathbf{R}$, defined as follows. Begin by putting all the intervals of the form (a, b), $(a, b]$, and so on in $\mathcal{F}$, where $b \geq a$. Then "close" $\mathcal{F}$ w.r.t. the operations (i), (ii), and (iii) above (that is, include in $\mathcal{F}$ all complements of these intervals, countable unions of these sets, complements

of these sets, and so on). This very large set $\mathcal{F}$ is by definition a σ-field and is called the Borel field.

For an interval (a, b), define the function λ^* as follows: let $\lambda^*((a, b)) = b - a$.

Theorem A.1   *There is a unique way of extending λ^* to a measure, λ, on $\mathcal{F}$.*

λ is called *Lebesgue measure.*

Note that λ is not a probability measure, since $\lambda(\Omega)$ is infinity.

2. Let $\Omega = [0, 100]$, and let $\mathcal{F}$ be the Borel field on Ω. Define, for an interval (a, b), $\mu((a, b)) = (b - a)/100$. As in theorem A.1, there is a unique way of extending this function to a measure, μ , on $\mathcal{F}$. Note now that $\mu(\Omega) = 1$, so $(\Omega, \mathcal{F}, \mu)$ is a probability space and μ is a probability measure. μ is called the *uniform measure* on $(\Omega, \mathcal{F})$.

The singleton sets consisting of just one point are all in the Borel field. Their measure under μ is zero. Indeed, any countable union of points is a set of μ-measure zero. There are even sets with an uncountable number of points of measure zero. So a set can be very large in cardinality, and yet have measure zero.

3. Let Ω be the set of real numbers describing the incomes of every household in the United States, a finite set. Let $\mathcal{F}$ be the set of all subsets of Ω (a finite set). For any subset A of Ω, define

$\mu(A) = $ the fraction of households in the United States whose income is a number in the set A.

Note that μ is a probability measure on $(\Omega, \mathcal{F})$: it satisfies criteria (1), (2), and (3) of the definition. (Think about countable additivity, which in this case reduces to finite additivity.)

μ is called a discrete measure, because it takes on only a finite number of values. In this application, μ is called the *income distribution* of U.S. households.

4. In social science, it is often useful to approximate large, finite sets (like the 150,000,000 or so incomes of households in the United States) by a continuum.

In fact, actual income distributions are often well approximated by a "continuous" distribution called the lognormal distribution, defined as follows. Let

$\Omega = \mathbf{R}_+$, let $\mathcal{F}$ be the Borel field on the Ω, and define the measure μ on a set $S \in \mathcal{F}$ as follows:

$$(\text{A.1}) \qquad \mu(S) = \int\limits_S \frac{1}{s\sigma(2\pi)^{1/2}} \exp \frac{-[\text{Log}(s/m)]^2}{2\sigma^2} ds,$$

where m and σ are parameters (positive numbers). It is certainly not obvious that μ is, indeed, a probability measure. Additivity is obvious, since the integral is an additive function, but the fact that $\mu(\Omega) = 1$ must be shown.

Many national income distributions in the world can be well approximated by suitable choice of the parameters m and σ.

The actual income distribution in the United States (of Example 3) has about 150,000,000 parameters—that is, one cannot specify the exact distribution without specifying the income of every household. The lognormal distribution has only two parameters! Thus if we can find a lognormal distribution that approximates the actual distribution, we have achieved a tremendously simplified description of the real world.

In particular, we can operate with the lognormal distribution analytically, whereas the exact income distribution of Example 3 is an extremely complicated function, which can only be studied by making arduous computations on a large-memory computer.

5. Suppose we have a population of agents who all have utility functions of the form $u(x, G) = x + \alpha \log(\beta G)$, where (x, G) are two goods, and α, β are positive parameters. An individual's type, then, is (α, β). There is a distribution of the parameters (α, β) in the population. How would this be stated formally?

Let $\Omega = \mathbf{R}_+ \times \mathbf{R}_+$, let $\mathcal{F}$ be the Borel field on Ω, and for any set $S \in \mathcal{F}$, define $\mu(S)$ as the fraction of society for whom $(\alpha, \beta) \in S$. Then μ is a probability measure: we say the traits (α, β) are distributed according to the probability distribution μ on Ω.

Definition Given a probability space $(\Omega, \mathcal{F}, \mu)$. We say *Statement $X(\omega)$ is almost surely true* if there is a set $S \in \mathcal{F}$, such that $\mu(S) = 1$, and $X(\omega)$ is true for all $\omega \in S$. We also say "$X(\omega)$ is true with probability one."

A.1.2 THE LEBESGUE INTEGRAL

We are given a measure space $(\Omega, \mathcal{F}, \mu)$. A function $\phi : \Omega \to \mathbf{R}$ is said to be an $\mathcal{F}$-*measurable function* iff, for any Borel set B of $\mathbf{R}$, the set $\phi^{-1}(B) \in \mathcal{F}$: the inverse images of Borel sets in **R** are measurable sets under μ. A real-valued function whose domain is a sample space is called a *random variable*.

We now define the integral

$$\int_\Omega \phi(s)d\mu,$$

which can be equivalently written as $\int_\Omega \phi(s)d\mu(s)$, or $\int_\Omega \phi(s)\mu(ds)$. The intuitive idea is that $\int_\Omega \phi(s)d\mu$ is the weighted sum of the function ϕ on the sample space Ω, where sets S in Ω are weighted by their "sizes," that is, their measures $\mu(S)$. If μ is a probability measure, then $\int_\Omega \phi(s)d\mu$ has the interpretation of the *average value* of ϕ on Ω, where events S in Ω are weighted by their probabilities $(\mu(S))$.

It is beyond the scope of these notes to give a precise definition of the Lebesgue integral, but you can, for practical purposes, think of it as follows. Partition the range of ϕ as illustrated in Figure A.1, and, for each element R_i in the partition, calculate its inverse image $\phi^{-1}(R_i)$, which is an element of $\mathcal{F}$, by hypothesis, and has measure $\mu(\phi^{-1}(R_i))$. Now take, for each i, an element $r_i \in R_i$ and add up:

$$\sum_i r_i \mu(\phi^{-1}(R_i)).$$

Now let the partition size go to infinity. This sum converges to the Lebesgue integral $\int_\Omega \phi(s)d\mu$.

The reader will recall that the Riemann integral has the interpretation of the area under the curve ϕ, while the Lebesgue integral has the interpretation of the average value of ϕ. If μ is *Lebesgue measure, then the Riemann integral and Lebesgue integral of a function are the same* (assuming both limits exist). So you may think of the Lebesgue integral as a generalization of the Riemann integral, where we may integrate with respect to measures other than the uniform (Lebesgue) measure.

Examples

1. Let μ be a probability measure. Consider the function $\phi(s) = s$. The Lebesgue integral $\int_\Omega \phi(s)d\mu = \int_\Omega sd\mu$ is called the *mean* of the measure μ. It is the average value of s w.r.t. the measure μ.

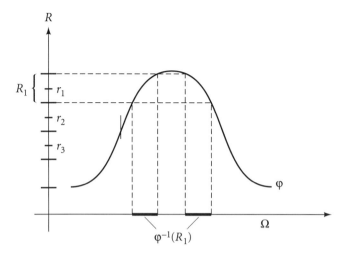

Figure A.1   The Lebesgue integral

Thus, for example, the *mean income,* if μ is an income distribution, is given by this formula.

2. Let m be the mean of a probability measure μ. We define the variance of μ by

$$\text{var}\,(\mu) = \int_\Omega (s - m)^2 d\mu.$$

This is a measure of the *average deviation from the mean* of elements in Ω.

3. Consider λ, Lebesgue measure. The integral $\int_\Omega \phi(s)d\lambda$, to repeat what was said earlier, is simply the familiar Riemann integral $\int_\Omega \phi(s)ds$ when the latter exists. Thus, like Molière's character Monsieur Jourdain,[1] you have been Lebesgue-integrating all your life, and didn't know it.

A.1.3 THE DENSITY FUNCTION

Let μ and ν be two measures on the measurable space $(\Omega, \mathcal{F})$. We say that μ is *absolutely continuous* w.r.t. ν iff whenever $\nu(S) = 0$, then $\mu(S) = 0$. If μ

---

1. Who was delighted to learn that he had been "speaking prose" his whole life.

and ν are each absolutely continuous w.r.t. the other, then they are said to be *equivalent* measures.

Examples

1. The lognormal probability measure is equivalent to Lebesgue measure on the positive reals.

2. Consider the discrete measure on $[0, 1]$ defined as:

$$\mu(S) = \begin{cases} \frac{1}{2} & \text{if } .25 \in S \text{ and } .75 \notin S \\[2mm] 0 & \text{if } .25 \notin S \text{ and } .75 \notin S \\[2mm] \frac{1}{2} & \text{if } .75 \in S \text{ and } .25 \notin S \\[2mm] 1 & \text{if } .25 \in S \text{ and } .75 \in S. \end{cases}$$

Check that this is a probability measure on $[0, 1]$.

The measure μ is not absolutely continuous w.r.t. Lebesgue measure on $[0, 1]$, since Lebesgue measure assigns a value of 0 to any point, while $\mu(\{.25\}) = 0.5$.

Theorem A.2 (Radon-Nikodym) Let μ be absolutely continuous w.r.t. ν on $(\Omega, \mathcal{F})$. Then there exists an $\mathcal{F}$-measurable function f such that, for any $S \in \mathcal{F}$,

(a) $$\mu(S) = \int_S f(s)d\nu$$

and, for any $\mathcal{F}$-measurable function ϕ,

(b) $$\int_\Omega \phi(s)d\mu = \int_\Omega \phi(s)f(s)d\nu.$$

This is an extremely useful theorem. Let the measure ν in the theorem be Lebesgue measure. Then the theorem says that if a measure μ is absolutely continuous w.r.t. Lebesgue measure, there exists a function f, such that for any function ϕ:

(A.2) $$\int_{\Omega} \phi(s)d\mu = \int_{\Omega} \phi(s)f(s)ds.$$

f is called the *Radon-Nikodym derivative* of μ, or the *density* of μ.

The formula (A.2) is in fact how we compute Lebesgue integrals—if their measures have densities. We convert them to standard integration problems via the formula (A.2).

Note   In fact, formula (a) of the Radon-Nikodym theorem can be derived from formula (b), as follows. For a given set $S \in \mathcal{F}$, define the random variable

$$\phi(s) = \begin{cases} 1 & \text{if} \quad s \in S \\ 0 & \text{if} \quad s \notin S. \end{cases}$$

ϕ is called the *indicator function* of S, and is usually denoted 1_S.

Now, from the definition of the integral, we have

$$\int_{\Omega} 1_S(s)d\mu = \mu(S) \quad \text{and} \quad \int_{\Omega} 1_S(s)f(s)dv = \int_S f(s)dv,$$

which together give us (a) from (b).

In fact, in many cases, the only way we have of defining a probability measure is by its density! For example, the normal distribution, which is a probability measure, is defined by its density. The lognormal distribution, described earlier, is defined by its density—the integrand in (A.1) above is in fact the density of the lognormal probability distribution.

Exercise   Consider Example 2, given just above the statement of the Radon-Nikodym theorem. Observe that μ does not possess a density; that is, there is no function f for which (A.2) is true.

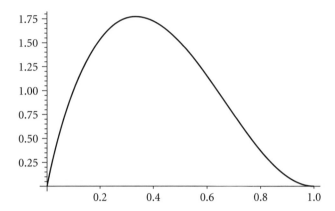

Figure A.2   The density of a beta measure

The density function is often graphed to illustrate the probability distribution. The "bell-shaped curve" is the density of the normal probability distribution on **R**.

In Figure A.2, I plot the density function of a useful probability distribution on the interval $\Omega = [0, 1]$, called the beta distribution. This is a two-parameter family of probability measures, whose density functions are given by

$$f(s; a, b) = s^{a-1}(1 - s)^{b-1}/\text{Beta}[a, b],$$

where a, b are real numbers, and $\text{Beta}[a, b]$ is the value of the "beta function." Note the role of $\text{Beta}[a, b]$ is just to normalize the density so that its integral over $[0, 1]$ is one. In Figure A.2, I have chosen $a = 2$, $b = 3$, and plotted the density f using Mathematica.

Example   Let f be the density of the probability measure μ. Then the mean, m, of μ is given by $m = \int_{\Omega} sf(s)ds$. (Follows immediately from above formulae.)

Remark   A common misinterpretation.
Consider the latest formula for the mean of μ, and f is its density. Suppose μ is an income distribution, and so s is a value of income. People often say that $f(s)$ is the "fraction of people with income s." This is wrong. The fraction of people with income s must be zero, since μ is absolutely continuous w.r.t. Lebesgue measure, which assigns measure 0 to any point. Indeed, you will note

that the value of density functions is often greater than 1, which makes this interpretation bizarre.

If μ is a continuous measure (that is, absolutely continuous w.r.t. Lebesgue measure), it is referring to a world with a continuum of people. The ratio $f(s)/f(t)$ has meaning: it is the ratio of the number of people with income s to the number with income t. This ratio can be finite, even if there are an infinite number of each type!

One convenient interpretation is to think of $f(s)$ as the *number* of people with income s, which is very large. Under this interpretation, $\int_\Omega sf(s)ds$ is the total income in the society. But we now divide by the total number of people, and that gives us average income in the society. Thus we effectively normalize the number of people in society to "one," letting that take the place of a very large number.

If you use this trick—thinking of $f(s)$ as the number of individuals with trait s—you will rarely go wrong in using density functions.

Referring to Figure A.2, suppose s is income, where the largest income in society is 1 (hundred thousand dollars). You might think of there being 175,000 people with incomes of .4 (that is, $40,000), and about 25,000 people with incomes of $80,000. It would not be correct, however, to say that "the fraction of people with income $40,000 is 1.75." To get the fraction of people with income in a certain interval we calculate the area of f under the curve on that interval, that is, the integral of the density over that interval.

A.1.4 THE (CUMULATIVE) DISTRIBUTION FUNCTION OF A MEASURE

Let $(\mathbf{R}_+, \mathcal{F}, \mu)$ be a probability space. Define the function $M : \mathbf{R}_+ \to [0, 1]$ by $M(x) = \mu([0, x])$. M is called the distribution function, or cumulative distribution function (CDF), of μ.

Note that M is just an abbreviated form of the measure—it tells us the measure of certain intervals. The function M is, of course, increasing.

Suppose that μ has a density f. Then, according to the Radon-Nikodym theorem, we can write

$$(A.3) \qquad \mu([0, x]) = M(x) = \int_0^x f(s)ds$$

Now, attack (A.3) with the fundamental theorem of calculus, and we have

$$M'(x) = f(x),$$

where ′ stands for derivative. Thus *the derivative of the distribution function is the density function.*

Formula (A.3) enables us to calculate the distribution function of various familiar measures (for example, the normal distribution).

Definition   Let $(\mathbf{R}_+, \mathcal{F}, \mu)$ be a probability space. The *median* of μ is that number q such that $\mu([0, q]) = 0.5$; or, if M is the CDF of μ, $M(q) = 0.5$.

For further elaboration of these concepts of probability theory, consult any advanced textbook on the subject, such as Durrett (1996).

A.2 Some Concepts from Analysis [2]

A.2.1 CONVEXITY

Let S be a set in $\mathbf{R}^n$. S is *convex* iff, for any pair of points $x, y \in S$, and any number $\lambda \in [0, 1]$ we have $\lambda x + (1 - \lambda)y \in S$.

Let $f : \mathbf{R}^n \to \mathbf{R}$. f is a *concave function* iff, for all $x, y \in \mathbf{R}^n$, and all $\lambda \in [0, 1]$, $f(\lambda x + (1 - \lambda)y) \geq \lambda f(x) + (1 - \lambda)f(y)$. f is a *convex function* iff for all x, $y \in \mathbf{R}^n$, and all $\lambda \in [0, 1]$, $f(\lambda x + (1 - \lambda)y) \leq \lambda f(x) + (1 - \lambda)f(y)$.

Thus linear functions are both convex and concave.

Let $f : \mathbf{R}^n \to \mathbf{R}$. f's *upper contour set at value* k is $\{x \mid f(x) \geq k\}$. f's lower contour sets are analogously defined.

It is easy to observe that the upper contour sets of a concave function are convex sets, and the lower contour sets of a convex function are convex sets.

Often, all we need to know about a function is that its upper contour sets are convex. This is a weaker property than concavity of f. We define:

A function $f : \mathbf{R}^n \to \mathbf{R}$ is *quasi-concave* iff all its upper contour sets are convex. A function $f : \mathbf{R}^n \to \mathbf{R}$ is *quasi-convex* iff all its lower contour sets are convex.

If $f : \mathbf{R} \to \mathbf{R}$, and f is monotone increasing or monotone decreasing, then it is easy to see that f is both quasi-concave and quasi-convex. Of course, such a function need not be concave or convex.

It is not difficult to show that:

Fact   A function $f : S \to R$ is quasi-concave on a convex set S iff for any pair $x, y \in S$, and any number $\lambda \in [0, 1]$, $f(\lambda x + (1 - \lambda)y) \geq \min[f(x), f(y)]$.

---

2. The concepts discussed here are all discussed in greater depth in the mathematical appendix of Mas-Colell, Winston, and Green (1995), to which the unsatiated reader is referred.

There is an analogous statement for quasi-convex functions, where the in-equality sign is reversed and the min operator is replaced by the max operator.

We have the following useful and easily proved

Fact   If $f : S \to T$ is a concave function and S is a convex set, and $x \in S$ is a local maximum of f, then x is a (global) maximum of f on S.

Let $a^1, a^2, \ldots, a^N$ be points (vectors) in $\mathbf{R}^n$. The *convex cone generated*, or *spanned, by this set of points* is $C = \{x \in \mathbf{R}^n \mid x = \sum \lambda^i a^i \text{ where } \lambda^i \geq 0 \text{ for all } i\}$.

Given the vector space $\mathbf{R}^n$, the *inner product* $\cdot$, or scalar product, is a function mapping $\mathbf{R}^n \times \mathbf{R}^n \to \mathbf{R}$, given by

$$x \cdot y = \sum_{i=1}^{n} x_i y_i.$$

Given a vector $v \in \mathbf{R}^n$, the set $\{x \in \mathbf{R}^n \mid v \cdot x = 0\}$ is a subspace of dimension $n - 1$. A subspace of dimension $n - 1$ is called a *hyperplane*. Conversely, given a hyperplane $S \subset \mathbf{R}^n$, there is a vector v such that $S = \{x \mid v \cdot x = 0\}$. v is called the *normal vector* to the hyperplane S. We also say that v is *orthogonal* to S. The normal vector is not unique, but it is unique up to scalar multiples. If $v \cdot x \geq 0$, we say that the vector x lies on the *same side* of the hyperplane (normal to v) as v; if $v \cdot x < 0$, we say that the hyperplane S *separates* v and x. More generally, given any two points x, y in $\mathbf{R}^n$, we say that the hyperplane orthogonal to v *separates* x and y if $v \cdot x > 0$ and $v \cdot y < 0$.

The next result is the basis of much of optimization theory. In particular, it is the key to our characterization of PUNE in Chapter 8.

Farkas' Lemma   *Let $a^1, a^2, \ldots, a^N, b$ be $N + 1$ vectors in $\mathbf{R}^m$. Then either*

(A) *there are non-negative numbers $\lambda^1, \lambda^2, \ldots, \lambda^N$ such that $b = \sum \lambda^i a^i$, or*
(B) *there is a vector $v \in \mathbf{R}^m$ such that $b \cdot v < 0$ and $a^i \cdot v \geq 0$ for all $i = 1, \ldots, N$,*

but never both A and B.

In words, Farkas' lemma says "either b is in the cone spanned by $\{a^1, a^2, \ldots, a^N\}$ or there is a hyperplane (orthogonal to the vector v) that separates b from all points in that cone—but never do both of these statements hold."

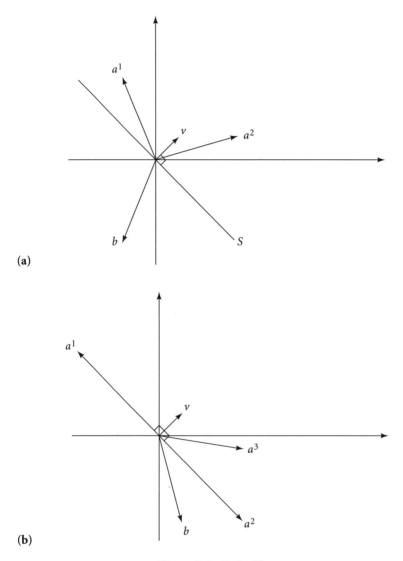

(a)

(b)

Figure A.3   Farkas' lemma

Figure A.3a illustrates Farkas' lemma. Here is a case where b is not in the cone spanned by a^1 and a^2, and the hyperplane S orthogonal to v separates b from the cone. Figure A.3b is another case covered by the lemma, although here the hyperplane does not "strictly separate" b from a^1 and a^2. (The hyperplane contains a^1 and a^2.)

Farkas' lemma is a special case of the more general *separating hyperplane theorem* (for which, see the mathematical appendix of Mas-Colell, Winston, and Green 1995).

Our application of Farkas' lemma requires an understanding of the directional derivative of a function. Let $f : \mathbf{R}^n \to \mathbf{R}$ be a differentiable function. The *directional derivative of f at x in the direction d is*

$$\lim_{\delta \to 0} \frac{f(x + \delta d) - f(x)}{\delta} \equiv D_d f(x).$$

Geometrically, this is the rate of change of f at x as we move toward x, in the domain of f, in the direction of d.

Fix x and d, and define the function $g(\delta) = f(x + \delta d)$. Observe that $g'(0) = D_d f(x)$. Now we can compute $g'(0)$ using the chain rule:

$$g'(0) = \sum f_i(x + 0d) d_i,$$

where f_i is the ith partial derivative of f. But this means that

$$D_d f(x) = g'(0) = \nabla f(x) \cdot d,$$

where $\nabla f(x)$ is the (row) vector of f's partial derivatives, evaluated at x. Thus we can say that f increases in value as we move away from the point x in the direction d if $\nabla f(x) \cdot d > 0$. (The statement is not "iff" because it could be that f increases in direction d at x but $\nabla f(x) \cdot d = 0$, which is the case if x is a local minimum of f.)

A.2.2 FIXED-POINT THEOREMS

While the mathematical foundation of optimization theory is the separating hyperplane theorem, the mathematical foundation of equilibrium theory is the fixed-point theorem. We employ two fixed-point theorems in the text.

Brouwer's Fixed-Point Theorem   *Let $A \subseteq \mathbf{R}^n$ be a compact, convex set, let $f : A \to A$ be a continuous function. Then f possesses a fixed point, a point $x \in A$ such that $f(x) = x$.*

We define a *correspondence* as a mapping $f : S \twoheadrightarrow T$, where the images of points in s under f are subsets of T. Thus we write $f(s) \subseteq T$.

A correspondence $f : S \twoheadrightarrow T$ is *upper hemicontinuous* iff, given any sequence of points $s^1, s^2, \ldots$ in S which converge to a point s^* in S, and points $t^i \in f(s^i)$, for all i, such that $\{t^i\}$ converges to a point t^* in T, then $t^* \in f(s^*)$.

A function is a single-valued correspondence.

Fact A single-valued correspondence is upper hemicontinuous iff, when viewed as a function, it is continuous.

Kakutani's Fixed-Point Theorem   *Let A be a nonempty convex, compact set in $\mathbf{R}^n$, and let $f : A \twoheadrightarrow A$ be an upper hemicontinuous correspondence of A into itself, whose images are nonempty convex sets. Then f possesses a fixed point, a point $a \in A$ such that $a \in f(a)$.*

The reader may consult Mas-Colell, Winston, and Green (1995, 953) for figures illustrating Kakutani's theorem.

Because of the *Fact* stated just above, Kakutani's theorem is a generalization of Brouwer's theorem. (A set consisting of one point is a convex set.)

Let $f : S \twoheadrightarrow T$ be a correspondence and let $g : S \twoheadrightarrow T$ be a correspondence such that, for all $s \in S$, $g(s) \subseteq f(s)$. Then g is said to be a *refinement* of f.

A.2.3 MISCELLANY

(1) The *implicit function theorem* is an important and standard result of advanced calculus. For a discussion, the reader may consult Mas-Colell, Winston, and Green (1995, 940–942) or any advanced calculus text.

(2) *The theorem of the maximum.* Consider the problem of maximizing a continuous function, f, on a compact feasible set, K, which lies in a larger set X. Suppose now that the set K changes with the value of a parameter vector, so we may more precisely denote it $K(q)$, where q is a parameter vector lying in some set Q. For each such parameter vector, there will be a nonempty set of *maximizers* of f, which we may denote $M(q)$; M is thus a correspondence mapping Q into X. We may also define the "value function," $v(q)$, which gives the value of f at its maximum on $K(q)$. The theorem in question asserts that if the mapping $q \twoheadrightarrow K(q)$ is continuous (as a correspondence), then the correspondence M is upper hemicontinuous, and the function v is continuous.

References

Abraham, David. 1981. *The collapse of the Weimar Republic.* Princeton: Princeton University Press.

Anderson, Dewey, and Percy Davidson. 1943. *Ballots and the democratic class struggle.* Stanford: Stanford University Press

Aumann, Robert. 1987. "Game theory." In *The new Palgrave,* edited by J. Eatwell, M. Milgate, and P. Newman. London: Macmillan.

Austen-Smith, David. 1996. "Electing legislatures." In *Collective decision-making: Social choice and political economy,* edited by Norman Schofield. Boston: Kluwer Academic Publishers.

——— 1997. "Interest groups: Money, information, and influence." In *Perspectives on public choices: A handbook,* edited by Dennis C. Mueller. New York: Cambridge University Press.

Austen-Smith, David, and Jeffrey Banks. 1988. "Elections, coalitions, and legislative outcomes." *American Political Science Review* 82, 405–22.

Baron, David. 1993. "Government formation and endogenous parties." *American Political Science Review* 87, 34–47.

Baron, David, and Daniel Diermeier. Forthcoming. "Elections, governments, and parliaments in proportional representation systems." *Quarterly Journal of Economics.*

Baron, David, and John Ferejohn. 1989. "Bargaining in legislatures." *American Political Science Review* 83, 1181–1206.

Berle, Adolf, and Gardiner Means. [1932] 1968. *The modern corporation and private property.* New York: Harcourt, Brace & World.

Besley, Timothy, and Stephen Coate. 1997. "An economic model of representative democracy." *Quarterly Journal of Economics,* February, 85–114.

Calvert, Randall. 1985. "Robustness of the multidimensional voting model: Candidate motivations, uncertainty, and convergence." *American Journal of Political Science* 29, 69–95.

Caplin, Andrew, and Barry Nalebuff. 1997. "Competition among institutions." *Journal of Economic Theory* 72, 306–342.

Claudin, Fernando. 1975. *The Communist movement from Cominform to Comintern,* pt. 1. New York: Monthly Review Press.

Coughlin, Peter J. 1992. *Probabilistic voting theory.* New York: Cambridge University Press.

Cukierman, Alex, and Allan Meltzer. 1991. "A political theory of progressive income taxation." In *Political Economy,* edited by A. Meltzer, A. Cukierman, and S. F. Richard. New York: Oxford University Press.

Davis, O. A. , M. H. De Groot, and M. J. Hinich. 1972. "Social preference ordering and majority rule." *Econometrica* 40, 147–157.

Downs, Anthony. 1957. *An economic theory of democracy.* New York: HarperCollins.

Durrett, Richard. 1996. *Probability: Theory and examples.* Belmont, Calif.: Duxbury Press.

Enelow, James, and Melvin Hinich. 1983. "On Plott's pairwise symmetry condition for majority rule equilibrium." *Public Choice* 40, 317–321.

———— 1989. "A general probabilistic spatial theory of elections." *Public Choice* 61, 101–113.

Evans, Merran, Nicholas Hastings, and Brian Peacock. 1993. *Statistical distributions.* New York: John Wiley & Sons.

Hamilton, Richard F. 1982. *Who voted for Hitler?* Princeton: Princeton University Press.

Hinich, Melvin J., and Michael C. Munger. 1997. *Analytical politics.* New York: Cambridge University Press.

Hirshman, Albert C. 1982. *Shifting involvements: Private interest and public action.* Princeton: Princeton University Press.

Hotelling, Harold. 1929. "Stability in competition." *Economic Journal* 39, 41–57.

Iversen, Torben. 1994. "Political leadership and representation in West European democracies: A test of three models of voting." *American Journal of Political Science* 38, 45–74.

Kalyvas, S. N. 1996. *The rise of Christian Democracy in Europe.* Ithaca, N.Y.: Cornell University Press.

Kitschelt, H. 1994. *The transformation of European social democracy.* New York: Cambridge University Press.

Klingermann, Hans-Dieter, Richard Hofferbert, and Ian Budge. 1994. *Parties, policies, and democracy.* Boulder, Colo.: Westview Press.

Korpi, Walter. 1983. *The democratic class struggle.* London: Routledge & Kegan Paul.

Laver, Michael, and W. B. Hunt. 1992. *Policy and party competition.* New York: Routledge.

Laver, Michael, and Kenneth A. Shepsle. 1996. *Making and breaking governments: Cabinets and legislatures in parliamentary democracies.* New York: Cambridge University Press.

Lindbeck, Assar, and Jorgen Weibull. 1987. "Balanced budget redistribution as the outcome of political competition." *Public Choice* 52, 273–297.

Lipset, Seymour Martin. [1960] 1994. *Political man.* Baltimore: Johns Hopkins University Press.

Llavador, Humberto. 2000. "Abstention and political competition." *Review of Economic Design* 5.

Luebbert, Gregory. 1991. *Liberalism, fascism, or social democracy.* New York: Oxford University Press.

Marhuenda, F., and Ignacio Ortuño-Ortín. 1995. "Majority voting and progressivity." *Investigaciones Económicas* 19, 469–473.

Mas-Colell, Andreu, Michael Winston, and Jerry Green. 1995. *Microeconomic theory.* New York: Oxford University Press.

Meltzer, Allan, and S. Richard. 1983. "A rational theory of the size of government." *Journal of Political Economy* 89, 914–927.

Nieuwbeerta, Paul. 1995. *The democratic class struggle in twenty countries, 1945–1990.* Amsterdam: Thesis Publishers.

Ortuño-Ortín, Ignacio. 1997. "A spatial model of political competition and proportional representation." *Social Choice and Welfare* 14, 427–438.

Ortuño-Ortín, Ignacio, and J. E. Roemer. 1998. "Endogenous party formation and the effect of income distribution on policy." Working paper.

Osborne, Martin. 1995. "Spatial models of political competition under plurality rule: A survey of some explanations of the number of candidates and the positions they take." *Canadian Journal of Economics* 28, 261–301.

Osborne, Martin, and Al Slivinski. 1996. "A model of political competition with citizen-candidates." *Quarterly Journal of Economics,* February, 65–96.

Palfrey, Thomas R. 1984. "Spatial equilibrium with entry." *Review of Economic Studies* 51, 139–156.

Persson, Torsten, and Guido Tabellini. 1994. "Is inequality harmful for growth?" *American Economic Review* 84, 600–621.

Plott, Charles. 1967. "A notion of equilibrium and its possibility under majority rule." *American Economic Review* 57, 787–806.

Poole, K. T., and H. Rosenthal. 1991. "Patterns of congressional voting." *American Journal of Political Science* 35, 228–278.

Przeworski, Adam, and John Sprague. 1986. *Paper Stones.* Chicago: University of Chicago Press.

Przeworski, Adam, Ernest Underhill, and Michael Wallerstein. 1978. The evolution of class structure in Denmark, 1901–1960; France, 1901–1968; Germany 1882–1933 and 1950–1961; and Sweden, 1900–1960: Basic data tables. University of Chicago. Photocopy.

Putterman, Louis. 1997. "Why have the rabble not redistributed the wealth? On the stability of democracy and unequal property." In *Property relations, incentives, and welfare,* edited by J. E. Roemer. London: Macmillan.

Riker, William. 1982. *Liberalism against populism: A confrontation between the theory of democracy and the theory of social choice.* San Francisco: W. H. Freeman.

Roemer, John E. 1994a. "A theory of policy differentiation in single-issue electoral politics." *Social Choice and Welfare* 11, 355–380.

———— 1994b. "The strategic role of party ideology when voters are uncertain about how the economy works." *American Political Science Review* 88, 327–335.

———— 1995. "Political cycles." *Economics & Politics* 7, 1–20.

———— 1996. *Theories of Distributive Justice.* Cambridge, Mass.: Harvard University Press.

———— 1997. "Political-economic equilibrium when parties represent constituents: The unidimensional case." *Social Choice and Welfare* 14, 479–502.

Schlesinger, James. 1991. *Political parties and the winning of office.* Chicago: University of Chicago Press.

Schorske, Carl. [1955] 1993. *German social democracy, 1905–1917.* Cambridge, Mass.: Harvard University Press.

Schultz, Christian. 1995. "The politics of persuasion when voters are rational." *Scandinavian Journal of Economics* 97, 357–368.

Shepsle, Kenneth A. 1991. *Models of multi-party electoral competition.* Chur, Switzerland: Harwood Academic Publishers.

Snyder, James, and Gerald Kramer. 1988. "Fairness, self-interest, and the politics of the progressive income tax." *Journal of Public Economics* 36, 197–230.

Strom, Kaare. 1990. *Minority government and majority rule.* New York: Cambridge University Press.

Tingsten, Herbert. [1941] 1973. *The Swedish Social Democrats.* Totawa, N.J.: Bedminster Press.

Wildavsky, Aaron. 1965. "The Goldwater phenomenon: Purists, politicians, and the two-party system." *Review of Politics* 27, 386–413.

Wittman, Donald. 1973. "Parties as utility maximizers." *American Political Science Review* 67, 490–498.

———— 1983. "Candidate motivation: A synthesis of alternative theories." *American Political Science Review* 77, 142–157.

———— 1990. "Spatial strategies when candidates have policy preferences." In *Advances in the spatial theory of voting,* edited by J. Enelow and M. Hinich. Cambridge: Cambridge University Press.

Young, Peyton. 1994. *Equity.* Princeton: Princeton University Press.

Index

abdication to radicals, 99–100, 101–102
Abraham, David, 209, 210n
absolutely continuous measure, 313–314
aggregate uncertainty, 3, 51; and Coughlin
    model, 134–144
agricultural proletariat, 212
almost surely, 311
American politics. *See* United States
AMNE. *See* average-member Nash
    equilibrium
Anderson, Dewey, 209
Assumption 1, 18
Assumption 2, 18
Assumption 3, 19
Assumption 4, 19
Assumption 5 (monotonicity), 29, 32, 68
Assumption 5′, 269
Assumption 6, 53
Assumption 7, 61, 68
Assumption 8, 61
Assumption 9, 69
Assumption 10, 104
Assumption 10′, 125
Assumption A, 157
Assumption B1, 174
Assumption B2, 177
Assumption B3, 177
Assumption B4, 182
Assumption B5, 184
Assumption C1, 194
Assumption C2, 195, 266
Assumption C2*, 196
Assumption C3, 198
Aumann, Robert, 39n
Austen-Smith, David, 277, 281, 282, 283n
average-member Nash equilibrium, 91–94;
    shortcomings, 94; for endogenous candidates,
    100–101

balanced-budget condition, 172
Banks, Jeffrey, 281, 282
Baron, David, 92, 284, 298, 299
Baron-Diermeier formulation, 298, 299, 302, 305
belief, associated with voter action, 286
bell-shaped curve, 316
Berle, Adolf, 27
Besley, Timothy, 95
best responses, 7, 63–64, 147, 157, 171, 278
Beta distribution of income, 273
beta function, 316
Borel field, 309–310
boundedly rational Nash equilibrium, 153
British Social Attitudes Survey, 201–202
Brouwer's fixed-point theorem, 321; applications,
    105
Budge, Ian, 38, 324
budget constraint: balanced, 172; individual, 174;
    in Luebbert models, 215, 216; in three-class
    model, 253; in three-party model, 300
Burr-Singh-Maddala distribution, application,
    92

Calvert, Randall, 76
candidate: motives, 17, 27; party control of, 27–
    28; choice of, 95; endogenous, 95–101. *See also*
    citizen-candidate
capitalists: party membership, 10–11; in Luebbert
    model, 210; utility function, 253; in three-class
    model of American politics, 253–254, 255,
    256; in coalition government, 299–304
Caplin, Andrew, 92
cardinal concept, 152
cardinally measurable, 143
CDF. *See* cumulative distribution function
Center (party), behavior in coalition government,
    290–296
Christian Democratic Party, 190–191

citizen: types, 14, 76; preference order over policies, 15; ideal policy, 20. *See also* polity; voter
citizen-candidate, 95, 101
class struggle: democratic, 209; in interwar Europe, 210–211
Claudin, Fernando, 230
CNE. *See* Condorcet-Nash equilibrium
coalition government model, 281–305; formation process, 282–284; with multidimensional issue space, 299–304
Coate, Stephen, 95
Communists, in three-party model, 230–241
communitarian issue, 190, 191, 192
complementary slackness conditions, 254, 302
concave function, 318
Condition (6.2), 106, 107, 108
Condorcet-Nash equilibrium, 6, 94; for endogenous candidates, 95–100; for Euclidean model, 99–101
Condorcet winner, 17, 179; strict, 17, 20–21, 30; nonexistence, 111
cone: of attractive policies, 180–181; convex, 319
consistent vote distribution: in three-party model, 285–287, 290–296; handling nonuniqueness of, 288; handling nonexistence of, 288–289
convex cone, 319
convex function, 318
convexity, concept of, 318–321
Corollary 3.1, 64–65
Corollary 3.2, 68
Corollary 6.1, 106
Corollary 9.1 (progressive policy wins), 184
correspondence, 321–322
Coughlin, Peter J., 6, 124, 127, 128
Coughlin model, 127–130; adaptation to aggregate uncertainty, 134–144
countable additivity, 309
covered set of policies, 146–147
Cukierman, Alex, 172
cumulative distribution function, 23, 317–318
cycling, 7, 82–89, 147, 171
Czechoslovakia, interwar politics, 211

Davidson, Percy, 209
Davis, O. A., 108
decent responses. *See* best responses
decreasing uncertainty theorem, 71
Definition 1.1 (political equilibrium), 15

Definition 1.2 (Condorcet winner), 17
Definition 1.3 (single-peaked function), 18
Definition 1.4 (ideal policy of citizen), 20
Definition 3.1 (decent responses), 63–64
Definition 3.2 (trivial Wittman equilibrium), 69
Definition 4.1 (economic equilibrium at tax rate t), 77
Definition 5.1 (average-member Nash equilibrium), 92
Definition 8.1 (party-unanimity Nash equilibrium), 149
Definition 8.2 (strict Downs equilibrium, regular Wittman equilibrium), 150
Definition 9.1 (strong party-unanimity Nash equilibrium), 179
Definition 10.1 (degree of uncertainty), 196
Definition 10.2 (ϵ-PUNE), 196
De Groot, M. H., 108
democracy: nonexpropriation of rich in, 9, 189–208, 279–280; perfectly representative, 90–91, 94–100, 259, 279; features of political economy of, 279–280
democratic class struggle, 209
Democratic Party: factions in, 10; as labor party, 252, 254; in three-class model, 252–258; redistributive tax policy, 276
Denmark, interwar politics, 211
density function, 313–317, 318; for three-party model, 234–237
Diermeier, Daniel, 298, 299
differentiability, 61
directional derivative, 321
disappointment, 82
discrete measure, 310, 314
distribution function. *See* cumulative distribution function
double median theorem, 54–55
Downs, Anthony, 1, 16, 27, 28
Downs equilibrium, 16–28; properties of, 1, 2, 46; shortcomings, 1–2, 3, 17, 26–28, 294; theorem and proof, 21–22; with identical preferences over income, 22–23; with variable preferences over public good, 23–24; with redistributed tax revenues, 24–25; and vote-maximizing model, 26–27; and median ideal policy, 52–55; unidimensional policy space with uncertainty, 52–55; ideal tax rate of median voter, 93; multidimensional policy space with certainty, 103–116; nonexistence in multidimensional issue space models,

106; with policies on boundary, 113–116, 123; nonexistence with party uncertainty, 124–126; multidimensional issue spaces with uncertainty, 124–144; when both parties play same policy, 141–143; strict, 150–151; in progressive tax model, 179

Durrett, Richard, 318

economic policy, and partisan dogmatism, 81

Einstein, Albert, 1

election: as simultaneous-move game, 146, 147; class analysis of, 209–211

electoral cycling, 82–89

electoral outcome, tie-breaking method for, 15–16

endogenous party: with unidimensional competition, 90–102; with multidimensional competition, 259–280

Enelow, James, 108, 131, 133

equivalent measures, 19n, 314

error-distribution model of uncertainty, 45–46; shortcomings, 47; applications, 52–53, 55–57, 60, 62–68, 69–71, 92–94, 124–125, 164–165, 166–170, 260–261, 269–276

Euclidean preferences, 26, 99–101, 106, 108, 119–122, 167–170

Europe: political competition in, 190–208; socialist parties, 209–211; three-class model of, 216–240; party representing capitalists in, 252n

Evans, Merran, 273n

Example 1.1 (voters with identical preferences), 22–23

Example 1.2 (citizens with two traits), 23–24

Example 1.3 (proportional taxation and equal redistribution of taxes), 24–25

Example 1.4 (voters with Euclidean preferences), 26

Example 1.5 (multidimensional type space), 33–35

Example 1.6 (parties with different preferences), 35–36

Example 1.7 (proportional taxation and equal redistribution of taxes), 36

Example 2.1 (discontinuous probability), 40–41, 46

Example 2.2 (multidimensional type space), 42–43

Example 2.3 (two-dimensional trait space), 43–44

Example 2.4 (two-dimensional issue space and trait space), 44–45

Example 3.1 (redistributive proportional income tax), 55–57; Wittman equilibrium for, 73–76; Downs equilibrium for, 74

Example 3.2, 57–61

Example (income, tax rate, and political extremism), 73–76

Example (labor-supply elasticity), 76–80

Example (partisan dogmatism and political extremism), 81

Example 6.1 (Euclidean preferences), 106

Example 6.2 (Euclidean preferences), 108

Example 6.3 (economic: tax rate and public good), 111–116

Example 6.4 (interior Wittman equilibrium), 118–119

Example (equilibrium between parties with factions that bargain), 155–158

Example 8.1 (generic regular Wittman equilibrium), 163–165

expropriation of rich, in democracy, 9, 189–208, 279–280

extremism, political, 73–76, 81

$\mathcal{F}$-measurable function, 311–312, 314

factions. See party factions

false consciousness, 189

Farkas' lemma: applications, 159, 162, 215, 271, 297; statement and illustration of, 319–321

Ferejohn, John, 284

finite-type model of polity, 14, 47–51; application, 134

finite-type model of probability: application, 213–216, 253–254

fixed-point theorems, 321–322

formateur, 283, 297, 299, 300–304

four-class model: definition for, 212–216; testing of, 218–230

Gallup, George, 200

German Social Democratic Party, 7, 153, 210, 230–231

Germany: socialists in, 209; interwar politics, 210–211; application of Luebbert's model to, 218–230; effect of Communist Party in, 237–241

Gini coefficient, 92

Goldwater, Barry, 154

Green, Jerry, 318n, 321, 322

Hamilton, Richard F., 209, 239, 241n
Hastings, Nicholas, 273n
Hessian matrix, application, 132–133
Hinich, Melvin J., 108, 131, 133, 147n
Hirschman, Albert C., 82
Hirschman effect, 85
Hirschman model of electoral cycles,
    82–89
historian, methods of, 243
Hofferbert, Richard, 38, 324
Hotelling, Harold, 16, 28
Hunt, W. B., 190
hyperplane, 319. *See also* separating hyperplane
    theorem

ideal point, 104
ideal policy, 3, 14, 20, 29, 79–80, 260
implicit function theorem, 322; application,
    109
incentive compatibility constraint, 174
income: as citizen trait, 13–14, 73–76, 81; citizen
    preferences, 55; after-tax, 172, 173; less than
    mean, 184
income distribution: skewness of, 93, 294; fair,
    144; in United States, 310, 311; approximations
    for, 310–311; fraction of people or number of
    people, 316–317
income tax rate. *See* tax policy
incomplete preference relation, 149
indicator function, 315; application, 129
indifference curve, 61, 169
indirect utility function over policy, 14
infinite-type model of polity, 14–15
infrastructure, 251, 252, 253, 299
inner product, 319
institutional approach, 146
interest group, 172; financial influence of, 277.
    See also reformist faction
issue. *See* policy
issue space. *See* policy space
Italy, interwar politics, 210–211
Iverson, Torben, 102

Kakutani's fixed-point theorem, 322;
    applications, 57, 65, 128, 132, 135
Kalyvas, S. N., 190
Kitschelt, H., 190, 191
Klingermann, Hans-Dieter, 38, 324
Korpi, Walter, 209n
Kramer, Gerald, 172

Labor Party, 190–191; absence of, in United
    States, 252, 258
labor supply: elastic, 76–80, 261; inelasticity
    assumption, 188
landed peasantry, 212
landowner, class of, 210
Laver, Michael, 190, 284
Lebesgue integral, 311–313
Lebesgue measure, 310, 313, 314; applications,
    108, 116, 177
Lee, Woojin, 198n, 244n, 263n
Left (party), 177; behavior in coalition
    government, 290–296
legislative behavior, 146
Lemma 1.1, 17–18
Lemma 1.2, 19
Lemma 1.3, 20
Lemma 1.4, 29
Lemma 3.1, 61–62
Lemma 3.2, 62
Lemma 3.3, 63
Lemma 3.4, 64
Lemma 3.5, 66–67
Lemma 9.1, 176–177
Lemma 9.2, 181–182
Lemma 9.3, 182
Lindbeck, Assar, 6, 124, 130, 131, 133
Lindbeck-Weibull model, 130–133
Lipset, Seymour Martin, 28, 209
Llavador, Humberto, 72, 198n
log concavity, 67–68, 157
lognormal distribution, 310–311, 315
lottery: preferences over, 152; equal-probability,
    298–299, 303
Luebbert, Gregory, 10, 209–211
Luebbert model, 10; with four classes, 212–
    216; with three classes, 216–218; supported
    by PUNE analysis, 242–243; derivations of
    formulae in, 244–250

Marhuenda, F., 172
Marx, Karl, 9n, 191
Mas-Colell, Andreu, 318n, 321, 322
maximum, theorem of, 322; application,
    66
maximum likelihood estimators, 264
mean (of measure), 312–313
Means, Gardiner, 27
measurable space, 309–311
measure space, 309

median ideal policy, 55; with Downs model, 52–55; relation to uncertainty, 79–80; one-dimensional, 106
median policy, 29, 37, 104
median voter, 23, 25, 61, 70, 259
median-voter theorem, 3, 259
Meltzer, Allan, 93, 172
militant faction: motivation, 7, 148, 154–155; equilibrium for ideal policy of, 148, 278; historical examples of, 153–154; in progressive tax policy model, 177, 178; in four-class model, 213; in three-party game, 296, 300–304
mixed-strategy equilibrium, in multidimensional game, 145–146
MLE. See maximum likelihood estimators
monotonicity axiom, 29, 32, 68
multidimensional Euclidean model, PUNEs in, 167–170
multidimensional policy space, 15, 299–304
multifaction game. See ROM game
multiparty politics. See coalition government model; three-party game
Munger, Michael C., 147n

Nalebuff, Barry, 92
Nash bargaining solution, 155; application, 144; unweighted, 156; weighted, 156–158, 163–165
Nash equilibrium: average-member, 91–94, 100–101; subgame perfect, 146; two-faction, 152–153; boundedly rational, 153. See also Condorcet-Nash equilibrium; party-unanimity Nash equilibrium
Nash product, 155
National Election Survey, 198, 263–264
Nazi Party, 211, 239
Nehring, Klaus, 184n
NES. See National Election Survey
Nieuwbeerta, Paul, 209n
noneconomic issue, use of, by political parties, 207–208
nongeneric equilibrium, 109
nonsingularity condition. See Assumption 10
nontrivial equilibrium, 196
normal distribution, 315, 316
normal vector, 319
Norway, interwar politics, 211

open ball, 20
opportunist faction: motivation, 7, 148, 154; historical examples of, 153–154; in progressive

tax policy model, 178; in four-class model, 213; in three-party game, 230, 296–297, 300–304
ordinal concept, 152
orthogonal vector, 319
Ortuño-Ortín, Ignacio, 72, 91n, 172, 279
Osborne, Martin, 72, 95

Page, Marianne, 187n
Palfrey, Thomas R., 72
paper stones, 209
partisan dogmatism, 81
party: as instruments of classes and interest groups, 1, 28; uncertainty of voter behavior, 3, 38; policy convergence, 3, 48, 141; payoff function, 15; victory as goal, 17, 27–28; control over candidates, 27–28; with polarized preferences, 29, 35–36, 69, 95–101; with consistent policy views, 38; set of responses, 63–64; concerned about fraction of votes, 72; effect of length of time in power, 84–85; abdication to radicals, 99–100, 101–102; and endogenous candidates, 100–101; as public institution, 146, 147; as coalition of factions, 148–155; tension in, 154; in progressive tax model, 177; use of noneconomic issues, 207–208; platform vector, 283; formateur, 283, 297, 299, 300–304. See also three-party game
party factions: bargaining among, 8, 145–171; in three-party game, 230, 296–304. See also militant faction; opportunist faction; reformist faction
party financing, 91
party formation, with private party financing, 276–277
party preferences, average or median, 95
party unanimity, concept of, 178
party-unanimity Nash equilibrium (PUNE): usefulness of, 12; criticisms of, 152; as bargaining equilibrium, 155–158; as generalization of Wittman equilibrium, 156–158; differential characterization of, 159–163, 297–298; with uncertainty in multidimensional policy spaces, 163–165; in unidimensional model, 166–167; in multidimensional Euclidean model, 167–170; for progressive tax model, 178–179; with religious and distribution issues, 192–198; unique, 193; nontrivial, 196; ϵ, 196–198; four-class model, 212–216; for Luebbert

party-unanimity Nash equilibrium *(continued)*
model with no class struggle, 216–218; iterative
solution method, 219, 255; computational
procedure, 237–240; for three-party model of
American politics, 254–258; with endogenous
parties (PUNEEP), 260–280; general existence
theorem, 277–279; for multidimensional
three-party game, 297–299
payoff function, 60; of political party, 15; in
Downs model, 17; conditional, quasi-concave,
67; for Wittman party, 282–290
Peacock, Brian, 273n
perfectly representative democracy, 90–91;
and Condorcet-Nash equilibrium, 94–100;
defined, 259; United States and, 279
Persson, Torsten, 93, 294
petite bourgeoisie, 10, 190; utility function, 253;
in three-class model of American politics,
253–254, 255; in coalition government, 300
platform vector, 283
Plott, Charles, 107
policy: differentiation in Wittman equilibrium,
70, 79; conditions for divergence of, 71–72;
meaning of subscripts and superscripts, 105;
distribution of national income as, 211; of
coalition government, 283. *See also* tax policy
policy preference, of voter, uncertain, 39–40
policy space, 2–3, 13, 39, 188; unidimensional, 3,
15, 25, 32, 52–72, 90–102; multidimensional,
15, 299–304; two-dimensional, 44–45;
rectangular, 105; trapezoidal, 112
political competition, 1; case of certainty, 13–16;
multidimensional in real countries, 190
political cycles, dynamic model of, 82–89
political equilibrium: general definition, 15–16;
Downs model, 16–28; with Condorcet winner,
17–18, 20–21; Wittman model, 28–36. *See also*
Downs equilibrium; party-unanimity Nash
equilibrium; Wittman equilibrium
politicians, characteristics of, 2, 27, 154
polity: modeling of preferences, 2, 13; finite- and
infinite-type models of, 14–15; classes in, 47.
See also citizen; voter
polling, 38
Poole, K. T., 190
probabilistic voting model, 127–130; of Lindbeck
and Weibull, 130–133. *See also* Coughlin
model
probability distribution, 311
probability measure, 309, 311

probability-of-victory function, 2, 5, 39;
discontinuous, 41, 42–43, 49; continuous, 43;
distinguished from expected fraction of vote,
45–46
probability space, 309
probability theory, basics of, 309–318
progressive taxation model: with democratic
political competition, 172–188; policy
definition for, 174; application to U.S. parties,
187–188. *See also* quadratic taxation model
property owner, responsible behavior of, 189
proportional representation, 46
proportional tax rate, 91, 164–165
Proposition 3.1, 68–69
Proposition 3.2, 69
Proposition 4.1, 73, 193, 279
Proposition 4.2, 78
Proposition 6.1, 105
Proposition 6.2, 105–106
Proposition 6.3, 122
Proposition 7.1, 127–128
Proposition 7.2, 134–135
Proposition 7.3, 138–141
Proposition 10.1, 197, 202
Proposition 10.2, 197, 202–203
Proposition 10.3, 198, 203–205
Przeworski, Adam, 190, 209, 218, 231
public good, 13, 55
publicity, 7, 148, 154
PUNE. *See* party-unanimity Nash equilibrium
PUNEEP. *See* party-unanimity Nash equilibrium,
with endogenous parties
Putterman, Louis, 189

quadratic taxation model, 269–276. *See also*
progressive taxation model
quasi-concave function, 18n, 318–319
quasi-convex function, 318–319

race, NES question on, 264n
racial issue, 9, 44–45, 191, 192; in endogenous
party model, 259–280
radical, abdication to, 99–100, 101–102
radical, rational for choosing, 100
Radon-Nikodym derivative (of measure), 315
Radon-Nikodym theorem, 314–315; application,
317
random variable, 312
ratio-scale measurable, 47n, 143
redistribution (issue), 190–192

refinement of correspondence, 322
reformist faction: motivation, 7, 148, 154–155; in ROM game, 148–171; gratuitous (inactive), 151–152, 234, 252; historical examples of, 153–154; in progressive tax policy model, 177, 178; in four-class model, 213; in three-party game, 296, 299
reformist political equilibrium, 28
regressive policy, 185
regular Wittman equilibrium, 150–151, 163–165
religion (issue), 81, 190–192; use of, by political parties, 207–208
religious position, 81
Republican Party: factions in, 10; in three-class model, 252–258; redistributive tax policy, 276
Richard, S., 93
Riemann integral, 312
Right (party), 177; creation of noneconomic issue by, 207–208; in three-party model, 230–241; in coalition government, 290–296
Riker, William, 146
Roemer, John E., 40, 47n, 57n, 68, 76n, 82n, 88, 91n, 143, 144, 155n
ROM game, 148–171
Rosenthal, H., 190
rural peasantry, 210
rural proletariat, 210

salience of values, 191–192, 200
sample space, 311
scalar product, 319
Schlesinger, James, 154
Schorske, Carl, 7, 153
Schultz, Christian, 40
SCP. See single-crossing property
separable, 105
separating hyperplane, 319
separating hyperplane theorem, 159, 321; application, 161
separating type, 95
sequential game approach, 146
Shepsle, Kenneth A., 281, 284
σ-field, 309
simultaneous-move game, 146, 147
single-crossing property (SCP), 61
single-peaked function, 18–19
Slivinski, Al, 95
Snyder, James, 172
Socialist Party: in Europe, 209–211; in three-party model, 230–240

social scientist, methods of, 243
solution manifold, 163
Spain, interwar politics, 210–211
spatial equilibrium, Hotelling model, 16
Sprague, John, 190, 209, 231
Stackelberg equilibrium, 146
state-space model of uncertainty, 39–45; general applicability, 45; applications, 53–55, 68, 177, 193, 281; nonexistence, 125
strict Condorcet winner, 17, 20–21, 30
Strom, Kaare, 284
strongness, 179
subgame perfect Nash equilibrium, 146
suffrage, effect of U.S. changes in, 189
Sweden: interwar politics, 211; effect of Communist Party in, 237–241

Tabellini, Guido, 93, 294
tax policy, 13–14; zero, 9, 197–198, 205; and political competition, 13–15; voter preference for, 14; in Downs political equilibrium, 22–25; to redistribute income, 24–25, 40–41, 279; uniform rate, 44–45, 251–258, 261–280; proportional rate, 55; extremes in, 74–76; and political cycles, 82–89; in progressive tax model, 172
tax-race model, 259–280
Theorem 1.1 (median ideal policy at Downs equilibrium; median voter theorem), 21–22
Theorem 1.2 (existence of Wittman political equilibrium), 29–32
Theorem 3.1 (existence of Downs equilibrium), 53
Theorem 3.2 (double median theorem), 54–55
Theorem 3.3 (existence theorem), 65–67
Theorem 3.4 (differentiated policies in Wittman equilibria), 69–71
Theorem 3.5 (decreasing uncertainty theorem), 71
Theorem 6.1 (singularity of Downs equilibrium), 106–107
Theorem 6.2 (singularity of Downs equilibrium), 108–111
Theorem 6.3 (nongeneric interior Wittman equilibrium), 116–118
Theorem 7.1 (singularity of Downs equilibrium), 125
Theorem 7.2 (singularity of Downs equilibrium), 126

Theorem 7.3 (existence of Downs equilibrium of Coughlin game), 128
Theorem 7.4 (existence of Downs equilibrium in Lindbeck-Weibull model), 132–133
Theorem 7.5 (existence of Downs equilibrium), 141–143
Theorem 8.1 (relationship among Downs, Wittman, and PUNE), 150–151
Theorem 8.2 (PUNE as Nash bargaining solution), 157–158
Theorem 9.1 (existence of strong PUNE), 182–184
Theorem 9.2 (both parties play progressive policies), 184–186
Theorem 10.1 (zero tax rate in PUNEs), 197, 205
Theorem 10.2 (existence of PUNEs), 197, 205–207
Theorem A.1 (definition of Lebesgue measure), 310
Theorem A.2 (Radon-Nikodym theorem), 314–315
three-class model: definitions for, 216–218; application to European politics, 216–240; testing of, 218–230; application to American politics, 251–258; budget constraint in, 253
three-party game: opportunist faction in, 230, 296–297, 300–304; Communists, Socialists, and Right in, 230–241; density functions for, 234–237; of American politics, 254–258; consistent vote distribution in, 285–287, 290–296; Wittman equilibrium for, 287–288, 290–296; reformist faction in, 296, 299; militant faction in, 296, 300–304; PUNE for multidimensional case, 297–299
Tingsten, Herbert, 209
trait space, two-dimensional, 23–24, 43–45
transfer payment, 251, 253, 254, 257, 304
two-faction Nash equilibrium, 152–153

uncertainty about voter behavior: models for, 3, 38–72; aggregate, 3, 51, 134–144; with unidimensional policy space, 52–102, 166–167; decreasing, 71; relation to policy differentiation and median ideal policy, 79–80; Downs model with, 124–144; with multidimensional policy spaces, 124–144, 167–170. See also error-distribution model of uncertainty; finite-type model; state-space model of uncertainty
uncovered set approach, 146–147

Underhill, Ernest, 218
unidimensional policy space, 3, 15, 25, 32, 52–72, 90–102; PUNEs in, 166–167
uniform measure, 310
United States: household income, 93n, 99, 186–187; presidential election, 154; income distribution, 165, 310, 311; household income, 186–187; limited suffrage in, 189; modeling of racial issue, 198–201; creation of noneconomic issue by Right, 207–208; three-class model of politics in, 251–258; absence of labor party in, 252, 258; fitting tax-race model to data of, 263–268; nonexistence of perfectly representative democracy in, 279
unweighted Nash-bargaining equilibrium, 156
upper contour set, 318
upper hemicontinuous correspondence, 322
urban middle class, 210
urban working class, 210
utilitarian social-welfare function, maximization, 144

value function, 322
victory: as goal, 17, 27; uncertainty of, 38. See also probability-of-victory function
vote distribution: in three-party model, 285–287, 290–296; handling nonuniqueness of, 288; handling nonexistence of, 288–289
vote fraction: expected, 45–46, 220, 316–317; in Coughlin model, 127–130; in Lindbeck-Weibull model, 131–132; maximization, 134–135
vote-maximizing model, and Downs political equilibrium, 26–27
voter: motivation, 1, 38, 50; median, 3, 23, 25, 61, 70, 259; party uncertainty of behavior of, 3, 38; preferences, 13, 39–40; as subset of citizens, 15; rationality, assumption of, 17; abstaining, 39; turnout, 39, 40–41, 46, 48; sincere, 231, 282, 284–285, 289–290; strategic, 282, 284–285, 289–290; belief and action, 286
voter type: and wage-earning capacity, 13–14, 73–76, 81; uncertainty of, 38, 39–41
voting: formulation of stochastic element in, 231–233; sincere or strategic, 284–287, 289–290, 301–302; consistent, 285–289

Wallerstein, Michael, 218, 252n
weather, and voter turnout, 39, 40–41, 46, 48
Weibull, Jorgen, 6, 124, 130, 131, 133

weighted Nash bargaining solution, 156–158, 163–165

Wildavsky, Aaron, 154

winner-take-all rule, 46

Winston, Michael, 318n, 321, 322

Wittman, Donald, 1, 28, 57n

Wittman equilibrium: properties of, 1–2, 69–71; with certainty and unidimensional policy space, 28–32; with certainty and multidimensional policy space, 34–36, 116–122; with uncertainty and unidimensional policy space, 55–61, 73–89; existence of, 61–69; with labor-supply elasticity, 76–80; with endogenous party preferences, 91–94; interior,

nongeneric, 116–118; generic, 118–119; with Euclidean preferences, 119–122; regular, 150–151, 163–165; as cardinal concept, 152; party-unanimity Nash equilibrium as, 156–158; payoff function for party in, 282–290; for three-party game (coalition government), 287–288, 290–296

workers, 10, 212; utility function, 253; in three-class model of American politics, 253–254, 255

worker-shopkeepers, in coalition government, 299–304

Young, Peyton, 172